Public Streets
for Public Use

Public Streets for Public Use

Edited by
Anne Vernez Moudon

with a Foreword by
Donald Appleyard

VNR VAN NOSTRAND REINHOLD COMPANY
NEW YORK

In memoriam
Donald Appleyard
Mania Seferi

Printed in the United States of America

Designed by Karolina Harris

Van Nostrand Reinhold Company Inc.
115 Fifth Avenue
New York, New York 10003

Van Nostrand Reinhold Company Limited
Molly Millars Lane
Wokingham, Berkshire RG11 2PY, England

Van Nostrand Reinhold
480 La Trobe Street
Melbourne, Victoria 3000, Australia

Macmillan of Canada
Division of Canada Publishing Corporation
164 Commander Boulevard
Agincourt, Ontario M1S 3C7, Canada

16 15 14 13 12 11 10 9 8 7 6 5 4 3 2 1

Library of Congress Cataloging-in-Publication Data

Public streets for public use.

   Bibliography: p.
   Includes index.
   1. City planning—Environmental aspects.
   2. Pedestrian facilities design. 3. Streets.
   I. Moudon, Anne Vernez.
HT166.P82 1987   711'.41   86-28124
ISBN 0-442-26404-6

Contents

Acknowledgments

Pierre Laconte and I first started exchanging information about streets in 1979. At the time, we were both researching development along streets to better understand the forces behind urban change, he at the Catholic University of Louvain, Belgium; I at the Massachusetts Institute of Technology. In 1980, Dr. Laconte, who is now Secretary of the Union Internationale des Transports Publics in Brussels, joined me in sponsoring a seminar at MIT, called "A Handle on Change." Discussants included Julian Beinart, Christopher Chadbourne, Christian Dame, Gary Hack, Phil Herr, Fernando Jimenez, and Christian Lasserre. A comparison of two case studies in Brussels, Belgium, and Cambridge, Massachusetts, confirmed our initial assumption that the analysis of streets as microcosms of a city reveals the dynamics of urban change. The seminar discussions also lead us to concur that in parts of Europe, and especially in the United States, the lack of coordination between transportation and city planning policy was eroding our cities' public environment.

In 1982, Dr. Laconte and I organized the International Institute at the University of Washington, called *Streets as Public Property: Opportunities for Public/Private Interaction in Planning and Design.* The conference speakers were Donald Appleyard, Dietrich Garbrecht, Roberta Brandes Gratz, Michael Harrison, Paulhans Peters, Amos Rapoport, and Richard Untermann. The Institute drew a much larger crowd than expected, attracting some two hundred participants from around the world. Proceedings were published in 1983, with thirty-six papers on subjects ranging from street design and planning theory to accounts of actual projects in different parts of the world. The event was supported by funds from the College of Architecture and Urban Planning at the University of Washington, the Land Use Study Group of the Catholic University at Louvain-La-Neuve, the Lincoln Institute of Land Policy in Cambridge, Massachusetts, the NATO Scientific Division in Brussels, the Committee of Thirty-Three in Seattle, and the Northwest Institute for Architecture and Urban Studies in Italy, also in Seattle. The National Endowment for the Arts provided a substantial grant that enabled us to reduce registration fees and to assemble the proceedings. For their personal interest in the quality of this event, special thanks are due to Myer R. Wolfe, Dean Emeritus of the College of Architecture and Urban Planning at the University of Washington, and to Michael Pittas, then director of the Design Arts Program at the National Endowment for the Arts. Also, the Institute would not have taken place without the many students and staff at the University of Washington and professionals in the Seattle area, who generously donated their time.

If the success of the Institute warranted a continuation of the work, Donald Appleyard's untimely death in 1982 made future efforts mandatory. In my mind, further research was required in at least two directions. Theories needed to be developed and tested to shed light on the many impacts of street design (among others, the role of streets in using, understanding, and remembering the city and the effects of street form on use and on urban socialization processes). And while such work necessarily requires many years for completion, one specific area seemed to cry out for immediate attention: the practical problems of North American streets, which, as public property, presented conditions and circumstances that were very different from their all too frequently cited European counterparts. That was to be the focus of this volume.

Work began with the participation of some ten of the original Institute's participants, whose research

7

addressed issues of street planning and design in North America. The other contributors were added along the way as the contents of the book evolved. I am indebted to Richard Dober and Charles Hutchinson, who endorsed the first proposal for this volume. Financial support for the production of this book came from the individual authors and their sponsors in homage to our colleagues Appleyard and Seferi. Because of the lack of funds, we exchanged most of our ideas by telephone or mail, a process I enjoyed immensely in spite of the absence of face-to-face contact. I am grateful to the contributors (including those whose work is not, for one reason or another, part of this volume) for this rewarding experience. Special thanks are extended to Sheila Appleyard for letting me reproduce Donald Appleyard's writings and to Peter Bosselmann, Randolph Hester, Allan Jacobs, and Melvin Webber for helping me respect Donald's legacy. Many of the ideas in the introduction came from the volume's contributors, especially Ronald Eichner, Kenneth Greenberg, Henry Tobey, Richard Untermann, and Charles Wolfe. We all benefitted from the editorial advice of Claire Frost and Sharon Tighe. Ann Heasly and Deborah Porte helped with last-minute research and graphic work. I am also grateful to the staff of the College of Architecture and Urban Planning, and particularly to Vicky Nicon for her day-to-day organizational assistance. The skills and efforts of Van Nostrand Reinhold's editors and designers greatly facilitated the production of this book.

My final acknowledgments are of Louisa Moudon Seferis (and indirectly, of course, her father) for sharing the proceeds of her treasure hunts along city streets and for enabling me to experience, once again, the world of small people.

Foreword

DONALD APPLEYARD

Streets have always been scenes of conflict. They are and have always been public property, but power over them is ambiguous, for the street has an open and easily changeable nature. Unlike buildings, with their defined activity areas and controlled entrances, the street is open to all. Its detailed design, however, can subtly favor one group over another. By changing the surface, by erecting a sign, by adding a bench, one obliges certain users at the expense of others. In Oxford, England, for example, a transit mall was created with a surface of paving slabs. Buses moved slowly among the freely wandering pedestrians. But the paving cracked under the weight, and so the central lane was changed to tarmac. With that surface change, pedestrians obediently confined themselves once again to the sidewalks.

Several competing population groups, establishments, public agencies, and professions vie with one another for control of the street space, each representing or claiming to be the public. The most powerful and well-established groups often win, but they do not by any means represent the public interest. For who is the public? I would define the public to be everyone. Not everyone can get what they want from the street, but it should be public policy to achieve the greatest good for the greatest number. And no one should be excluded. In particular, it should be the

This foreword was presented as a keynote lecture at the *Streets as Public Property* conference, held at the University of Washington in May of 1982, and published in the conference proceedings (A. V. Moudon and P. Laconte 1983). It was adapted from chapter 5, *Identity, Power, and Place* (Unfinished manuscript. Berkeley: University of California, Institute of Urban and Regional Development 1982). This work was interrupted by Professor Appleyard's tragic death. Gratitude is expressed to Professor Randolph Hester for helping to edit this text—ED.

policy of public agencies and their representatives to support the weaker users of the streets—pedestrians, residents, children, old people, the handicapped, and the poor—because the powerful can generally look after themselves.

Urban designers have the opportunity to offer a new view of what streets are all about. Traditionally, highway engineering, which until recently dominated the management and design of streets, has tended to support only the travellers who use streets and especially those with motorized vehicles. Urban designers can view streets more broadly; they are for all users and for many more purposes than simply transportation. It is important, though, to understand the full range of groups that participate in streets and, conversely, the full range of opportunities that streets can offer to each individual. It is the urban designer's and the highway engineer's task to work out ingenious solutions for the design and use of street spaces and to optimize the participation and satisfaction of the maximum possible numbers of different people and groups.

I will begin by outlining the major conflicts that occur over the use of streets and affect the following groups of people:

1. Travellers (automobilists, truck drivers, public transit riders, pedestrians, cyclists, and so on)
2. Bystanders (especially merchants, residents, industries, and institutions).
3. Public agencies (public works, police and fire services)
4. Residents
5. Engineers
6. Urban designers (architects and landscape architects)

Because the nature of these conflicts on center-city streets is often quite different from neighborhood streets, I will avoid generalities by distinguishing between these two contexts in the following discussion.

TRAVELLERS VERSUS BYSTANDERS

Travellers who occupy the street space usually want to pass through it as quickly as possible to reach their destination. Occasionally they stroll and browse, or they cruise around, looking for their route or for a parking space. In city centers bystanders are often represented by commercial establishments that wish to attract customers by displaying wares along the street front or placing signs to catch the attention of passing traffic. Yet competing merchants do not want to let the traveller pause and ponder in the street space—better to get the window shopper past all other uses and directly to a particular store. Other uses, however, such as offices or institutions, do not need to attract so much attention.

Many of these bystanders are powerful: they own large pieces of land and build huge buildings. They often dominate the street with monolithic stone and concrete walls in the interests of their own display, privacy, or defense. In these cases, travellers, especially pedestrians, are the sufferers. As William Whyte has revealed, lunchtime pedestrians on New York streets have few places to sit; they stride through shadowed and congested sidewalks and attempt to find whatever seating is available in arid plazas, meager spaces, and even on spiky railings.

In neighborhoods the power relationship of traveller to bystander changes. The residents seek sanctuary in residential neighborhoods, but the travellers do not allow it. Here it is usually the traffic that oppresses the residential bystanders, creating dangers for children and noise and pollution that intrude into residents' homes, diminishing the quality of their daily lives. Of course, here more than in the central city bystanders are at other times travellers. The same people play different roles.

TRAVELLERS VERSUS TRAVELLERS

Of all the traveller groups in downtown streets, pedestrians are the weakest, especially children and the elderly. Then there are those who travel on fragile, nonmotorized vehicles—cycles, wheelchairs, and the like. The most powerful vehicles on streets are auto-

mobiles, trucks, and buses. This power hierarchy has virtually confined pedestrians to sidewalks in most cities. An extreme example of such oppression is the center of Osaka, Japan, where all pedestrians are confined to sidewalks by street railings and can only cross the downtown streets on high pedestrian bridges. Much of the new shopping is underground, sometimes three stories below the surface, while the traffic flows uninterrupted through the downtown area as if it were a ground-level freeway.

Some cities, usually those of medium size, have attempted to reverse this hierarchy by pedestrianizing a few of the main streets. Were this hierarchy to be changed, with the "smallest" travellers, pedestrians, bicyclists, and drivers of small, slow-moving vehicles, at the top, the streets would have far greater capacity and the centers of cities would be much more lively.

On neighborhood streets drivers are usually the most powerful travellers. Even though these users may be infrequent, their speed and unpredictable presence enable them to dominate the street space even when they are nowhere in sight. This almost sinister domination renders the millions of acres of residential street space in our cities unavailable to travellers other than the occasional cyclist. Pedestrians and children are mostly confined to the sidewalks. Attempts to share the street space by slowing the automobile, as in the Dutch *Woonerf* and the German *Wohnbereich*, are important because they offer greater use of the street space to other modes of transportation. Trails and streets specially designed for bicycles follow parallel policies.

BYSTANDERS VERSUS BYSTANDERS

In center cities, there is a trend for larger-scale uses to supplant smaller-scale establishments: offices and banks replace stores, restaurants, and other quasipublic uses; new buildings replace historic buildings. Downtown streets are consequently being deadened. Fewer entrances and lack of display frontage result in blank walls, bored pedestrians, and, ultimately, danger from increased crime. Housing has long ago been excluded from the centers of most American cities, although attempts are now being made to bring some housing back into downtown areas through mixed-use ordinances. Other cities are trying to conserve historic landmarks, though usually only the most highly rated of these survive. This kind of conservation does help to preserve the smaller scale that characterized earlier buildings and streets.

On neighborhood streets bystander conflicts usually occur between local merchants who want as much traffic as they can get and the residents who would like to restrict both traffic and parking for outsiders. Other institutions, such as hospitals, schools, clubs, and even funeral homes, also conflict with the desires of residents because they generate both traffic and parking, which spread into the neighborhood.

PUBLIC AGENCIES VERSUS RESIDENTS

In many cities public works agencies have, until recently, supported the needs and demands of travellers. Streets have been used to allocate public space for motorized traffic, while sidewalks are for pedestrians. The whole paradigm of traffic engineering has been directed at expanding the capacity of streets to accommodate ever-increasing numbers of automobiles. Many public works agencies have operated on the assumption that traffic would increase by 3 percent per year into the distant future. And so the principal measures of street use are traffic volumes and capacities. Few measures of other vehicle or pedestrian use are made. Changes in streets are in the direction of widening them to increase traffic flow and speed.

Public works agencies have developed a whole system of rules for the use of traffic control devices and other aspects of street design. But these are created (as with stop signs) mostly to facilitate traffic flow by assigning priorities to different routes. Although quite restrictive in their use, they are not easily available to the public. Recently, in California, traffic control devices installed by individual cities were ruled illegal because they did not appear in the state's *Manual of Uniform Traffic Control Devices*. New devices can be inserted in this manual only when they are approved by a committee composed entirely of engineers appointed by the State Department of Transportation. Obviously, the public has no representation on this committee.

Fire and police departments want to keep the streets open for emergencies. They argue that public safety must be the first consideration for public amenity, even though emergencies are relatively rare. Here communities must estimate the relative risks of adding time to delivery of emergency services. At the same time, many emergency service agencies could be more flexible in their use of equipment and routes. In one California city, the fire department insists that two hook-and-ladder fire trucks be able to pass each other between parked cars on every new residential street. This inevitably leads to streets that are about sixty feet wide from curb to curb. An example of an alternative approach is one Dutch city that is experimenting with the use of jeeps as fire trucks in neighborhoods with narrow streets. In Berkeley barriers used for traffic control have an "undercarriage preventer," a device that prohibits cars from passing while allowing trucks to do so. But the fire chief travels in a car and objects to them. If he would use a truck, there would be no problem.

Since public works, or sometimes parks and recreation departments, have been in charge of street maintenance, they have been able to control all changes to the streets, paralyzing bystanders and residents who feel helpless to change their streets and who have no incentive to look after them. But since public works and other agencies, like the police, have restricted budgets, streets have increasingly become no-man's-lands, uncared for by residents or public agencies.

Residents therefore have a new opportunity to take over their streets.

TRAFFIC ENGINEERS VERSUS URBAN DESIGNERS

Since street design has traditionally been the domain of the highway engineer, the urban designer's recent interest in streets can be seen as an attempted invasion of professional territory. Conflict and friction are likely. Each profession has its own set of values, concerns, and blinders. Highway engineers have been concerned with traffic function, safety, and cost of facilities. They are not especially interested in, nor do they understand, aesthetics, and they are little concerned with the problems of adjoining uses. While these values are changing, safety, function, and cost remain the "bottom line" for engineers. Urban designers, on the other hand, value amenity and aesthetics; they have a pedestrian orientation and worry less about safety and costs.

An example of the difference in approach is the use of speed humps. The engineer will tend to design a speed hump solely for the purpose of slowing the traffic in a safe and cheap way. These humps can be quite ugly—lumps of asphalt that convey a negative, controlling impression to the drivers. The urban designer favors more pleasant humps, perhaps made of bricks, that can also serve as raised crosswalks for pedestrians. The latter solution would thus serve more purposes. It is a multidimensional rather than a unidimensional approach.

But the urban design approach also has its weaknesses. In Delft, an urban designer responsible for a *Woonerf* did not like speed humps, yet without them the traffic could not be slowed down. As a result his scheme looked pleasant but was ineffective from a traffic viewpoint. The limitations and styles of each professional approach must be understood. Some architects in Germany are now saying that street landscaping in the style of the *Woonerf* spoils the formal quality of the street, even though residents like the new design. Historic conservationists sometimes argue that the original streets were somehow "good" and should not be changed. In one city, the lines of the original sidewalks have been retained, although the street has been narrowed. These professional and expert viewpoints may not always be in accord with one another. More seriously, the need of the residents and bystanders may be ignored in favor of professional values.

REPRESENTATION, TRADE-OFFS, AND INGENUITY

What does this outline of actors and conflicts mean for the design and redesign of streets and their vehicles?

First, it is important that all major and minor groups be *represented* at all stages of the planning and design process. All needs and values should be understood. And the weakest, in terms of political and economic power and in terms of raw physical power on the street, should be supported. On downtown streets those who take up less space, those who enhance public life and interaction (smaller establishments, pedestrians rather than people in automobiles), those who have no other choices may be given some weighted priority.

The economist sees the resolution of these different demands in terms of *compromise* and *trade-offs*, but the urban designer and planner can offer *creative ingenuity* and the ability to serve several group needs within a limited space. By designing the street to be used to capacity, each group can be attracted by its particular amenities; new functions and meanings can be imagined that will return the street to the center of public life and make it once more the arena for supporting the culture of cities.

Introduction

ANNE VERNEZ MOUDON

This book is as much about cities as it is about streets. Much has been said recently about what urban streets are, could be, and should be. *Public Streets for Public Use* continues the discussion, upholding as its central thesis that streets can and should be more than automobile traffic channels. Consequently, this book examines streets as networks of public urban space that can organize and unify cities. As networks, streets become powerful tools for urban planning and design.

What are streets? Amos Rapoport asserts in chapter 5 of this volume that streets are most commonly defined as physical entities, "the more or less narrow, linear spaces lined by buildings found in settlements and used for circulation and, sometimes, other activities." Streets are generic, pervasive elements of cities. They are, along with their antecedents, roads, often older than the human settlements they serve (Rykwert, in Anderson 1978). Urban residents have had a stake in streets, relying on their presence to go about their daily lives. In the newspapers, streets are synonymous with the unruly aspects of urban scenes—street people, street gangs, demonstrations, and accidents. Yet the press also reflects their positive associations with parades, sidewalk cafés, vendors, and outdoor performers. Celebrated in literature, music, and the movies, streets embody social life and its memories. Yet, ironically, streets are so common that Bernard Rudofsky noted in his seminal 1969 book that "the Library of Congress [had at that time] no book . . . ever written about the street proper."

More than any other element of the urban infrastructure, streets both record and determine the history of city form. A connoisseur reading a street map can at once unveil many aspects of a city's history, including when and how quickly it developed. Moving along a city's streets, one can readily discern much of the residents' life-styles, visions, and opportunities

for the future. Thus, streets and their layout reflect the societies that have created them. This book emphasizes the streets of North American cities, the special circumstances of their history, and the opportunities they offer today.

Street space can be conceptualized in two ways: either as individual streets—which, in chapter 28 of this volume, Lucien Kroll likens to a cloth stretched between buildings—or as networks of streets that irrigate the city and its different parts. To consider streets as individual spaces is to think of the characteristics of the *space* that links urban activities. The perception of streets as networks, on the other hand, leads to an understanding of their temporal dimensions, linking urban activities *in time* as well as in space.

Are streets public? In this country, according to strict legal analysis, street *land* (as property) is often in private ownership, but the public improves and maintains most street *space* (as territory). Important also, the public controls the *use* of the street (above, on, and below the hard surface). In theory, therefore, streets are for public use. However, in practice, most streets in this country's cities are dominated by only one "branch" of the public, the automobile.

Accordingly, engineering and public works departments have guided the development and management of streets under a mandate to ensure conflict-free circulation. Another task of these public agencies is to provide the necessary services—water, sewer, telephone, electricity, police, fire, and emergency protection—to every individual property in the city. Over time, utilities, including most drainage, have been moved underground to make room above, thereby further increasing the efficiency of the street's circulation function. In this spirit, the public has allowed (and paid for) most streets to be topped with a smooth, "wall-to-wall" asphalt cover and lined with a panoply of lights and signs either guiding the motorist or, in the tradition of great commercial streets, reminding him or her of what to buy.

The ever-increasing proliferation of cars (in the United States, one car for every two human beings) tells us that engineering and public works departments have indeed done their job: people can drive from place to place. But the relative convenience and efficiency of car travel has not been without side effects. Donald Appleyard (1981) has shown how increasingly difficult it is to live along streets with traffic. The proliferation of commercial malls (some five thousand in the United States alone [Kowinski 1985]) tells us that we can no longer shop on our streets. In Rudofsky's words, "air-conditioned [commercial] 'malls' do not qualify as streets; they are buildings" (1969: 20). Both in shopping and living functions, traffic is an impediment not only to pedestrian movement, but to ordinary social interactions (Wolfe 1962; Appleyard 1981). Further, we cannot work on our streets. In fact, just about every function in the city has, over the past forty years, tried to avoid the negative impact of the contemporary street.

Streets designed for cars have greatly altered our experience of the city. Zooming over expressways (which are increasingly kept behind continuous acoustical walls or sunken between retaining walls), we now only peek at high-rises or hills in the foreground. Even where traffic speed is limited, we see little of the residents' lives because streets are lined with garage doors and blank walls, a phenomenon that Richard Untermann calls our "environmental blinders" in chapter 8. A lack of regard for the pedestrian's comfort and safety keeps away the few who would otherwise make use of streets.

Grady Clay notes in chapter 6 how many streets are now " 'down time'—stretches of the urbanized environment where learning is at minimum . . . [between] the new Citadels." Our cultural, social, and economic life is now contained in (or constrained by) these citadels or islands, which are socially as well as spatially restricted. They are in the *private* domain, often locked up and closed to the people "that do not belong" (Jacobs 1980). This is true of downtowns as well as suburban malls, office buildings, and housing projects of the rich and the poor alike. These islands are forbidding ghettos where we appear as a captured society, whether confined within them or encapsuled in our cars.

What are the streets of the future? There are reasons to believe that many future streets will be "down time." Two-thirds of new office development over the past decade has taken place in the suburbs, in citadels surrounded by seas of parking and reached by stern, multilaned expressways or streets. Growth in these suburban "activity centers" has been so demanding that many communities now tax employers in order to build more streets. Given the staggering amount of existing roads in these suburban areas, as well as the unlikelihood of building transit systems as alternatives to automobile transport, many more all-inclusive megadevelopments linked by environmentally poor roads will, sadly, develop in the future.

Yet there are reasons why many streets can and should be open to uses that serve the public at large, not only drivers. Already, several suburban centers are aggressively controlling growth, taming the presence of cars, and reinforcing the pedestrian environment—see chapter 16 by Don Miles and Mark Hinshaw. In many cases, new streets are combined with public open space and commercial development that favor pedestrians (Moudon, in Beedle 1986).

Costs also limit the future of automobile-dominated streets. As federal funding dwindles and local traffic engineering departments assume the entire costs of street planning, it will become public knowledge that motorists contribute only 60 percent of annual expenditures. Moreover, this figure represents only 30 percent of the long-term capital and operating costs of roads (see chap. 20, by D. B. Lee). When motorists are made to pay for the actual expense of such indulgence, they are more likely to look for others with whom to share the cost of the roadway.

Societal costs are becoming more evident in communities fighting the impact of the automobile. Hazards such as noise and air pollution now stand as high on the list of documented problems as the threats that traffic poses to human life. Fifty percent of air pollution is attributed to car traffic (Gakenheimer 1978), and the environmental role of streets can no longer be denied.

Slowly the politics of street use and management are changing. Five percent of people actually walk to work, while just as many use public transit (Hirsch, in City of Boulder 1981). And at least 25 percent of people in our society do not drive, either by choice or because they are too old, too young, or handicapped. These constituencies are increasingly vocal and are gaining a better representation in city management (Urban Planning for Children Project 1986).[1] Their demands go hand in hand with the consolidation of new life-styles. Single parents and parents in the small, two-income family cannot forever transport children by automobile. Children need to be autonomous, and to a large extent, their autonomy depends on safe streets. The elderly also require safe streets, maintained through the presence of pedestrians who can provide surveillance, as well as through the restriction of threatening automobiles.

In spite of claims that communication technology

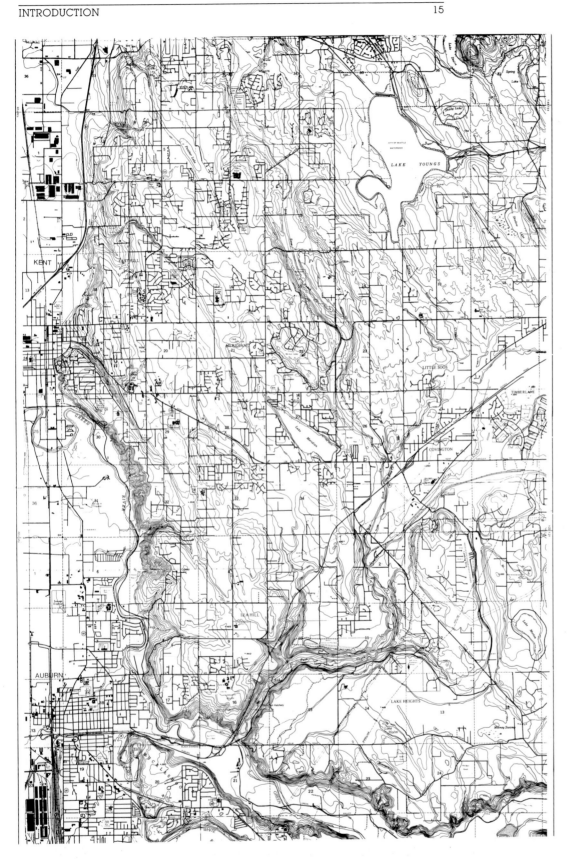

Street patterns in King County, Washington.

would eliminate needs to consider location for functional reasons, proximity and location remain important considerations in decisions relating to residence, school, and work. For many, the substantial time spent on the road for commuting, shopping, chauffeuring, and so on can be reduced only by a fine mix of activities within close proximity of either home or work or both. This in turn leads to higher densities. Increasingly, then, land-use and transportation issues must be considered together. Again, urban street networks linking activities in space and time are at the center of controversy. Finally, demand for environmental quality is emerging even from people who continue to drive extensively.

For these reasons, many streets of the future will need to be reclaimed for use by the public at large. Rethinking street use, however, means rethinking many of the characteristics of our society. The contributors to this book show that there are alternatives to the private islands, ghettos, and freeways. Cities with cars can be vital, rich in public life and in opportunities for face-to-face contact for the child, the aged, and the nondriver alike. *These environments, however, do not come naturally and must be cultivated.*

Changing planning policy. The car is not the enemy, nor is the elimination of cars the solution. It is our *societal bias* toward cars that must be questioned. The business of streets can no longer belong singularly to engineering and public works departments. Also, the public must confront ambiguities and outright contradictions in its demands: the same person who wants ease and speed as a driver, but who objects to the lack of safety for the pedestrian, must examine priorities. Street use must be allocated accordingly, and cars made to share the roadway. In effect, the function of the street must be expanded to its full social, economic, and environmental significance. As Donald Appleyard (1981) noted, streets must be more than *channels* for car transportation; they must also accommodate people on foot, on bicycles; they must be a social *place* for people to meet face to face; and they must bring additional green space to communities.

Changing the role of the street in the city also requires a critical examination of the city planning function. Because streets embody movement, access, and public life, they play a major role in the management and transformation of cities. Haussmann and his followers in the nineteenth century understood both the organizing and integrating powers of street space over the fabric of cities. In chapter 7 of this volume, Charles Wolfe explains how the regulatory role of the urban street during the Middle Ages and at the beginning of the modern period marked special turning points in the history of urban form. Yet over time planners have consistently worked to increase the speed with which people move. In using the various technological breakthroughs that allowed vast numbers of people to cover long distances rapidly, planners have moreover separated street function from daily, more sedentary activities.

The modern planner's approval of transportation as the street's dominating function has fit within a larger theory of city planning that dissociates the various pieces of the city. The ensuing segregation of urban elements, such as land uses and transportation modes, stemmed from an overreaction to the complexities of the new industrial and postindustrial city and a desire to control these complexities. Hence, rather than continuing the nineteenth-century tradition, which used streets as catalysts for the transformation of cities, modern planners have focused on sectors within the city, as reflected in land-use plans and area plans, and on controlling private development, as reflected in zoning codes (see chap. 22, by R. B. Eichner and H. Tobey). The result is that streets have become a void in the minds of city planners. Transportation planning has been made separate from city planning and, accordingly, streets separate rather than link the different pieces of the city.

City planners, working together with engineers, architects, and landscape architects, need to conceptualize streets as networks of public open space. Neil Klopfenstein and Linda Snyder discuss the repercussions of such a concept on rapidly growing Alaskan cities (chap. 11). Thinking of streets as open space networks helps integrate many aspects and problems of cities, from the control of air quality to the improvement of public transit—see Anne Spirn's chapter 26 and Lorne Cappe's chapter 24, respectively.

All contributions to this volume show how street design and urban design can and must be integrated at several levels once again. Most challenging are the changes in the ways street-use decisions take place. Clearly, the public must be directly involved. As Donald Appleyard's foreword warns, however, considering streets in the public domain makes their use and management difficult. For, as he shows, "the public" is a complex set of actors with diverging views and different values. As a means of resolving the many conflicting demands, he recommends sorting out the issues between downtowns and neighborhoods, where the needs for street space are different. Yet public conflicts, rather than stifling the planning process, should in fact enliven it, resulting in what Mark Francis has called "democratic" streets (chap. 1). Democratic streets are not only multifunctional but they also change over time in response to evolving public claims for the space.

Further probing the process of street-use decision making, Douglass Lee, in chapter 20, proposes to return to the notion of streets as private goods, managed according to private-sector mechanisms. In chapter 19 Richard Untermann argues that current street standards, devised almost exclusively by transportation specialists, emerge as significant impediments to the public use of streets. Steve Dotterer shows how in Portland, Oregon, the public is directly involved in interpreting street standards (chap. 12). The street design process, in itself a complex affair involving many different professionals, is discussed by John Owen in chapter 21 and by Ronald Eichner and Henry Tobey in chapter 22.

The making of better streets obviously requires better technical knowledge about street design. In the dense areas of cities, human health and comfort must be achieved through an emphasis on environmental quality over efficient car travel. Peter Bosselmann (chap. 15) and Harvey Bryan and Susan Stuebing (chap. 25) introduce tools for considering climate and light as important determinants of comfort. Good street design can better protect people from exposure to air pollution, as shown by Anne Spirn's research in chapter 26. Also, implementing a street design policy requires creative financing. Capital improvements for streets can be shared by several public agencies often aided by private developers, as Kenneth Greenberg's case study of Toronto (chap. 14) illustrates.

Streets in North American cities. Several aspects of the American city facilitate the redesign of its streets. First of all, an inordinate amount of urban land—from 30 to as much as 60 percent—is allocated to streets, not including freeways or other designated high-speed roads. While congested parts of cities, such as automobile-oriented suburban centers and crowded downtowns, are perhaps difficult to reclaim, urban streets in America are, for the most part, not subject to the "stress" that is put upon streets in older European cities. The abundance of streets makes it realistic to rethink the use of street space for many activities other than automobile traffic. In chapter 23, Beatrice Ryan discusses the particularly exciting possibility of vacating this space.

Second, streets are the most pervasive public open areas in American cities, where outdoor plazas, squares, and even parks have not developed in a significant way. (The only other open space found in the same frequency is the parking lot, unfortunately in the private realm!)

Third, the relative youth of the American city holds some promise. Infrastructure maintenance has not been an important agenda item in new American cities, and delayed action in this area will soon require large amounts of resources to restore existing streets. As it makes financial sense to rethink the role of streets, other considerations can be included as well. Lucien Kroll's chapter examines how meaningful public places—where people congregate spontaneously and where they customarily walk to carry on daily activities—build on the bits and pieces of the city's social history. In newer American cities, opportunities to cultivate history are just emerging now. As such cities formed, cars quickly dominated, stifling opportunities for public events and contributing to the dearth of public plazas, squares, or other areas for people to gather. Yet there are signs of change. In Cambridge, Massachusetts, for instance, a number of so-called squares are named after people with a special place in local history. Spatially speaking, these squares are destitute—mere street intersections, places that have neither been nor are conducive to social events. Yet, named after local personalities, they attest to the significance of place in the community. A seed has been planted; the idea of the public place is being realized. And however primitive, it is cultivated in the appropriate location because intersections are *the* public space in American cities.

New public space is now emerging in American cities, sometimes in a grand way. Some 300 years after its inception, Harvard Square, the intersection of several major thoroughfares in Cambridge, is just now being "made" into a public place. In Portland, Oregon, the subject of chapter 13, by Michael Harrison, Pioneer Square is yet another example of a newly created public plaza. (Yet restructuring public space is a lengthy, laborious process—as documented in this volume by Elizabeth Rivers and David Streatfield [chap. 18]. We should also remember that it took at least 400 years of repeated design activity, which followed a few hundred more years of just "using the space" to make Piazza San Marco in Venice!)

A fourth aspect that lends itself to reshaping the role of American streets is evidence of a mature automobile society. Cars are smaller, and automobile speed is gradually being reduced. The roadway could foreseeably become smaller too, with little effect on traffic. (The Swedes have actually *reduced* the network of arterial roads serving Stockholm over the past decade—see chap. 10 by Marina Botta.) The public now recognizes the benefits of walking and bicycling, and several cities are actively working to make modes of transportation other than the car an integral part of transportation policy. Greater numbers accept car pooling and shared parking. In many ways, a subtle revolution is taking place: although the car remains the principal mode of transportation, it no longer is *symbolically* the most rewarding method of moving about. Several cities have survived long beyond "D day," when planners projected that cars would be at a standstill. Yet many urban areas forestalled the car's demise by lowering the standards attributed to car transportation. Not only did they reduce the space reserved for cars, whether moving or parked, but they allowed the speed of automobile travel to decrease and the costs of maintaining a car within the city to rise dramatically. A comparison with some of the world's most congested cities—New York, Paris, Rio de Janeiro, Mexico City—shows that acceptable standards for cars are culturally bound and change considerably over time. We may be doomed worldwide to choke with our cars, but in cities the phenomenon can be controlled.

Fifth, there are signs that the value of old-fashioned public streets is being missed. Citizens who have been denied basic public rights in shopping malls and other private, often indoor, streets, are taking their grievances to court. And in some cases, the courts have ruled in favor of granting people full public access and rights in malls that are "functionally equivalent" to downtown areas (Woodcock 1984).

The structure of the book. The material in this book is divided into issues related to the appropriate use of urban streets, and approaches toward designing, developing, and managing truly public ones.

The first part, *Better Streets*, examines people in streets. Robin Moore (chap. 3) and Brenda Eubank-Ahrens (chap. 4) give special emphasis to the needs of children, a largely unrecognized, yet extensive, group of street users. In chapter 2, Norman Pressman summarizes the European experience with streets for pedestrians. Chapter 5, by Amos Rapoport, addresses the cultural variations in the levels of socialization and in the interactions between pedestrians and drivers as a prelude to understanding the environmental needs and behavior of pedestrians.

Part 2, *Better Cities*, focuses on streets as important open space networks permeating cities. Street networks are shown to be, in the words of Grady Clay (chap. 6), "great common carriers of information for a democratic society" and "rewarding educational instruments," as well as powerful tools to regulate urban form and development. Contributors to this part also raise issues related to U.S. suburbs and gridded cities.

Part 3, *Streets Reclaimed*, reviews several cases of cities where deliberate efforts have been made to open the use of streets to a large cross section of the population. These case studies display the multifaceted aspects and inherent complexities of real-world decisions regarding street design or implementation. The seductiveness of these new design ideas is enhanced by an understanding of how they have been executed. Cases cover both citywide and areawide approaches to the reclamation of streets.

Part 4, *Considering the Future*, is a collection of ideas, strategies, and tools to transform streets into varied types of public spaces. The contributors discuss issues concerning the formulation and implementation of design policy and offer many suggestions regarding safe, socially responsive, comfortable streets. This material provides the necessary ingredients to develop a public policy for the use of street land.

Many tasks remain. For example, a more detailed examination of parking policy will soon be necessary. Cars are parked during 97 percent of their life (Mackey 1984), and as the moving car comes increasingly under control, issues related to the parked car will also become prominent. Notwithstanding specific issues, this work shows that to expand the function of the street to its full social and economic significance, urban planners and the public must conceive of streets as the primary unifying element of the city. Streets are "the great urban outdoors" (Rudofsky 1969), the publicly controlled land bank that American cities have always lacked. Much can be gained by focusing city planning and design on this public territory.

NOTE

1. In Seattle, Washington, KidsPlace, an ongoing project of the mayor's office, is a children's lobby that gives this normally nonvocal population group the opportunity to express its needs and to obtain special amenities through legislation.

REFERENCES

Anderson, S., ed. 1978. *On Streets*. Cambridge: MIT Press.
Appleyard, D. 1981. *Livable Streets*. Berkeley: University of California Press.
Beedle, L. S., ed. 1986. *Advances in Tall Buildings*. New York: Van Nostrand Reinhold.
City of Boulder, Transportation Division. 1982. "Feet Accompli: Linking People with Places." *Proceedings of the Third Annual Pedestrian Conference*, 7–8 October.
———. 1984. "The City on Its Feet." *Proceedings of the Fifth Annual Pedestrian Conference*, 20–21 September.
City of Boulder, Transportation Division, and Denver Regional Council of Governments. 1981. "Two for the Road: The Urban Pedestrian." *Proceedings of the Second Annual Pedestrian Conference*, 12–13 October.
Eichner, R., and H. Tobey. 1982. "Urban Streetscape Analysis." Draft final report submitted to the Federal Highway Administration, January 15.

Gakenheimer, R. A. 1978. *The Automobile and the Environment: An International Perspective.* Prepared by the Organization for Economic Development. Cambridge: MIT Press.

Jacobs, A. B. 1980. "They're Locking the Doors to Downtown." *Urban Design International* 1, no. 5 (July/August): 24–38.

Kowinski, W. S. 1985. *The Malling of America: An Inside Look at the Great Consumer Paradise.* New York: William Morrow.

Mackey, P. 1984. *La Conception du stationnement en fonction de l'économie urbaine.* Report. Quebec City: Division des études intermodales, Service des études, Ministère des Transports, February.

Moudon, A. V., and P. Laconte, eds. 1983. *Streets as Public Property: Opportunities for Public/Private Interaction in Planning and Design.* Seattle: University of Washington, College of Architecture and Urban Planning.

Public Technology, Inc., and City of Boulder, Transportation Division. 1983. *Proceedings of the Fourth Annual Pedestrian Conference.* Washington D.C.: U.S. Department of Transportation's Technology Sharing Program.

Ramati, R. 1981. *How to Save Your Own Street.* Garden City, N.Y.: Doubleday, Dolphin Books.

Rudofsky, B. 1969. *Streets for People.* Garden City, N.Y.: Doubleday, Anchor Press.

Urban Planning for Children Project, and Swaback, J. 1986. *Planning Sacramento: Views of Students and Parents.* Sacramento, Calif.: Urban Interdependencies.

Wolfe, M. R. 1962. "Shopping Streets and the Pedestrian Rediscovered." *AIA Journal* (May): 33–42.

Woodcock, J. 1984. "Public Access to Private Property: The Preservation of First Amendment Rights." Student paper, Department of Urban Design and Planning, University of Washington, Seattle.

PART ONE

Better Streets

1.
The Making of Democratic Streets

MARK FRANCIS

"It is the idea of the street, not the reality, that is important..."
—A. P. Smithson, 1970

Streets are an important part of the landscape of everyday life. People rely on them for such daily activities as travel, shopping, and interaction with friends and relatives. Much social life and learning occurs along streets. Yet there is now growing concern that American streets are becoming "privatized," denying people basic rights of access, use, and enjoyment. Empirical research, historical analysis, and some demonstration projects (Rudofsky 1969; Whyte 1980; Appleyard 1981; among others) begin to show that good streets are democratic streets—streets that have meaning for people, invite access for all, encourage use and participation, are loved, and are well cared for by their users. These basic qualities of street democracy may be vanishing from our towns, cities, and neighborhoods (fig. 1-1).

In this chapter I will briefly review the history of street life and culture. I will discuss and critique recent design theories and applications including "pedestrianization," "livable streets," and "private indoor streets." Finally, I will introduce an alternative perspective, "democratic streets," which provides a broader and more holistic view of street culture.

STREET DEMOCRACY IN HISTORY

Several historical influences may help to explain America's ambivalence toward streets and their complex role in public culture. J. B. Jackson, in his observations on the evolution of the American landscape (1972), suggests that the grid that shaped much of rural and urban form in America was largely intended

The preparation of this chapter was funded, in part, by a grant from the University of California Agricultural Experiment Station. All photos and graphics are by the author unless otherwise noted.

as a democratic tool to distribute land and define the boundaries between public and private worlds. The grid created the systems of streets and street space as we now know them and gave form to the rural farmstead and urban neighborhood. Early public spaces, such as the commons, were not legally protected because they were understood as part of the public domain.

Early immigrants brought memories of lively European streets that influenced street life in such urban centers as New York City and Boston. Those streets were more democratic than our current ones. While dirty, overcrowded, and often dangerous, they were the center of public life, having been accessible to and used by all types of people. Unfortunately, however, the environmental problems of early urban streets were never resolved, in part because many people chose to leave the city in search of a better life outside. Leo Marx, in *The Machine in the Garden* (1964), claims that an idealized, romanticized view of nature may be partly responsible for suburbanization, the rise of privacy in American life, and the resulting decline in public culture. A majority of Americans believed, as many still do, that the countryside could provide a more pleasant, supportive living environment than the city.

Street democracy also declined with the rise of mass transit, followed by increasing speeds in transportation and, eventually, by the automobile. Not only did the automobile provide the means for people to move away from heavily trafficked streets to the suburbs, but it took people away from direct involvement with the streets themselves. Traffic engineering, with its concerns for efficient traffic movement, became a powerful shaper of city form and continues to dominate decision making regarding streets today. The result has been a decline in the attractiveness and desirability of urban streets (fig. 1-2).

1-1. A lively democratic street in Copenhagen, Denmark, which mixes diverse activities and users.

The past two decades have seen increased interest in the role public space and the street can play in shaping public culture. The demonstrations of the 1960s used streets as a stage for political and social change. Since then, also, street activities, such as street vending, outdoor eating, walking, and bicycling, have increased. Local concern with controlling traffic speeds and improving public transit are further indicators of increased interest in the street as community space. Developers, recognizing the economic potential of the affluent moving back to the city, have reinvested in city centers on a large scale.

RECENT APPROACHES TO STREET DESIGN

Changes in attitude toward city life over the past twenty-five years have supported considerable design, planning, and management activity in transforming urban streets into more safe, secure, and comfortable places. New forms of urban streets have emerged, including "pedestrianized" streets, auto-restricted zones, malls, traffic-managed neighborhood streets, and, more recently, "privatized" indoor commercial streets. Advances in research and practice have contributed useful principles regarding street life and culture that can be generally placed in one of the following three frameworks.

Pedestrian Streets

"Pedestrianization" is the strongest and most influential of the street redesign movements that have

1-2. The problem of the urban American street, as pictured in New York City. Eighty-five percent of city street space is devoted to moving vehicles and 15 percent to pedestrians.

changed the public environment of many cities. Inspired by successful efforts in Europe, American planners set out to revitalize declining downtowns by closing or restricting main streets to traffic and constructing elaborate and expensive pedestrian malls. Labelled by some as the "malling of America," the movement involved the construction of over 150 malls in large and small cities across the United States during the 1960s and 1970s (Brambilla and Longo 1977; Kowinski 1985). Considerable design and research work has documented the impact, both positive and negative, of pedestrianization efforts (Breines and Dean 1975; Brambilla and Longo 1977).

The pedestrian movement has experienced several historical shifts in intent and application. The pedestrian mall proposals of the 1950s and 1960s sought to reduce the negative impact of cars on shoppers. In the 1960s and early 1970s, emphasis was placed instead on creating elaborately landscaped and furnished downtown malls, which catered more to the comfort of pedestrians than to the needs of shoppers.[1]

As commercial ventures, downtown malls were not always successful. For example, merchants found that the mall did not lure shoppers back from suburban shopping centers. Several cities, such as Sacramento, California, have replaced strictly pedestrian malls with "mini-malls," where other forms of traffic, for example, buses, "light rail," and taxis, are allowed during certain periods (Knack 1982) (fig. 1-3).

In the mid-1970s auto-restricted zones became popular. Entire downtown districts were accorded priority access for public transit and people on foot. Bus routes were brought closer to the hearts of downtowns, and cars permitted only at selected times, such as evenings and weekends. Examples of this period, found in downtown Boston, Burlington, Vermont, and Portland, Oregon, have been commercially successful (fig. 1-4).

A few small towns and wealthy commercial areas have developed some of their neighborhood streets for shopping. These efforts have often been influenced by the historic preservation movement, where build-

1-3. The K Street mall, Sacramento, California, one of the early pedestrian malls in the United States: a. before demolition; b. after demolition for light rail in 1985. (Photos: Frieder Luz)

a.   b.

1-4. Washington Street in Boston, Massachusetts, after implementation of an auto-restricted zone.

ings are restored to their original or idealized nineteenth- or twentieth-century character. Building uses have been transformed, with corner drug stores and neighborhood grocery stores replaced by expensive boutiques selling clothes, records, and gourmet foods.

The pedestrianization movement both at the downtown and neighborhood scale remains a commercialization effort committed to maximizing retail sales by creating a more comfortable relationship between moving vehicles and shoppers. Retail sales and private control often ensure the success of these projects, while qualities such as commercial diversity, public access, and street life are ignored.

Livable Streets

A second, smaller movement in street design and management falls under the broad theme of street "livability" or "sociability" (Levine 1984). Pioneered by environmental design researchers such as William Whyte (1980) and the late Donald Appleyard (1981), the "livable streets" movement recognizes the importance of the street environment for the social life of cities. It emphasizes opportunities for greater safety, security, and social contact, particularly on residential streets, where traffic and street quality directly affect residents' satisfaction (Appleyard and Lintell 1977). As in the pedestrianization movement, design and planning innovations from Europe have served as a form of inspiration. For example, the Dutch *Woonerf*, or "play street," is viewed as an effective way to reduce traffic speed and provide for social activities, such as ball play, sitting, and communal use of neighborhood space (Royal Dutch Touring Club 1978) (fig. 1-5).

While popular in Europe, and with some planners and social scientists elsewhere, the livable streets movement has had limited application in the United States, due in part to the reluctance of many public works departments to turn control of the street back to the people. Livable streets efforts here have focused on speed-reducing traffic devices, such as speed bumps and barriers. And even those minimal efforts have been applied only to selected neighborhood environments. Comprehensive efforts that incorporate pedestrian space, reduce traffic, and allow for extensive user participation—such as those found in the Netherlands, Germany, and Norway—have not been extended into the larger public environment of cities in the United States.

Private Indoor Streets

In a third street prototype, the enclosed private street, public pedestrianization techniques, such as auto restriction and extensive landscaping, have been applied indoors. The return of affluent suburbanites to the city has fostered the development of many comfortable and revitalized urban areas. This process, commonly known as "gentrification," creates social enclaves in cities, resulting in the "suburbanization" of downtowns and neighborhoods with new developments such as indoor malls and enclosed atriums. The returning suburban gentry has also brought the forms of social control that have guarded and protected the suburban mall from undesirables. Labelled by some critics as the "Rousing of America" (after the highly publicized projects by the Rouse Corporation in Boston, Baltimore, and, more recently, New York City) this trend has yielded new part-private, part-

1-5. Neighborhood street in Stavanger, Norway, redesigned for children's play and slower traffic speeds.

1-6. Suburban mall concept applied to city center at Quincy Market, Boston, Massachusetts.

public spaces surrounded by boutiques and restaurants that many urban designers see as models for the rebuilding of declining downtowns (Barnett 1978) (fig. 1-6).

In contrast to the openness and plurality of urban streets, these new developments stand aloof from the everyday city environment. These projects often treat the nearby street as a hostile place, either to be ignored or guarded against with gates and even armed guards. Public policy and funding have supported this move toward "privatized" public space. For example, authors of the highly acclaimed San Francisco Downtown Plan (San Francisco Dept. of Planning 1985), under pressure from developers, have allowed en-

closed pedestrian and atrium areas to be counted as public outdoor space (fig. 1-7).

As with the earlier "pedestrianization" movement, the privatization of the urban landscape remains largely a commercial venture where retail sales determine the social design of public space. Private developers have now moved indoors, where they can better control use and users.

At the same time, most streets in traditional neighborhoods and shopping areas remain untouched, at the mercy of traffic, and economically and ecologically unhealthy. Some are homes for transients and other unwanted citizens. The creation of privileged urban enclaves thus contributes to larger social prob-

1-7. New downtown indoor atrium street space, Oslo, Norway.

lems, while it works against the ideal of a democratic city with social and economic diversity.

There are signs that the privatization process may also be taking place in some European cities and towns—traditionally the models of democratic urban space. French environmental psychologist Perla Korosec-Serfaty (1980) has labelled this process "museumization," where natural public spaces, such as squares and small plazas in older towns in France, are being turned into nicely preserved but socially changed places. The atrium movement is now very popular in some parts of Europe and Japan, with large enclosed interior malls completed in several cities, including Paris, Amsterdam, and Tokyo. The international flavor of the privatization movement raises basic questions about the future role streets will play in supporting public life.

DEMOCRATIC STREETS: AN INITIAL DEFINITION

The decrease in plurality of public space, as shaped by current practices of urban design, and the growing trend of privatization, together create a troubling gap between the social goals and manifest results of current design and development initiatives. A broader and more holistic concept of "good" streets is needed.

The alternative perspective is "democratic" streets. Incorporating some aspects of pedestrian and livable streets, the concept of democratic streets is grounded in the notion of public use. It recognizes streets as playing larger social, economic, and ecological roles in towns and cities.

A democratic street is one that reflects the history as well as the social and economic diversity of the larger neighborhood and city. Friendly to pedestrians and livable for residents, it also reflects social justice, economic health, and ecological vitality. The democratic street does not exclude the automobilist but provides space for vehicles by striking a more equitable balance with other street users, namely, pedestrians and bicyclists. Like the livable street, it stresses safety and comfort. Yet the democratic street also emphasizes the access and needs of many different kinds of people, provides opportunities for discovery and challenge, and actively encourages user manipulation, appropriation, and transformation.

Street democracy grows out of the concept of *publicness*. While the concept of privacy has been well developed and legally protected in modern society, publicness is a relatively new concept that recognizes one's right to free and unlimited access to public places. Publicness is the foundation of street democracy, providing the framework in which a true public culture can develop and flourish.[2]

What specific ingredients are needed to create a democratic street? Past research on the quality of street life reveals some important characteristics.

Jane Jacobs (1961), one of the early advocates of democratic streets, made planners aware that the "eyes on the street" were important in creating a sense of place and security in neighborhoods. Observations of her own street in Greenwich Village encouraged her to advance important principles of street quality and democracy, such as the need for streets to support contact, safety, and child use.

Kevin Lynch, another keen observer of urban life, argues in *A Theory of Good City Form* (1981) that we have five basic public space rights: presence, use and action, appropriation, modification, and disposition.

These rights, simply stated, are that people should not only have access to a public space, but also freedom to use, change, and even claim the space, as well as to transfer their rights of use and modification to other individuals. Lynch's spatial rights provide an effective measurement of the street's publicness and democracy.

Based on the work of Jacobs, Lynch, Appleyard, and others, we can further define democratic streets as ones that are well used and that invite direct participation, provide opportunities for discovery and adventure, and that are locally controlled and broadly accessible.

What follows is a discussion of specific ingredients of street democracy that are useful for evaluating existing streets or for designing new ones.

USE AND USER DIVERSITY

Healthy streets are used by different people for a variety of activities. Yet streets are often designed primarily for one group or for a particular function, such as walking or driving. A lively and successful street demands a balanced mix of different user groups and activities.

User diversity exists when a variety of age groups and social classes can interact in a place, or at least tolerate one another without major physical or social controls. As Stephen Carr and Kevin Lynch have noted (1981), a healthy balance between freedom and control is needed to minimize user competition. For example, security problems in midtown Manhattan plazas (such as Exxon's) prompted plaza managers to redesign the spaces, with the aim of excluding low-income users and attracting more affluent ones. Yet a successful public place is one where users of different backgrounds can coexist without one group dominating another.

As Whyte has pointed out (1980), people-watching is one of the primary activities shared by different classes of people in public space. For the sake of diversity, it ought to be encouraged. Such simple amusements as walking, talking, eating, and sports also give a street diverse life. Unfortunately, planners have attempted to relegate these activities mainly to parks, restaurants, and public buildings. We need to bring them back to the street.

Failure of pedestrian malls can be traced to one social group's lack of tolerance for others that have been attracted by new amenities. In the case of the K Street mall in Sacramento, California (Becker 1973), pedestrianization failed to attract suburban shoppers downtown as long as existing elderly and teenage users found the mall to be a comfortable place for "hanging out." In 1982, after a decade of debate, merchants and planners agreed on a plan that sacrificed pedestrian improvements (and the undesirable users they bring) and improved transportation to the mall, introducing streetcar traffic on K Street.

The social success of the *Woonerf*, as documented in Leiden, Holland (van Andel 1985) and in Hannover, West Germany (Eubank-Ahrens 1985; see also chap. 4) results from the deliberate redesign of street space to foster user diversity. Both postconstruction evaluation studies found that more small children used the street space after the *Woonerf* was first built, whereas adult users spent more time in the space following reconstruction. These empirical findings support previous theories maintaining that a balanced diversity of use and users is needed for urban space to become truly public.

ACCESSIBILITY

Kevin Lynch (1981) and J. B. Jackson (1984) claim that a space is "open" only when it is publicly accessible. A fenced-in area along a waterfront, for example, cannot be classified as open space; the area may be vacant but it nonetheless prohibits public entry. As Lynch and Jackson suggest, degrees of publicness are crucial for classifying space. Such criteria extend beyond mere physical considerations to encompass humanistic concerns. Designers should use accessibility criteria as guidelines in determining whether a new project adds to or subtracts from the public landscape of the city.

Research on children's access to the outdoors has offered clues to the effect of public access on human development in general. Hart (1978), studied children's use of the public landscape, both in a small Vermont town and in New York City neighborhoods. He found that the environmental competence of children is directly related to their ability to gain safe access to built and natural environments. The space directly near the home environment was found to be especially important. Yet home-based recreation is still poorly planned on many neighborhood streets (Brower 1973), although safe and easy access to nearby street spaces continues to be a major factor in residential satisfaction (Appleyard 1981).

PARTICIPATION/MODIFICATION

Direct participation of street users in the design and management processes will help people establish an *ongoing* attachment to streets. Considerable advances have been made in the development of participatory methods that allow street users to involve themselves directly in the creation and maintenance of neighborhoods and urban centers (Francis 1979).

Streets also need to be modified by their users to fit the changing activities and needs of the community. Loose parts, such as toys and sports equipment, can encourage children to use the street environment (Nicholson 1971). Elements brought out by residents or merchants, for example, movable chairs and planters, can contribute to a sense of local control and responsibility for the street environment. Recent research has documented that users who develop vacant lots into community gardens and plant flowers and vegetables on sidewalks often encourage other people to participate in the improvement and care of the rest of the street (Francis, Cashdan, and Paxson 1984).

Direct, active engagement in modifying the nearby environment can have an important impact on a person's development and improve his or her competence in other aspects of life (fig. 1-8).

REAL AND SYMBOLIC CONTROL

Streets work democratically when people feel a sense of control over them. Conversely, streets fail when people perceive them as belonging to the "city" or when they seem to be controlled by no one (Francis 1987). Control is real for residents who maintain the sidewalk or street trees; it is symbolic when residents feel that their private space, such as their front yard or entrance, extends into the public environment (Hester 1984).

Largely ignored as an element of street design and management in the United States, control has been part of the success of European streets for centuries. It allows direct negotiation of the conflicting values of different publics. For example, the concern of merchants for a safe environment often competes with the needs of local teenagers for a place to socialize. The environmental values of children and adults are often quite different, as found in a study of a new neighborhood in Davis, California (Francis 1983). This study used an action-research approach employing methods such as favorite-place analysis and ideal landscape mapping, to design a new playground. Researchers discovered that adults wanted a clean and safe play structure while children wanted opportunities for playing with dirt, water, and natural elements. A participatory approach allowed for these two groups to educate and negotiate with one another directly to create a solution that provided elements from each group.

TRAFFIC MANAGEMENT

Traffic management is also an important ingredient of street democracy. Considerable research has demonstrated that control of traffic speed contributes to one's attachment to or detachment from a residential street (Appleyard 1981). For example, fear of auto

a.

b.

1-8. Residents taking control of street by planting trees in street space: a. Davis, California; b. West Germany.

traffic is largely responsible for parents restricting children's use of the street space in front of houses (Sandels 1975). Appleyard and Lintell (1977) determined that resident satisfaction with neighborhood streets in San Francisco depended in large part on traffic volume and speed. They also found greater social contact among residents on streets with less traffic. Ongoing traffic management is needed in order for other democratic elements, such as use, access, and participation, to be effective.

SAFETY/SECURITY

Peoples' concern about traffic is only part of their need to feel safe on a street. Like the auto driver, the pedestrian assesses the hazards of a street before deciding whether or not to use it, and street democracy depends on his or her sense of security.

The effect of crime on street satisfaction is an important yet poorly understood dimension of city life. Fear of being assaulted or robbed, which is particularly acute for women, can be a major barrier to street use, especially at night. Drug sales commonly take place on streets and create a sense of insecurity for pedestrians. Often there is a gap between real and perceived crime that restricts a person's use of the public environment.

Many who are concerned with safety, especially merchants and developers, have argued persuasively for the development of private streets. Democratic streets, however, must strike an appropriate balance between safety and qualities denied by privatization, namely, discovery and challenge. This is particularly important for children. Risk and discovery contribute to their individual development and environmental competence, and a sense of safety can be maintained without removing the street's challenges.

GROUND FLOOR-STREET RELATIONSHIP

In democratic streets a social connection links ground floor building uses to the adjacent street space. A public street has a healthy relationship between private or semipublic life inside buildings and the public world outside (Fischer 1981). Whyte (1980) argues that "dead" uses, such as businesses without display windows, banks, offices, parking garages, and storage areas with blank walls, should not be placed along the

1-9. Activity mapping of pedestrians, bicycles, and autos in downtown Davis, California. (Source: Francis 1984: 21–35)

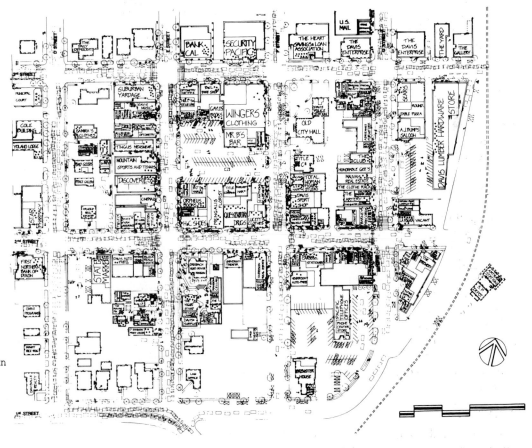

LEGEND

- One Observed Pedestrian Street Crossing
- Moving Bicycle
- Parked Bicycle
- Moving Vehicle
- Vacant Parking Space

public street. On the other hand, uses such as news-stands or restaurants can enhance street life. Activity-mapping techniques have been developed that allow the ground floors of buildings to be designed in harmony with existing street uses and physical elements (Francis 1984) (fig. 1-9).

In residential neighborhoods there is a greater recognition of the importance of home-based recreation in everyday life (Brower 1973). For example, the placement of kitchen windows and other lived-in spaces overlooking the street, as well as of building elements, such as ledges and stoops that encourage sitting, can enhance the social life of the street and improve the sense of safety for residents.

COMFORT

A street needs to be comfortable to be democratic, and comfort involves adequate shading from hot summer sun and extreme temperatures, as well as solar access during cold days. The latter requirement is especially important. It was paramount, for example, in the recently approved San Francisco Downtown Plan (San Francisco Dept. of City Planning 1985), which stipulated that the physical form of new office buildings was to be determined by the solar access provided to the adjacent street environment (see chap. 15, by P. Bosselmann).

Adequate and comfortable seating space is also essential. William Whyte's recommendations for providing "sittable space" (1980) are particularly useful for design and management. One can use a "comfortability" factor to gauge the potential success of a new public space or street environment.

ECOLOGICAL QUALITY

The role of natural systems in urban environmental quality has been a neglected aspect of city and street design, as shown in theoretical work by Hough (1984) and Spirn (1984; see also chap. 26). A democratic street is an environmentally healthy one. Air and noise quality affect one's attachment to a street and should be carefully monitored and controlled through traffic management.

A healthy street is in turn a green one. Vegetation and plant materials contribute to clean air, buffer noise, and add visual relief (fig. 1-10). As documented by the research of Appleyard (1981), most street users value natural vegetation and rate trees as one of the street's most desired elements. Thus, trees, plants, and animals need to be reintroduced to street environments to help create greater user comfort and satisfaction.

ECONOMIC HEALTH

Related to ecological health is a need for streets to be economically healthy. A democratic street is one

1-10. Trees adjacent to urban paths and streets in London, England, add visual interest and clean air.

where businesses and land values prosper, and where abandonment, vacant lots, and disinvestment are discouraged. Yet economic health needs to be balanced with other dimensions of street democracy, such as diversity of uses and users, participation, and controlled traffic speeds. One type of business should not be allowed to take over, especially as a wide range of business activities can contribute to an image of prosperity.

ENVIRONMENTAL LEARNING AND COMPETENCE

Democratic streets are places where we learn to deal more competently with our everyday environment (Ward 1978); they communicate much about the economy and social structure of urban life (see chap. 6, by G. Clay). Researchers have shown that much of a child's learning takes place close to home (Carr and Lynch 1968; Hart 1978. See also chap. 3, by R. Moore). The street should be a comfortable setting where learning by children, teens, and the elderly alike can take place naturally. The experience and interpretation of the street by all age groups is critical to the continued education and development of an urban society.

The "town trail" concept, developed in Britain, exploits the educational potential of the street cheaply and innovatively (Goodey 1975). Reference material was prepared to help people understand the town environment as they walked along a designated route. The maps and guidebooks were designed to provide visitors of all ages with an incisive history of the town (see chap. 3, by R. Moore, note 2). The town trail approach has useful and inexpensive applications in the United States.

LOVE

Perhaps most important, streets need to be loved. Although difficult to measure, meaning and memorability are hallmarks of the successful street. A democratic street is rich with associations, a place you want to come back to, like the Champs Elysées in Paris or Times Square in New York. Democratic streets also mirror the history of a place, providing a connection between people and previous street use and revealing the larger social and political world in which the street exists.

Memories of favorite childhood street environments can be important sources of current design ideas. For example, one can map a favorite street to launch a participatory design and management process for a neighborhood or downtown street (Appleyard 1981; Francis 1981).

CONFLICT

Efforts to make streets democratic will unavoidably invite conflict because democratic streets, by their very definition, require greater user participation and negotiation. Street publics, as outlined in Donald Appleyard's foreword to this volume, will need to articulate and defend their values more clearly. Designers can play a significant role in translating the everyday experiences and values of people into concrete plans (see chap. 21, by J. H. Owen, Jr.). As a result of this process, streets will become stages for more diverse urban life and activity.

EXAMPLES OF SUCCESSFUL DEMOCRATIC STREETS

Given these dimensions of street democracy, which streets stand as successful examples? Based on a recent survey of public-space research (Carr, Francis,

Rivlin, and Stone n.d.), several places may be considered prototypes.

Davis Farmers' Market, Davis, California

On Saturday mornings and Wednesday afternoons, farmers back up their trucks against the curb along C Street adjacent to Central Park, and residents of Davis turn out for the biweekly ritual of buying fresh fruit and vegetables. At first glance, the market is a place to purchase locally grown produce directly from farmers. However, a visitor does not take long to discover that much more goes on here. The market also serves as one of the central meeting places for the residents of this university town; it is a place to bump into friends, share news, lobby city officials, and obtain anything from fresh bagels and cut flowers to political information. As customers arrive, the sidewalk becomes a block-long promenade. The play area in the park is quickly filled with small children, dropped off by parents who go on to do their shopping (fig. 1-11).

Robert Sommer has observed some of the public qualities of markets, of which there are now over fifty in California: "Farmers' markets are among the most social spaces in America today. People are there to buy, barter, converse, and watch the spectacle. In designing and modifying urban parks, there is a need to provide space and facilities for such gatherings to help build and preserve a sense of community" (1981: 26).

Grand Street Waterfront Park, Brooklyn, New York

On a vacant lot at the end of Grand Street, near the East River in Brooklyn, Grand Street Park is an active part of the social life of the community (Francis, Cashdan, and Paxson 1984). Designed as a "drive-in park" by landscape architects Philip Winslow and Norm Cohen of the New York City Parks Council, the area is a local setting for community dances, teenage courting, and midnight views of the Manhattan skyline. Grand Street Park was designed and built with active participation by people in the neighborhood. It is a democratic place that is at the same time community controlled and publicly accessible (fig. 1-12).

Early on, the designers realized that the vacant lot was already well used. Their observations of the undeveloped park explains some of its social and community success:

Though much of the street-ending was heaped with refuse, visitors were coming and we spent hours watching what they did. The results were extremely useful. We

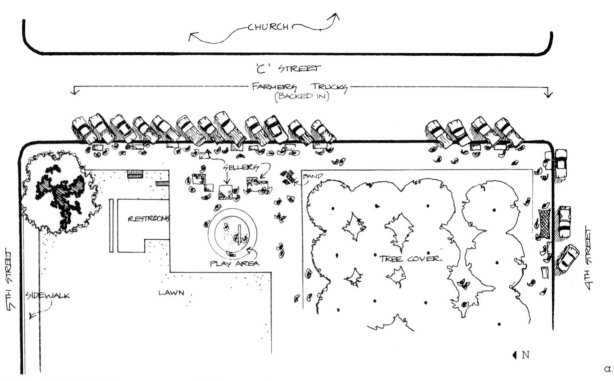

◀ N

a.

1-11. Davis Farmers' Market, Davis, California: a. plan; b. farmers selling locally grown vegetables along C Street.

discovered that most of the visitors were children ages 6 to 16 who invariably headed straight for the water's edge to explore, throw stones in the river, etc. Adults on foot usually went to the point with the highest elevation where they stood quietly for a few minutes while enjoying the view. We learned that many visitors, in cold weather or warm, during the day or night, drove as close to the water as possible and stayed in their cars, looking on the river. We saw no reason to disrupt these existing uses by construction of the park; rather, we would seek to preserve and enhance them. They were activities we would expect to be popular after the site was improved (Cohen 1979: 43).

Woonerf, Delft, Netherlands

As one enters the traffic-protected *Woonerven* in the Netherlands, one immediately recognizes that something special is going on. Cars are moving at pedestrian speeds, and the street floor has been redesigned without curbs to allow for free pedestrian and bicycle flow. In *Livable Streets* (1981: 306), Donald Appleyard summarizes the features of the Dutch *Woonerf*: "You may walk anywhere on a road within a 'woonerf' and children may play anywhere; . . . anyone who drives a car or rides a moped . . . must not impede pedestrians. But pedestrians and children at play should not

b.

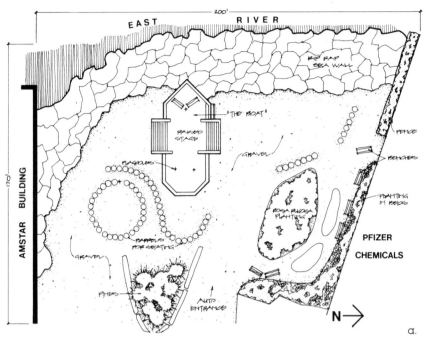

1-12. Grand Street Waterfront Park, Brooklyn, New York: a. plan; b. cars at "drive-in." (Drawing: Lisa Jovanovich)

obstruct or unnecessarily impede cars; and parking is only permitted where 'P' is painted on the street, parking elsewhere is forbidden." Now, over 800 of these traffic restricted zones have been developed in Dutch neighborhoods (fig. 1-13).

Gogate Walking Street, Røros, Norway

In Røros, a small historic town in the center of Norway, a thoroughfare running alongside is closed during the day to create a *gogate*, or "walking street." A feature of other Scandinavian countries, the *gogate* can be used by traffic only during the evenings or in the harsh winters (fig. 1-14). Limited vehicle use has enabled the street to keep much of its local character: neighborhood-oriented shops are located along its two-block length; restaurants have set out picnic tables for use by anyone; vendors with carts occupy the middle of the street, where they sell hand-crafted goods to tourists; and the local recreation department has placed inexpensive and portable play equipment in the street for use by children.

a.

b.

1-13. Dutch *Woonerf* street concept applied both to <u>a.</u> old, and <u>b.</u> and <u>c.</u> new neighborhoods in Delft.

c.

MEASURING STREET DEMOCRACY

Clearly, every street or network of streets has its own level of democracy, and a variety of techniques are useful in assaying this quality (Jacobs 1985). Some of the more effective traditional research methods involve the observation of street use with behavior mapping techniques, including counts of pedestrian and bicycle flow, tracking of street users, mapping of physical elements on the street, and overlaying behavioral data (Project for Public Spaces 1981). Other, more interactive methods include the preparation by users of mental maps that feature what they like or dislike in a street; favorite-place analyses that illuminate the varied preferences of children, teenagers, and adults; group mapping or workshops on street quality; and user and nonuser surveys or questionnaires.

A DEMOCRATIC PROCESS FOR MAKING AND MANAGING STREETS

How can we ensure that streets are planned and preserved for democracy? Democratic streets are not possible without a democratic process charged with shaping their character and form. The failure of past attempts may rest in part with the absence of such an ongoing management process.

Street designers and managers should recognize that good streets are not designed but evolve over time (Seamon and Nordin 1980; Moudon 1986). Typically, streets are designed without provision for ongoing evaluation and necessary adjustments. While careful planning can enhance street quality, successful streets also result from a variety of social, economic, and political forces.

New public commissions must be developed that decentralize the control of streets; public works departments and traffic engineers need to share management responsibilities with interdisciplinary professionals, intergovernmental task forces, and, most important, local user groups. To this end, evaluation could be centered on areas, such as storefronts, where people can easily participate in the process.

Streets, in other words, cannot be successful without a new form of street politics that requires users and interest groups to negotiate directly with one another and share power in a continuous and open process. A democratic process, however, demands several additional—and essential—measures: the current privatization trend of the public environment must be reversed—cities have to recognize that downtown and neighborhood development projects must directly contribute to public street life; greater public education and understanding of street quality needs to be developed through the encouragement of public participation; and cities must explore ways to allocate space more equitably so that full public access, use, and enjoyment of downtown and neighborhood streets is ensured (see chap. 10, by M. Botta). A special effort needs to be made to improve the publicness of private indoor commercial spaces (fig. 1-15).

With much of the public life of cities still taking place on streets, they will continue to be places where public culture is developed and nurtured. Street democracy may be an important way to create a truly healthy and lively public environment.

1-14. Children and parents using play equipment in *gogate*, Røros, Norway.

1-15. A friendly, democratic street in Sweden.

NOTES

1. See Brambilla and Longo (1977) for a review of the goals and results of the pedestrian movement in the United States and Europe.
2. The concept of "publicness" was first developed by Lynn Paxson and Alan Forest in a study of the waiting room of Grand Central Station. Their research was part of a doctoral seminar in environmental psychology taught by Leanne Rivlin and myself at the City University of New York (1979).

REFERENCES

Alexander, C., S. Ishikawa, M. Silverstein, M. Jacobsen, I. Fiksdahl-King, and S. Angel. 1977. A *Pattern Language*. New York: Oxford University Press.

Appleyard, D. 1981. *Livable Streets*. Berkeley: University of California Press.

Appleyard, D., and M. Lintell. 1977. "The Environmental Quality of City Streets: The Residents' Viewpoint." *AIP Journal* 43, no. 2 (March): 84–101.

Appleyard, D., and K. Lynch. 1974. "Temporary Paradise?

A Look at the Special Landscape of the San Diego Region." Report prepared for the Planning Department of the City of San Diego.

Barnett, J. 1978. *Urban Design as Public Policy*. New York: Harper & Row.

Becker, F. 1973. "A Class-conscious Evaluation: Going Back to Sacramento's Mall." *Landscape Architecture* 64: 295–345.

Brambilla, R., and G. Longo. 1977. *For Pedestrians Only*. New York: Whitney.

Breines, S., and W. Dean. 1975. *The Pedestrian Revolution: Streets without Cars*. New York: Vintage.

Brower, S. 1973. "Streetfront and Sidewalk." *Landscape Architecture* 63: 364–69.

Carr, S., and K. Lynch. 1968. "Where Learning Happens." *Daedalus* 97: 4 (Fall).

———. 1981. "Open Space: Freedom and Control." In *Urban Open Spaces*, edited by L. Taylor. New York: Rizzoli.

Carr, S., M. Francis, L. Rivlin, and A. Stone. (N.d.) *Qualities of the Public Environment of Cities*. Book manuscript in preparation.

Cohen, N. 1979. "Park Design: Who Makes the Decisions?" In *Bronx River Current*. New York: Bronx River Restoration Corporation (Fall).

Cranz, G. 1981. *The Politics of Park Design*. Cambridge: MIT Press.

Eubank-Ahrens, B. 1985. "The Impact of *Woonerven* on Children's Behavior." *Children's Environments Quarterly* 1: 39–45.

Fischer, C. 1981. "The Public and Private Worlds of City Life." *American Sociological Review* 46: 306–16.

Francis, M., ed. 1979. *Participatory Planning and Neighborhood Control*. New York: Center for Human Environments, City University of New York.

———. 1981. "Designing Landscapes with Community Participation and Behavioral Research." *Landscape Architectural Forum* 2: 14–21.

———. 1983. "Some Differences between Child and Adult Design Values in Open Space Projects." *Childhood City Quarterly* 10: 20–24.

———. 1984. "Mapping Downtown Activity." *Journal of Architectural and Planning Research* 1: 21–35.

———. 1987. "The Park and Garden in the City: Some Different Meanings Attached by Users to a Public Park and Community Garden." *Landscape Journal* (in press.)

Francis, M., L. Cashdan, and L. Paxson. 1984. *Community Open Spaces*. Covelo, Calif: Island Press.

Goodey, B. 1975. "Urban Trails: Origins and Opportunities." *Journal of the Royal Town Planning Institute* 61: 29–30.

Hart, R. 1978. *Children's Experience of Place*. New York: Irvington Press.

Hester, R. 1984. *Planning Neighborhood Space*. New York: Van Nostrand Reinhold.

Hough, M. 1984. *City Form and Natural Process*. New York: Van Nostrand Reinhold.

Jacobs, A. 1985. *Looking at Cities*. Cambridge: Harvard University Press.

Jacobs, J. 1961. *The Death and Life of Great American Cities*. New York: Vintage.

Jackson, J. B. 1972. *American Space*. New York: Norton.

———. 1984. *Discovering the Vernacular Landscape*. New Haven: Yale University Press.

Knack, R. 1982. "Pedestrian Malls: Twenty Years Later." *Planning* 48, no. 11 (December): 15–19.

Kowinski, W. S. 1985. *The Malling of America*. New York: William Morrow.

Korosec-Serfaty, P. 1980. *The Main Square: Functions and Daily Uses of Stortget, Malmo*. Lund, Sweden: ARIS.

Levine, C. 1984. "Making City Spaces Lovable Places." *Psychology Today* (June): 56–63.

Lynch, K. 1981. *A Theory of Good City Form*. Cambridge: MIT Press.

Marx, L. 1964. *The Machine in the Garden: Technology and the Pastoral Ideal in America*. New York: Oxford University Press.

Moudon, A. V. 1986. *Built for Change: Neighborhood Architecture in San Francisco*. Cambridge: MIT Press.

Nicholson, S. 1971. "Theory of Loose Parts: How Not to Cheat Children." *Landscape Architecture* (October): 30–34.

Project for Public Spaces, Inc. 1981. "What Do People Do Downtown? How to Look at Mainstreet Activity." New York: Project for Public Spaces, Inc.

Rivlin, L., and M. Francis, eds. 1979. "Provisions for People: Grand Central Station and Citicorp Study." New York: Center for Human Environments, City University of New York.

Royal Dutch Touring Club. 1978. *Woonerf*. The Hague, Netherlands: Royal Dutch Touring Club.

Rudofsky, B. 1969. *Streets for People*. New York: Doubleday.

Sandels, S. 1975. *Children in Traffic*. London: Paul Elek.

San Francisco Department of City Planning. 1985. *The San Francisco Downtown Plan*. City of San Francisco: San Francisco Department of City Planning.

Seamon, D., and C. Nordin. 1980. "Marketplace as Place Ballet." *Landscape* 24: 35–41.

Sommer, R. 1981. "Farmer's Market Resurgence: Landscape Design Implications." *Landscape Architectural Forum* 2 (Summer): 26–31.

———. 1983. *Social Design*. Englewood Cliffs, N.J.: Prentice-Hall.

Spirn, A. W. 1984. *The Granite Garden: Urban Nature and Human Design*. New York: Basic Books.

van Andel, J. 1985. "Effects of Children's Outdoor Behavior on Physical Changes in a Leiden Neighborhood." *Children's Environments Quarterly* 1:46–54.

Ward, C. 1978. *The Child in the City*. New York: Pantheon.

Whyte, W. 1980. *The Social Life of Small Urban Places*. Washington, D.C.: Conservation Foundation.

2.
The European Experience

NORMAN E. P. PRESSMAN

Most European city centers have been returned to the pedestrian, as examples in Switzerland, France, Germany, the Netherlands, Denmark, and England attest. Pedestrian zones often coincide with historic medieval centers that exhibit the qualities inherent in a fine-grained urban tissue; both reflect the spatial diversity and human scale that are so vital to our physical and psychological well-being. Although pedestrian zones were first pioneered in town centers, they have recently found their way into residential neighborhoods. There, they are instrumental in protecting the pedestrian domain from automobiles, returning public open spaces and streets to people, and creating environments that can once again become agents of social contact, reflection, and vitality. The automobile may have been accommodated by vast underground and multistory car parks, but the pedestrian has been given priority.

A sensitivity to the human condition and its expression in physical terms characterizes a "new" urbanity in city planning and design. Priority is given to the qualitative aspects of urban life, with a focus on increasing and improving urban activities. Urbanity is associated with the notions of *savoir-faire la ville* (knowing how to plan and design the city) and *savoir-vivre en ville* (understanding how to enjoy and use the urban environment) (Biennale de Paris 1980).

Essential to both notions is the social activity of the city. Public collective spaces bear witness to the need for social intercourse. The agoras, fora, and squares of the past had been designed and used for the exchange of information, material goods, and ideas (Smith 1977). The "new" urbanity preserves the activities as well as the structures of the old, for which four hierarchies of socially intensive space can be designated (Smith 1977):

1. Formal space (civic and religious plazas, as, for example, Piazza San Marco, Venice; Place de la Concorde, Paris; and Piazza del Campo, Siena)
2. Casual space (public and informal commercial squares, as, for example, the harbor at Vieux Port, Marseilles, and Bahnhofplatz, Zurich)
3. Protective space (intimate, sheltered, meeting places for sitting, daydreaming, and chatting, as, for example, Place des Vosges, Paris; semipublic courts immediately off the Kalverstraat, Amsterdam; and Kappelerhof, Zurich)
4. Linear space (shopping streets, arcades, and promenades, as, for example, Souk at Marrakesh; the Milan Galleria; the Paseo at Palma de Majorca; Bahnhofstrasse in Zurich; and Eaton Centre in Toronto)

For design purposes, the conceptualization and evaluation of any of the street spaces above can be approached from two fundamental perspectives. One emphasis is on urban form and the use of streets (and specifically on pedestrian environments, where environment is meant as space and artifact). The other is on the "real-life," day-to-day user experience (experiential realm). The former is rooted in the formalist tradition of city planning embodied in the works of Camillo Sitte, while the latter is an outgrowth of the behavioral schools of psychological thought and is closely linked with developments in the fields of man-environment studies. In the words of R. K. Jarvis:

The visual artistic tradition speaks in aesthetic, abstract terms . . . . At the other end of the spectrum urban design analysis based on social usage may hardly include any reference to the appearance of a place at all; behavioural matters and their congruence or incongruence with the surroundings predominate (1980: 51).

THE URBAN-SOCIAL STREET

Boulevardiers, or "men about town," came into existence in Paris in the 1820s, where they elevated street life to the apex of social activity. The phenomenon of the *flaneur* was produced. It is suggestive that *loiterer*, which has a distinctly sinister meaning, is one translation of "*flaneur.*" A more acceptable translation is *stroller*, although strolling is more likely to occur in a park than along a street (Bedarida and Sutcliffe 1980: 391).

Varied street life was also sustained in Paris by a multiplicity and mix of land uses and high residential densities throughout the nineteenth century and up until the present day. Recently, however, the tradition of the "stroller" has been revived outside of Paris —witness Dufferin Terrace and rue St. Jean in Quebec City; the Yorkville area of Toronto; Dizengoff Street in Tel Aviv, which is converted to car-free use one day a week; and the hundreds of streets throughout the world that have already been turned into exclusive or partial pedestrian malls in central-city zones. Entire citywide precincts, exemplified by the Secteur de la Cathédrale in Strasbourg, France, have also become part of the new urban scene.

Yet many streets still remain neglected spaces of the public realm and are viewed merely as conduits for traffic. In fact, some engineers preposterously insist that the pedestrian remains one of the few major impediments to free and efficient traffic flow in cities.

Today, cars—not people—are the biggest obstacle to good streets. Streets need to be safe for adults and children, for those who cycle and walk. Streets must also function as part of the symbolic environment, epitomizing the community sense of place and expressing collective territoriality. As Donald Appleyard observes, none of this is possible as long as the automobile retains its supremacy over all other forms of transportation:

> [People] should not be forced to withdraw from the street because of the discomforts caused by traffic. The street environment should have places where people can sit, converse and play . . . . All streets have a history . . . without undue nostalgia, a street's history [could] be recorded, were residents able to begin seeing it as a "place" rather than a "channel." Residential streets should be destinations, not routes (1980: 33–39).

In fact, the pedestrian strolling about his neighborhood represents one of the essential ingredients of urbanity and of a meaningful social existence. What

is essential, to paraphrase the words of Gertrude Stein, is getting the "there" there, and keeping it there.

General Approaches for Accommodating the Pedestrian

While North American streets have enhanced pedestrian use largely as part of the economic revitalization of downtowns, traffic-free zones in Europe were created for a variety of reasons: a more efficient management of traffic to ameliorate mobility in the core; the conservation of the architectural tissue; the improvement of residential conditions; the beautification of the environment; the desire to achieve meaningful social spaces with a strong sense of identity; the shaping of environments that bring people together and stimulate spontaneous discourse and human contact; and the strategic control of environmental pollution. These goals have been achieved through either or a combination of two general approaches: relegating shopping primarily to urban centers and constraining traffic in residential neighborhoods.

The hundreds of inner-city pedestrian areas created to revitalize European downtowns have helped contain automobile traffic and thus eliminated a major source of visual and atmospheric pollution. As part of this effort, historic public spaces have been returned to their former uses and are slowly reassuming their original character. Lively commercial streets are filled with buyers and window shoppers, and sidewalk cafés are jammed with customers. Moreover, the success of traffic containment in the dense urban cores has sparked a new movement—the restraint of traffic in residential zones to protect the character of these areas. Known in Germany as *Verkehrsberuhigung* (literally, traffic "tranquilization" or traffic "taming"), this idea is a logical extension of Western Europe's extremely successful examples of pedestrian planning.

Traffic-control devices used to restrict the volume, speed, composition, and direction of traffic, and even to limit access to residential sectors, have assumed two basic forms. The first, passive, psychological controls, normally involve signs and rely on obedience and enforcement if they are to prove effective. While allowing flexibility for drivers and access to emergency vehicles, they do not ensure that through traffic will be curtailed within neighborhoods. The second, physical controls, comprise obstacles such as diverters, cul-de-sacs, barriers, and so forth, which are more effective and exert greater control over driver behavior. These systems often create "traffic cells" or "protected neighborhoods," limiting access and frequently segregating pedestrian from vehicular flows and thereby restricting motorcar movements to peripheral and arterial roads.

The Dutch *Woonerf*

The most recent and interesting of the "protective devices" is the *Woonerf*, or residential yard (see chap. 4, by B. Eubank-Ahrens). This unique idea, which involves the conversion of residential streets into pedestrian-dominated, collective spaces (called *Woonerven* in the plural), has proved extremely popular: by the end of 1979, over eight hundred *Woonerven* had been implemented among more than two hundred Dutch cities, with many eager residents requesting yet more. The program has now been adopted at the national level by the Netherlands' Ministry of Transport and Public Works.

The *Woonerf* concept is generally applied in residential areas, where traffic destination is limited to the designated spot and where traffic flows at the rate of 100 to 150 vehicles per hour during the peak period (Wynne 1980). A *Woonerf* street acquires two principal characteristics that differentiate it from all other hitherto used "neighborhood protection" devices.

The street becomes a space shared by pedestrians and cars, where pedestrians rather than motor vehicles have the dominant role. The automobile is tolerated strictly on the basis of "good behavior," as its traditional mastery over the street environment is restricted by physical barriers and legal means. For example, although the roadway is shared, the right-of-way legally belongs to the pedestrian. Each *Woonerf* is clearly marked at its entrances and within its precinct, and cars that are not destined for the area are strongly induced to confine their movements to peripheral, higher-speed roads. The quality of the neighborhood is upgraded, for not only is through traffic reduced, but drivers in the *Woonerf* must maintain a speed limit of ten to fifteen kilometers per hour (Royal Dutch Touring Club 1978).

The *Woonerf* therefore accommodates cars yet makes them feel fundamentally unwelcome. Other techniques used to do this include the elimination of both straight-line streets and curb separations; the selective positioning of street furniture and children's play equipment; and the creation of public open space and generous parking areas (Wynne 1980; see also chap. 27, by P. Bosselmann).

Some residential neighborhoods in the Netherlands and Sweden are now being protected from through traffic by hydraulic gates that block access to private cars but allow buses (as well as pedestrians and cyclists) to enter. The weight of the bus activates a pressure system that in turn engages a horizontal wheel causing the gate to swing open. The mechanism is so designed that a private car, because of its relatively light weight, cannot activate the gate, which returns automatically to its closed position after a bus has passed. Such physical barriers are proving extremely useful in areas where motorists have developed a habit of disregarding "buses only" signs and where there is insufficient legal enforcement of such traffic regulations.

As a result of these features, *Woonerven* are safer than conventional public streets. Special planting and visually interesting paving materials give them a pleasing appearance. Also, they exhibit a stronger social cohesiveness. They can serve as auxiliary play space (in some cases, the only play space) for children and they offer adults possibilities for sitting, daydreaming, chatting, and exchanging glances with neighbors and passersby. The street thus has the potential of becoming part of the social realm and of fostering more social interaction and recreation than do car-oriented urban streets. The overall design philosophy of the *Woonerf* is to create a type of "gestalt" message that streets belong to residents. In the Netherlands, for example, the particular traffic-control devices are left for residents of the streets to determine through a sophisticated process of citizen participation.

Experiments in Other European Countries

West Germany is also engaged in a number of important projects directed at neighborhood upgrading and protection. Known as the *Wohnbereich*, the German *Woonerf* is similar to its Dutch precedent. Each city chooses the techniques and devices to be employed within its neighborhoods but all strive toward the same end: they seek to establish greater stability, participation, and social contact and to ensure that drivers will indeed travel through these areas very slowly and carefully. As in the Netherlands, such measures induce a sense of belonging, greater neighborhood pride, better maintenance, and more stable play patterns among children.

Switzerland has slowly adopted a variation of the *Woonerf* system in Basel, Zurich (where it has been present for several years), and other towns. It is variously called the *Wohnstrasse* or *rue résidentielle*.

Belgium and France have just commenced to explore *Woonerf*-type schemes, or *rue libre*. They are concerned with accommodating different behavior patterns among drivers and residents as well as with responding to different urban layouts. In Scandinavian countries—Norway, Denmark, Sweden, and Finland—"traffic tranquilization" programs and neighborhood protection schemes have evolved simultaneously and are viewed as an integrated process of neighborhood planning.

The underlying idea of the *Woonerf* concept is to reestablish the social character of the street and to make it public territory, as it used to be prior to the mass ownership of the automobile. In this context, one expects that neighborhood relations will be improved and that street residents will become part of a more cohesive community; all the more so, since citizen participation is essential for the proper implementation and maintenance of such programs.

WHAT HAVE WE LEARNED?

Over the past twenty years, urban designers have conducted an unusually large number of experiments to create pedestrian-oriented environments in residential neighborhoods and town centers, with the ultimate objective of making cities more livable. The following list is a summary of the most salient aspects of these environments:

1. *Woonerf* areas integrate car and pedestrian use of the street space in residential neighborhoods.
2. *Woonerf*-type systems cannot properly evolve without a high degree of public participation.
3. The introduction of innovative legislation heralding greater rights for pedestrians and urban dwellers, and the enforcement thereof, is imperative.
4. The conversion of former automobile streets into pedestrian malls, networks, and precincts is now an acceptable concept to the public.
5. Stop signs are beginning to appear at mid-block to slow and divert traffic movement where no intersections or road junctions exist.
6. "Sleeping policemen," or speed bumps, effectively discourage other local traffic movements.
7. Neighborhoods can be protected from through traffic by the use of hydraulic gates blocking access to private cars but permitting buses, cyclists, and pedestrians to enter.
8. Individual components are designed to enhance the visual character of the street. Objects such as paving, litter bins, seating furniture, signage, lighting, planting, and fencing can all emphasize quality and human scale.
9. Sophisticated visual guidance systems are now being introduced to assist visitors and local residents in finding points of interest, urban institutions, and place locations, as well as in using the public transportation systems (the case of Basel, Switzerland, is exemplary).
10. Heritage buildings are being preserved to enrich the street environment in city centers and other densely populated areas.
11. The urban environment is being regarded as a totality rather than as a series of piecemeal policies, programs, and interventions.
12. Strong political commitment is needed for ideas to be actualized.
13. The designation of long-range capital money for future maintenance has become essential.
14. Small-scale, low-cost amenities often go a long way toward improving a town's environment in functional and aesthetic terms and in setting up demonstration projects for future urban action.
15. The street scene is not relegated only to shopping areas and landmark features: all streets, walls, alleys, and open spaces are critical to the improvement of environmental quality.
16. The public has access to and mobility within the designated pedestrian areas.
17. Timing, project management, and skills of insertion into the urban setting are prerequisites for success.
18. Traffic-free zones are integrated with regional and townwide public transit systems.
19. Zoning that extends beyond commercial activities and provides the elements that will draw a healthy population cross-section is critical to the success of animated pedestrian public spaces.
20. The ability to accommodate changes in use over time are central to the zone's vitality.[1]

CONCLUSIONS

Increasing attention will be paid to the quality of life in our urban centers and residential neighborhoods. Yet the problems inherent in the urban environment are obviously not specific to a single nation, much less to a single city; approaches adopted by one community or country can be adapted by another.

In Western Europe, and more particularly in the Federal Republic of Germany, the process of taming traffic is no longer questioned and there remains very little antagonism regarding such action. The difference between the European and North American attitudes can be linked to the fact that the urban tradition (appreciation and resultant use of urban amenities and institutions) has been and still continues to be much more deeply rooted in the European value system (Council for International Urban Liaison 1979). If North Americans were to develop a much closer affinity to the urban rather than the suburban life-style, more humane environments would inevitably evolve.

Streets and public spaces, whether of the climate-controlled or open-air variety, are critical elements in helping us to achieve a sense of importance within our highly mechanized, technological society. In the words of Bernard Rudofsky (1977: 6), "The main task for the towns now is to elevate the pedestrian street from a design concept to a social institution. The newly created legroom might even encourage the nation to take the necessary steps toward an urban utopia—A Declaration of the Rights of the Pedestrian."

Public initiative constitutes a key element of the strategy to develop more humane areas within the city, especially areas that are now on the border of economic decline. Economically, healthy districts are attracting more intensive uses as well as design gestures that effectuate both aesthetic and functional improvement. The private sector is being offered every incentive to contribute its share, and its efforts are being coordinated with those representing the public interest. The result, over the long term, must inevitably be a more livable urban environment.

NOTE

1. For items 16 through 20, see "Keys for Pedestrian Success" in *Urban Innovation Abroad* (Council for International Urban Liaison 1979).

REFERENCES

Appleyard, D. 1980. "Livable Streets: Protected Neighborhoods?" *Urban Design International* 1, no. 5 (July/August): 33–39.

Bedarida, F., and A. Sutcliffe. 1980. "The Street in the Structure and Life of the City." *Journal of Urban History* 6, no. 4 (August): 379–96.

Biennale de Paris. 1980. *Urbanité*. Paris: Section Architecture (3 March).

Council for International Urban Liaison. 1979. *Urban Innovation Abroad*. Special supplement. Washington, D.C.: Council for International Urban Liaison, September.

Jarvis, R. K. 1980. "Urban Environments as Visual Art or as Social Settings." *Town Planning Review* 51, no. 1 (January): 50–66.

Royal Dutch Touring Club. 1978. *Woonerf*. The Hague, Netherlands: Royal Dutch Touring Club.

Rudofsky, B. 1977. Foreword to *For Pedestrians Only*, by R. Brambilla and G. Longo. New York: Whitney Library of Design.

Smith, P. F. 1977. *The Syntax of Cities*. London: Hutchinson.

Wynne, G., ed. 1980. *Learning from Abroad, Traffic Restraints in Residential Neighborhoods*. New Brunswick, N.J.: Transaction Books.

3.
Streets as Playgrounds

ROBIN C. MOORE

Great differences exist between adults and children in their perception and use of the outdoor environment. One of the greatest relates to residential streets. To adults, streets are functional resources: the quickest way from A to B or a good place to park the car. Sometimes, if lined with trees, they are valued as an aesthetic enhancement. Children see streets differently, as play opportunities discovered in lampposts, curbstones, gutters, inspection chamber covers, overhead wires, parked cars, trees, piles of leaves, flights of steps, gates, bollards, hedges, retaining walls, driveways, building entrances, bus stops, mailboxes, street signs, and benches. Children measure the environmental quality of streets by the presence or absence of these mundane objects, not by the ease of traffic flow and parking. Nonetheless, traffic has a critical effect on street playability (fig. 3-1).

STREET PLAY IS HERE TO STAY

Think back to your own childhood for a moment and recall what your favorite play places were. I guarantee that street-related spaces will come to the minds of most readers. Self-reflection is a worthwhile source of understanding, but we do not have to stop there. A clutch of scientific studies conducted in the past fifteen years back up personal recollections and reinforce what any good pair of eyes can still witness: in any present-day residential area inhabited by children, children make substantial use of streets and street-related spaces.

Cooper Marcus (1974: 202), who studied children's activity in St. Francis Square, a multifamily housing

All photographs are by the author unless otherwise noted.

3-1. In Stoke-on-Trent, England, two children chat on the flight of steps leading up to their house, while keeping an eye open for friends in the street below.

district in San Francisco, mapped 44 percent of play occurring on paved areas and 12 percent on perimeter sidewalks. Francis (1985: 36–38) noted 20 percent of

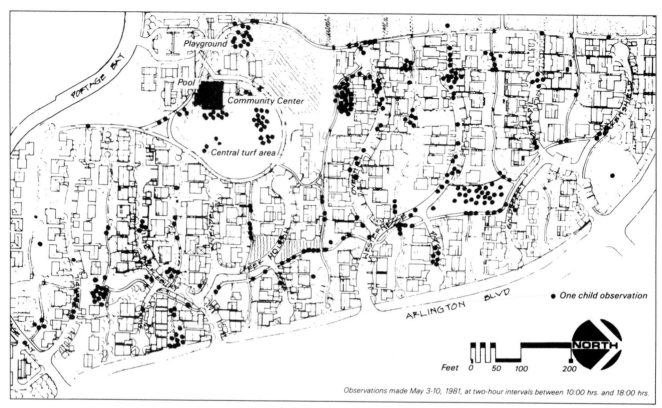

One child observation

Feet 0   50   100   200

Observations made May 3-10, 1981, at two-hour intervals between 10:00 hrs. and 18:00 hrs.

a.

3-2. Consistently high levels of children's use of streets, sidewalks, and pedestrian paths are illustrated by behavior maps of contrasting neighborhood settings in a. Davis, a low-density Californian suburban town, and b. Leiden, a high-density Netherlands town. (Source a.: Francis 1985: 37; source b.: van Andel 1985: 49)

children's activity happening on streets and a further 24 percent on bicycle/pedestrian paths in Village Homes, a suburban neighborhood in Davis, California (fig. 3-2a). A study by van Andel (1985: 46–54) of the effects of environmental improvements on the use of open space in a neighborhood in Leiden, the Netherlands, dramatically illustrates the persistence of street and sidewalk play. Sidewalk play remained the same (44 percent) before and after changes were made, even though some of the pavements were substantially upgraded. Street play, which was initially 22 percent, decreased to 17 percent after the changes, primarily because two newly installed play areas attracted activity (fig 3-2b). We can conclude that, even though faced with many attractive alternatives, a substantial number of children still make the street their playground.

Further results suggest that streets and sidewalks are but two of the most popular items within a broader category of hard-topped circulation spaces woven in-

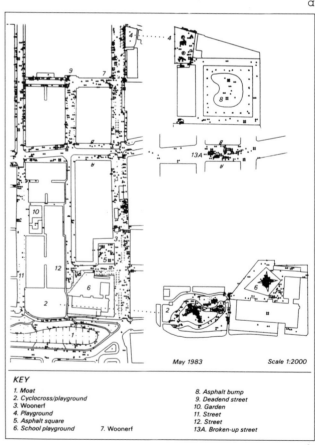

May 1983   *Scale 1:2000*

KEY

1. Moat
2. Cyclocross/playground
3. Woonerf
4. Playground
5. Asphalt square
6. School playground   7. Woonerf

8. Asphalt bump
9. Deadend street
10. Garden
11. Street
12. Street
13A. Broken-up street

b.

to the fabric of residential areas. Traffic-segregated pathways, parking areas, and garage courts also represent appealing places for play. For example, the well-known study by the British Department of the Environment, *Children at Play* (1973: 18,20), showed that 23 percent to 41 percent of observed activity occurred in garage courts and miscellaneous paved areas in five out of six housing sites of varying density. Becker (1976), in a study of four multifamily housing developments, found 22 percent to 38 percent of child activity on pathways. Björklid, in her analysis of two Stockholm housing estates, found that in one estate, Tanto, 63 percent of all children's play took place on asphalt and concrete surfaces, 10 percent occurred on paths, and 8 percent in entrance spaces related to parking (1982: 140–41). In the other estate, Plankan, Björklid mapped 20 percent activity on paths. Gibbons and Stirling's study of Stevenage New Town (n.d.) showed a whopping 48 percent of children's play on streets in the older, nontraffic-separated neighborhoods. Equally dramatic was the evidence that even in the highly segregated neighborhoods, 17 percent to 18 percent activity still occurred on streets. Moore and Young's review (1978), which included the results of a number of smaller studies from both sides of the Atlantic as well as those just cited, concluded that between one-quarter and one-half of observed neighborhood outdoor activity occurred on streets, pathways, and associated hard-surfaced circulation areas.

The foregoing data relate to "actual use," but this is not the only method of assessing children's relationship to the physical environment. Vital information comes from children's own responses—how they perceive their behavior and how they feel about their surroundings.

One out of five children interviewed in a study of three British neighborhoods said streets and associated spaces were their preferred after-school play areas (Moore 1986). When asked where they went to meet other children, 23 percent of the ninety-six children in the study referred to the same spaces. One in three of their drawings of favorite places included streets—the sixth most frequently mentioned element of a total list of sixty (figs. 3-3 and 3-4). Finally, Holme and Massie (1970: 140) reported that among mothers interviewed, 21 percent from Stevenage and 64 percent from Southwork (London) said their children usually played on the street. (However wary we must be of the accuracy with which parents can report activity on behalf of their children, the figures are suggestive.)

Why Streets Are So Attractive

Kids *do* play in streets—all kinds of streets—and nothing that planners, parents, or city officials can do will stop it. Indeed, there is every reason for celebration, for streets are the social hub of the neighborhood, where children meet, learn about each other and their adult neighbors, and investigate their surroundings.

The high levels of use and positive values replicated in these studies in a number of countries can be explained by two phenomena: children's close proximity or ease of access to such spaces and the hard, linear

3-3. Life in a dead-end street: <u>a.</u> eleven-year-old girl playing catch with her sister in a Stoke-on-Trent, England, cul-de-sac; <u>b.</u> the girl's drawing beautifully illustrates the many activities and traditional games possible in such a street, where traffic speeds are low and passage intervals long. (Source <u>b.</u>: Moore 1986: 105)

a.

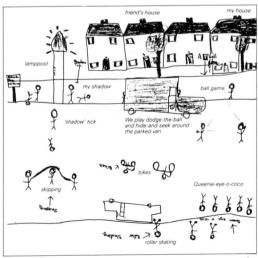

b.

a.

3-4. Indicators of street playability:
a. "race line" painted by a girl and
her friends on a street in moderate-
density Berkeley, California; b.
drawing by the same girl shows the
street race lines, sidewalks, and
adjacent friends' houses as favorite
places to play. (Source: Childhood
Use of the Urbanizing Landscape
Project 1979)

b.

play surfaces that children prefer for many everyday games and play activity. Asphalt and concrete do not get muddy; they make a smooth surface for wheeled toys, bikes, and roller skates; and they have excellent ball-bouncing characteristics (fig. 3-5). What makes streets especially attractive, however, is their high degree of accessibility to children of both sexes and all ages. Streets fall within the *habitual* range of childhood territory; that is, they are close enough to home to be used every day within the severe time con-

straints under which most children live. Streets are available during the cherished intervals between school and the evening meal, between the completion of homework and darkness, between wet weather and domestic chores, between waking and a family outing (fig. 3-6).

When friends have to synchronize their free time, opportunities for play can become severely limited indeed. Realistic choices boil down to staying indoors, playing in adjacent streets, or (depending on the type

a.   b.

3-5. Hard surfaces in the traffic environment attract children's play: <u>a</u>. ball games in a garage court in Stevenage New Town, England; <u>b</u>. wheeled-vehicle play on a sidewalk in Berkeley, California. (Photo <u>b</u>.: Bruce Levin.)

3-6. Street play is especially important to girls, as illustrated by these San Francisco sidewalk scenes: <u>a</u>. skipping in a warm patch of sunlight—the rope tied to a handy drain pipe; <u>b</u>. ball play cornered between front steps and garage doors—a universal childhood activity with very modest spatial requirements.

a.

b.

a.

of housing) finding niches in private yards and gardens or in the shared open space of apartment buildings.

In private yards and gardens, however, parents often do not tolerate anything except quiet, nonphysical play for fear of unacceptable noise levels or damage to fragile plants. Such spaces are often too small to accommodate more than one or two children, and neighboring children may feel too intimidated to enter the private territory of another family. Private yards and gardens may not be available to apartment-dwelling children altogether; if they are, the amount and, particularly, the quality of space are notoriously variable. Sometimes this reflects inherent site constraints and opportunities, a point well illustrated by Björklid's 1982 study. One of the estates (Tanto) was sited on steep terrain where many natural features (trees, rocky topography, wild vegetation, slopes) were retained and used by children; the other (Plankan) was built on level ground with no such natural advantages. In Plankan, the onus fell on those responsible for site planning and design to understand the play needs of future residents and to find creative ways to support them physically. But the product of their imaginations was no match for what nature had provided in Tanto. The resulting large, flat, barren, hard-surfaced areas were a good deal less interesting than the surrounding streets.

Finally, it is important to stress another very pragmatic reason why streets and sidewalks are so important in the lives of children. They are the means by which children, for whom walking is the almost uni-

b.

3-7. Well-differentiated street environments enable children to "play along the way" as they move around neighborhood and city: a. walking on walls in San Francisco; b. leapfrogging bollards in Stoke-on-Trent; c. twirling around railings in Stoke-on-Trent; d. the varied street interactions of a Berkeley, California, child on her way home from school, as illustrated by this behavior map. (Source d.: Hara and Levin 1973)

c.

versal mode of transportation, travel around the neighborhood and city. In the Department of the Environment's study of British neighborhoods (1973: 18, 20), 93 percent of the children said they got to their favorite after-school places by foot; but this does not mean they *walked* in the adult sense of the word. Out on the street, children hop, skip, jump, climb, crawl, leapfrog, balance, skate, slide, run, chase, hide, pounce, sit, lean, and twirl. They play along the way to any destination as they investigate with mind and body every opportunity presented by the street-as-gymnasium (fig. 3-7).

Streets fill an especially important role in children's loose-knit social structure by providing a locus for peer contact a few steps from home. Streets and street corners are important meeting places. When traffic density is low and streetscape diversity high, children are drawn to an environment that is extremely well adapted to their needs. Seen in this light, the notion of "keeping the kids off the streets" seems highly unrealistic, not to mention undesirable. Street play is a universal cultural phenomenon that will occur even if traffic levels are high and space differentiation low.

KAYLA'S TRIP HOME FROM SCHOOL
At the time these observations were made by Tod Hara, a landscape architecture student at the University of California, Berkeley, Kayla was a seven-year-old attending John Muir School. With her consent, the trip was made on November 2, 1972 (Election Day). It covered approximately 0.6 miles and took forty-five minutes (the observer alone took twenty minutes).

1 Kayla and her friend Simon crossed Claremont Avenue, helped by the traffic monitor.
2 Picked up garbage and said, "People throw a lot of garbage on the street."
3 Stopped by a water puddle and found a half-drowned butterfly.
4 Splashed along the water lying against the curb (from the rain that had fallen earlier).
5 Picked some leaves off a tree.
6 Stopped at Dennis's house and dropped the garbage there (from 2, above).
7 Saw a flag of the United States on the street and asked a passerby why it was there.
8 Crossed Piedmont Avenue without looking around.
9 Noticed that the stream of water on the street was getting smaller. Climbed on a truck parked on the street.
10 Both children picked a leaf out of the stream, wrote their names on it with mud, washed their hands in the stream, and walked through the mud.
11 Found Simon's parents' car parked in the gas station, on which Kayla had written "let me be washed" on her way to school that morning. Kayla took a drink of water at the fountain.
12 Crossed College Avenue (a major four-lane arterial) very carefully and continued down Webster Street.
13 Took a "short cut" that involved: going into the entrance courtyard of an apartment building on the corner; going under a stairway; and crawling through a hedge of bamboo to re-emerge on Webster Street (hardly a short cut!).
14 Stopped by a car with a McGovern bumper sticker on it; talked about the mock election they had had in the classroom, then drew signs on the wet car.
15 Walked between two houses and went into the small play area of a private day-care house. Played on the swings and seesaw.
16 Kayla arrived home.

John Muir School

CLAREMONT AVENUE

Dennis's house

PIEDMONT

Gas station

COLLEGE AVENUE

WEBSTER STREET

"Short cut"

Play area

Kayla's house

d.

Designated playgrounds can add important play opportunities and attract activity but they cannot substitute for the immediacy of the street. Streets have always been used for close-to-home play and will surely continue to be so in the future.

Banning Play Is No Answer

General play is frequently banned in housing projects, or specific activities are prohibited, such as ball play and bike riding. Even tobogganing was not permitted on the Tanto slopes (Björklid 1982), which seems unimaginable for a Swedish child living through long northern winters. Moreover, a full 20 percent of activities recorded by Björklid (1985) were officially forbidden—an extraordinary state of affairs that, at best, must have produced much petty friction between housing managers, parents, and children; at worst, it represented an ongoing situation of repression and victimization. Contrary to the popular notion that children get a kick out of breaking the law, most are far more likely to feel guilty when doing forbidden things—even games, like ball play, that should legitimately be considered part of the child's developmental *right to play*. As Verkerk and Rijpma (1984) argue, banning play is no answer. When anti-play attitudes are built into law and promulgated by housing managers, they reinforce a pervasive, authoritarian control over children's lives and can greatly diminish the many opportunities for creative self-learning available outdoors.

Streets are not the only places suitable for play. Many, in fact, are unsuitable because of traffic and social dangers or because they are too far from home. Some residential areas and housing projects provide attractive park and playground facilities and occasionally offer excellent community activity programs. These are choices that can equal and often surpass the attraction of the street, but, sadly, they are few and far between. In all too many instances, either playgrounds are not available or they are so poorly sited or limited in what they provide that they are no match for local streets.

Well-intentioned adults designate playgrounds as spaces where children "ought" to go, but children do not necessarily follow these implicit (or explicit) directives. Indeed, many of the sources cited earlier, illustrating the generally heavy use of streets, also demonstrate the light use commonly made of designated play areas. At best, they fulfill only part of the full range of children's play needs. At worst, they are an irrelevant waste of money. The term *playground* covers an enormous range of facilities, from fully staffed "adventure playgrounds" and "playparks," providing young people with a multitude of opportunities for creative engagement with each other and their physical surroundings, to barren wastelands of asphalt, most commonly found (ironically) in urban schools.[1] Given the choice, few children play there, except to pursue specific activities suited to large hard-surfaced areas, such as bike riding and ball games.

Most children I have worked with are in favor of conventional playgrounds and use them as a place to meet new kids or to rendezvous or socialize with friends. Standard equipment like swings, slides, roundabouts, and climbing structures often are a pretext, or an enjoyable backdrop. Their main purpose for being there is social. Unfortunately, most conventional playgrounds are too far away from children's homes to make everyday use feasible. Streets, on the other hand, are invariably present (fig. 3-8).

The Street Playground

Some children are "pushed" toward streets because of the lack of play opportunities elsewhere. Others are "pulled," even if other play spaces are available, by the special attractions of the street not duplicated

3-8. Low-trafficked suburban "courts," as opposed to playgrounds, offer an attractive, secure play environment, as expressed in this favorite-places map drawn by a girl in suburban Walnut Creek, California. (Source: Childhood Use of the Urbanizing Landscape Project 1979)

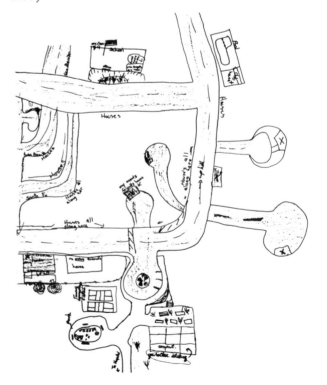

elsewhere. Streets are especially important to girls because their families do not allow them to wander far from home alone in most, if not all, countries where research has been done. All children like to be where the action is, where the life of the community takes place—where trees get trimmed, fire engines come clanging, and dogs wander.

The street is a world as exotic as it is familiar. There, children play in the interstices between parked cars, along the curbside ecotone of gutter rivers, down "bottomless" storm drains, among insect life of sidewalk verges, in jungles of front fence vegetation, and on grandstand stoops. Among the myriad and inexhaustible supply of toys are maple and sycamore seed "helicopters," mayflower peashooters, horse chestnut "conkers," and wonderful rubbish put out for pickup. Children who play on the street witness the comings and goings of tradespeople, mailpersons' surprises, tree trimming crews, hole diggers unearthing mysterious pipes, and the quotidian details of their neighbors' domestic lives. The street playground offers leaves for shuffling, railings and boarded fences to run sticks along, patches of dirt for constructing imaginary landscapes, and occasional building materials, such as sand piles (fig. 3-9).

The minutiae of neighborhood life exist in the narrows between flowing traffic and private homes. Here vital meetings occur between resident children and children just moved in, perhaps from a foreign culture or nationality. More and more children are migrating with their families from rural regions to the world's cities. Some are the children of parents relocated by our increasingly mobile society or moved to a strange place to study. In each case, streets will be the spaces where first steps toward new friendship, socialization, and multicultural integration take place through play (fig. 3-10).

MAKING STREETS LIVABLE FOR CHILDREN

Conserving and Enhancing Fronts

Front is a traditional British working-class term used to describe the space between the boundary of the private home environment (such as the front door or frontyard fence) and roadway (fig. 3-11). Fronts include all those oddball, leftover spaces where the larger community environment intersects with the private domain of the family. They are people-environment ecosystems that provide an essential ingredient of all other healthy ecosystems: *diversity*. Because of their physical diversity, fronts support the

varied quality of children's social life; their attributes and opportunities need to be recognized and conserved in old residential streets and carefully designed into new ones to maximize use by children. The number and variety of physical differentiations, such as those listed in the opening paragraph of this chapter, enhance play opportunities on individual streets. Hilly topography is an added influence because it results in more banks, steps, and retaining walls around streets and adjacent buildings. This further increases children's play repertoires, including games with roller skates, go-carts, and toboggans, and helps perpetuate local street-play traditions (fig. 3-12). Furthermore, streets that work best are connected to a subsidiary network of "side," "back," and "front" spaces of many kinds that greatly extend the variety of children's behavior. As argued by Ward and Fyson (1973) and by Hirst (1983), improved streetscapes need to be integrated into neighborhood networks of pathways, greenways, and urban trails for educational as well as recreational purposes.[2]

Reducing Vehicle Speed and Increasing Passage Interval

Traffic density is the severest constraint on the use of the roadway by children. In fact, use becomes unfeasible above a very low level of traffic density. Zerner's 1977 study contains examples of street-stringing games that could occur only when traffic was slow and the passage interval more than twenty minutes or so (amounting to, in other words, less than three vehicles per hour). The criteria of slow speed and long interval are likely to be met only in narrow alleyways or dead-end streets (fig. 3-13). Provided traffic speed remains slow (at a walking pace of three to four miles per hour), children can play chasing and hiding games across the full width of the street, even with shorter vehicle passage intervals. Bike riding and ball play can continue under even more adverse conditions. But at passage intervals of less than five minutes and speeds in excess of ten miles per hour, play can no longer span the full right-of-way and has to remain on either side.

For the most part, children are mindful of traffic constraints on their street behavior. Even so, danger always lurks in the form of unexpected events and exceptions to the normal pattern of traffic flow. For this reason, we need a street management policy that favors children in order to reduce these and other risks by appropriate measures. The greatest danger, of course, is faced by children who live on streets where traffic is so bad that even the minimum levels of playability are not met, yet who play there nonetheless because they have nowhere else to go. Those streets

3-9. Street environments function as children's social centers—exemplified by these scenes from Berkeley, California: <u>a.</u> a temporary campground between two parked cars; <u>b.</u> a girl's map illustrates the diverse stimulations of the street; <u>c.</u> map author, swinging on the street tree in front of her house with a friend; <u>d.</u> a street sign becomes a challenging climbing object and rallying point on the street. (Photo <u>a.</u>: Bruce Levin; source <u>b.</u>: Childhood Use of the Urbanizing Landscape Project 1979; photo <u>d.</u>: Barbara O'Mahoney)

a.

b.

c.

d.

3-10. A multi-ethnic group perched in a San Francisco street meets to blow bubbles.

3-11. Street "fronts" offer children opportunities to interact with their environment: <u>a.</u> sweeping autumn leaves; <u>b.</u> sandplay in the gutter; <u>c.</u> hunting wildlife in an overgrown front garden.

a.

b.

c.

3-12. The effect of topography on street play: go-cart and Big Wheel race each other on a hilly street in San Francisco.

3-13. A narrow, dead-end alley in San Francisco's Chinatown helps support traditional games (notice the "stringing" behind the children, possible only at very low traffic levels).

may require drastic intervention to improve conditions, but all streets where children play and move through the city must be made safer to reduce the number of young lives lost or young bodies maimed. It is an issue no less important than seatbelt and impaired-driving laws.

Improving Street Performance for Children's Play

Woonerven and similar measures also enhance the use of streets by children (see chaps. 2, 4, and 27 and Eubank-Ahrens 1985). Donald Appleyard's *Livable Streets* (1981), which incorporates his own pioneering research together with that of Stina Sandels (1968) and Charles Zerner (1977), contains examples from several countries of successful attempts by local communities to make residential streets more habitable. The examples show how vehicle speed and passage interval can be controlled by appropriate measures combining "necks," "sleeping policemen" (bumps), "jogged" lines of travel, and varied surface treatments. Improvement is achieved by measures such as limiting the flow of through traffic, reducing speed limits, and changing roadway alignments. Of critical importance is the legal priority accorded to pedestrians.

Narrowed streets and cul-de-sacs reduce traffic speed and increase the security of children who fear being hit from behind. These measures also keep through traffic on through streets and off internal neighborhood streets. The assumption is that residents and tradespeople conversant with the street and its users will keep a sharper lookout for playing chil-

dren than will fast-moving strangers seeking a shortcut.

Principal objectives of these efforts are to control the noise, pollution, and visual impact of neighborhood traffic and to reinstate some of the social functions that local streets once enjoyed before automobiles took over. Obviously, children stand to benefit greatly from such actions. The study by Eubank-Ahrens of two *Woonerven* in West Germany (1985, and see chap. 4), supports this claim. Her results clearly indicate how street improvements led to more and more diverse street use by children. Opportunities for street improvement are especially obvious in older housing areas where traffic levels are moderate and where streets are generously laid out and have interesting configurations that already stimulate imaginative play.

Community Participation: The Key to Success

Once we accept that children *will* use neighborhood streets as playgrounds, we confront the inevitable policy issue of how to upgrade street quality. Wherever possible, the community of users—above all children—needs to participate in replanning and redesigning street environments, especially given the number of examples of constructive participation methods throughout the world (fig. 3-14): Appleyard (1981) offers detailed guidance; the Norwegians have instituted a model of youth involvement in planning (Hongrö 1983); Berkeley, California, has set a precedent for cities in the United States with a similar program (Moore Iacofano Goltsman 1985); and the Livable

3-14. Children need to participate in a genuine manner in the replanning and redesign of residential street environments. An example is the McKinley Commons community design workshop conducted in Berkeley, California, as an environmental education project by a class of elementary school children (the street, McKinley Avenue, was adjacent to their school): a. getting a feel for the size of the street compared to the size of the human body; b. the results of a traffic survey conducted by the children; c. reviewing a map of the neighborhood, after a trip to the planning department at city hall, to see how McKinley Avenue related to other streets; d. children working on a model showing changes they

a.

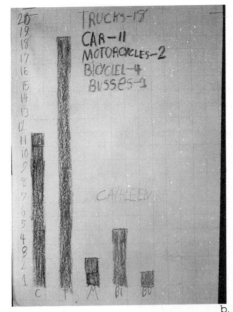

b.

c.

d.

e.

wanted to see in the street; e. detail of the model, showing many additional trees, trash cans, a play tunnel *(top)*, a barbeque gazebo *(bottom)*, and benches and a central fountain *(white circle)*; f. mock-up of the fountain—part of a full-size simulation of the proposed changes to see how they would work. At the time of writing, the community was still waiting for the changes to be implemented on the ground—a situation difficult for children to influence directly, since they have no political power.

f.

Streets Project, conducted by Jeff Oberdorfer in Santa Cruz, California (1982), provides a useful case study of an effective participatory approach involving business interests and other groups in the community.

An extensive array of participation techniques have been developed and documented in recent years (Hart and Moore 1982–83). One of the most creative ways of achieving participation, and helping all age groups break away from stereotype images of the street, is "animation." In Europe, animation is practiced by local artists and other specially trained professionals who instruct communities in the social, economic, and political processes that shaped their environment and who help them to control their surroundings. Although the methods and contexts used in animation vary from community to community, the process essentially develops a local culture that is alive and relevant to the present yet grows out of the past and is oriented toward the future.[3]

In the long run, collaborative approaches toward environmental problem solving will be far more effective than holding on to the unrealistic notion that children can be banned from any part of their local surroundings. Children are very resourceful when they want something badly enough (fig. 3-15). Educating children about road safety—in other words, teaching them to accommodate themselves to traffic —is certainly worthwhile, but it is a very limited strategy. For one thing, as Stina Sandels's 1968 research showed, children's acuity does not fully develop until the age of twelve or so. Only then, in the final years of childhood, are they fully equipped biologically to judge the speed and distance of oncoming traffic.

The ever-rising costs of running a car and the resurgence of interest in the quality of life in urban neighborhoods will mean, as Appleyard suggests, the renaissance of street space as a significant social resource for all ages. Urban streets *can* be humanized; the balance between the needs of people and the needs of motor vehicles *can* be redressed. Many successful examples already exist. We must make a greater effort to ensure that children's needs are not only recognized but thrust in the forefront and represented by children themselves.

NOTES

1. *Adventure playgrounds* were developed in Europe after World War II. Typically, they are fenced-in areas where indoor and outdoor activities of a challenging, adventurous, and exploratory nature for children of all ages are supervised by one or more play leaders. The construction

of "huts" and "camps" in children's self-planned communities and the presence of animals are two main components. Lately, the term has been misapplied to playgrounds that do not fit this description.

Playparks originated in Sweden, particularly Stockholm, and later developed in London and other European cities. Normally sited in a public park, housing estate, or schoolyard, a typical playpark provides a park-like setting for children's informal play along with a variety of equipment and animation programs designed to fulfill the broad spectrum of child development needs. The social needs of accompanying adults are also recognized in the provision of comfortable sitting areas and adequate shelter.

2. *Urban trails* (along with *urban study centers*) were developed in the United Kingdom during the 1970s as part of the British environmental education movement. They consist of defined pathways along routes that were chosen for the way they expose users to significant historical, cultural, social, economic, visual, artistic, and architectural aspects of the city or neighborhood. Thus, they represent an educational potential of street environments (see chap. 1, by M. Francis)

3. See Westland and Knight's *Playing Living Learning* (1982) for details regarding animation groups.

REFERENCES

Appleyard, D. 1981. *Livable Streets*. Berkeley: University of California Press.

Becker, F. D. 1976. "Children's Play in Multifamily Housing." *Environment and Behavior* 8, no. 4: 545–74.

Björklid, P. 1982. *Children's Outdoor Environment*. Stockholm: Stockholm Institute of Education.

———. 1985. "Environmental Diversity in Housing Estates as a Factor in Child Development." *Children's Environments Quarterly* 1, no. 4: 7–13.

Childhood Use of the Urbanizing Landscape Project. 1979. Report for Landscape Architecture Department, University of California, Berkeley. (Available from the author, North Carolina State University, Department of Landscape Architecture, Raleigh, NC 27695-7701.)

Cooper Marcus, C. 1974. "Children's Play Behavior in a Low-Rise, Inner-City Housing Development." In *Man-Environment Interactions*, edited by R. C. Moore, vol. 12, *Childhood City*. Milwaukee: Environmental Design Research Association (EDRA).

Department of the Environment. 1973. *Children at Play.* Design Bulletin 27. London: Her Majesty's Stationery Office.

Eubank-Ahrens, B. 1985. "The Impact of *Woonerven* on Children's Behavior." *Children's Environments Quarterly* 1, no. 4: 39–45.

Francis, M. 1985. "Children's Use of Open Space in Village Homes." *Children's Environments Quarterly* 1, no. 4: 36–38.

Gibbon, J., and D. Stirling. (N.d.) "Aspects of Traffic-separated Housing Layouts." Edinburgh: Edinburgh University Architecture Research Unit.

a.

b.

3-15. Children can be very resourceful in changing the traffic environment to suit their needs, especially when adults collaborate: <u>a.</u> a "clubhouse" built by a group of children in a garage court behind an apartment building (surrounded by four-lane arterial highways) in Oakland, California; <u>b.</u> researchers (off camera), parents, and children sit around one of the favorite-places map, while parents (in their role as animators) explain how they helped the children collect clubhouse building material and negotiate permission with the apartment building manager to allow the clubhouse to be constructed.

Hara, T., and B. Levin. 1973. "Street Anthropology." In *Living Kid City*, edited by R. C. Moore, P. Ford, and C. Malcolm. Berkeley: University of California, Department of Landscape Architecture.

Hart, R., and R. Moore, eds. 1982–83. *Childhood City Quarterly* 9, no. 4;10, no. 1. Double issue on participation techniques. (Available from Center for Human Environments, City University of New York Graduate Center, 33 West 42d Street, New York, NY 10036.)

Hirst, L. 1983. "Another Look at Town Trails." *Bulletin for Environmental Education*, no. 150 (November): 23–27. (*Bulletin for Environmental Education* is published by Streetwork, Notting Dale Urban Studies Centre, 189 Freston Road, London W10, 6TH.)

Hongrö, K. 1983. "Children and Youth Plans in Municipal Planning: Some Norwegian Experiences." Paper presented at Play 2000 Conference, Munich, July. (German-language version published in *Spielräume für Kinder in der Stadt*. Pädagogische Aktion e.V., Schellingstr. 109a, 8 München 40, Federal Republic of Germany.)

Holme, A., and P. Massie. 1970. *Children's Play: A Study of Needs and Opportunities*. London: Michael Joseph.

Moore, R. C. 1986. *Childhood's Domain: Play and Place in Child Development*. London: Croom Helm.

Moore, R. C., and D. Young. 1978. "Childhood Outdoors: Toward a Social Ecology of the Landscape." In *Children and the Environment*, edited by I. Altman and J. F. Wohlwill. New York: Plenum Press.

Moore Iacofano Goltsman. 1985. "Berkeley Youth Downtown Planning Project: Findings and Recommendations." (Available from the firm, 1824 Fourth Street, Berkeley, CA 94710.)

Oberdorfer, J., and Associates. 1982. "Livable Streets for the Downtown Neighborhood: A Plan to Improve and Protect the Residential Street Environment in Downtown Santa Cruz." (Available from the firm, 122 Princeton Street, Santa Cruz, CA, 95060.)

Sandels, S. 1968. *Children in Traffic*. London: Paul Elek.

van Andel, J. 1985. "Effects on Children's Outdoor Behavior of Physical Changes in a Leiden Neighborhood." *Children's Environments Quarterly* 1, no. 4: 46–54.

Verkerk, J., and S. Rijpma. 1984. "Playgrounds: An Emergency Provision?" Rotterdam: Municipality of Rotterdam, Department of Sports and Recreation.

Ward, C., and A. Fyson. 1973. *Streetwork: The Exploding School*. London: Routledge and Kegan Paul.

Westland, C., and J. Knight. 1982. *Playing Living Learning*. State College, Penn.: Venture Publishing.

Zerner, C. 1977. "The Street Hearth of Play." *Landscape* 22, no. 1: 19–30.

4.
A Closer Look at the Users of *Woonerven*

BRENDA EUBANK-AHRENS

"Democratic freedom" is a phrase commonly used to explain the absence of speed limits on highways in West Germany. Yet, also in West Germany, automobile traffic is often strictly controlled in urban residential areas. The same German automobile club that fights against speed limits has actively promoted traffic management in neighborhoods and has supported the transformation of urban streets into *Woonerven* (see chap. 2, by N.E.P. Pressman). One can only speculate about the psychological needs and economic interests behind the opposition of speed limits on highways. In contrast, the recognition of the need for traffic restrictions to foster the quality of life in urban neighborhoods may be traced to a growing environmental awareness. Open space is a scarce resource in a densely populated country like Germany. Cities cannot continue to expand spatially and consume what little undeveloped land is left. In order to combat further suburban expansion, efforts are made to improve existing urban neighborhoods. The principal drawbacks of these neighborhoods, especially for families with children, are the hazards and stresses caused by traffic and the lack of access to usable open space near the home.

As a result, traffic management, combined with increased open space for play, socialization, and leisure, are seen as two essential components of the livability of existing neighborhoods. Traffic plans are developed for entire residential precincts to eliminate through traffic and to reduce driving speeds. The means used to implement these plans include erecting traffic signs; rerouting traffic by using diagonal barriers at intersections, cul-de-sacs, or one-way streets; and slowing traffic by building humps or bumps, elevating intersections, or narrowing traffic lanes. These ac-

tions require varying amounts of physical change. One of the most elaborate physical interventions involves converting local distributors into *Woonerven* within the street hierarchy. Local streets that were formerly dominated by moving and parked motor vehicles are thereby made available for use by residents (figs. 4-1 through 4-4).

Since 1979, numerous studies have evaluated the impact of diverse traffic controls on environmental quality (noise, air pollution, microclimate, and driver behavior) (see chap. 15, by P. Bosselmann). Results of experiments are reported by federal ministries and research commissions (Minister für Wirtschaft, Mittelstand und Verkehr 1979; Bundesminister für Raumordnung, Bauwesen und Städtebau 1980a; Bundesforschungsanstalt für Landeskunde und Raumordnung 1983; and Umweltbundesamt 1985). Flade, Müller, and Ratschow (1982) and van Andel (1984–85) considered children's play in connection with *Woonerven*. Baier and Poth (1983) recorded the density of street activity in five neighborhoods with varying types of traffic controls. But the impact of street redesign on the behavior of nonmotorized users either has been neglected or dealt with only superficially. Little is known about the relationship between

4-1. Official German traffic sign marking the beginning and end of a *Woonert*. Note how the sharing of street space by various users is depicted graphically.

All photos and graphics are by the author.

4-2. *Efforts are made to provide more usable open space for social and leisure activities.*

4-3. *Streets that were formerly dominated by traffic are made available for use by residents.*

4-4. *Woonerven* allow children to play across the full width of the street.

specific street designs and their support of street use. This led me to begin an independent study of the effects of *Wooneren* on neighborhood street life.

THE NEIGHBORHOOD

I chose Linden-Süd, a neighborhood in Hannover, as an appropriate case study for several reasons. First, urban renewal, begun there ten years earlier, had pro-

gressed to a point where streets were actually being rebuilt with the aid of federal funds. Second, I would be able to study two streets, Haspelmath and Ahrberg, both before and after their redesign into *Wooneren*. Linden-Süd was, also, interesting as a case study because it enjoyed the services of an open space advocacy planner. The Hannover Planning Department viewed the neighborhood as a setting for play and was in the process of developing a network of *Wooneren* and other open spaces throughout the neighborhood to invite use by all ages (fig. 4-5). Planners intended

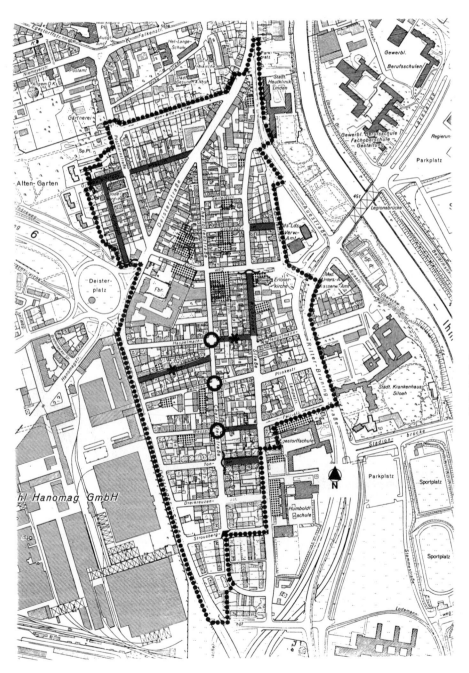

4-5. Map of Linden-Süd showing the open space improvements completed by 1983 and the two streets studied before and after redesign.

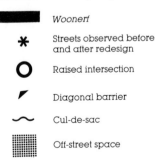

Features of Public Open Space in 1983

▬	*Woonerf*
*	Streets observed before and after redesign
O	Raised intersection
◤	Diagonal barrier
∿	Cul-de-sac
▦	Off-street space

the improved distribution of open space to provide more freedom of choice for leisure activities and more opportunities for social contact. The department was supportive of my work and wanted to use the results of my design evaluation.

Located near the center of Hannover, Linden-Süd is a high-density, mixed-use area with, for the most part, multifamily housing from the turn of the century (fig. 4-6). Traditionally a working-class neighborhood, today it is over-represented by elderly Germans and young guest workers (25.7 percent of the residents are foreigners, as compared with 8.5 percent in the rest of Hannover). The relevant characteristics of this population give a picture of limited mobility: many people do not have the means, time, or inclination to travel to outlying park areas and are dependent on the immediate residential surroundings for outdoor activities.

The rehabilitation plan for Linden-Süd was based on the existing street pattern. Wherever feasible, old housing was renovated, and new buildings were made to conform in scale and material. Measures to improve neighborhood open space included redesigning block interiors, reusing empty lots and other leftover spaces, creating new and renovating existing playgrounds, forming new squares, and redesigning streets into *Woonerven*. A traffic management scheme with a system of one-way streets and traffic-control barriers (including raised intersections on the main street) was implemented to prevent trucks and automobiles from taking shortcuts through the area on the way to the city center. As a result, most traffic in the neighborhood became local, and speeds were reduced. A question remained: given the reduced amount of traffic, how did the redesign of streets into *Woonerven* contribute to the fulfillment of open space needs?

THE STUDY

I decided to study behavior and outdoor activities on Haspelmath and Ahrberg streets before and after redesign (figs. 4-7 through 4-12). I selected those particular streets because of the fortuitous timing of their reconstruction. Although their redesign into *Woonerven* gave them a more distinctive appearance, they were in no way special streets in the neighborhood.

The observed section of Haspelmath Street is considerably shorter than that of Ahrberg Street and has correspondingly fewer residents. However, its central location, two day-care centers, and two small food stores account for a high pedestrian flow. All buildings on Haspelmath were constructed recently. Ahrberg Street, on the other hand, is a purely residential area composed of old buildings. Small brick houses, built in the 1850s by a nearby factory for its workers, have been rehabilitated. The street terminates at a major highway, beyond which lies an impenetrable manufacturing complex; thus the street itself represents both the source and goal of most pedestrian movement. However, since more residents live on Ahrberg Street, there are more potential users than on Haspelmath Street.

As to my observation method, my goal was to leave undisturbed the normal flow of events in the street. I sat inconspicuously in a parked auto and recorded the behavior of only those persons who chose to remain in the street for more than one minute. Because a *Woonerf* is meant to change the nature of street use from a channel for car traffic to a place for people, evidence of users opting to stay in the area warranted special attention. Also, I assumed that necessary activities, such as carrying out the trash, waiting for a ride, or doing construction work, would take place

4-6. Linden-Süd is a turn-of-the-century neighborhood in Hannover with mixed land uses.

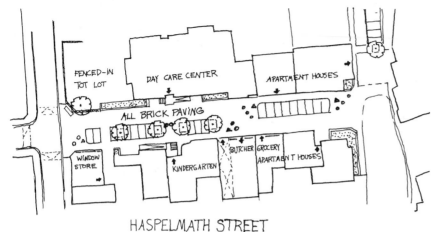

HASPELMATH STREET

○ Bollards
▯▯▯ Parking places
🌳 Trees with raised bases
△ Street lights
♣ House entrances

N

0   10   20   30   40

4-7. The Haspelmath Street *Woonerf* in plan.

4-8. Haspelmath Street, looking east: <u>a.</u> before redesign (bare of trees, littered, and with a monotonous road surface in need of repair); <u>b.</u> after redesign (brick paving unifies buildings and street).

a.

b.

4-9. Haspelmath Street, looking west: <u>a.</u> before redesign; <u>b.</u> after redesign (parking is allowed only in the specially marked spaces; bollards prevent parking elsewhere).

a.

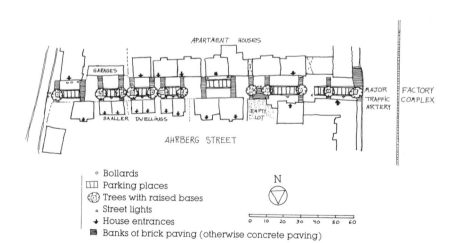

b.

4-10. The Ahrberg Street *Woonerf* in plan.

a.

b.

4-11. Ahrberg Street, looking west: <u>a.</u> before redesign (with narrow sidewalks and automobiles parked haphazardly along curbs); <u>b.</u> after redesign (pedestrian-scale lighting, rows of trees, and the grouping of parking spaces give the street a more distinctive appearance).

a.

b.

4-12. Ahrberg Street, looking east: <u>a.</u> before redesign (wide street space is reserved for traffic); <u>b.</u> after redesign (a bend in the traffic lane draws the driver's attention to the special *Woonerf* situation).

regardless of the particulars of street design. Such activities were therefore not recorded. In contrast, however, leisure activities such as playing, relaxing, communicating, observing the activities of others, and so on, would only occur where the street's physical and social qualities were supportive. The presence of leisure activities could therefore serve as an indicator of environmental quality.

Each observation period lasted one hour. I noted the number of individuals in the street, including their gender, ethnic origin, and approximate age. As far as groups were concerned, I recorded their size, main activity, location on the street, postures, the physical elements they used, and the forms of interaction that took place.

OBSERVATION RESULTS

Number of Users and Their Length of Stay

If one reason for transforming streets into *Woonerven* is to draw more people into the street space, another, perhaps more important, purpose is to enhance the experience of street users. Hence, increases in the number of people in the streets after redesign were checked against increases in the length of stay (or, amount of time people spent on the streets), which indicates increased visual, social, or functional offerings of the street environment.

Observations of people who repeatedly went in and out of buildings confirmed that most of the users who chose to spend time in the street were residents. The actual number of stationary users increased after redesign on Ahrberg Street but not on Haspelmath Street (fig. 4-13). However, on both streets I observed

4-13. Number of individuals and their length of stay on the streets, based on thirty-six hours of observation before and after redesign. Season, weather, day of week, and time of day were carefully controlled.

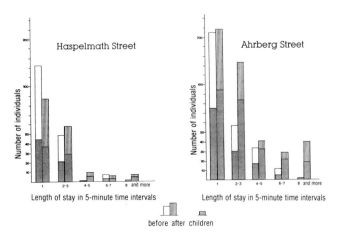

increases in the length of time that individuals spent in the *Woonerven*. These increases were more dramatic in Ahrberg Street because more people lived there. Longer lengths of stay were established for children, teenagers, and adults (table 4-1).

TABLE 4-1.

MEAN LENGTH OF STAY IN TERMS OF AVERAGE NUMBER OF FIVE-MINUTE TIME INTERVALS OBSERVED

| | HASPELMATH STREET | | AHRBERG STREET | |
	BEFORE	AFTER	BEFORE	AFTER
Children	1.79	2.54	1.94	3.02
Teenagers	2.00	2.50	1.94	5.00
Adults	1.23	2.03	2.08	3.32
Elderly	1.75	1.20	1.88	2.90
Total	1.61	2.34	1.98	3.11

Ages of Users and Types of Activities

In considering the *Woonerven's* contribution to open space needs, one must realize that different user groups have varying demands. It would have been valuable to differentiate users according to both their life-cycle stage and their life-style (for example, to establish their daily schedule determined by family, work, education, and so on). However, because my method was limited to observation and nonverbal communication, only approximate age groups could be determined. These proved to be a key factor for analysis.

Children were the principal users of the streets for leisure (table 4-2). An important part of the daytime population of a residential neighborhood, children spend most of their time playing. Preschoolers are especially dependent on the quality of the environment near their home to fulfill their needs for movement and exploration, and to experience and learn from the outdoors (see chap. 3, by R. C. Moore). Indeed, children understood the *Woonerven* as new settings for play: the number of children using the streets increased substantially after redesign.

Teenagers characteristically spend most of their leisure time with their peers, and meetings of teenagers

TABLE 4-2.

USERS: NUMBER AND PERCENTAGE OF TOTAL OBSERVED POPULATION (BY AGE GROUP)

| | HASPELMATH STREET | | | | AHRBERG STREET | | | |
	BEFORE	(%)	AFTER	(%)	BEFORE	(%)	AFTER	(%)
Children	71	39	79	46	125	49	249	64
Teenagers	21	11	44	26	16	6	8	2
Adults	62	34	38	22	91	36	88	23
Elderly	28	16	10	6	24	9	42	11
Total	182	100	171	100	256	100	387	100

often take place in streets (Erke and Eubank-Ahrens 1983). At teenage gatherings, some members invariably show off and try to attract the attention of others; they often intend to provoke adults. Yet what adults may view as pointless "hanging around" and "roughhousing" seem to be necessary behavioral outlets for juveniles who are seeking identity and territory in the transition from childhood to adulthood. A few juvenile residents did meet and interact in the observed street sections, however, these particular *Woonerven* did not, as a whole, become popular meeting places for teenagers. Perhaps the audience there was not large enough. Also, locations that did become meeting points were more public and thus less closely controlled by the families. A popular teenage meeting point in Linden-Süd was in a *Woonerf* near a playground on a main pedestrian route. Apparently, the street sections observed were too far off the beaten track to support opportunities for chance meetings and for public behavioral displays.

Although adults were well represented in both streets, redesign did not increase street use by this age group. With the exception of the unemployed, adults have, on normal days, only small blocks of free time. The working and studying population spends a great deal of time outside of the neighborhood, while housewives with children and many single parents are housebound. The very fact that adults have little time for recreation explains why they primarily use the street space close to their homes. As Brower pointed out (1977), people choose such spaces not so much for their intrinsic quality as for their location. This appeared to be true in the streets observed: clearly their redesign could not affect the ability of adults to participate in street life.

Retired elderly persons have lots of time at their disposal, and their choice of open space for leisure activity depends very much on their physical capabilities. Other research has shown that active elderly often take extensive excursions of long duration to city parks and green belts. Those who are physically weaker are dependent on open space available in the immediate residential surroundings. In fact, many older people often compensate for their own inactivity by observing the doings of others. Those who feel frail and vulnerable are afraid of verbal or physical assault. They desire contact, but at a safe distance. Elsewhere in Linden-Süd, I saw senior citizens gladly appropriate benches that were protected and had an interesting view (even at street intersections and playgrounds). The *Woonerven* studied did not appear to support use by the elderly, perhaps because of the lack of appropriate seating. Not recorded (because they were not present in the street) were older people who watched the street and communicated with ac-

quaintances from within the safety of their own homes. This occurred often in Ahrberg Street, where houses featured windows that were positioned directly at street level.

Impact of *Woonerven* on Leisure Activities

The categories of activities observed were derived both from the relevant literature and from exploratory observations of public open space in Linden-Süd (table 4-3). In contrast to country outings or trips to the swimming pool, for instance, leisure activities that take place on streets and near homes do not require special effort or equipment. They are spontaneous, casual, and often of short duration. Their nature is such that most subjects, if asked, would not be able to recall them; most people would not cite the short conversation with the neighbor on the way to the mailbox as an example of how they spent their leisure time. The opportunity for verbal communication and for experiencing people and events is generally what makes streets attractive to urban residents.

Figure 4-14 shows that children's play was the chief street activity. (How the *Woonerf* design proved supportive of this will be discussed in more detail later.) A major activity for teenagers, adults, and the elderly, both before and after redesign, was verbal communication in the form of chance meetings and spontaneous conversations.

A surprising finding was the high frequency of vehicle maintenance by single adults in the Ahrberg Street *Woonerf*. This activity, engaged in beyond the bounds of necessity to the point where it must be recognized as a preferred working-class pastime, apparently fulfilled the need for a constructive hobby (and perhaps was also undertaken to save money). Vehicle maintenance can be an interactive pursuit, resulting in consultations with others on procedures, conversations with passersby, and contact with nearby children. Other grown-up activities, such as active recreation, passive relaxation, observing people and events, looking at store windows, as well as some forms of antisocial behavior, were recorded infrequently.

The willingness of residents to take care of the public property was also worth observing. Planners had hoped street renovation might influence this tendency. For example, in his book *Defensible Space* (1972), Oscar Newman projected that street redesign might help define the street as a territory for which residents would feel responsible. He argued that residents might not only be more willing to maintain and personalize a *Woonerf* than an ordinary street but that their exercise of social control might extend to reducing rowdiness and vandalism. Yet studies of a possible

TABLE 4-3.

PRINCIPAL STREET ACTIVITIES AND CORRESPONDING BEHAVIOR CATEGORIES

PRINCIPAL ACTIVITIES	MAIN BEHAVIOR CATEGORIES	PRINCIPAL ACTIVITIES	MAIN BEHAVIOR CATEGORIES
Boys kick soccer ball Girls play "keep away" with ball Children swing on tree supports Boys balance along top of low wall Small child digs in planter boxes Children ride up and down the street with bicycles Children take turns riding in go-cart Girls play a word-guessing game Turkish children sing, dance, and clap hands Children play doctor, patient lies on street Children act out scenes with dolls Girls pretend to be in a Turkish wedding A discarded umbrella is used as a parachute Small child eats ice cream and watches others Children argue among themselves	CHILDREN'S PLAY (activities of children only)	Men wash and polish their cars Man repairs auto Foreign men examine new van Young man disassembles motorcycle Student repairs bicycle	VEHICLE MAINTENANCE
		Elderly woman sweeps street	MAINTAINING PUBLIC OPEN SPACE
		Housewife steps out for a breath of fresh air Man stands in driveway and watches children play	INACTIVE RELAXATION OBSERVING PEOPLE AND EVENTS
		Young men play badminton in the street	ACTIVE RECREATION
		Couple stands and looks into store window	BUILDING-RELATED ACTIVITY
Neighbors coming out of their houses meet by chance Women arriving home stand around and talk Retired man stands around and talks to passersby Elderly woman in window talks to someone on the street	COMMUNICATION (activities of teenagers, adults, and elderly)	Drunks urinate in the bushes, yell, and fight Watermain breaks, and all run to see the incident Car accident occurs and crowd develops A political organization sponsors a party	ANTISOCIAL AND OTHER BEHAVIOR

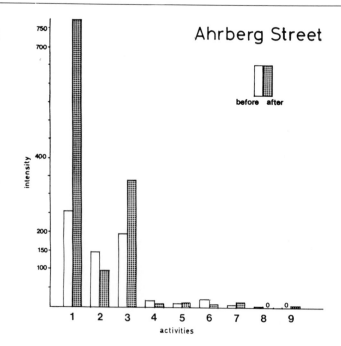
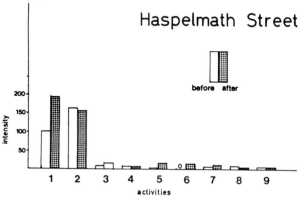

1. Children's play
2. Communication (teenagers, adults, and elderly)
3. Vehicle maintenance
4. Observing people and events
5. Maintaining public open space
6. Active recreation
7. Inactive relaxation
8. Building-related activity (looking at store windows)
9. Antisocial and other behavior

4-14. Activities observed before and after redesign.

increase in the residents' willingness to maintain the public space as a *Woonerf* are inconclusive. Systematic documentation of littering patterns, personalization of facades and streets, and so on, would be required to understand better the relationship between street design and maintenance.

At this point, it must be concluded that the limited range of leisure activities exhibited by adults is a realistic effect of redesigned residential streets. If urban streets allow for a great deal of social interaction, they do not provide the privacy, withdrawal, and contemplation of, or communion with, nature that are characteristic of parks, community gardens, or visually protected private open space. The public nature of streets invites social control to the extent that it may in fact inhibit adult leisure activities.

Children's Play

As to the positive development of children's play in *Woonerven*, not only did more unsupervised children stay longer after *Woonerven* were built, but play became more complex. (In fact, the observations of children's activities required more lengthy and complicated coding after redesign.) Increases were noted in games requiring more space and good playing surfaces (such as ball games); in other physical-motor, large-muscle play (jumping, climbing, running, and so forth); and in the use of bicycles and toy vehicles (table 4-4). Children living in Ahrberg Street who, before redesign, played space-saving rule games, such as hopscotch, and word-guessing games with markings on the sidewalk, became involved in more spatially extensive types of play. In both *Woonerven*, as the number of children on the streets increased, the amount of purely verbal communication also rose dramatically. Further improvements in the nature and diversity of play were suggested by the increased development of role and fantasy play, entertaining, music making, and dancing.

The unusual amount of physical-motor, small-muscle play recorded in Haspelmath Street reflects the activity of several small children who dug in planters at the base of an apartment house for long periods of time. Yet those planters became less interesting after redesign of the street: the more generous physical and social amenities in the *Woonerven* encouraged small children to explore the environment at large.

Spatial Behavior

LOCATION OF PLAY AND PHYSICAL ELEMENTS USED

Shifts in the areas where children played are clearly visible in the behavior maps constructed before and after street redesign (figs. 4-15, 4-16). Children used

TABLE 4-4.
INCIDENTS OF STREET PLAY (BY TYPE)

TYPES OF PLAY	HASPELMATH STREET		AHRBERG STREET	
	BEFORE	AFTER	BEFORE	AFTER
Ball games	3	26	27	93
Other physical-motor, large-muscle play	14	18	5	75
Physical-motor, small-muscle play	19	9	3	12
Play involving bicycle or toy vehicle	4	25	14	112
Rule games (other than ball games)	9	16	70	7
Role and fantasy play, entertaining, music making, dancing	4	16	0	80
Passive behavior, such as watching playmates	10	4	23	63
Social play, communication as main activity	49	58	104	309
Total	112	172	245	751

all 432 time samples

the *Woonerf* in its entire width, including the former traffic lane. Spaces protected by bollards inspired especially intensive use. The highest intensity of play was observed in Ahrberg Street, where a protected area of the street adjoined an empty lot that had been made available to the neighborhood. The expansion of play activity in the street space confirms the value of *Woonerven* as added usable open space.

The physical elements used by children were related to the type and location of play. The sidewalk zone was used intensively in Haspelmath Street before redesign, primarily because of attractive features such as recessed house entrances, ramps, and stairs. The sidewalk was used much less on Ahrberg Street because it did not have those features before redesign.

Children's play in *Woonerven* demonstrated more interaction with the physical environment, particularly with street furnishings (fig. 4-17). The substantial increase in the use of "play props" was connected with the burgeoning use of bicycles and toy vehicles. Special props and "found objects" were also used in fantasy play.

LOCATION OF TEENAGERS', ADULTS', AND ELDERLY'S ACTIVITY AND PHYSICAL ELEMENTS USED

Although verbal communication among grown-ups did not increase with the redesign of the streets, the latter did have an effect on areas where communication took place (fig. 4-18, 4-19). While not directly tied to street furnishings, adult communication occurred within the street zone near the buildings (formerly the sidewalk) (table 4-5, fig. 4-20). By creating more areas protected from pedestrian and traffic flow, but near

4-15. Behavior map of children playing in Haspelmath Street: <u>a.</u> before, and <u>b.</u> after physical changes were made.

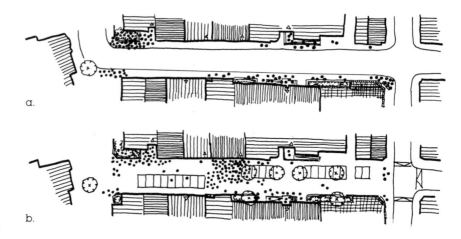

a.

b.

4-16. Behavior map of children playing in Ahrberg Street: <u>a.</u> before, and <u>b.</u> after physical changes were made.

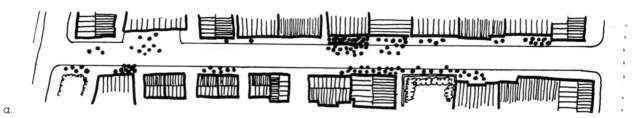

a.

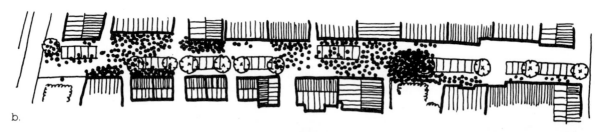

b.

4-17. *Woonerf* street furniture supports children's play in Haspelmath Street.

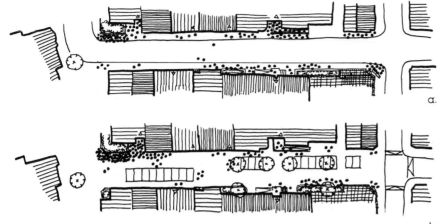

4-18. Behavior map of communication among teenagers, adults, and the elderly in Haspelmath Street: <u>a.</u> before, and <u>b.</u> after redesign.

4-19. Behavior map of communication among teenagers, adults, and the elderly in Ahrberg Street: <u>a.</u> before, and <u>b.</u> after redesign.

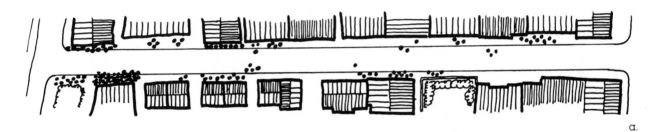

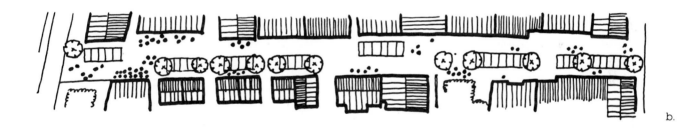

TABLE 4-5.
PHYSICAL ELEMENTS AND SPACES USED (BY AGE GROUP)

	HASPELMATH STREET		AHRBERG STREET	
	BEFORE	AFTER	BEFORE	AFTER
ELEMENTS USED BY CHILDREN:				
Border zone (building features, house entrance, windows, etc.)	81	45	4	84
Street furnishings (bollards, trees, tree supports, etc.)	6	41	0	106
Large impermanent objects (cars, garbage containers, etc.)	0	3	0	15
Special props (toys, bicycles, found objects, etc.)	6	67	64	316
ELEMENTS USED BY TEENAGERS, ADULTS, AND ELDERLY:				
Border zone (building features, house entrance, windows, etc.)	49	84	83	237
Street furnishings (bollards, trees, tree supports, etc.)	16	3	0	15
Large impermanent objects (mostly motor vehicles)	18	30	36	340
Special props (bicycles, sports equipment, etc.)	12	18	29	34

all 432 time samples

house entrances, *Woonerf* design supported some spatial expansion of verbal communication among adults.

Behavior maps of activities other than children's play and grown-up communication show that such pastimes as observing people and events, street sweeping, passive relaxation, and window shopping continued to occur in the street zones near the buildings after redesign (figs. 4-21, 4-22). Only a few spontaneous games took place in the former traffic lane area. Since *Woonerf* design involves the relocation of parking, vehicle maintenance was moved into central areas of the streets. With the increased pursuit of vehicle maintenance, more large, permanent objects, such as cars, were drawn into grown-up activity.

Woonerven as Places for Interaction

Interaction (between two or more persons) refers both to physical and verbal exchanges. The observations of the two streets showed few isolated individuals engaged in leisure-time activities (table 4-6). Because of increases in the length of stay on the street after redesign, the amount of observed interaction increased correspondingly. The increase in the size of groups found in *Woonerven* also facilitated interaction. In Haspelmath Street, the number of groups remained constant, but individual groups became larger after redesign. In Ahrberg Street, there was a considerable increase in the number of small and large groups (table 4-7).

Given more contacts and larger groups in *Woonerven*, one may ask who the "new" actors were. Clearly children made up the groups that interacted most.

TABLE 4-6.

FREQUENCY OF INTERACTION (FOR STREET USERS INVOLVED IN LEISURE ACTIVITY)

	HASPELMATH STREET		AHRBERG STREET	
	BEFORE	AFTER	BEFORE	AFTER
No interaction	29	49	84	286
Interaction	280	342	444	1003
Total	309	391	528	1289

all 432 time samples

TABLE 4-7.

FREQUENCY OF INTERACTION (BY GROUP SIZE)

	HASPELMATH STREET		AHRBERG STREET	
GROUP SIZE	BEFORE	AFTER	BEFORE	AFTER
One person	38	47	117	245
Two persons	75	68	43	187
Three to five persons	33	60	63	144
Six and more persons	3	0	11	22

TABLE 4-8.

FREQUENCY OF INTERACTION (BY AGE GROUP)

	HASPELMATH STREET		AHRBERG STREET	
	BEFORE	AFTER	BEFORE	AFTER
No interaction				
Child alone	17	28	29	96
Teen alone	3	7	0	20
Adult alone	5	5	46	143
Elderly alone	4	9	9	27
Interaction				
Children	92	131	139	569
Teenagers and children	4	50	16	0
Teenagers	36	42	28	6
Child/teenagers with adults/elderly	33	69	120	211
Adults and/or elderly	115	50	141	217
Total	309	391	528	1,289

all 432 time samples

Not only did interaction among children increase in *Woonerven*, but so did the frequency of contacts between younger and older people (table 4-8). Thus, it appears that the *Woonerf* provides the essential element of street life that Jane Jacobs advocated (1961): added opportunities for children to be in contact with the adult world.

Of course, some negative contacts also occurred among the inhabitants of Linden-Süd. In changing neighborhoods, conflicts invariably arise between the established social order and newly arriving residents. Certainly, the influx of foreign workers can be expected to create tensions among children as well as adults (in 1979, 61.8 percent of Linden-Süd's foreign residents were under six years of age). This situation is also likely to be aggravated by conflicts engendered by the different behavior of various age groups, which have an impact on the usability of public open space.

Although *Woonerven* cannot be expected to solve all social problems, it was worth examining the impact that increased interaction could have on better tolerance for ethnic diversity and for the behavior of different age groups. Observation showed, however, that little interaction among the different ethnic and age groups took place both before and after redesign of streets (table 4-9). In Haspelmath Street, interaction was predominantly among the German majority. In Ahrberg Street, the many foreign families interacted with each other. The apparent increase in ethnic interaction in Ahrberg Street was due in part to the continual presence of the children of a large Turkish family who had no inhibitions about talking to whomever came by (fig. 4-23). While such contact could be stimulating for the children, it cannot necessarily be attributed to ethnic relations.

4-20. Communication took place from window to street both before and after redesign of Haspelmath Street.

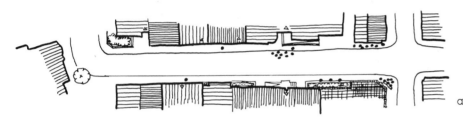

a.

4-21. Behavior map of activities other than play and communication in Haspelmath Street: <u>a.</u> before, and <u>b.</u> after physical changes were made.

b.

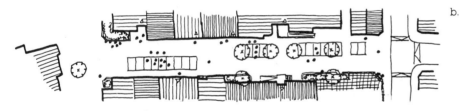

4-22. Behavior map of activities other than play and communication in Ahrberg Street: <u>a.</u> before, and <u>b.</u> after physical changes were made.

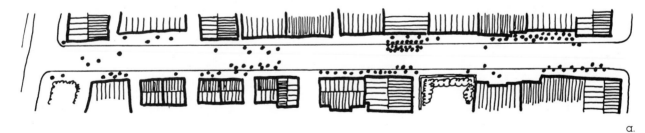

a.

b.

TABLE 4-9.

FREQUENCY OF INTERACTION (AMONG ETHNIC GROUPS)

	HASPELMATH STREET		AHRBERG STREET	
	BEFORE	AFTER	BEFORE	AFTER
No interaction	29	49	84	286
Interaction among Germans	175	245	97	108
Interaction among foreigners	81	91	300	687
Interaction among Germans and foreigners	24	6	47	208
Total	309	391	528	1,289

all 432 time samples

CONCLUSIONS

Whether *Woonerven* are worth the economic investment remains uncertain. Certainly, it is not enough merely to redesign and rebuild isolated streets. A network of *Woonerven* needs to be developed along with other types of open spaces to make an impact on a neighborhood. The results of this study indicate that *some* of the anticipated positive social and behavioral consequences of redesigning streets are true. *Woonerven* proved to be more than transportation channels for cars; rather, they are places suited for pedestrian use, where more people chose to stay on the street for longer periods of time after redesign. As designed and built in Linden-Süd, *Woonerven* were particularly supportive of children's play. Children (and, indirectly, their parents) seemed to feel more secure, allowing for a proliferation of types of play. Children gained more contact with adults, which would not have been possible in playgrounds or other isolated play facilities. Play and verbal communication expanded spatially, and involvement with the physical environment generally increased, making the streets more lively.

On the other hand, street redesign did not yield far-reaching social consequences for adults. If interaction and verbal communication are extremely important in streets, their occurrence and intensity may not be directly influenced by design. One can argue that the willingness of adults to interact beyond spontaneous contacts depends too much on common interests for street design and furnishings to make a difference.

Of course, it is possible to blame the lack of adult and elderly interaction on the shortcomings of the particular designs in Linden-Süd. The *Woonerven* there may be too undifferentiated in their appearance; also, the amount of vegetation may be insufficient. As plans were reviewed in public hearings, residents put pressure on planners not to reduce the number

4-23. Turkish children play in the empty lot opened up for neighborhood use in the Ahrberg Street *Woonerf*.

of parking places, thereby restricting the amount of space left for adornment, planting, furnishings, and so on. Residents showed little interest at the time in creating flower beds in front of their houses because many individuals did not have the time or money to maintain such "luxuries." During the public deliberations, only practical necessities prevailed, as, for example, the provision of underground pipes and cables, which then severely limited potential locations for trees.

In the final evaluation, *Woonerven* must be rated positively for the benefits they yield to children's environments. That children are so dependent on their immediate residential surroundings, and therefore so disadvantaged in the modern, car-dominated urban environment, confirms the critical importance of improved street design for this age group. *Woonerven* clearly provide more behavioral options for children at their home base.

REFERENCES

Baier, R., and R. Poth. 1983. *Wirkungsanalyse von Massnahmen zur Wohnumfeldverbesserung im öffentlichen Raum*. Aachen: Institut für Stadtbauwesen, Technische Hochschule Aachen.

Brower, S. 1977. *The Design and Management of Neighborhood Parks*. Baltimore: Department of Planning, City Planning Commission.

Bundesforschungsanstalt für Landeskunde und Raumordnung. 1983. *Flächenhafte Verkehrsberuhigung: Zwischenbericht*. Report No. 8/9. Bonn: BLR.

Bundesminister für Raumordnung, Bauwesen und Städtebau. 1980a. *Massnahmen zur Verbesserung des Wohnumfeldes*. Bonn: BRBS.

————1980b. *I. Kinderfreundliche Umwelt, II. Kinderspiel im Strassenraum*. Report No. 03.087. Bonn: BRBS.

Erke, H., and B. Eubank-Ahrens. 1983. *Jugendtreffpunkte*. Braunschweig: Abteilung für angewandte Psychologie.

Flade, A., P. Müller, and A. Ratschow. 1982. *Verbesserung der Spielmöglichkeiten von Kindern auf öffentlichen Strassen im Wohnumfeld: Vorheruntersuchung*. Darmstadt: Institut für Wohnen und Umwelt.

Hester, R. T. 1975. *Neighborhood Space*. Stroudsburg, Pa.: Dowden, Hutchinson & Ross.

Jacobs, J. 1961. *The Death and Life of Great American Cities*. New York: Random House.

Minister für Wirtschaft, Mittelstand und Verkehr. 1979. *Verkehrsberuhigung in Wohngebieten, Schlussbericht über den Grossversuch des Landes Nordrhein-Westfahlen*. Düsseldorf: MWMV.

Neeskend, J., G. Versteijben, and J. Kpopman. 1982. *Woonerven: Bijdrage aan een beter Woonmilieu*. Nijmegen, Netherlands: Institut voor toegepaste Sociologie.

Newman, O. 1972. *Defensible Space: Crime Prevention through Urban Design*. New York: Macmillan.

Umweltbundesamt. 1985. *Forschungsvorhaben Flächenhafte Verkehrsberuhigung: Erste Erfahrungen aus der Praxis*. Berlin: Umweltbundesamt.

van Andel, J. 1985. "Effects on Children's Outdoor Behavior of Physical Changes in a Leiden Neighborhood." *Children's Environments Quarterly* 7: 46–54.

Whyte, A. 1977. "Guidelines for Field Studies in Environmental Perception." Technical note 5, *Man and the Biosphere*. Paris: UNESCO.

5.
Pedestrian Street Use:
Culture and Perception

AMOS RAPOPORT

The major question to be addressed in this chapter is: What are the variables that influence the use of streets by pedestrians, or, more specifically, which perceptual qualities of streets influence such use? Since comparative approaches tend to clarify matters, these perceptual characteristics will be contrasted with those desirable for high-speed traffic. This chapter is a summary and synthesis of some previous work as well as of a major project on streets still in progress. In dealing with the question of pedestrian street use, several specific questions will be addressed:

1. What is a street, and how can a cross-culturally valid definition be derived?
2. What is the role of culture, and of rules, in defining behaviors appropriate to streets?
3. How can we classify the variety of street behaviors so that those perceptual characteristics supportive of various behaviors can be derived?
4. How can we formulate a more detailed set of physical characteristics that are perceptible and that support walking?

It will be suggested in the chapter's conclusion that not only is this comparative approach extremely useful for analyzing streets, but as is the case in much of my recent work, I take it to represent a paradigm for valid design in general.

WHAT IS A STREET?

It is quite clear, as I have repeatedly argued, that, in order to be valid, design must be based on theory.

All drawings are by the author.

In turn, valid theory must be based on proper generalizations about environment-behavior interaction. Such generalizations only become reliable when they, in turn, are based on the very broadest evidence possible. This involves the use of the most extensive historical data; the use of all forms of design, including vernacular, "primitive," and so on; and the use of cross-cultural data.

All these types of evidence, particularly the use of cross-cultural data (which the other two categories presuppose), require that the units used in analysis and in any comparisons be appropriate. In anthropological terms, such units must in the first instance be at the *emic* level; in other words, they must be fully embedded in the cultures in question and seen in their terms. Only then can units be derived for use in comparisons. That is to say, one needs to use *derived* etic units; what must be avoided is the use of *imposed* etic units.[1] (The undesirable consequences of this have been demonstrated for cities [Wheatley 1971], for privacy [Rapoport 1976, 1977], and for dwellings [Rapoport 1980a].)

In these terms, the definition of a street is far from self-evident (Rapoport 1973). That setting called *street* needs to be defined in such a way that the type of comparison desired can be made validly. For some purposes it can be defined morphologically; from another perspective it may more usefully be designated as a setting for a particular set of activities (Rapoport 1980a). This would then determine whether the common notion of *street* is an adequate descriptive category or whether it should be defined in terms of a public-private continuum or in terms of activities and uses. In other words, is a morphological definition in terms of "a linear space between buildings" useful, or would a definition in terms of "that setting in which a specified set of activities occur" be more useful (as an analogue of the dwelling in Rapoport 1980a)? If the latter is the case, a compound may be the most relevant unit to compare with a street in some cases; in others, analogous activities may take place in restaurants, pubs, coffee shops, or dwellings. This, then, would affect the discussion of the street as a behavior setting and the choice of units to be used in the analysis. Any such discussion would also need to include the cultural definition of rule systems for appropriate public behavior (see the next two sections) and also the different "space splits" or domain definitions respectively corresponding to what cognitive anthropologists have called reality splits or cognitive domains.

It is this problem of what one could term functional nonequivalence, and the failure to relate environmental form to cultural norms, that is at the root of the weakness of otherwise insightful studies of the street by various designers (Rudofsky 1969). Definitions, however, depend on the purposes for which they are used. In this chapter, I will assume that even though streets are difficult to define (as are cities [Rapoport 1980b], dwellings [Rapoport 1980a], or units of settlement [Rapoport 1981]), there are such units that are comparable across cultures. While it is desirable to use a *derived* etic, I will use an *imposed* etic for two reasons: First, the principal activity with which we are concerned is walking, for which *street* is commonly the accepted unit in many cultures; second, the imposed etic is based on the observation that *street* is a well known and accepted setting (Barker and Barker 1961; Barker and Schoggen 1973) and that this definition, which we all commonly use, is *morphological.* Thus, for the purpose of this discussion, *streets are the more or less narrow, linear spaces lined by buildings found in settlements and used for circulation and, sometimes, other activities.*

THE USE OF STREETS

The main concern is with the use of streets by pedestrians but, as I will show below, one needs to approach the topic more broadly. The activities that occur in any setting are a function of culture, primarily of a set of rules that are part of the culture in question. These not only define the setting itself, but also define both the repertoire of activities available to members of that culture and that subset of activities appropriate in specific settings. For example, in the case of streets, this is clearly a major question, particularly since the presence or absence of certain activities depends on how the street is seen in terms of front/back or public/

private oppositions. Moreover these rules then lead others to attribute meaning to the street: to judge it, for example, as a "slum" (Rapoport 1977), because "hanging out" on the streetfront in the United States communicates a negative image, even to people who so use the street (Brower 1977: 9). In that case use conflicts with the rules of the majority culture, those rules being related to front/back and public/private.

From the perspective of environment-behavior research, the relation of people and environments is the result of complex interactions among cultural, environmental (physical), and perceptual variables. This also applies to the specific set of activities that occur in that environment called *streets* and, specifically, to the pedestrian use of streets. The following list enumerates some of the many variables involved in pedestrian street use:

1. *Technology.* In places where wheels, or even riding animals, were unknown or known but little used, walking was extremely prevalent, since the only alternative—being carried—was available only to a small minority.
2. *Safety*, whether from traffic or crime (especially, *perceived* safety).
3. *Environmental variables*, such as noise, fumes, congestion, quality of paving, and so forth.
4. *Climate and weather* (for example, season, shade or sunlight), although these are clearly modified by culture.
5. *Topography*, for example, hills, slopes, and so on, which may, however, affect certain people—for example, the elderly or handicapped—differentially. (We are thus dealing with "*perceived* topography.")
6. *Distance* to a given goal, or, more correctly, cognized, subjectively defined distance.
7. *Availability and presence of services*, such as shops, cafés, kiosks, toilets, seats, and so on.
8. *Culture*, which defines settings, rules for appropriate behavior, and so on.
9. *Physical, perceptual characteristics*, for example, adequate complexity levels and adequate interest that may be supportive of the particular activity in question.

In general, walking and other street activities are mainly a function of the last two variables—cultural and physical. The remainder of this chapter will, therefore, concentrate on them, starting with the role of culture.

CULTURE AND STREET USE

As noted, activity in any given setting is primarily culturally based in that it is the result of unwritten rules, customs, traditions, habits, and the prevailing lifestyle and definition of activities appropriate to that setting (Rapoport 1969, 1977, 1979a, 1979b). Note that while I have listed technology in a separate category above, it is, strictly speaking, part of culture.

Accordingly, the use of streets by pedestrians has to do not only with accepted levels of physical exertion but also with attitudes of sociability or reserve. For example, if reserve and anonymity are the accepted norms, then settings encouraging sociability will be seen as inhibiting; if the contrary is true, then the same settings will be seen as supportive. In addition, in cases in which sociability is acceptable, those settings that are appropriate will further influence the activities that occur in a street (Rapoport 1982c). This, then, is partly a function of design; in other words, two major sets of variables with which this chapter deals both play a part. Thus, designing the best Italian hill-town street or Greek island plaza will have no effect if particular uses are seen as generally undesirable or as inappropriate in public settings. If, however, there *is* a desire to use streets for walking or promenading and plazas for sitting, then certain physical configurations are much more likely to be supportive than others, while those that are antithetical may be so inhibiting as to block such behavior completely. But even appropriately designed settings will be used or not used depending on the culturally established rules.

Note, however, that rules can change with general changes in the culture and that they can also change in a given case. For example, a residential block in Milwaukee may be used for a block party, but only on the Fourth of July. In effect, the situation is redefined, and previously inappropriate behavior becomes appropriate in a new context and changes accordingly (Rapoport 1979c). In the same physical milieu, ball games, eating, drinking, cooking, and socializing become acceptable. Note also that different subgroups who dominate areas of a city may define appropriateness differently. Thus, in Baltimore, the same design worked for one group that used back areas, such as backyards and center block parks, for socializing, but not for another that used the street region (Brower and Williamson 1974; Brower 1977). As already seen, (Rapoport 1977, 1982b), other groups may then read meaning into these "inappropriate" activities and see such a place as an undesirable "slum." That is to say, they may stigmatize it.

I hypothesized as early as 1969 that there were two major kinds of street use, two major "styles" of urban space use; I have since elaborated this (Rapoport 1977, chap. 1; chap. 2: 91–96; and chap. 5), citing some more recent empirical work (Becker 1973; Thakudersai 1972, among others). Members of some cultures and subcultures do seem predisposed to use streets and plazas for many more activities than members of other groups, either seeking greater public involvement or turning many streets into semiprivate settings —or both, as seen in the case of India, for example.

Thus, in comparing a fictitious small town in Britain ("Yoredale") with one in the United States ("Midwest"), researchers found pedestrian activities to be much more important in the former (Barker and Barker 1961: 458). The setting category *streets and sidewalks* was used a total of 77,544 hours per year in Midwest versus 300,000 in Yoredale—a 400 percent greater use in the latter, although it had a smaller population. In terms of the popularity of public settings, Yoredale streets came first, with 21.33 percent of public behavior, whereas Midwest's were third, with 7.76 percent of behavior (Barker and Schoggen 1973: 415, 425). I expect that if one were to compare Britain with other cultures, such as France, Greece, Italy, Brazil, or India, the difference would be even more striking.

Consider India as a final example of the effects of culture on street use. On one hand, many of its highways and major roads seem to be treated as extremely public—in fact, almost as free occupancy space. Thus, the pavement may be used for drying grain or dung, working, talking, or engaging in a wide variety of commercial activities. However, other streets, particularly in small, homogeneous residential areas, variously called Mahallas, Paras, Pols, and Bustis depending on the region, are semiprivate, so that, effectively, only residents have access. *Their* rules apply, and a whole different set of activities takes place in them, many of which are appropriate in our culture only to the dwelling and other buildings.

At first sight, the streets provide a setting for what seems to be a bewildering variety of activities and correspondingly diverse sounds, smells, and sights. A confusing mixture of animals, people, bicycles, rickshaws, trucks, and buses moves continuously. Activities are intermingled at an extraordinarily fine grain and in close juxtaposition. The streets are full of a great variety of people in all sorts of costumes, not only walking and riding but standing, sitting, squatting, and lying down; sleeping, cooking, eating, getting their hair cut or getting shaved; doing laundry, fixing bicycles or tires, manufacturing things, sewing, playing, chanting, arguing, bargaining—even praying. The contrast to streets in, say, Beverly Hills, California, where even walking is regarded with suspicion, could not be greater.

Note, however, that the streets yet display a high degree of cultural specificity. There are clear differences in activity among regions in the country, as well as among different groups within a single region or city. Frequently, in high-status areas inhabited by high officials or professionals (often occupying the old English "civil lines"), the streets are empty and quiet, resembling those found in comparable areas in Britain and the United States. (In the latter, in turn, there are subgroups using streets in ways contrary to majority norms.) This distinction in India reflects two traditions: the indigenous and the colonial (King 1976).

Without elaborating this point further, I would summarize the argument of this section as follows: cultural variables are primary for any activity, including walking and others, occurring in streets. It is culture that structures behavior and helps explain the use or nonuse of streets and other urban spaces—or of other settings. Thus, the use of streets by pedestrians is primarily culturally based, since physical environments do not determine behavior. Physical environments, however, can be supportive or inhibiting. Given this culturally based predisposition toward obeying unwritten rules of proper street use, people can also be influenced by physical variables. The particular physical, especially perceptual, qualities of these urban spaces, which broadly have to do with complexity, characterize settings that are facilitating rather than inhibiting and thus support pedestrian activities. Hence, given a particular cultural context, certain physical and perceptual characteristics are needed to provide that environmental quality appropriate for pedestrians. This can be seen in Brasilia, where street life is much more prevalent in the squatter settlements; in the disappearance of pedestrian activities in French housing projects (Rapoport 1977); and, again, in India. There I recently compared two environments in the same city inhabited by identical populations in terms of ethnicity, caste, socioeconomic level, and life-style. One environment was full of pedestrian activities as described before; the other made them impossible. Thus, environments, while never determining positively (they cannot *generate* behavior), can be so inhibiting as effectively to block behavior—in this case the pedestrian use of space—and thus can be *negatively* determining (Rapoport 1983a).

It thus becomes necessary to turn to those physical characteristics of streets that are of primary interest to designers. But before doing so, it is necessary briefly to discuss the various activities that are found in streets.

STREET ACTIVITIES

Activities are highly varied even when considered at their manifest level in any one culture and among cultures. Equally or even more varied are the ways in which they are carried out—as well as where, when and including or excluding whom. The association of any given activity with others—in other words, how it forms an activity system—varies even more. Most variable of all is the most latent aspect—what activities mean (Rapoport 1977, 1982b).

However, with regard to streets, even the most highly varied set of activities and their characteristics, manifest and latent, can be discussed in terms of three broad classes:

1. *Nonpedestrian Movement.* This consists mainly of wheeled vehicles (in our own culture, mainly motorized vehicles). In other cultures and periods, animals may be involved—either carrying riders or on their own (for example, cows in India).
2. *Pedestrian activities*, which can further be subdivided into two principal types:
   (i) *dynamic* pedestrian behavior, mainly walking and strolling. These are comparatively constant in nature; culture influences how acceptable walking is, who walks, where, when, how fast, and with whom.
   (ii) *static* pedestrian activities—sitting and standing, squatting, lying down, eating, playing, working, sleeping, and so on. These tend to vary greatly with culture and many of those acceptable in India, for example, would not be acceptable in the United States.

If one wishes to concentrate on physical, perceptual variables the question then becomes: What are the characteristics of the physical environment that will constitute supportive environments for the various classes of activity? One could begin with any, but I will stress pedestrian behavior, particularly walking, since that is my current interest, although I will contrast the requirements for walking with those for static pedestrian activities and, in more detail, with those necessary for fast vehicular movement. This comparison should clarify both; it also leads to lessons that I believe to be highly relevant to urban design.

PEDESTRIAN-SUPPORTIVE SETTINGS

The particular aspect to be discussed is what I have called the *perceptual* separation of pedestrians and motorists, in contrast with the *physical* separation that is usually considered (Rapoport 1982a). When variables other than physical separation are considered, they tend to be restricted to matters of noise, fumes, and the like. When complete separation is not at issue, the concern is still with some form of physical separation—overpasses or underpasses—or with other forms of physical manipulation barriers, such as channeling, controlling crossing points, or slowing down traffic through physical devices or legislation, as in the *Woonerven* of the Netherlands (*Ekistics* 1978: 417–22). More recently, there has been some discussion of the physical facilities that encourage the use of spaces (Whyte 1980).

The notion of *perceptual separation* addresses a different topic: the very different perceptual characteristics that settings for pedestrians and vehicular traffic require. (A few studies have addressed some requirements for pedestrian spaces [Khisty n.d.; Lozano 1974; Joardar and Neill 1978].) It does this by concentrating on the perceptual requirements of pedestrian spaces and the contrasting ones needed in spaces for motorists. The stress is thus on the perceptual rather than cognitive level, or on dealing with the experiential, sensory aspects leading to interest and exploration, rather than with imageability and clarity leading to orientation, subjective distance, and the like (Rapoport 1977).

In summary, the argument is as follows: pedestrian behavior, like any activity, is a function of two major sets of factors, cultural and physical. As we have already seen, any activity is primarily culturally based in that it is the result of unwritten rules and customs, traditions and habits, and the prevailing life-style and definition of behavior appropriate to given settings. Regarding pedestrian behavior, there are two major "styles" of street use, with some cultures predisposed to use urban spaces for many more activities than others. Also included in "culture" is the level of technology, which is to say, the availability or nonavailability of animal, mechanical, or other forms of transport or conveyances.

Physical factors include those characteristics of settings that are supportive of the activity in question. In this case, a set of perceptual characteristics can be broadly described as having to do with *complexity*, which, in a given cultural context, will maximize and encourage walking. In other words, given a set of cultural rules, certain perceptual characteristics are needed for such settings to work. Clearly, other physical characteristics exist (which have already been mentioned). Among these may be the size of a town (Gump and James n.d., and others); safety—whether from traffic or crime; climate, sunshine, and shade; topography (which may influence people differentially, such as hills in the case of the elderly); distance; and the presence of services, such as food, shopping, toilets, or seating.

These last will not be discussed. The question that will now be addressed is which perceptual characteristics of environments are supportive for walking. Note that we are *not* discussing environments *causing* walking; the relationship is not a deterministic one. Rather, settings are either supportive or inhibiting, although, as already pointed out, some can be so inhibiting as to block behavior. Thus, they can be negatively determining (Rapoport 1977, 1983a).

A detailed discussion of the nature of supportive environments in general would be inappropriate here (however, see Rapoport 1979d, 1980c, and 1983b). But one can ask three major questions about any supportive environment: What is supported? How is it supported? By what is it supported? In this case the hypothesized answers are: *Walking is being supported; it is done, other things being equal, by maintaining high levels of interest; this is achieved through high levels of perceptual complexity.*

These perceptual characteristics are hypothesized as increasing the *pleasure* of walking by stimulating exploratory activity. We are thus not dealing with the manifest or instrumental function of safety but with the latent functions of pleasure, delight, interest, exploration, ludic behavior, and the like (on this use of manifest and latent, see Rapoport 1977 and 1982b). While environments are not determining but supportive, they can also be seen as catalysts (Wells 1965). In other words, they elicit previously inhibited behavior. Note that this can also sometimes be achieved by physical separation, particularly where there is a tradition of pedestrian behavior and where, as in many traditional cities in Europe, the perceptual characteristics of pedestrianized areas frequently happen to be like those proposed here, and unlike those of U.S. pedestrian malls.

The effect of environment on behavior can also be considered another way: through the notion of *habitat selection*. Like other organisms, people match perceived characteristics of environments against certain needs, expectations, norms, desires, and images so as to try to make consistent desired characteristics of a particular setting with a particular behavior pattern (Rapoport 1977, chap. 2; 1982a).

In this connection, walking is an interesting activity because it has remained essentially unchanged since the origin of our species. This suggests the possible existence of a clear evolutionary baseline. Unlike other travel modes, pedestrian behavior is millions of years old and it evolved in settings of a particular level of complexity (see the arguments, in other connections, of Boyden 1974, 1979; Hamburg 1975; Dubos 1966, 1972; Tiger and Fox 1971; and Fox 1970, among others. See also Rapoport 1979a and 1979b). Note also that since the evolutionary *perceptual* baseline is still generally valid, the criteria derived for other travel modes, for example, high-speed motor traffic, will be equally valid if based on these same perceptual needs and characteristics. Thus, in terms of habitat selection, it is likely that even if people are "unaware" of their needs, they will respond to those characteristics being discussed and walk more in settings possessing them.

Thus, the underlying notion, summarized in Rapoport (1977: 207–47) and based on extensive research literature, is that human beings, like most organisms, process information and, in doing so, seek certain levels of information input at certain perceptual rates that depend on the individual (and his culture) and on the activity in question. These preferred levels can be described as constituting complexity (contrasted with the extremes of deprivation and boredom, chaos, and overload). Note that with regard to complexity, there seems to be a difference between liking and preference, as opposed to interest and exploration. Liking seems best described by an inverted U-curve (where there is an optimum), whereas interest seems best described by a monotonically rising line (although there is probably an upper limit when overload is approached or reached [Rapoport 1977: 212, fig. 4.7]).

Since the U-curve seems to apply to preference and the straight line to time of exploration, they likely describe two different sets of pedestrian spaces. Recall that there are two types of pedestrian activity and hence two types of supportive environments: those related to walking or strolling (dynamic spaces, such as streets), and those related to sitting and standing (static spaces, such as plazas). It is likely that interest is the principal criterion for the former and liking the

principal criterion for the latter; these spaces may have different desirable characteristics, particularly since liking is more influenced by *meaning*. Thus, liking is more (although not exclusively) a matter of associational qualities than interest, which is more (although not exclusively) a matter of perceptual qualities. An example is the frequent liking of *green* spaces for sitting (Rapoport 1977: 207–40). Hence, also, the important role of other people and culturally appropriate and acceptable activities while sitting or standing. Note once again that *cultural variability is likely to play a larger role in static pedestrian behavior than in walking.*

Both settings are pedestrian; while they differ from each other, both differ from settings for vehicular traffic. I will concentrate on dynamic spaces—streets—although the same approach is applicable to static spaces and to traffic spaces. In other words, the same type of analysis will reveal which qualities are supportive of the different activities.

While the discussion will concentrate on perceptual aspects, it will touch on the associational qualities of dynamic spaces. For example, the effectiveness of arcades as pedestrian settings is based on both perceptual and associational variables. Not only are the levels of complexity inside and outside the arcade very different and suitable for the types of movement concerned (as we shall see), but the highly enclosed, sheltered, and almost nurturant arcaded space; its uses, such as shops, restaurants, and so on; its very different spatial quality; its enclosure and separation from, yet visibility to, traffic; its freedom of movement and slow tempos, contrasted with the adjoining speed and linear flow of traffic—all provide a clear contrast in meaning. One is clearly in a human rather than nonhuman space (Rapoport 1970), in a pedestrian rather than machine space (Horvath 1974) (fig. 5-1).

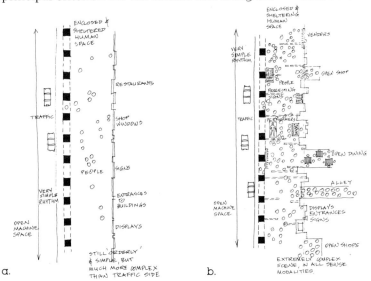

5-1. Two examples of arcaded streets among many throughout the world: a. Rue de Rivoli, Paris; b. composite, Singapore, early 1960s. (Redrawn from Rapoport 1977: 221)

Similarly, the raised sidewalks in Paris do more than provide different and appropriate perceptual experiences to the two classes of users: by putting pedestrians *above* ground rather than underground (and in what is clearly an important place, as opposed to an overpass, which is clearly a second-class place), they communicate meanings about relative importance, status, and the like. They set a context and define a situation (Rapoport 1979c) and hence work in the associational realm as well as in the perceptual one. It is, however, likely that many of the characteristics that provide appropriate perceptual complexity also tend to communicate the appropriate meaning, most simply that the raised sidewalks are a desirable pedestrian space (fig. 5-2).

Given these distinctions, let us turn back to the central issue of perceptual characteristics. There is clearly a continuum of travel modes and conditions and associated complexity levels (walking, bicycling, slow driving, and fast driving, as well as various public transport modes, such as bus, train, and subway). Each has different requirements for complexity levels, in other words, different perceptual characteristics that can be specified. Moreover, driving on a narrow road lined by trees is different from driving on a road through open country or through mountains; an urban freeway is different from a rural one; driving on a surface or elevated road is different from driving through a tunnel—all in terms of the perceptual characteristics that are desirable.

The point is made most clearly, however, by picking two extremes—walking, strolling, and sauntering on the one hand, as opposed to fast, urban motor traffic on the other hand—and deriving the perceptual characteristics desirable in these contrasting settings. Although my interest is in pedestrians, I can clarify the whole issue by contrasting their needs to motorists'. In discussing urban pedestrian streets and urban highways, the perceptual variables considered will be mainly *visual*, although environmental perception is

multisensory (Rapoport 1977: 184–95). Moreover, *the nonvisual senses are particularly important in pedestrian spaces*, since there is opportunity to experience and appreciate them; while driving one tends to be isolated from those nonvisual variables. They thus add greatly to the desirable complexity of such settings by providing many more potential noticeable differences in various sensory modalities (Rapoport 1977: 229–30). Also, while complexity in all settings, and especially in pedestrian settings, is achieved both through fixed feature and semifixed feature elements (as well as through nonfixed feature elements, meaning other people), only fixed feature elements will be discussed here. While the semifixed elements may, in fact, be most important, they can be fit easily into the conceptual framework. Also, they are less under the control of the designer.

THE PERCEPTUAL CHARACTERISTICS OF PEDESTRIAN VERSUS VEHICULAR SPACES

The specific suggested perceptual characteristics that should distinguish pedestrian spaces from those designed for motor traffic can be derived from the variable speed of travel and the different ways of perceiving the environment: free and flexible for pedestrians, constrained and "tunnel" for motorists. (For more detail, see Rapoport 1977: 240–47.)

Notions such as information processing and channel capacity suggest that complexity is best expressed in terms of noticeable differences. What is important is the *rate* of information, or, the number of noticeable differences per unit time. Thus, speed plays an important role in the perception of noticeable differences and hence of complexity. It can, therefore, be asserted that pedestrians and motorists differ greatly in the way they perceive urban environments.

Perception of the city is dynamic and sequential. The city is experienced over time and its image is made up of the integration of successive partial views, each of which, however, must be noticeably different, and never wholly predictable.[2] This integration of partial views is affected by speed and the nature of the environment, both of which influence the rate of noticeable differences. Assuming that the environment provides potential noticeable differences, speed influences how often noticeable differences occur, how long they are seen, and, hence, whether they are observed. Subtle cues need a slow pace, yet driving is not only fast, but it also demands concentration, leaving little time or capacity to appreciate the environment. Pedestrians thus have a much better awareness of places and clearer ideas of the meaning and ac-

5-2. Raised sidewalk, Boulevard St. Dennis, Paris. One of several such boulevards in the city. (Redrawn from Rapoport 1977: 246)

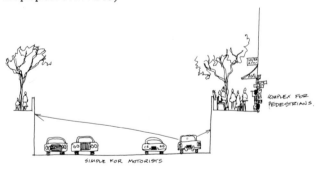

tivities in the city than have either drivers or users of public transport. Because of the lower speed and lower criticality of their movement, pedestrians can perceive many more differences in form and activity. Pedestrians are also less insulated from multisensory information, whose dimensionality is increased by the active nature of walking.

This suggests that for different speeds, different cues and different levels of complexity should be designed. For example, streets with arcades can provide different levels of complexity for motorists and pedestrians. Long pedestrian underpasses, with white, shiny, tiled walls are much too featureless at pedestrian speeds; the apparent rate of progress is reduced by the lack of noticeable differences and adequate levels of information. The roadside strip is too complex and chaotic at driving speeds while residential streets seen at slower driving speeds or at pedestrian speeds are too monotonous; there is a reversal of needed levels of complexity related to speed. A roadside strip, full of parking lots and large elements, is extremely open spatially and provides inadequate information to pedestrians, since there are few visible changes; at slow speeds there is a low rate of information, few noticeable differences, and the environment is boring (fig. 5-3).

The perception of complexity is thus related to the number of noticeable differences per unit time and hence to speed. Speed also influences the way people organize discrete stimuli into groups. At high speeds, elements are grouped into simple chunks, while at slow speeds more discrete elements are perceived. High speed makes a complex environment too chaotic; a simple environment, interesting at high speed,

becomes monotonous at slow speeds. Complexity in a traffic tunnel and simplicity in a prison yard are both undesirable. In all these cases the *perceived* complexity of spaces is more constant than their *designed* complexity, because of the variability of speed. Thus high-speed environments need to be designed with much lower complexity than slow-speed environments, and the elements need to be composed differently (as will be shown later).

Fine detail and small differences are picked up by central vision, while peripheral vision detects motion and its importance increases at high speeds. Thus elements close to a rapidly moving observer, particularly if they are complex, can be made distressing by greatly exaggerating apparent speed. Movement itself, as it affects perception and creates sequences, can be understood in terms of noticeable differences. Movement through an environment can be described in terms of transitions, "emergence from behind," sequences, and transformations. This can only happen when there are noticeable differences, so that on a featureless plan or a completely featureless tunnel, and in a vehicle with no kinesthetic cues to speed and movement, the apparent rate of movement would be much lower than in an environment rich in transitions and noticeable differences. In other words, complexity depends on the number of changes or noticeable differences per unit time, including changes of any uniform, or uniformly varying, attribute, such as rate, direction, slope, curvature, color, enclosure, smell, sound, light, and temperature. All analyses of an urban environment in terms of transitions and sequences, while easily interpreted in terms of noticeable differences, must include a consideration of how fast they occur. Given a certain number of noticeable differences per unit length, it is clear that at lower speeds an environment would tend to be simplified, while at higher speeds it would tend toward more complexity (fig. 5-4).

At pedestrian speeds, the perceiver is free to explore the environment using all sensory modalities. This leads to some increase in complexity if potential noticeable differences are present. It follows that settings for high and low speed should be perceptually quite different. The subtleties of traditional high-style or

5-3. Speed and noticeable differences. Roadside strip covered: <u>a.</u> in a five-minute walk; <u>b.</u> in a five-minute drive. (Redrawn from Rapoport 1977: 241)

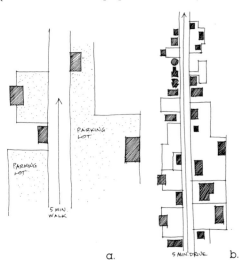

5-4. Speed and noticeable differences. (Redrawn from Rapoport 1977: 242)

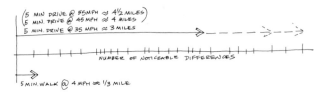

vernacular architectural or urban design cannot be appreciated at high speed; neither can a freeway at walking speed. At driving speeds, the time available to obtain information is also greatly reduced. The need is thus for large-scale elements and infrequent broad and smooth rhythms. The pedestrian receives very different input—it is fine grain, he can vary the rate, he can look around and stop to observe detail, he is aware of the environment all around him in all sense modalities. Motorists' perceptions are affected by the length of time each element is in view and also by the criticality of the task. The pedestrian has each element in view as long as he wishes and can satisfy his interest in it because of the low criticality of this task. When pedestrians are harassed by traffic, their task becomes more critical and they cannot perceive the environment in the way appropriate to their speed. This is a common design problem.

Urban light and sign systems have different effects at different speeds, as anyone who has experienced a highway strip at night at high speed knows. The effects of speed on highway and road design have been discussed (Tunnard and Pushkarev 1963; Appleyard, Lynch, and Myer 1964; Carr and Schissler 1969), but the general effects on perception or on the design of pedestrian spaces have not been considered. The important conclusion is that pedestrian and high-speed environments are perceptually incompatible, so that the conflict is not only between cars and pedestrians, but between fast and slow speeds and also between such types of movement as smooth and jerky or straight and irregular.

To repeat, an environment that is comfortably stimulating from a car becomes monotonously boring on foot, while what is interesting on foot becomes chaotic in a car. The Shambles at York is a good pedestrian environment, while the Egyptian Pyramids are ideal at car speeds. More generally, the medieval city is pedestrian; Ville Radieuse and its progeny are for motorists. The two environments need to be quite different in terms of noticeable differences and perceptual organization: at high speeds one needs distant views, simplicity and a large scale, while at slow speeds one needs a small scale, intricacy, and complexity. It can also be shown that as speed increases, not only do tasks become more demanding and concentration increases, but several other things also happen (Tunnard and Pushkarev 1963: 172–74). These include changes in the distance of the point of focus, which changes the relation of objects to the route and narrows peripheral vision, so that changes are required in the relation of side elements to the route as a result of the need to avoid "tunnel vision." Foreground detail fades, so that elaborate detail is both useless and undesirable. Finally, space percep-

tion becomes impaired, which influences the placing of elements to avoid "looming." In general, then, the requirements for both the high- and low-speed environments, as well as for dynamic or static pedestrian spaces, can be specified in perceptual terms (Rapoport 1977: 240–47).

For high-speed environments, these include gradual curves, long views, regular rhythms, wide symmetrical spaces, generally low complexity, gradual modulation, and a restricted complexity range. For pedestrian movement, the opposite is true. Pedestrians need sudden changes in direction, short views hiding and gradually revealing other views, irregular rhythms, narrow asymmetrical spaces of high enclosure, generally high complexity, and a wide complexity range.

In somewhat more detail, it would follow that, for motorists, building setbacks should be greater than for pedestrians and should not be uniform. Uniform and consistent surroundings confound orientation, confuse destination location, and reduce curiosity, since they do not provide noticeable differences. The shapes of the visual fields on either side of the road should be similar, that is to say, symmetrical. Although one side is always dominant, the visual field never expands equally on both sides. Distances between peripherally and foveally viewed elements should be large scale and simple. Elements along the road should provide information at an intermediate rate with gradual transitions—sudden contrast between high- and low-information environments should be avoided; although areas of differing complexity are still needed, the transitions among them should be gradual. There should be a smooth continuous succession of such areas, with their intensity decreasing as speed increases. Generally, then, as speed increases, the number of noticeable differences in the environment should decrease and setbacks should increase. As traffic intensity increases, the perceptual complexity of the environment should be reduced.

Pedestrians can use, and they desire, much more acute and abrupt transitions in space, sensory experience, light levels, sounds, and all other sense modalities. Only they can notice and respond to the variety of stimuli that can be used in a rich, opulent environment. The characteristics of pedestrian spaces, which also follow from the discussion generally, and those of high-speed spaces can be illustrated and combined (fig. 5-5).

Note that we are only discussing perceptual variables. Many other considerations will also play a role. For example, activity will also modify these relationships, since play and exploratory, as opposed to grimly purposeful, behavior will need very different levels of

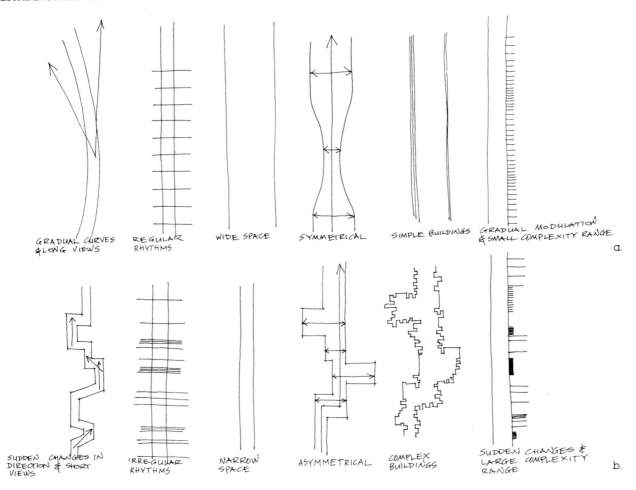

GRADUAL CURVES
& LONG VIEWS

REGULAR
RHYTHMS

WIDE SPACE

SYMMETRICAL

SIMPLE BUILDINGS

GRADUAL MODULATION
& SMALL COMPLEXITY RANGE

a.

SUDDEN CHANGES IN
DIRECTION & SHORT
VIEWS

IRREGULAR
RHYTHMS

NARROW
SPACE

ASYMMETRICAL

COMPLEX
BUILDINGS

SUDDEN CHANGES &
LARGE COMPLEXITY
RANGE

b.

5-5. Perceptual characteristics for: a. motorist, and b. pedestrian spaces. (Redrawn from Rapoport 1977: 244)

complexity at given speeds. Walking or driving for pleasure or to a job are all very different. People may thus select different environments for apparently similar activities, depending on the context and the situation as well as the culture; but the difference between slow- and high-speed environments will persist.

At the scale of the city, the existence of many levels of complexity and their appropriate relationship to the context is important. For example, designers could modulate complexity levels to reflect the nature of areas and their activities, their importance in the urban hierarchy, and the speed at which they will be perceived (fig. 5-6). It has already been noted that pedestrians rarely look above eye level in enclosed urban spaces, where perception of detail is almost inevitable. Given the needs of drivers as described, their movement channels should be simple, and it is freestanding elements and tops against the sky, and clusters of tall buildings that become important (fig. 5-7).

We have already seen that pedestrian spaces them-

selves can be separated into movement and rest spaces, dynamic and static spaces. This is an example of the need for specificity; to say *pedestrian spaces* is not really enough (neither can one ignore cultural variables and the specific activities that follow). As suggested, these two forms of pedestrian spaces may require different perceptual characteristics: movement spaces need to be linear, narrow, and winding so that they entice with hidden views and encourage walking, strolling, and sauntering; while rest spaces need to be more static and wider (although still enclosed), frequently green, provided with sitting spaces, and so on. Such spaces, whether plazas or avenues, encourage visual exploration—mainly of other people—from one place and need to act as a stage for social behavior. It is people who become objects of interest, providing the requisite complexity levels. Thus streets that seem excessively broad, like the Champs Elysées in Paris, Dizengof Street in Tel Aviv, or Paseo Colon in Barcelona, provide human interest through their outdoor cafés, which narrow

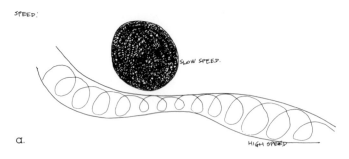

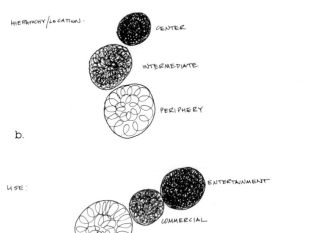

5-6. Complexity and context at the area level: <u>a.</u> speed; <u>b.</u> hierarchy/location; <u>c.</u> use. (Redrawn from Rapoport 1977: 245)

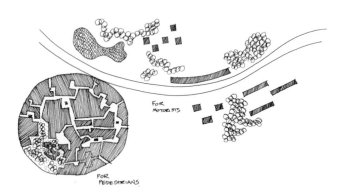

5-7. Pedestrians and motorists—separation by perceptual needs. (Redrawn from Rapoport 1977: 246)

the pavement, creating more appropriate pedestrian movement spaces. They also become complex as the result of people, tables and chairs, awnings overhead, sounds and smells, and so forth. Moreover, pedestrians and seated people see and are seen. In many cities, as in the Plaka in Athens, one finds the contrast of narrow shopping and pedestrian streets with wider rest spaces, often with trees, where cafés, *tavernas*, tables, and markets are found, although these spaces can still be remarkably small. In Athens, one also finds vast spaces like Parliament Square, which have parts that become satisfactory static pedestrian settings—but this is another topic.

CONCLUSION

The argument concerning the cultural and perceptual aspects of pedestrian street use can best be summarized in visual form (fig. 5-8). Rather brief and condensed, this argument simplified what is a more complex set of issues that ideally require greater development, elaboration, and even qualification. However, I believe that, even in its simple form, it is both valid and useful.

Nothing more need be said about its validity. Regarding its usefulness, two concluding comments can be made. The first one is general: Design is culture-specific (Rapoport 1979d, 1980c, 1983b). Therefore, any design requires the identification of the cultural characteristics of the group or groups in question, their unwritten rules about permitted activities, and acceptable settings and situations for such activities. The argument in this chapter is thus a specific instance of a more general model about the nature of design which, if used, would prevent some rather unfortunate designs. It would also avoid unlikely arguments, which imply that if we built Greek Island town streets and plazas, people would use them the way they are used in the Greek Islands.

Second, however, through the concept of supportive environments, and also through the argument about evolutionary constancies, it *does* suggest that any cultural predisposition that exists for pedestrian activity (or any other activity) in a given place will usually be greatly helped by appropriate design. It also suggests that in this specific instance such appropriate design is related to what can broadly be described as appropriate levels of complexity. It also provides some fairly specific suggestions of what these might be, which become a hypothesis to be tested (as any design must be). Moreover, it suggests that one type of urban design analysis that is extremely useful is in terms of rates of speed of movement. While it goes without saying that this needs to be complemented by many others, it finally suggests that we think of the urban system as a system of settings for systems of activities (Rapoport 1977, 1982c) which, in this case of streets, are distinguished in terms of rapid movement, slow movement, and static behavior, each with its appropriate perceptual qualities.

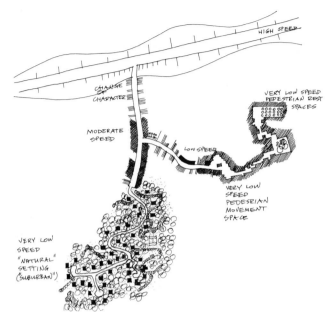

5-8. Complexity and speed: motorists and pedestrians. (Redrawn from Rapoport 1977: 247)

An urban street (and road) system based, in the first instance, on such an analysis and set of considerations would work better than current ones in terms of supporting the widest possible range of culturally appropriate behaviors—which, moreover, can be specified for any milieu (see Beverly Hills or India!). This would lead to much more satisfactory street design. It would also, when combined with other human considerations with which I have dealt elsewhere (Rapoport 1977), provide a framework for cities that would be much more varied, complex, interesting and supportive, and hence more satisfactory, than current cities tend to be.

NOTES

1. In *etic* operations, the *observer* judges the information, concepts, and analyses used, whereas in *emic* operations, the *native informer* judges the observer's description and analyses—ED.
2. This is the reason why I argue that the concept of "mystery," which is seen by Stephen Kaplan as a separate characteristic of the environment, is, in fact, an aspect of complexity.

REFERENCES

Appleyard, D., K. Lynch, and J. Myer. 1964. *The View From the Road.* Cambridge: MIT Press.

Barker, R. G., and L. S. Barker. 1961. "Behavior Units for the Comparative Study of Culture." In *Studying Personality Cross-Culturally*, edited by B. Kaplan. New York: Harper and Row.

Barker, R. G., and P. Schoggen. 1973. *Qualities of Community Life.* San Francisco: Fossey-Bass.

Becker, F. D. 1973. "A Class-conscious Evaluation: Going Back to Sacramento's Mall." *Landscape Architecture* 64, no. 1 (October): 448–57.

Boyden, S. V. 1974. "Conceptual Basis of Proposed International Ecological Studies in Large Metropolitan Areas." Mimeo, Australian National University, Canberra, Australia.

———. 1979. *An Integrative Ecological Approach to the Study of Human Settlements.* (MAB Technical Note 12). Paris: UNESCO.

Brower, S. 1977. *The Design and Management of Neighborhood Parks.* Baltimore: Department of Planning, City Planning Commission (August).

Brower, S., and P. Williamson. 1974. "Outdoor Recreation as a Function of the Urban Housing Environment." *Environment and Behavior* 6, no. 3 (September): 295–345.

Carr, S., and D. Schissler. 1969. "The City as Trip: Perceptual Selection and Memory in the View from the Road." *Environment and Behavior* 1, no 1 (June): 7–36.

Dubos, R. 1966. *Man Adapting.* New Haven: Yale University Press.

———. Dubos, R. 1972. "Is Man Overadapting to the Environment?" *Sydney University Union Recorder* 52, no. 6 (April 13).

Ekistics. 1978. Vol. 45, no. 273 (November/December). Special issue on people-oriented urban streets.

Fox, R. 1970. "The Cultural Animal." *Encounter* 35, no. 1 (July): 31–42.

Gump, P. V., and E. V. James. (N.d.) "Child Development and the Man-Made Environment: A Literature Review and Commentary." Mimeo, Lawrence: University of Kansas, Department of Psychology.

Hamburg, D. A. 1975. "Ancient Man in the Twentieth Century." In *The Quest for Man*, edited by V. Goodall. New York: Random House.

Horvath, R. J. 1974. "Machine Space." *Geographical Review* 66, no. 2 (April): 167–88.

Joardar, S. D., and J. W. Neill. 1978. "The Subtle Differences in Configuration of Small Public Spaces." *Landscape Architecture* 69 (November): 487–91.

Khisty, C. J. (N.d.) "Planning of Pedestrian Facilities Using Behavior Circuits." Mimeo, Washington State University, Pullman, Washington.

King, A. D. 1976. *Colonial Urban Development.* London: Routledge and Kegan Paul.

Lozano, E. E. 1974. "Visual Needs in the Urban Environment." *Town Planning Review* 45, no. 4 (October): 351–74.

Rapoport, A. 1969. *House Form and Culture.* Englewood Cliffs, N.J.: Prentice-Hall.

———. 1970. "The Study of Spatial Quality." *Journal of Aesthetic Education* 4, no. 4 (October): 81–96. Reprinted in *Architectural Association Quarterly* 10, no. 1 (1978): 45–50; footnotes in vol. 10, no. 2.

———. 1973. "Some Thoughts on the Methodology of Man-Environment Studies." *International Journal of Environmental Studies* 4: 135–40.

———. 1976. "Socio-cultural Aspects of Man-Environment Studies." In *The Mutual Interaction of People and Their Built Environment*, edited by A. Rapoport. The Hague: Mouton.

———. 1977. *Human Aspects of Urban Form.* Oxford: Pergamon Press.

———. 1979a. "On the Cultural Origins of Settlements." In *Introduction to Urban Planning*, edited by A. J. Catanese and J. C. Snyder. New York: McGraw-Hill.

———. 1979b. "On the Cultural Origins of Architecture." In *Introduction to Architecture*, edited by J. C. Snyder et al. New York: McGraw-Hill.

———. 1979c. "On the Environment and the Definition of the Situation." *International Architect* 1, no. 1: 26–28.

———. 1979d. "An Approach to Designing Third World Environments." *Third World Planning Review* 1, no. 1 (Spring): 23–40.

———. 1980a. "Towards a Cross-culturally Valid Definition of Housing." In *Optimizing Environments (Research, Practice and Policy)*, edited by R. R. Stough and A. Wandersman. Washington, D.C.: Environmental Design Research Association.

———. 1980b. "Cross-cultural Aspects of Environmental Design." In *Human Behavior and Environment Vol. 4; Environment and Culture*, edited by I. Altman, A. Rapoport, and J. F. Wohlwill. New York: Plenum Press.

———. 1981. "Some Thoughts on Units of Settlement."

Ekistics 48, no. 291 (November/December): 447–53.

———. 1982a. "On the Perceptual Separation of Pedestrians and Motorists." In *Road Safety—Research and Practice*, edited by H. C. Foot et al. Eastbourne: Praeger.

———. 1982b. *The Meaning of the Built Environment—A Non-Verbal Communications Approach.* Beverly Hills, Calif.: Sage.

———. 1982c. "Urban Design and Human Systems: On Ways of Relating Buildings to Urban Fabric." In *Human and Energy Factors in Urban Planning—A Systems Approach*, edited by P. Laconte, J. Gibson, and A. Rapoport. (NATO Advanced Study Institute, Series D, Behavior and Social Science No. 12). The Hague: Nijhoff.

———. 1983a. "The Effect of Environment on Behavior." In *Environment and Population (Problems of Adaptation)*, edited by J.B. Calhoun. New York: Praeger.

———. 1983b. "Development, Culture Change and Supportive Design." *Habitat International* 7, nos. 5–6: 249–68.

Rudofsky, B. 1969. *Streets for People.* Garden City, N. Y.: Doubleday.

Thakudersai, S. G. 1972. "Sense of Place in Greek Anonymous Architecture." *Ekistics* 34, no. 204 (November): 334–40.

Tiger, L., and R. Fox. 1971. *The Imperial Animal.* New York: Delta.

Tunnard, C., and B. Pushkarev. 1963. *Manmade America: Chaos or Control?* New Haven: Yale University Press.

Wells, B.W.P. 1965. "The Psycho-social Influence of Building Environment: Sociometric Findings in Large and Small Office Spaces." *Building Science* 1: 153–65.

Wheatley, P. 1971. *The Pivot of the Four Quarters.* Chicago: Aldine.

Whyte, W. H. 1980. *The Social Life of Small Urban Spaces.* Washington, D.C.: The Conservation Foundation.

PART TWO
Better Cities

6.
The Street as Teacher

GRADY CLAY

It is the Road which determines the sites of many cities and the growth and nourishment of all. It is the Road which controls the development of strategies and fixes the sites of battles. It is the Road which gives its framework to all economic development. It is the Road which is the channel of all trade and, what is more important, of all ideas. In its most humble function it is a necessary guide without which progress from place to place would be a ceaseless experiment; it is a sustenance without which organized society would be impossible; thus, and with those other characters I have mentioned, the Road moves and controls all history.

—Hilaire Belloc
The Road

That we have travelled a long distance from such deterministic views and a long time from 1923, when Belloc wrote these words, does not reduce their power or conceal the strategic mind at work in a large field. One of the great English essayists of the first half of this century, Belloc was nothing if not absolutely certain and a master of the sheer crescendo of utterance in argumentation. His grasp of geography, though bearing traces of the British empire-building tradition, was often firm and occasionally brilliant.

Modern readers must struggle with Belloc over many a detour and diversion, for the English personal essayists, of whom few still practice the art, were devotees of the telling aside, the byways and by-the-ways of exposition. Belloc's intriguing book *The Path to Rome*, first published in 1902 and repeatedly printed in paperback, tells us as much about Belloc's encounters with folk, drink, and oddities along the way as it does about the way itself. That was Belloc's way of operating: anecdotal, diversionary, reflective from various distances and viewpoints.

He would be among the first to welcome with erudite derision the modern wave of analysts of the street, road, and highway. Of their preoccupation with efficient movement, their charts and questionnaires, their paradigms and parameters he would have little but epigrammatic scorn. Yet, without my attempting to push him ahead of his time, he was, I think, offering a rare insight into the cultural functions of street,

All photos are by Grady Clay unless otherwise noted.

road, and highway, which we would do well to consider today. Particularly revealing was his plumbing the depths of the historical process by which tracks became trails became paths became pathways, ways, wagon and carriage roads, well-travelled routes, and eventually today's Autoroutes across Europe and Interstates across the United States.

Above all, it occurs to me, after taking a second look at some of Belloc's work, that he was viewing street and road as a palimpsest of past and present, a teller of tales for all who care to look, a schoolbook both continental in scope and transferrable across cultures. Without this conviction I would be foolish indeed to bring Belloc kicking and screaming across the Atlantic and into the great North American scene of street, road, highway, and multimodal transit systems. (However, I expect Belloc must have welcomed the no doubt considerable royalties from his book sales in North America.) Belloc's closest model in current literature is James/Jan Morris, the transsexual journalist whose mastery of the long-distance trip in essay form for *Rolling Stone* and other media is as well-fitted to modern dress as was Belloc's to more old-fashioned modes.

From Belloc's pioneering Road to the modern American street is not as long a leap as one might suppose, given certain universals about all linear means of transportation and most especially about the street as it is situated in contemporary urban territory. In this essay, I assume that the street is the great common carrier of information for a democratic society; an educational device of huge dimensions, giving off great volumes of lessons, examples, warnings, admonitions; a living and inescapable classroom penetrating all phases of life. My view is further conditioned by assuming that our knowledge about the Street (in which term I include Road and Highway) is socially conditioned, so that only by supreme effort can we think of it much beyond its simplistic function of getting us from here to there.

We have been brainwashed by at least a half-century of "research," all of it designed to prove that getting from here to there quickly by personal vehicle is the fundamental human activity of the twentieth century. Vast sums of money have cascaded through state highway departments, research institutes, and universities to ratify trends rather than to explore alternatives. My own bookshelves—reflecting an abiding interest in highway development—are crowded with studies of the impact of the Houston Freeway on land values and the like, reinventions of the wheel to suit every local whim and budget.

If one of the major revolutions in history was the multiplication of the amount of food one man could produce in one day's time, then another revolution surely is the multiplication of places that a human being can occupy or modify in the space of a day's travel. That first revolution lay in the multiplication of sustenance; the next in the multiplication of presence.

In this multiplication table, the street speaks a universal language: its signals are part of everyday learning; its rules for movement are among the most widely understood of all public codes of conduct; and even its most bizarre variations offer, upon close examination, familiar goings-on.

The School of the Street offers kindergarden-to-graduate-level curricula, evidence, texts, and tests. To matriculate in the School of the Street, one must take determined steps that go beyond merely venturing down the sidewalk of one's own street—even though Jane Jacobs showed masterfully what a large curriculum is offered by any complex street system and how much is to be learned in front of one's own house. (Her pre-Toronto location, Hudson Street, Manhattan, has gone down in urban history as one of the great Learning Streets. See her *Death and Life of Great American Cities* [1961] for a more complete lesson.)

Marshall McLuhan reminded us in *Understanding Media* (1964) that, "for the West, literacy has long been pipes and taps and streets and assembly lines and inventories . . . things in sequence and succession." The road and the printed word he dismissed as "our older media." Implicit in McLuhan's writings—as in those of his mentor, the Canadian economist Harold

A. Innis—was his conviction that transportation and personal movement-through-territory was a dying form of communication, fast being supplanted by television and the electronic grid forming the Global Village (his capitals, not mine). The world he attempted to describe would soon be moving information to the body, rather than vice versa.

But now, twenty years after *Understanding Media*, the mass movement of persons from Here to There persists, and neither McLuhan's brilliant insights nor the rise thus far in the price of oil seems able to diminish the world's appetite for movement—by personal vehicle, if possible, and by any means, where necessary. Human movement itself shows such power as a learning device that I doubt it can ever be fully replaced by electronic substitutes. Street scenes will change, perhaps beyond all recognition, but differences between places will continue to require humans to exploit or escape those differences—as tourist, as entrepreneur, as military invader, or as refugee.

Photography changed the presence of places by moving them to the easy chair, the desk or slide show, and later the television screen. This truncation of places-in-the-round to places on a flat surface left out feeling, smelling, movement, experiment—all those elements of "being there" that were the essence of thereness.

But in considering how such a scene, this locus of movement—the North American street—can operate as a fully rewarding educational instrument, we must approach it in a structured way, organize it as a replicable experience, and record it in ways that prove meaningful and useful beyond the classroom's walls. In this essay, I wish to examine Street, Road, and Highway collectively as a public educational medium and to do so in three ways: first, as a mode of communication in which the language we use is an essential part; second, by taking a look at special methods of examination; and, finally, by speculating upon Street-Road-Highway as laboratories for universities.

Along the way, we must take note of "down time" —stretches of the urbanized environment where learning is at a minimum, where street frontage gives over to open parking lots or closed-off parking garages; and where a form of design exists called "Riot Renaissance," with no stores, no shops, few doorways along one street and none along the next block. Along the way, we must also observe the rise of the new Citadels —those multipurpose megastructures containing convention halls, hotels, indoor race tracks, sports arenas, and parking ramps—self-consciously designed to capture customers and keep them spending their time and money indoors, well removed from the street. Few major American cities are without these new zones of confinement, which reduce the sidewalk population of the streets around them. Scores of them have been deposited at the edge of town or used to clear away slums adjacent to the old Downtown—with devastating impact on their neighborhoods (fig. 6-1).

Let me now reinforce this discussion with the lamentation that our language is still imprecise and deficient in dealing with Street, still stuck at the level of prescientific discourse that preceded Linnaeus's great codification of plant and animal names in the eighteenth century. Here before our very eyes is a definitional entity that we name Street: "A generally levelled, linear, artificially lighted, and paved surface, extended across territory in a continuous and often straight direction, bounded on either side by curbings or other tangible limits, and offering unlimited or partial access to its surface from adjoining properties [my construction]." Having said all that in schoolmarmish fashion, I am obliged at once to utter qualifications and emendations. Thousands of small-town, unpaved, rocky streets in the Americas admit to no such rigidities, being dusty in summer, muddy in winter, impassable after rains, and of random width and direction. I am being deliberate in using such a formal definition of the urbanized street, for reasons soon to come.

Meanwhile, what about the nomenclature for all those variations and subspecies of Urban Street? What of those things called Main Street, Main Drag, Shopping Strip, Back Alley (Laneway, in Toronto), Front Street, Back Street, Side Street, Dock Street, Structural Street (a nice example from Allan Jacobs's book *Looking at Cities* [1985])? What about Connector, High Tech Corridor, Mansion Row, Skid Road (popularized as Skid Row), Cross-Town (with Con-

nector understood but silent), Fashionable Shopping Street (as in Worth Avenue, Palm Beach; Regent Street, London; Rodeo Drive, Los Angeles; rue de Faubourg, Paris; Fifty-seventh Street, New York City)?

Not to mention those endless subdivisions into Fire Lane, Express Bus Lane, Fast Lane, Deceleration Lane, Bicycle Lane, Loading Ramp, Runaway Truck Ramp, No Parking and No Standing Zones, Towaway Zone, Carriageway (also known as Cartway), Verge, Gutter and Valley Gutter, Access Road, and Pull-Outs, and then off to Easements and Rights-of-Way of infinite variation, Driveways, Sidewalks and Walkways. As we proceed into the outskirts, we again confront Trails, Paths, Cowpaths, Ways, and the increasing obscurities of hinterland routes. Beyond the outskirts the Dirt Tracks, Raceways, Racetracks (dog, horse, and auto), and Drag Strips flourish. Hobbyists pursue each other in gymkhanas, autocrosses, point-to-point races, cross-country steeplechases, fox hunts, and drag hunts off to the far horizons. Closer to the Main Road, we encounter the large acreages where Motel Complexes thrive, where a dozen dealers jostle for customers in the new Auto Shopping Complex, with its own internal Streets, Ramps, Hardstands, and so on.

All this nomenclature suggests that the School of the Street properly begins with the language of the street, and here I do not mean the language of the gutter. I look upon the street as an educational enterprise, partly institutionalized and partly open to the most outrageous assumptions and interventions. Its rules of movement are among the most widely understood of all codes of public conduct. Within this broad context, one should view the trip and the walk as

6-1. Albany, Georgia, circa 1985. The civic arena surrounded by acres of empty parking just outside the built-up city shows "confinement" at work—everybody is gathered into one huge structure. Pulled off the streets and sidewalks, attendees have no lessons to learn, no messages to understand, only distance from a potentially enriching environment.

mechanisms by which each of us learns to adjust, cope, memorize, and habituate; to replicate experience and generalize from it; to invent experience and go with it.

Linnaeus, the great Swedish botanist, organized "the sovereign order of nature" with a naming system that still spans the natural sciences of our day. If the study of urban objects and processes is to advance beyond its present contentiousness, then the sovereign order of the man-made urban environment will need all the intensity of gaze and discrimination of nomenclature that we can muster. And for our study to proceed much beyond name-calling, we must recognize that the order of the street is continuous, that the street exhibits the ancient order of history that Hilaire Belloc revelled in, and that it displays emerging orders, both of magnitude and specialization, which we have only begun to put into some useful order.

One of the more intriguing aspects of street evolution is that its evolutionary order is far more apparent to the naked eye (though not to the naked mind) than was the evolution of plants and animals. Unless we live on a farm, go to the zoo, go to the jungle (with an exemplary guide to chop a path), or go to the laboratory and textbook, we see too few examples of animals in an ordinary life to arrive at evolutionary conclusions from visible evidence.

Not so on the street. A single daily commute from suburb to city center, an eye-filling trip to the airport, or a strongly held gaze at the passing roadside can uncover more historical evidence of evolution than the mind can digest.

Evidence of this evolutionary process, however, is scattered far and wide among many disciplines, and in recent years much of it has been generated by the historical preservationists. Off in other directions, the environmental psychologists are taking their own cut at the subject, while traditional planners and designers pursue their own objectives, using their own special lingo. Street literature and research methods run in all creeds and colors. Where does one find a multidisciplinary university course in Visible Evidence? Where does one find the same intensity of broad, scholarly gaze fastened upon a famous street (Fifth Avenue, New York; Market Street, San Francisco; North Wells, Chicago; Peachtree, Atlanta) as is regularly fastened upon single buildings of renown?

Without attempting to lay down my own favorite tactic upon so volatile a subject, I do suggest that use of the cross-section trip through metropolitan areas is as revealing to the modern observer as the first cross section of human tissue was to the anatomist Vesalius, or as the Valley Section was to the botanist-ecol-ogist-planner Patrick Geddes—to whom we shall shortly return.

As we move down the street itself, ten generations of cars pass by a hundred generations of advertising fashions, and a thousand variations in roadside building styles fill the windshield in an hour's trip. The evidence is so thick we recoil, we block it out; school is over, the mind closes shop for the rest of the trip. William Ewald, in his seminal book, *Street Graphics* (1971), recounts a 1968 study of Baltimore County drivers: "Under normal driving conditions, the occupant of a moving car can seldom handle more than ten items of information at a time." Yet at thirty miles per hour (2,640 feet per minute) both driver and passenger are confronted with 1,320 items of information —words, phrases, signs, symbols, diagrams, directions, and admonitions. This comes to approximately 440 words a minute—about double the average person's reading speed. No wonder most road users learn to blank it all out, to write it all off as a confusing blur (fig. 6-2). (Ewald's solution, which needs not detain us unduly, was to ration roadside messages by zoning, so as to protect drivers from excess diversion from the road itself.) Yet behind all that razzle-dazzle of the street-road-highway, an emerging order exists there waiting to be found.

Linnaeus would remind us students of street life that certain criteria hold true for the searching gaze. We must consider birth, nutrition, aging, movement, and internal propulsion; all of these criteria, it appears to me, operate as observably in street life as they do in animal and vegetable existence. Street evolution is far more clear in the school of the street than is biological evolution, yet the former has attracted little of the scholarly apparatus that surrounds the latter. Should we not think of today's street as the link between ancient paths and trails and tomorrow's megastructure? The street itself will take many forms beyond those envisioned by architect Louis Kahn, when he said "the street wants to be a building"—one that Kahn himself would design. But the ancient pathways persist over most of those human settlements we call cities. And in the evolution of those paths—once sufficiently recorded—there lies a new form of evolutionary theory waiting to be discovered. When such a theory finally develops, I suspect it will revolve around a single vital criterion, accessibility, from which all other attributes flow.

The street itself is a place of complex behavior and specialization and cannot be understood apart from its denizens and their habits. Increasingly, street space is preempted by the "world cars" of the 1980s (fig. 6-3). These look-alike contenders jostle for right-of-way with mobile earth movers, garment workers'

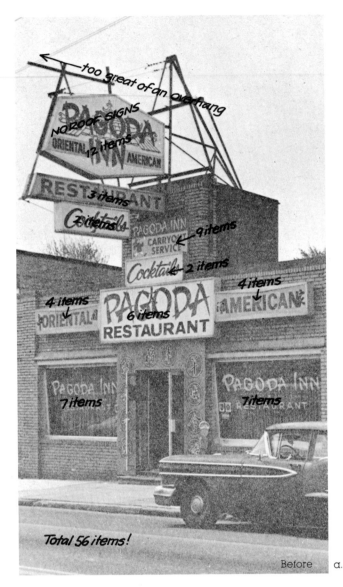

simple, inexpensive

with a flourish!

Before   a.   After   b.

6-2. How to trim down the number of commercial messages from the roadside: a. example of message overdose; b. two ways to reduce it. (Source: Ewald 1971: 91–92)

carts, motorized deliverymen, mobile-home transporters, backhoes, front loaders, gas-guzzlers, and a host of incipient minivehicles. While the city street grid attempts to accommodate all these vehicles, specialized streets, and streets-within-streets arise, as demarked by Express Lanes, Bus Lanes, Truck Routes, Mass-Transit Streets, Loading Zones, and special rights-of-way. Small personal vehicles—the horse, bicycle, and motorbike—have long demanded street and parking space. Now comes the "Trike," the three-cylinder commuter car.

But perhaps no one (to my knowledge, at least) has put upon street life the burden of explication that Linnaeus, two hundred years ago, put upon life in its

biozoological senses. There is yet to be found a fully documented and logical order of streets.

Contrast this, if you will, with the intensity of gaze fastened upon the street's mechanical denizens, the automobile, especially by the sports car magazines. From years of captivity to this narcotic subspecies of literature, I can testify to the endless permutations of specialized language—terms, depiction, description, comparison, and codification that are bought, sold, traded, and given currency by practitioners and observers alike. From the fastidious Museum of Modern Art down to endless local galleries, public museums give testimony to the object—the car—with their predictable exhibitions of the world of the car. That

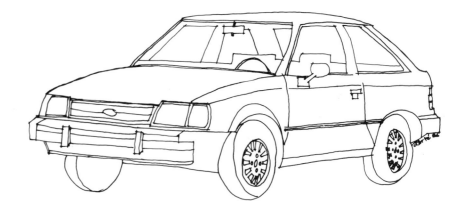

6-3. World car. (Sketch: Deborah Porte)

world turns out to be mostly the car itself, its couture and that of its drivers: a celebration of mechanical commodity. Few museums or historians, until lately, have paid much attention to the world beyond the car. No doubt it was the Arabian oil embargo and the first brisk whiff of shortages that encouraged a new wave of road historians to begin publishing their observations of the road, highway, motel, and tourist facilities in the 1970s, encouraged by J. B. Jackson's essays on the stranger's path and the evolving strip, which appeared in *Landscape* during the 1960s. Closer to the racetracks, the great Henry Manny III, a columnist in *Road and Track* magazine, was one of the most versatile linguists of that field, relishing the wordplay involved in a run through the gears, run-in, test run, trial run, trial spin, running off the track (as distinguished from an off-track run), or run for your money (as distinguished from a run for The Money).

Beyond learning the language of the street, future theorists of street meanings can find no better mentor than the great Scottish biologist Patrick Geddes and no better example adapted to the modern metropolis than his Valley Section (fig. 6-4).

Geddes's Valley Section was first exhibited in a grand civic panorama designed for the now-famous Cities Exhibition at Chelsea, London, in 1911. His painting showed a typical seventeenth- to eighteenth-century valley in cross section, with a fishing village port at the right and the landforms slowly ascending upward to the left through town streets, outskirts, hopfields, vineyards, and market gardens. The painting depicted cattle, arable and sheep farms on higher

6-4. Patrick Geddes's great "Valley Section," a pioneering description of a nineteenth-century port fishing village and its tributary region and an early version of the Metropolitan Cross Section described in this essay. (Source: Geddes 1950: 166–67)

grounds, then upland hunters, foresters, gold miners, and quarry workers on the mountains. It featured the perfect epitome of the perfect town form. From the woods came game and pelt; off the pastures the cattle were led down the paths and streets into the slaughterhouse, the cobbler's shop, and onto the ships; off the fields came the harvests for miller, baker, and town grocer. The whole, in short, was a progressional pageant from start to finish, a complete story in one picture.

But even the most cursory study of the Geddes epitome showed that such a cross section as an educational device can tell only part of the story of the modern city and its street system. Geddes's town was an old-fashioned processor of raw materials. Today's American city has become a processor of power and information. To understand that power firsthand, to tap that information, one must traverse the whole city, the whole metropolitan area as a continuous experience from outer trail to path to road to street, into the very city center, and out the other side. This completed experience forces the student-learner to confront the Whole Thing, the "city" as a complex educational enterprise, with various forms of learning available at each stage. The processing of local crops in the Geddes diagram is but a small part of today's picture.

There was no way, I concluded from a study via cross section of thirty-three North American cities in 1972 to 1973, that one can come to grips eye-to-eye, firsthand, with the complex metropolis, short of inventing and then following such a cross-section trip in a single, unifying journey. This approach could be considered Montessorian—handy for dealing with an environment rich in manipulative materials. One should look to it as a form of transactional analysis, a running encounter that requires both homework and on-site skills. It is a learning experience of high order, although it can be much simplified in scale and adapted to grade-school children, as has been done by members of the British Town and Country Planning Association with their Town Trails (Goodey 1975) (fig. 6-5).

In order to make the most of a cross-section analysis as a learning device, one must consider and plot out a route that performs as follows:

1. It must follow one general direction, not doubling back upon itself. In this way it would resemble the familiar geographer's traverse, a time-tested learning device for recording a linear experience through new territory.
2. As a corollary, it must form a continuous, easily described experience, using certain routes as a "spine" for the trip.

3. It should span the full range of daily commuting, exploiting the full size of the "commutershed." The ideal cross-section route thus begins at the outer limits of commuting (generally considered the zone in which at least 5 percent of job holders commute into the metropolitan area) and ends at the opposite outer limits—usually, but not invariably, 180 degrees in the opposite direction.
4. It should deal with the Center, whether the historic city center, the civic center, or the geographic center, where all roads once came together at a historic crossroads; it could be the original Town Landing, Zero Milestone, Court House Square, or other designated central place.
5. It must cope with the zone or neighborhood that is the major source of exportable goods and services and therefore the essential source of local income from distant markets.
6. It must explore a dying area—slums beyond recall, an abandoned warehouse district based on cost advantages long gone, a mill district undermined by foreign competition, Mansion Row on the skids.
7. It should encounter at least one growth area where booming firms burst through their walls and workers' parking expands all bounds, where land development is under way, and where roadside billboards announce zoning changes and new construction to come.
8. It should offer transactions with the Best Address, where fashion and ambition dictate that the new wealthy jostle for space with old families or carve out their own turf, where foreign-car agencies cluster, and where the spoor of status-striving rests upon vegetation, house style, and decor.
9. It should bring us into at least visual contact with the major geographic feature of the area, be it the closest navigable water or the dominant local peak or escarpment.
10. The ideal cross section will touch a historic part of the city, perhaps an entire district—sufficient evidence to tell the studious what might further be pursued (figs. 6-6, 6-7).
11. Finally, the course should be fun. This is the wild card in the deck, the subjectivity among those objective criteria. My own tactic has been to give close consideration to my own attention span, to my own capacity for boredom. If the route turns boring, turn off. And this opens up another axiom: To turn is to learn. Moving off a predictable or familiar route increases the intensity of one's gaze, the receptivity of one's senses. If one turns into threatening territory, pupils dilate, muscles tense, sweat exudes—and learning speeds up (fig. 6-8).

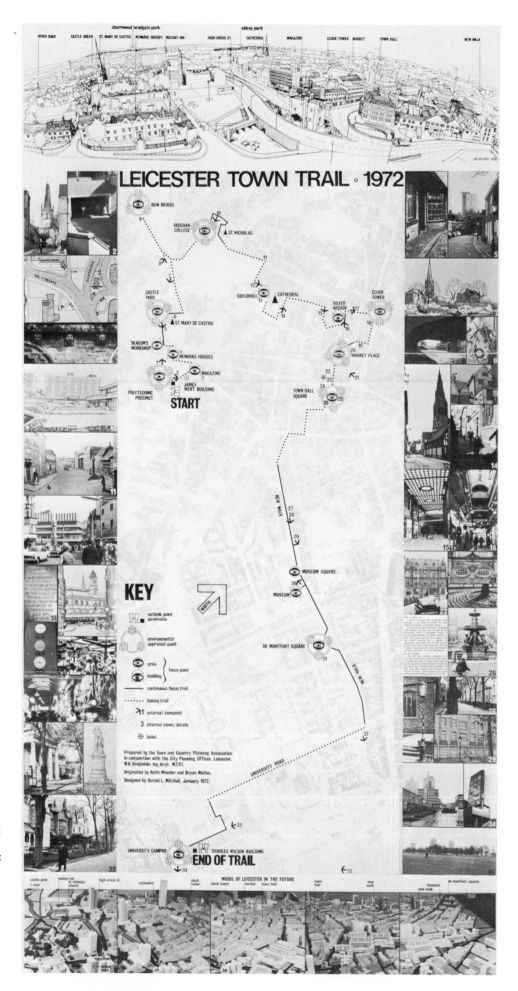

6-5. Leicester Town Trail, another pioneering effort in using the town as a teaching device. (Source: Town and Country Planning Association 1972)

a.

b.

6-6. <u>a.</u>, <u>b.</u>, and <u>c.</u> In these Old Louisville back-alley scenes, garages, stables, and other outbuildings have been demolished, backyards gravelled, and new parking spaces tucked up close to the house because of residents' fear of crime.

c.

103

6-7. Informal expansion of alleys and private hardstands offer clues to increasing population density in a once-elegant neighborhood where old mansions have been converted. Often, where alleys turn (as above), the hardstands become targets for anonymous parkers from a distance.

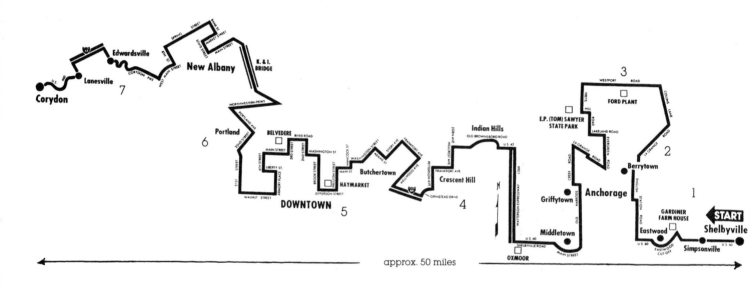

approx. 50 miles

1. Jogs in route touch original curvy-swervy route of old highway before the road-straighteners got at it in the 1930s. Here the old roadside is revealed: an early settler's house converted to a suburban plant nursery.
2. Berrytown and Griffytown, post-Civil War black communities, settled around sites of old plantations.
3. Ford truck plant, first blue-collar impetus for this suburban sector.
4. Route is now inside 1900 city limits, directed past old and new housing and signs of gentrification.
5. I-64 cuts through bucolic backwater of old quarries and roars alongside new riverfront hotels and office towers.
6. Zig-zag route through transition area (right) was once all white, but West Walnut is partly black. K & I Bridge is now blocked to auto traffic, so I-64 Bridge is best for views of river traffic, which creates many city jobs.
7. You are now in the Indiana Knobs, a replay of Appalachian-type land and settlement patterns, where everything hangs out along the highways.

6-8. The Cross-Section Trip offers a formal, well-structured experience in "reading" a metropolitan area to anyone travelling a carefully chosen route. This one, from the Kentucky county-seat town of Shelbyville (at right) to Corydon, the original state capital of Indiana, approximately 45 miles away (at left), is plotted to touch significant generators of Louisville's urban form.

To fulfill all of the aforementioned criteria, one should pursue at least one Main Drag, preferably that special variation I call Alpha Street. Most cities east of the 100th meridian had their start along a river that brought settlers and trade. They then extended their old streets toward higher ground, usually at right angles to the original landing place. Careful observers can "read" the generations of occupants and economic activities along the old main route, the one that starts down by the original Town Landing; meanders through the dying Mill District, then through the city center, office district, and Court House Square; proceeds uphill along the decaying Mansion Row (see the Men's Club, watch the funeral parlors take over the old mansions); and then merges with the Auto Strip toward suburbia. Not all Main Drags will be so accommodating, but they bear close inspection. (Since I fastened myself on it, Alpha Street has assumed an utter and predictable reality for me. I take delight in looking for the Alpha Street wherever I travel. I can be sure that it will not be listed in the city directory, and that few if any books—beyond anecdotal tracts pitched to visiting conventioneers—will mention it. So one is left to dig it out of the city's fabric as a current discovery: Genesee Street in Utica, New York; St. Charles in New Orleans; Main Street in Houston; Meridian Street in Indianapolis.)

In Louisville, Kentucky, Alpha Street is Third Street (fig. 6-9). Close to the original landing place on the Ohio River—where hundreds of river packets once competed for space—the *Belle of Louisville* occasionally shares berth with a few other tourist and excursion boats. Up above the river landing, Main Street once was home to brokers, warehousemen, commission agents, banks, and shippers working off the river. Today, landlords compete for boutiques and tourist-oriented shops. Their original customers long gone, several stores were taken over during and after World War II by pornographic displays, which puritan-minded downtown promoters were attempting to remove in the 1980s. A state-financed convention center—a security-minded citadel with few entrances —muscles into the scene, turning its back on the neighborhood. A mile from the river, a former town mansion is boarded up. Shortly after being photographed it was razed to get spaces for a nearby Theater Square project. Old Automobile Row had seen better days before most of its dealers moved to suburban strips, now replaced by equipment dealers and other "interim users." After its original owners sold out and the street began "going commercial," an old mansion featured add-ons typical of "cash-register drawer architecture." The "duke's mixture" of old mansion, postwar low-rise "garden apartment," and a high-rise for the elderly built in the 1970s, marks a

transition zone between the commercializing conversion district and Mansion Row, where old houses more or less maintain their original shape. The Ferguson mansion, once the city's finest downtown residence, was converted into an undertaker's parlor and later remodelled and expanded for the Filson (historical) Club. Now a landmark structure, a drive-in filling station dates from the 1920s (when Mansion Row began its slow descent). Today it serves yuppies and others who renovate the area's old mansions into apartment buildings.

In common with many educational experiences, a full cross-section trip does tend to screen out the hard parts: it smooths everything down to automobile grades. Any cross-section traveller may find himself choosing routes that eliminate the dead ends, the rough terrain, the spectacular views. No matter what one may intend at the start, beginning cross sectioners unconsciously tend to follow straight lines and hence become captives to a geometry that may not correspond to a city's basic structure. But, of course, the truly experimenting student will stop the car, get out, and explore as necessary afoot and afresh. Often the hidden spaces just off the main routes tell a different story, allowing the student to compare what is up front with another reality out back.

But beyond such personal or schoolish adventures, should we not ask ourselves: How can universities themselves tap into the School of the Street—beyond supporting all those hundreds of forays by click-counting and tape-recording students following the footsteps of William H. Whyte Jr.'s marvelous movies of people-on-the-street?

Private universities that own their own streets are prime candidates for such experiments as I envision. They can manage certain streets as open-air laboratories for experiments in crowd, vehicle, space, and a combination of learning, experience, and management. Most such spaces, as I have encountered them, became experimental only during the riots and mass meetings that were part of Earth Day and the Vietnam War protests of the 1970s. American streets seldom become educational media except for two forms of messages: commercial (advertising) and control (government rules and regulations). To encounter six blocks of a major thoroughfare that have been exclusively reserved for one set of messages is almost unthinkable, on campus or off, and I will admit that the first examples that come to mind flourished during a semidictatorial election campaign in Mexico City, where some major highways were dominated by Get-Out-and-Vote billboards. But we need to know such things as how the street can be made to perform more fully its many educational functions. And where better to begin than on the university campus itself? In

6-9. A trip along Alpha Street in Louisville, Kentucky: a. the *Belle of Louisville;* b. stores along Main Street; c. storefront pornography advertisement; d. convention center; e. boarded-up town mansion; f. Old Automobile Row; g. old mansion with add-ons; h. Mansion Row with new uses; i. Ferguson mansion in process of being reconverted; j. drive-in filling station and converted mansions *(in rear).*

a.

b.

c.

d.

e.

f.

g.

h.

j.

such fashion, the School of the Street could become far more the mixed media than we have so far explored. It would be instructive, just for starters, to see how students of engineering, urban design, architecture, and public art would handle a given block-long "street" of their own design. So far as I have observed, all such experiments have been confined to special events (the Big Game, Homecoming, the Beaux-Arts Ball, and so on), with little effort to examine the evidence for its larger lessons. My own experience, as an outsider being driven off Madison, Wisconsin's State Street which, unbeknownst to me, had become student Turf, offers a memorable example of special purpose. Looking farther, how can that after-hours white elephant, the multilevel parking garage, become an extension of the classroom? A television and computer hookup for every car, piped-in heat or air conditioning for the car occupants, pickup and delivery service by trike or bike?

We continue to go through each new Age of Confinement and its ensuing reactions. Sociologist Robert Gutman believes television merely takes people off the street and into the home, and is thus just another force inhibiting street life—an inevitable follow-up to early sanitation laws and social reforms that swept beggars, peddlers, garbage, kids, and tramps off the streets and into institutions. The department store and elevators conspired to pull adults off the sidewalks into buildings; the modern "Citadel," which I referred to earlier, reinforces the trend to depopulate the street. Traditional architects and their buildings are so inward directed that street life around buildings is a second-class activity.

But to lament all this merely reinforces our need to view the street from the reformist tradition. It is not merely the inevitable byproduct of our latest mode of transport, but a vital part of the learning and testing system for the larger society. We can look back at the outpouring of federal, state, and local funds into traffic/transport/movement studies since World War II as an expensive episode in single-purpose thought. Such a look gives us both time to reflect and to prepare for a new wave of studies and examples that show how the street can perform to the fullest extent its many educational functions.

REFERENCES

Belloc, H. 1923. *The Road*. British Reinforced Concrete Engineering Co. Ltd. Manchester, England: C. W. Hobson.

Ewald, W. 1971. *Street Graphics*. Washington, D.C.: The American Society of Landscape Architects Foundation.

Geddes, P. [1915] 1950. *Cities in Evolution*. Reprint, New York: Oxford University Press.

Goodey, B. 1975. "Urban Trails: Origins and Opportunities." *Journal of the Royal Town Planning Institute* 61: 29–30.

Jacobs, A. 1985. *Looking at Cities*. Cambridge: Harvard University Press.

Jacobs, J. 1961. *The Death and Life of Great American Cities*. New York: Random House.

Linnaeus [Linné, Carl von]. 1751. *Philosophie Botanique*. Stockholm: Apud Godofr Kiesewetter.

———. 1977. *Systema Naturae*. Stockholm: Rediviva (Nordiska Bokhandeln, Distributor).

McLuhan, M. 1964. *Understanding Media*. New York: McGraw-Hill.

Town and Country Planning Association. 1972. *Bulletin of Environmental Education*. London: Town and Country Planning Association. January.

7.
Streets Regulating Neighborhood Form:
A Selective History

CHARLES R. WOLFE

Throughout recorded history, streets have structured neighborhood space. Whether fully owned by the public or comprising only an easement in the public's favor, local streets, historically, have been recognized by governments as a versatile tool for exerting control (Jackson 1980). J. B. Jackson has posited the "rediscovery" of the street as a medieval phenomenon, the result of Western Europe's reinvention of the wheeled vehicle in the eleventh century. This rediscovery yielded governmental recognition of the street as a flexible control device. Further, the eventual placement of utilities under the street "gave the street a permanence which it had never previously had, so that it became more important than the property on both sides of it" (Jackson 1980: 123).

This chapter builds on the Jackson model by examining the history of a second, more contemporary "rediscovery" of the street premised on the advent of another wheeled vehicle, the automobile. This profoundly influential by-product of the industrial revolution helped architects and planners within the American reform movement to focus on the creation of humane and safe conditions within and about residential streets and open spaces. Their efforts have left a lasting impression on the planning and replanning of the urban local area, and on the underlying legal concepts, such as subdivision ordinances and planned unit developments, that guide and implement the local area's new and continued development.

The history to be traced here begins with the Neolithic village and ends circa 1929, with the burgeoning neighborhood planning movement in the United States. By the 1920s, the premise of safety, a key element in Donald Appleyard's more contemporary volume, *Livable Streets* (1981), had spurred numerous studies of the best methods for designing, reordering, or legally implementing plans for the physical neigh-

borhood. The efforts culminated in the simplest and best known of such schemes, Clarence Perry's Neighborhood Unit, which used streets and public spaces to structure neighborhood space: arterials created a neighborhood periphery and internal streets were scaled according to use to control the flow of traffic through the area. The scheme encouraged the use of curvilinear streets and common open spaces within residential blocks (Perry 1929a, 1929b, 1939).

Perry, the synthesizer of various reform precursors, grew to recognize the crucial importance of determining appropriate legal implementation methods for his plan. After his death, the American Public Health Association (APHA) standards for neighborhood planning adopted much of his scheme, especially the standards that addressed "layout for vehicular and pedestrian circulation" (APHA 1960). Along with the APHA, Federal Housing Administration regulations and countless subdivision and planned unit development ordinances incorporated standards of population, recreation, education, site planning, and construction that found their roots in Perry's research. Thus, thousands of suburban housing developments nationwide reflect Perry's formula and, consequently, they reflect the historical traditions of premising regulation upon the street and implementing an ideally improved physical superstructure on the urban local area.

THE CLASSICAL MODEL AND THE FIRST "REDISCOVERY"

The premise of local area development and redevelopment, with emphasis on the ideal form and function of streets and public spaces, owes allegiance to the evolution of public rights, which assumed recognizable form even before the advent of the Greek city-state. Mumford noted how the city's embryonic structure, consisting of the house, shrine, cistern, public way, and agora, was primitively expressed in the form of the Neolithic village (Mumford 1961).

Although some evidence exists of classical Greek codifications analogous to the modern municipal ordinance (Ward-Perkins 1974), physical manifestations of the public interest are most apparent in the Greek agora. As far as we know, the agora served as marketplace, place of assembly, and setting for ceremony and spectacle. Around it stood the meeting place of the city council, magistrate offices, temples, altars, fountain houses, courts, and public halls. Many authors have recounted the town planning exploits of Hippodamus of Miletus, who is credited for a grid-based urban model most employed in Greek colonial cities (Morris 1972; Ward-Perkins 1974; Wycherley 1962). Of particular interest is Hippodamus's layout of Piraeus, the port of Athens. There, archaeologists discovered a primitive, on-site "ordinance" in a number of boundary stones, which delimited the area available for public use with the simple inscription, "I am the boundary of the agora" (Wycherley 1962: 57). Similarly, inscriptions by the ministers responsible for agora maintenance required cleanliness of agora and streets. As Ward-Perkins has written of Greek practices:

Among [certain widely accepted principles and practices] we find a basic distinction between public and private property (often including the right of expropriation when in the public interest); the nomination of magistrates . . . to supervise the public domain, including such vital services as streets . . . *and a mass of detailed provisions regulating the uses and abuses of private property* [emphasis added] (1974: 16–17).

The rights of the public, albeit limited to the most fundamental concerns, evolved through Hellenistic times to the Roman emphasis on passable roads and government by civic entities. The rectangular layout of the Roman military camp, with named streets crossing at right angles, was the foundation of numerous towns and was complemented by the *pomerium*, a reserved belt of land adjacent to town walls where no buildings could be placed (Mumford 1961). Roman practice thus created standards. For example, Vitruvius's *Ten Books of Architecture* (trans. 1960) provided both a model for street layout, which was concerned with proper orientation to the winds for public hygienic purposes, and a model for the forum that contemplated provision for adequate passage, scaling according to population, and the placement of private offices so as to be convenient and to generate public

revenue. From Roman law emerged the still-prevalent premise that the municipality is trustee for the community, a premise that is the foundation for municipal regulation of the street: "[Streets] are not the property of the [municipal] corporation for if they were the corporation could exclude the whole world from the use of them—on the contrary, the use of them belongs to the whole world." (McQuillin 1981: 663). Accordingly, Lewis Mumford (1961) has detailed how traffic jams became subject to regulation in Rome in the first century B.C. and how a succession of emperors expanded such regulation once wheeled traffic became common throughout the empire.

As wheeled traffic disappeared in Western Europe with the decline of Roman civilization, the feudal and religious order that followed erased most concern with widespread standards of government and brought a return to village life (Pirenne 1952; Saalman 1968). By the eleventh century, villages again grew to town status, and ruins were transformed to encroaching buildings that allowed little room for passage between them (Saalman 1968). Yet the reborn wheeled vehicle demanded adequate streets to reach growing open marketplaces, and, in response, statutes governed streets widths, frontage lines, and building height. As J. B. Jackson has aptly described, this "rediscovery" of the classical street emerged from "a new kind of urban plan, based not simply on the dominance of a small number of important buildings and streets, but on street as a direct link between the private domain—home or place of work—and the life of the town" (1980: 64). Private structures and property were once again bisected by public spaces, although perhaps in a more irregular fashion than Jackson would admit. As a result, the municipality's classical role returned and became a direct precursor to today's American city proceeding under the police power:

Almost at once town authorities recognized the street as a versatile tool for exerting control. In one town after another, ordinances regulated the height of buildings, the pitch of their roofs, their construction, even their design, which had to be suited to the social standing of their occupants. . . . In the additions to existing towns and in most of the new towns, the dimensions of the law were prescribed, and all houses were taxed on the basis of their frontage. The fact that each house owned half of the width of the street in front of it encouraged each household to expand its activities into the street and to use the space for its convenience. As a consequence the civic authorities legislated questions of health and safety (Jackson 1980: 64–65).

As Jackson has further recounted, "the discovery of the street as a predeterminant of city growth and development . . . produced increasingly orthogonal town patterns, based on right angles and perpendicular lines" (1980: 64). This gridiron system of rectilinear subdivision was a major element of planned colonial and military towns of medieval Europe, such as the *bastides* of France, England, and Wales (Morris 1972). Similarly, the street in gridiron form became a characteristic of colonial towns overseas. Spanish settlers in the New World applied the grid dictated by the Laws of the Indies to new town sites (Morris 1972; Reps 1965; Sutter 1973). In a manner similar to the earlier specifications of Vitruvius, the Laws of the Indies established standards for the placement of streets, squares, and structures, which served as a precedent for further urban development in North America. Other North American colonial towns exhibited the gridiron form. Planned towns such as Philadelphia and Savannah were likely influenced by contemporary European examples of rectilinear plans (Reps 1965).

The grid was perpetuated through land reform in the post-Revolutionary United States. The inherited English system of property law was streamlined as "speculation of raw land [became] almost a national lottery" (Friedman 1973: 207). In the new democracy, land ownership transcended class boundaries, making the elaborate forms of English land law unsuitable (Friedman 1973). Rapid land speculation was furthered by the survey system imposed on the American West by the Land Ordinance of 1785, which established the "national grid" that spawned the rectangular street system of new American towns. As John Reps has noted (1965), the grid-based 1811 Commissioners' Plan for New York City facilitated traffic congestion, overbuilding, and land speculation and ignored open space needs. The New York City plan and the national grid foreshadowed the countless gridded settlements that appeared both on the land and within speculators' brochures as the United States grew westward.

Rapid land speculation within the gridded city was often accompanied by lack of attention to open space, and the monotony of the grid was compounded by substandard housing conditions and the characteristic absence of light and air in growing urban industrial areas (Lubove 1962). Such declining conditions within the gridded American industrial city led reformers to propose a variety of social, economic, and physical approaches to urban problems in the late nineteenth and early twentieth centuries (Wiebe 1967). In this spirit, early planners rediscovered the street as a determinant of neighborhood form.

THE SECOND "REDISCOVERY": HISTORICAL MODELS FOR LIVING WITHIN THE GRID

The second "rediscovery" of the street evolved from nineteenth-century utopian efforts to cure the substandard residential and working conditions of the industrial revolution. Model planned industrial villages provided planners with examples of environments where issues of density, allocation of amenities, and standards for neatness and beauty had been considered (Benevolo 1967; Reps 1965). The romantic railroad suburbs of the late nineteenth century displayed curvilinear street plans, landscaped streets and open spaces, cul-de-sacs, and deed restrictions, which combined to form a readily perceived community (Mumford 1968; Reps 1965). Ebenezer Howard's Garden City, popularized in 1898, included the concept of the ward, which, in the planner's words, "should in some sense be a complete town by itself" (Howard 1965). Howard's ward, like Clarence Perry's later neighborhood unit, was bounded and defined by arterial streets. However, scholars disagree whether smaller scale, local areas existed within plans for the first Garden Cities in Great Britain (Mumford 1968; Osborn 1969).

In the early twentieth century, following the popularization of the Garden City ideal in the United States, social reformers and planners addressed the problems of increasing population densities and dangers brought about by the advent of the automobile. Further, such reformers sought to alleviate the monotony of the grid and the impracticalities resulting from its imposition without regard to terrain. Finally, reformers addressed the lack of public and semipublic parks and open spaces characteristic of the gridded industrial city (figs. 7-1, 7-2).

In order to assure safety and to return light, air, and a sense of nature to the city, social reformers and planners suggested new street patterns and scales within and outside the grid, including curvilinear streets, a hierarchy of streets scaled according to use, and manipulation of the block to allow for interior open spaces and parks. Purposeful planning for neighborhood life turned away from a focus on the city as a whole (Mumford 1968). Rather, the neighborhood focus employed a vision of the street that fostered a local orientation, safety of children, and convenient access to local business, church, and school. Recognizing the crucial role of streets in determining conditions on abutting properties, reformers employed street design and redesign as a planning tool for imposing order on the rapid urbanization that occurred in the late nineteenth and early twentieth centuries.

Raymond Unwin, an early Garden City planner,

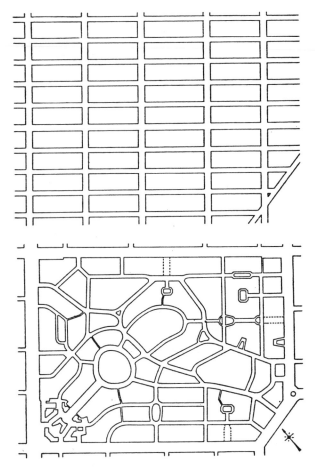

7-1. Gridiron *(above)* versus curved neighborhood street systems. (Redrawn from Perry 1929: 88)

was a major figure in the second "rediscovery" and pioneered the use of the street in structuring residential space. He directly influenced Americans in the community planning movement, such as Perry, Clarence Stein, Henry Wright, and Frederick Law Olmsted, Jr. His most noted contributions were made between 1905 and 1914 with Barry Parker at Hampstead Garden Suburb. Hampstead was universally admired for its handsome groups of buildings and the use of buildings to define public spaces (Unwin [1911] 1971). Unwin's planned community was flanked by arterials, within whose boundaries business uses stood segregated from the residential and public areas. Unwin emphasized open views; small, open spaces "where folk may repair from the bustle of the street to stop and rest awhile;" and the various "places" about which buildings were grouped (Unwin [1911] 1971: 228, 284) (fig. 7-3).

Unwin's emphasis on a hierarchy of "roads and street, . . . lane and way, . . . the pedestrian close

and walk, [and] mere paths" was instrumental in restoring the legality in Great Britain of the "pedestrian close," or cul-de-sac, by means of the Hampstead Garden Suburb Act of 1906. "[F]or residential purposes," he noted, "particularly since the development of the motor car, the cul-de-sac roads, far from being undesirable, are especially to be desired for those who like quiet for their dwellings" ([1911] 1971: 393).

With equal foresight, Unwin forecasted the need for street design. In his famed pamphlet, "Nothing Gained By Overcrowding" (circa 1903, in Unwin [1911] 1971: 381), he addressed the issues of density and lack of open space within the grid. Unwin illustrated how greens, play areas, and allotment gardens within street blocks could replace unneeded street allocations and pavement without extra cost or sacrifice of the number of housing units. This illustration became an influential tenet of American neighborhood and community planning thought and forms the basis for the superblock of today.

At the time of Unwin's major works, American city planning circles had yet to adopt a small-scale focus. The planning profession was dominated by the City Beautiful movement and by the "make no little plans" spirit of City Beautiful forefather Daniel Burnham. However, a new, more socially conscious generation was growing in strength, motivated by housing, hygiene, and smaller-scale site-planning concerns. Between 1907 and 1911, the housing-reform and city-planning movements converged, and planners developed a design-oriented approach to crowded, substandard housing conditions that included attention to the relationship of the street to abutting structures and lots (Lubove 1962).

Although termed "wistful garden city rhetoric" by later critics (Lubove 1962: 245), lectures and writings of the time supplied apt evidence of the second "rediscovery" of the street. In his "Address on City Planning" at the 1909 First National Conference on Planning, Frederic Law Olmsted, Jr. described the negative socioeconomic effects of street planning that did not address the aesthetic, spatial, and economic impacts on abutting homes and property (Lubove 1967). At the 1911 First National Conference on Housing, he offered counsel and solutions reminiscent of the Unwin approach at Hampstead Garden Suburb, which would later be standardized by Clarence Perry's neighborhood unit: a distinction between thoroughfares and neighborhood streets, the provision of light and air in the form of district open spaces, and the preplanning of intermediate streets as a cure to housing ills (Olmsted 1911).

Simultaneously, other planners stressed the virtue of the local street and open space. Theorist Charles Mulford Robinson stressed "neighborhood foci,"

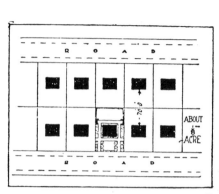

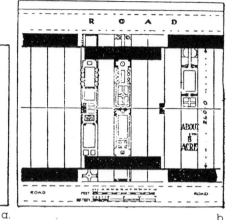

a.

b.

7-2. Conventional neighborhood layouts versus community planning principles: a. detached houses centered on plots, with eight houses to the acre; b. plan showing extra depth of garden and distance among houses built in groups; c. groups of small gardens designed to produce total effect. (Source: Unwin (1911) 1971: 350, 358)

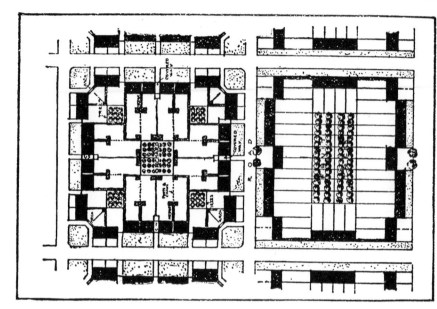

c.

building groupings to preserve neighborhood open spaces, allotment gardens, and playgrounds "located inside the block" (Robinson 1916). *A City Plan for St. Louis*, by George Kessler and Henry Wright (1907), recommended the grouping of various public, semi-public, and private institutions about a common neighborhood center to "develop a neighborhood feeling." John Nolen's various plans emphasized street location, block location, playgrounds, open space, and building regulation (Nolen 1908; Scott 1971). His later plans provided for well-defined institutional and residential centers (Hancock 1960).

Other, often lesser-known, planners also participated in the second "rediscovery" of the street (Comey and Wehrly 1939). William Manning's 1912 Goodyear Heights, outside of Akron, Ohio, featured a public square at the center of a hierarchical and curvilinear street pattern. Grosvenor Atterbury's 1915 Indian Hill, in Worcester, Massachusetts, offered a community center, discouraged through traffic, and "contained the nucleus of the neighborhood unit idea." Arthur C. Comey's 1914 plan for Billerica Garden Suburb, under the auspices of the Massachusetts Homestead Commission, was a hopeful attempt to adopt the Garden suburb to American conditions. In Beloit, Wisconsin, the Beloit Model Homes Company developed a subdivision employing the interior of blocks as parks in advance of the more noted "superblock" of Wright and Stein (Yeomans 1916). In the early 1920s, architect Andrew J. Thomas employed the interior garden court in several shallow coverage apartment developments (Lubove 1963).

World War I gave government-sanctioned expression to such planned residential communities as Brooklawn, New Jersey; Cradock and Hilton Village, Virginia; and Buchman in Chester, Pennsylvania (Comey and Wehrly 1939; Scott 1969). Yorkship Village (later Fairview), in Camden, New Jersey, was

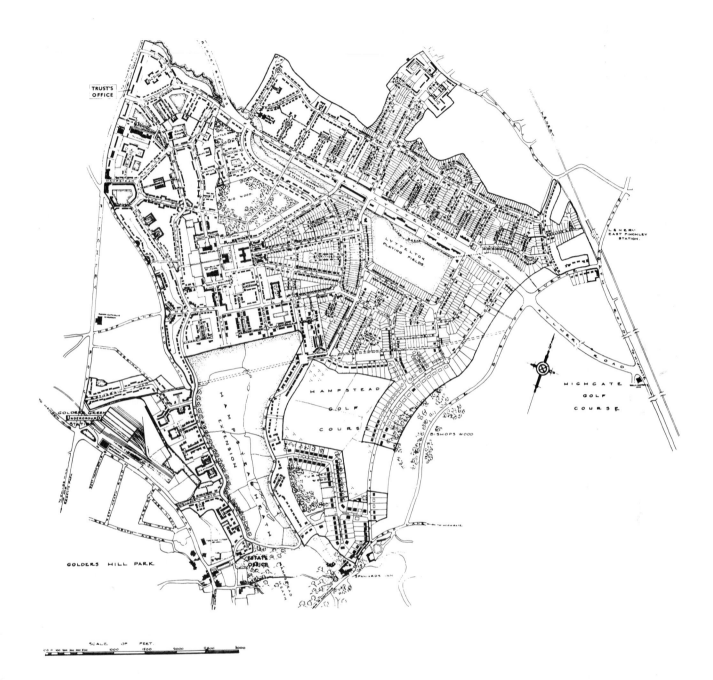

HAMPSTEAD GARDEN
SUBURB

7-3. Plan of Hampstead Garden Suburb. (Courtesy Hampstead Garden Suburb Trust)

planned by Electus D. Litchfield and became the best known of the group. The symmetrical plan mixed straight arterial approaches with curvilinear residential streets and focused on the centrality of Yorkship Square. The plan combined institutional, residential, and commercial uses about the square, and allocated space for a park, school, and community center.

These examples experimented with site planning techniques and service delivery concerns and they represented a general attempt at self-containment in the Garden City and suburban tradition. None achieved a widespread effect on the American real estate market; nor did it specifically articulate clearly stated standards in the manner of Perry's later approach. Yet these early experiments in suburban planning produced the methods and ideals today credited to Perry, including the manipulation of the street and its surroundings in the public interest.

Even more crucial to the history of this second "rediscovery" of the street, and to Perry's later synthesis, were two efforts that fully indicated the planning concerns of the early twentieth century. The first was Forest Hills Gardens in New York, the 1911 collaboration of Frederick Law Olmsted, Jr. and Grosvenor Atterbury. The second was a 1913 competition for the design of a quarter-section of the Chicago grid, which brought the tools of the planned Garden suburb within urban boundaries.

At Forest Hills Gardens, Olmsted chose to emphasize the central role of the local street:

> Probably the most notable characteristic of Forest Hills Gardens will be the cozy domestic character of these local streets, where the monotony of straight wind-swept thoroughfares which are the New York conception of streets, will give place to short, quiet, self-contained and garden-like neighborhoods, each having distinctive character (quoted in Robinson 1916: 171).

Clarence Perry's unrelenting pride in the conceived success of Forest Hills Gardens contributed substantially to the formation of the neighborhood unit theory. Nowhere was this more clear than in his street-oriented statement of intent to the Regional Plan of New York staff in 1922:

> I have been interested in making a study of the community unit because the development at Forest Hills has been so extraordinarily interesting. There is a community somewhat set off by its physical plan and rather different architectural features. It appears boulevards and wide arterial streets are often decisive features in fixing a community (Regional Plan Association Papers 1922).

Perry's response to Forest Hills was consistent with the Olmsted emphasis on the local street. Especially remarkable to Perry was what Olmsted had promised

as distinctive: a street layout designed according to the perceived needs and convenience of residents (Perry 1929b). Station Square, the stopping place of Manhattan commuter trains, was this layout's focal point and shopping nexus. Other prominent features were the straight approaches of Ascan and Continental Avenues, arterials that later brought cross traffic through the community (probably unforeseeable at the time of planning); Greenway South and North, the definitional, curvilinear hub that converged on the central Station Square, framing the one-and-one-half-acre green that was used as the Garden City's nominal civic center; and two small parks, part of the six originally planned. These "cozy streets and open spaces" were publicized in copies of the site plan made available to potential residents (Perry 1929b).

Two years after Forest Hills provided the exemplary application of Garden City thought to the United States, several architects and landscape architects attempted to apply Garden City ideals to a Chicago urban neighborhood setting. In December 1912, the City Club of Chicago staged a competition for the design of a quarter-section of the Chicago grid (Yeomans 1916). Mumford has summarized the competition's focus as being on "the process of integrating the domestic areas of the city and relating their housing to markets, schools, churches, and other institutions that serve the local area rather than the city as a whole" (1968: 65). The various entries expressed street planning as a fundamental element of the integration process.

The competition's collection of plans displayed the clear influence of the Garden City movement, especially the Hampstead and Forest Hills precedents. Alfred B. Yeomans, a Chicago landscape architect who edited the competition's publication (1916), acknowledged new attention to the planned development of the local area premised on the increasingly comprehensive role of the street. He noted that the "purely mechanical extension of existing street systems is giving way to scientific methods of development based on a careful study of the probable economic, social and aesthetic needs of prospective inhabitants" (Yeomans 1916).

Several of the entries emphasized the role of the local street system and public open spaces. The first-prize entry, by Chicago architect Wilhelm Bernhard, contained a community center and stressed deterrence of through traffic from surrounding Chicago. Arthur C. Comey, the second-prize winner, employed the English allotment garden within blocks, with houses facing inward, an intermediate street system for local use, recreation spaces, and buildings grouped about small parks.

Other entries took up more directly the question of

integration with the surrounding city, thereby starting a debate on the worth of isolated communities at variance with the surrounding grid. This debate has regained importance today. Landscape architect G. C. Cone noted that the proposed neighborhood was not destined to exist independent of Chicago's entirety (Yeomans 1916). He argued for retention of the grid-iron throughout, foreshadowing today's defenders of continuity within the grid and implying that the imposition of a curvilinear scheme would negatively isolate the community from the prevailing pattern of development (fig. 7-4). Nonetheless, he emphasized the use of interior-block open space and the community center. Similarly, William Drummond, a Prairie

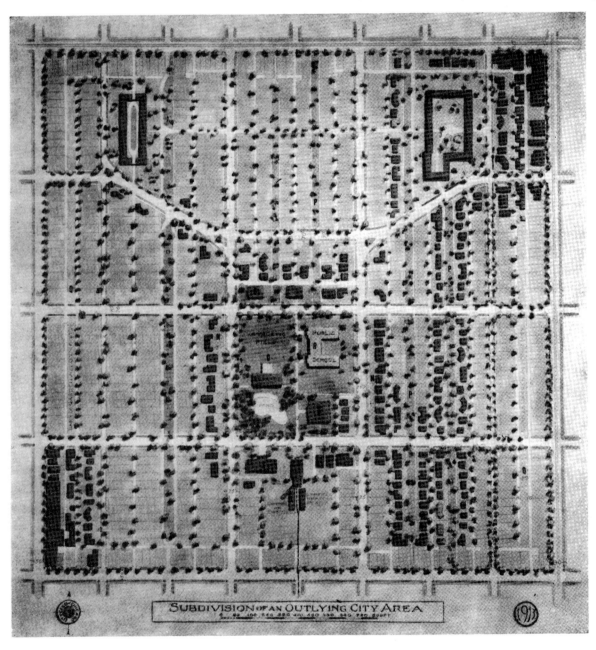

D. Streets with narrow pavements on either side and parkway in middle	H. Two-story cottage	N. Large residence lots	Q. Barn segregation strips
	L. Central heating plant	O. Recreation center	R. Public school
	M. Business buildings	P. "Streets" without pavements	S. Semipublic buildings

7-4. G. B. Cone's Chicago competition entry. (Source: Yeomans 1916: 34)

School architect and disciple of Frank Lloyd Wright, proposed grid-based "neighborhood units" with allotment gardens and interior courts (fig. 7-5).

These designs were but a fraction of the Chicago competition's entries. Yet they exhibited best the perceptive synthesis of reform ideals and site planning sensitive to the uses of the street within the new arena of the urban neighborhood. In response to such efforts, the competition provided a "Sociological Review of the Plans" by Dr. Carol Aronovici, then director of the Bureau of Social Research of Philadelphia and a lecturer on housing and town planning at the University of Pennsylvania. Aronovici cautioned that the new, local street plans within specific areas should not proceed without determination of "the relationship that this area is intended to bear to the whole" (Yeomans 1916: 117).

Aronovici, like many of today's urban designers, saw virtue in the grid. He viewed the abandonment of the gridiron street system as a possible symptom of an "artificial and radical" attempt to set the planned community off from its surroundings. Thus, he urged the location of public and semipublic buildings on the community's periphery rather than grouped about local community centers, so as to preserve contacts with adjacent neighborhoods. Finally, he was especially troubled by the interior-block allotment garden, for which he saw no role in an urban setting of varied social composition, a diversity of preferences, and high land values. He perceptively identified problems inherent in public regulation and ownership of inner-block open spaces and saw the necessity of assuming community maintenance of public areas:

The whole question of "shut-in spaces," whether they be parks, playgrounds or allotment gardens, is one that should be carefully weighed. The line of cleavage between public and private ownership, between public and private maintenance, should be sharply drawn. While I am heartily in favor of extending the bounds of public ownership, I am opposed to common ownership that is not coupled with common responsibility (Yeomans 1916: 122).

7-5. W. Drummond's Chicago competition entry: <u>a.</u> bird's-eye view; <u>b.</u> typical city block. (Source: Yeomans 1916: 37, 41)

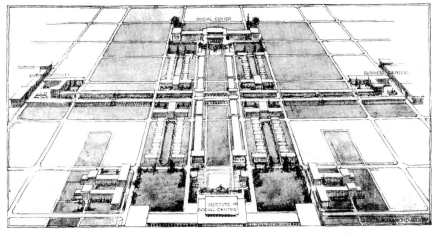

a.

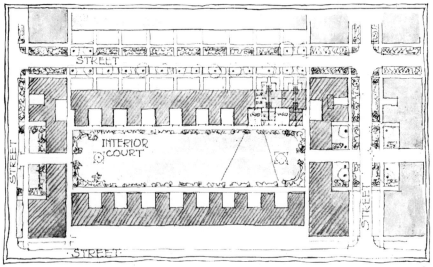

b.

The 1920s saw the second "rediscovery" of the street proceed to new levels of sophistication. Community and neighborhood planning evolved toward identifiable theory and standards and produced the most memorable responses to the proliferation of the automobile. During this decade, Clarence Perry developed and refined his neighborhood unit hypothesis. Simultaneously, his contemporaries Henry Wright and Clarence Stein supplied Perry with practical examples of inner-block recreation space, pleasant residential character, and innovative, community-oriented architecture. Stein and Wright inherited the tradition outlined thus far and gave special emphasis to "the possibility of preserving open spaces for natural green, for recreation, for light, for healthful living, and for spacious and beautiful living without additional cost" (Stein 1966: 22).

Henry Wright has been duly credited with adapting to "American conditions" the cost-efficient use of open-block interiors espoused in Unwin's "Nothing Gained by Overcrowding." His practical separation of pedestrian from vehicular traffic, in partnership with Stein, is well documented (Stein 1966). At the same time, he was a major theoretical contributor to the second "rediscovery" of the street. In his unpublished "No Mans Land of Real Estate" (Wright 1919), he parodied the narrow lot, wide street platting methods then common in the United States and urged that lot division, street platting, and structure placement should be considered hand in hand. He wrote that "the consideration of the kind and location of the buildings must determine first as far as possible the *street* position but always the *lot division*."

In 1921, Wright set forth his conception of ideal residential planning, which included innovative group housing, open space, and topography sensitive to relationships with the street:

> Rather narrow areas of occupancy would be established on either side of a main avenue of service and communication along and adjacent to which would be shops and garages. Laid off at right angles with this would be areas of varying size, based on natural subdivisions to be taken over as sites for group developments. Between these series of groups and more or less parallel to the line of principal communication as determined to some extent by topography, would be strands of open territory in close relation to the residential groups. These areas would preserve, as far as possible, the natural landscape, except for providing sites for educational, recreational and community buildings, with playgrounds, and whenever possible including golf courses and other suitable features (Wright 1921: 323).

By 1925, Wright offered "Six Planks for a Housing Platform," a more refined version of his planning ideals in a Perry-like formula that revealed commu-

nity planning as far more than "a mere mechanical structure of laying out lots." Much of his approach was drawn from a 1923 unpublished report undertaken with Stein and New York realtor Alexander Bing for their newly formed City Housing Corporation (Wright 1923).

The report was an exemplary attempt to restructure neighborhood form by varying the gridiron street pattern to yield additional public space. The authors outlined "a proposed garden community," urged "better homes surrounded by adequate recreation and garden space," and criticized the wastefulness of the gridiron street system. Their plan specified functional interrelationships, the amount of space devoted to each use, and streets scaled according to use. The plan limited the amount of land devoted to street use to 21.5 percent of total land area, rather than the ordinarily "wasteful" 40 percent, and employed the resulting open space for five categories of recreational space: block interiors, playgrounds, a community center, parks, and parklike buffer zones on the periphery.

Wright and Stein further criticized grid-based subdivision practices in an American Institute of Architects' Committee on Community Planning Report (reprinted in Lubove 1967). The report emphasized that the young planning profession and early planning legislation had yet to address the relationship of streets and plot layout to the planning and grouping of structures. The report blamed the design constraints of the grid for the monotonous appearance of the American residential street.

> The sameness of the plots, the absence of special sites, the sidelong approach to every building, great or small, inconspicuous or monumental, all tend to stifle the imagination of the architect and to do away with even such small variations or setbacks as might relieve the monotony of the continuous rows of houses that are so characteristic of our American cities. It is in its effect upon residential planning . . . that the American block and lot have exerted a positively baneful effect (Reprinted in Lubove 1967).

The authors' principles were applied at Sunnyside Garden Apartments in New York City and at Radburn, New Jersey (Stein 1966).

While Stein and Wright developed their community planning approach, Clarence Perry's parallel neighborhood unit was well under way. Beginning in 1921, Perry, veteran of the community center movement and well versed in the applied sociology of Charles Horton Cooley, teamed with his Russell Sage colleagues for work on the ambitious Regional Plan of New York and Its Environs (Regional Plan Association Papers 1921–29). What began as Perry's general inquiry into recreational facilities planning in 1922, ended as the neighborhood unit study published in Volume 7 of the *Regional Survey* in 1929. In his 1922 general inquiry, Perry suggested several studies, one of which would "discover the area . . . under given population, racial and social conditions, in which a local voluntary organization concerned with matters of common interest most naturally arises and flourishes" (Regional Plan Association Papers 1922). This concern produced his presumably earliest synthesis of the elements of self-containment and local association as they related to streets and other modes of transport.

The object of Perry's study was initially called the "community unit," and the study itself emphasized physical redefinition of existing inner-city neighborhoods. At an early stage, Perry developed alternate unit approaches premised on a residential neighborhood with no particular site restrictions, a residential neighborhood adjacent to industry, and an "apartment house unit" (Regional Plan Association Papers 1923). Noted Plan staff members commented favorably on Perry's neighborhood orientation and boundary study proposal and suggested application to undeveloped suburban settings (Regional Plan Association Papers 1922). In this context, staff members, such as Frederick Law Olmsted, Jr., concentrated on the regulatory role of the street. Olmsted suggested the regulation of subdivision fees in urbanizing areas, so that neighborhoods that indulged in excess street width and inadequate recreation space would be levied higher fees in scale with their deficiencies. Thomas Adams, a noted town planner and general director of plans and surveys for the Regional Plan, addressed the role of municipal legal powers in the implementation of Perry's 160-acre neighborhood units within surrounding gridded arterials. He recommended that Perry examine local residential zoning practices to assure the compatibility of the unit scheme thereto and that he confer with "the father of zoning," Edward Bassett, with regard to zoning practices.

Adams, who by 1928 appeared more concerned with accommodating new rather than existing neighborhoods, understood that replatting the grid into a superior model for neighborhood form was achievable on a large scale only if municipal powers could be employed to guide the effort (Regional Plan Association Papers 1924, 1928). Otherwise, the unit concept would be nothing but an ideal for large landowners developing entirely new communities on parcels not subject to land-use controls. Adams recognized that in order to impose a physical structure and social life on the 160 acres framed by gridded arterials, it would be necessary to determine how zoning could control the nature and placement of buildings and uses along those arterials.[1] Perhaps consequently, Bassett and others developed model planning legislation pursuant to Regional Plan research that included attention to a planned unit residential development. Such legislation was enacted in New York State, but remained unused for over thirty years (Krasnowiecki 1965).

Notwithstanding Adams's prophetic advice and contemporaneous legal developments, Perry concentrated on the social aspects of the neighborhood and did not clearly emphasize legal methods of implementation for his neighborhood scheme until the early 1930s (Perry 1933). His 1939 *Housing for the Machine Age* contained a chapter on legal implementation methods, which suggested the use of municipal eminent domain authority and of police power to apply the neighborhood unit concept to existing and developing urban areas. The volume included a suggested "Neighborhood Improvement Act" reminiscent of modern utility improvement district legislation.

As noted at the outset of this chapter, Perry's neighborhood unit standards gained widespread acceptance (Dahir 1947). In the United States, the neighborhood unit was applied during the 1930s at Radburn, New Jersey, the Greenbelt Towns, and Baldwin Hills Village (Dahir 1947). After adoption by the American Public Health Association, elements of the unit scheme were borrowed by professional groups and government agencies, incorporated into zoning and subdivision ordinances, and employed in the post-World War II design of new towns in the United States and abroad (Banerjee and Baer 1984; Osborn and Whittick 1963).

The neighborhood unit became an integral element of British planning. Patrick Abercrombie supported the unit approach in his *County of London Plan* (1943) and *Greater London Plan* (1944). The Reith Committee Report, which established the guiding principles for British new towns, generally endorsed the unit concept (Shaffer 1970). The New Towns Act of 1946 furthered this endorsement, and numerous new town neighborhoods displayed elements of the Perry model (Osborn and Whittick 1963). The unit concept was more recently applied to the American new towns of Columbia, Maryland, and Reston, Virginia (Banerjee and Baer 1984).

Nonetheless, it was not until the acceptance in the 1960s of flexible zoning devices, such as the planned unit development, that the self-contained Garden City ideal advocated by Wright, Perry, and others gained a firm legal method of implementation. Planned unit development ordinances allow a departure from the rigid separation of uses characteristic of Euclidean zoning; they encourage self-contained, mixed-use districts with careful attention to internal street patterns and the relationship of uses (Anderson

1977). Model planned unit development ordinances contain statements of objectives descended from the ideals of Perry and previous reformers, including a mixture of housing types and lot sizes, usable recreation space, convenience in location of commercial areas, preservation of the natural environment, and efficient land use involving small street and utility networks (Anderson 1977; Krasnowiecki et al. 1965).

The second "rediscovery" of the street yielded non-Euclidean, mixed-use communities, with careful attention to a hierarchy of curvilinear streets, ample public spaces, and amenities with tasteful placement of abutting structures. Presumably, attention to aesthetic and safety considerations produced a conducive residential climate. For much of this century, the gridiron was conquered by standards espoused by Perry.

Ironically, the widespread acceptance and institutionalization of reformers' second "rediscovery" of the street in the form of the neighborhood unit may have fostered a third "rediscovery" centered upon the virtues of the grid (see chap. 9, by A. V. Moudon and R. K. Untermann). Contemporary studies such as Appleyard (1981) suggest skepticism regarding neighborhood redevelopments premised upon curvilinear street patterns and internal open spaces. In the spirit of the above-noted critics of the Chicago Competition in 1916, today's urban designers debate how best to use streets to integrate a neighborhood with the surrounding urban area and prevailing development patterns.

As Cone and Aronovici forewarned in 1916, an emphasis on scaled, curvilinear streets diminishes attention to the relationship of the neighborhood to the city as a whole. Densely trafficked, the new high-speed arterials that surround neighborhoods in effect separate one from the other, transforming them into islands with no-man's-lands in between (see chap. 8, by R. K. Untermann). Further, regardless of street layout or dimension, the automobile has not been adequately constrained. As a result, even narrow, curvilinear streets have failed to foster the socially conducive setting of which Perry dreamed. Modern critics, such as Appleyard (1981), concluded that safety and livability are not entirely dependent on street hierarchies or separation of vehicular and pedestrian traffic; the speed, noise, and amount of vehicular traffic, all important elements of livability, are to be managed by traffic control devices, public education, law enforcement, and vehicle redesign. Finally, the separation of pedestrian and vehicular traffic in the many low-density neighborhoods where cars and their drivers are the "regular" life on the street, has so isolated the few pedestrians as to make their environment unsafe. Ironically, drivers are, for this limited

number of pedestrians, an important element of surveillance.

Thus, those who debate the parameters of today's third "rediscovery" of the street need not debate the aesthetic concerns of curvilinear versus grid. Today's planners must, like their forebears, utilize the street as a legal and planning tool to structure neighborhood form and appearance. Yet they must assure a functional, continuous layout that integrates vehicles and pedestrians and must avoid neighborhoods that turn inward on themselves. Given these considerations, the gridiron, so maligned in the recent past, may have a new life.

NOTE

1. It should be observed that Adams's "Planning and Subdivision of Land," which also appeared in the 1929 *Regional Survey*, fulfilled his prescription more sufficiently than Perry's contribution to the same *Survey* volume. Laden with illustrations of the New York region's existing conditions and self-contained communities, Adams's effort to explain proper subdivision practices for unbuilt areas may have been a direct response to Perry's often shallow use of historical examples and frequently elementary tone.

REFERENCES

American Public Health Association. 1960. *Planning the Neighborhood.* Chicago: Public Administration Service.

Anderson, R. M. 1977. *American Law of Zoning.* Vol. 2. Rochester, N.Y.: The Lawyers' Cooperative Publishing Co.

APHA. *See* American Public Health Association.

Appleyard, D. 1981. *Livable Streets.* Berkeley: University of California Press.

Banerjee, T., and W. C. Baer. 1984. *Beyond the Neighborhood Unit.* New York: Plenum Press.

Benevolo, L. 1967. *The Origins of Modern Town Planning.* London: Routledge and Kegan Paul.

Comey, A. C., and M. Wehrly. 1939. "Planned Communities." *Urban Planning and Land Policies.* Washington, D.C.: U.S. Government Printing Office.

Creese, W. L. 1966. *The Search for Environment, the Garden City: Before and After.* New Haven: Yale University Press.

Dahir, J. 1947. *The Neighborhood Unit Plan, Its Spread and Acceptance.* New York: Russell Sage Foundation.

Friedman, L. M. 1973. *A History of American Law.* New York: Simon and Schuster.

Hancock, J. L. 1960. "John Nolen: The Background of a Pioneer Planner." *Journal of the American Institute of Planners* (November): 304–5.

Howard, E. 1965. *Garden Cities of Tomorrow*. Cambridge: MIT Press.

Jackson, J. B. 1980. *The Necessity for Ruins*. Amherst: University of Massachusetts Press.

Kessler, G., and Wright, H. 1907. *A City Plan for St. Louis*. St. Louis: The Civic League of St. Louis.

Krasnowiecki, J. Z. 1965. "Planned Unit Development: A Challenge to Established Theory and Practice of Land Use Control." *University of Pennsylvania Law Review* 114 (November): 47–97.

Krasnowiecki, J. Z., R. F. Babcock, and D. N. McBride. 1965. "The Model State Statute." *University of Pennsylvania Law Review* 114 (November): 140–70.

Lubove, R. 1962. *The Progressives and the Slums*. Pittsburgh: University of Pittsburgh Press.

———. 1963. *Community Planning in the 1920s: The Contribution of the Regional Planning Association of America*. Pittsburgh: University of Pittsburgh Press.

———. 1967. *The Urban Community: Housing and Town Planning in the Progressive Era*. Englewood Cliffs, N. J.: Prentice-Hall.

McQuillin, E. 1981. *The Law of Municipal Corporations*. Vol. 10. Willamette, Ill.: Callaghan and Company.

Morris, A.E.J. 1972. *History of Urban Form*. New York: John Wiley.

Mumford, L. 1961. *The City in History*. New York: Harcourt Brace Jovanovich.

———. 1968. *The Urban Prospect*. New York: Harcourt Brace Jovanovich.

Nolen, J. 1908. *San Diego: A Comprehensive Plan for Its Improvement*. Boston: George H. Ellis.

Olmsted, F. L., Jr. 1911. "Housing and City Planning." In *Housing Problems in America*. Proceedings of the First National Conference on Housing, New York City.

Osborn, F. J. 1969. *Green-belt Cities*. New York: Schocken.

Osborn, F. J., and A. Whittick. 1963. *The New Towns*. Cambridge: MIT Press.

Perry, C. A. 1929a. "The Neighborhood Unit." In *Neighborhood and Community Planning*. Volume 7, *Regional Survey of New York and Its Environs*. New York: Regional Plan of New York and Its Environs.

———. 1929b. "Planning a Neighborhood Unit." *American City* 41 (September): 124–27.

———. 1933. *The Rebuilding of Blighted Areas*. New York: Regional Plan Association.

———. 1939. *Housing for the Machine Age*. New York: Russell Sage Foundation.

Pirenne, H. 1952. *Medieval Cities: Their Origins and the Revival of Trade*. Princeton: Princeton University Press.

Regional Plan Association. 1921–29. *Papers*. Department of Manuscripts and Archives, Cornell University, Ithaca, N.Y.

Regional Plan of New York and Its Environs. 1929. *Regional Survey of New York and Its Environs*. New York: Regional Plan of New York and Its Environs.

Reps, J. W. 1965. *The Making of Urban America*. Princeton: Princeton University Press.

Robinson, C. M. 1916. *City Planning*. New York: G. P. Putnam's.

Saalman, H. 1968. *Medieval Cities*. New York: George Braziller.

Scott, M. 1969. *American City Planning since 1890*. Berkeley: University of California Press.

Shaffer, F. 1970. *The New Town Story*. London: MacGibbon and Kee.

Stein, C. S. 1966. *New Towns for America*. Cambridge: MIT Press.

Sutter, R. E. 1973. *The Next Place You Come to*. Englewood Cliffs, N.J.: Prentice-Hall.

Unwin, R. [1911] 1971. *Town Planning in Practice, An Introduction to the Art of Designing Cities and Suburbs*. Reprint, New York: Benjamin Blom.

Vitruvius. 1960. *The Ten Books of Architecture*. Translated by M. H. Morgan. New York: Dover Publications.

Ward-Perkins, J. B. 1974. *Cities of Ancient Greece and Italy: Planning in Classical Antiquity*. New York: George Braziller.

Wiebe, R. H. 1967. *The Search for Order*. New York: Hill & Wang.

Wolfe, C. R. 1982. *Clarence Perry and the Neighborhood Unit Reconsidered: Perspectives on Precedents, Formulation and Development*. Master's thesis, Cornell University.

Wright, H. 1919. *Papers*. Department of Manuscripts and Archives, Cornell University, Ithaca, N.Y.

———. 1921. "Shall We Community Plan?" *Journal of the American Institute of Architects* 9 (October): 123.

———. 1923. *Papers*. Department of Manuscripts and Archives, Cornell University, Ithaca, N.Y.

———. 1925. "The Road to Good Houses." *Survey Graphic* 54 (21 May): 167.

Wycherley, R. E. 1962. *How the Greeks Built Cities*. New York: W. W. Norton.

Yeomans, A. B., ed. 1916. *City Residential Land Development*. Chicago: University of Chicago Press.

8.
Can We Pedestrianize the Suburbs?

RICHARD K. UNTERMANN

"Mom, can I use the car for a few minutes to run to the drugstore? Need some aspirin." "Hey, Dad, can I borrow the car to visit Bill? Be back in a couple of hours." "Gee, think I'll pop down to the newsstand and buy tonight's paper." "Say, Sally, want to take a spin and get a bite of dinner?" Suburban life revolves around the car. It is essential for virtually every activity, including, work, shopping, school, and entertainment. As a result, the suburban street has grown to serve one user, the automobile. Most suburban streets have wide, smooth surfaces; soft, gentle curves; and generous turning radii—all geared to move large volumes of traffic at relatively high speeds. To be a pedestrian, a bicyclist, or a vendor on one of these streets is to be a fish out of water.

Our metropolitan streets may provide good access for people with motor vehicles, but how good is debatable, since we have no other model for comparison. Car access takes time and exacts both personal and community costs. Yet, although the automobile clearly cannot be eliminated, one can, over a period of time, encourage substitute land use and the development of other transportation modes.

The automobile has become a powerful deterrent to socially responsive streets. Cars isolate people. They detach users from their environment and often inspire heedless behavior on the part of drivers. Suburban roads have become two-dimensional channels with no other purpose than to move as many vehicles as quickly as possible. Little concern is left over for the way the road looks, feels, or fits into a community, and little attention is focused on providing safe, efficient access for those without a car. Given the dearth of spaces where people can congregate and interact, public streets can be places for socializing if a "walk-

ing speed" environment is returned to the streets. However it is accomplished, people ought to spend less time in cars and more time in face-to-face situations where they can be part of a community.

IS PEDESTRIANIZATION POSSIBLE?

Our suburban communities evolved in direct opposition to the needs of pedestrians and cyclists. They are linear, disbursed, and single-functioned. Many follow a modified "Radburn Plan," with small, mostly residential, subdivisions that merge at arterial roads (see chap. 7, by C. R. Wolfe). The neighborhood, in turn, joins an even larger arterial to become part of a community. Yet, while Radburn has an internal pedestrian system, most suburban subdivisions serve no public pedestrian needs. Arterial streets are the only routes that reach parks, goods, and services, but, for most pedestrians and bicyclists, they are dangerous and uncomfortable. Walking requires safety, concentrated, mixed land uses, and a variety of activities and services within reasonable distance of home (see chap. 5, by A. Rapoport).

Eliminating "Environmental Blinders"

Suburban communities continue to develop into inward and private worlds. This phenomenon stimulates the development of many attractive, but private, "mini-environments" and forces the use of what I call "environmental blinders." Each suburban household develops a series of favorite mini-environments for playing, working, shopping, and living. Mini-environments are, for instance, one's home, office, favorite restaurants, shopping mall, athletic club, and so on.

123

Each mini-environment is selected in accordance with the individual's taste and budget. But people travel *between* these privileged places in the isolation of their cars, putting on their environmental blinders because the streetscape often is too unsightly to warrant any sort of inspection.

Environmental blinders reinforce a feeling that people—even neighbors—who pass by on foot or bicycle are merely obstructions to efficient travel. As a pedestrian, I sometimes become angry at cars that will not stop for me; as a driver, the object of fury reverses, and I become irritated at pedestrians who want me to stop for them. Either situation generates hostility, primarily because when there are no travel options other than driving, drivers become detached and selfish.

Signs of Change

Would it be possible to satisfy daily needs on foot or by bicycle? Aerial photos of many a suburban community show the close relationship that actually exists between residential developments and community services. A surprisingly high percentage of suburban homes are within easy (up to three miles) bicycle distance of shopping, schools, parks, offices, bus stops, and some workplaces. Many are within walking distances (up to half a mile).

There are other encouraging signs. New apartment construction has shifted the balance in many communities toward higher-density life-styles. For instance, the 1980 census notes that almost one-half of the new units in suburban communities are designed for more than one family.

Multifamily areas are ideal for enhancing pedestrian opportunities; they concentrate density which, in turn, encourages nearby convenience stores, restaurants, transit, and office developments. Were sidewalks to connect these services to nearby apartments, residents would be able to lessen considerably their dependence on the automobile.

The number of elderly and young people living in suburban counties fully supports the need for alternative transportation modes. Many subdivisions are nearly forty years old and include a surprising number of "original settlers" who are now in their sixties. According to census reports, over 8 percent of suburban residents are elderly.

Increasing numbers of people are responsive to walking. Many have vacationed in Europe and admired traffic-free places. They like being in safe areas that are free of traffic problems, like shopping centers. Bicycles are extensively used on weekends, and a number of roads have been widened slightly and striped to facilitate bicycle travel. Sidewalks are beginning to appear on many streets. Last, many suburban communities are instituting extensive transit systems (see chap. 16, by D. C. Miles and M. L. Hinshaw). Although all of these are yet minimal changes, they suggest that an increasing number of people without vehicles will be on the streets. For them, "pedestrian islands," such as shopping centers and main shopping streets, are not enough. Reliance on the automobile must be reduced, and streets need to be converted for safe, convenient access by foot, bicycle, or bus.

The need is increasingly felt to make the total suburban environment more usable for children, elderly, and other people without cars. I asked a friend recently what his sixteen-year-old child was going to do this summer. He replied, "He's going to work if we can figure out how to get him to work." Most parents find it difficult to minimize the task of transporting their children from place to place. Yet often there is no other way for children to travel long distances safely. The "family taxi" is a part of bringing children up and an important reason to make our larger communities more accessible.

A BROAD-BASED APPROACH

The conversion of streets to serve broad public purposes will require adjustments in the way we plan and deliver land-use and transportation services. It will also require a broader perspective on the part of decision makers and particularly transportation engineers. The real opportunities for future suburbs will come when we deal with cars, reduce speeds, revise road standards, and design streets, parking, and pedestrian areas more carefully. Opportunities will also stem from supporting pedestrians and bicyclists through mixed land uses, increased density, public transit, sidewalks, and so on (fig. 8-1).

If we had to pay attention to the environments through which we drive and if we truly had to respect the people who live, work, or walk on those streets, we might not drive so speedily. One way to increase our attention span is to convert all streets to serve the needs of elderly people and children, who cannot drive. Converted streets would also benefit residents who presently live along busy streets and who would enjoy quieter days, cleaner air, and safer foot travel— in short, a healthier environment.

Arterial streets should be the main target of a program to cater streets to the public because they interconnect residential districts with community services and activities. Like their namesakes, the arteries of the body, they provide access to all community goods and services. Changes will occur if equal, safe access is provided for all transportation modes and all users,

8-1. Opportunity: many uses can be found for wide, empty streets.

including those choosing to travel by foot, bicycle, or bus; moreover, a sense of community will be reinforced by fitting streets in with complementary land uses that support local community needs. Streets must look, feel, and work as part of a particular community.

Supporting the Pedestrian

Streets as public places are especially important in most higher-density residential neighborhoods, which are often severely compromised by heavy traffic. In apartment districts, the absence of sidewalks and a lack of concentrated services force residents to use cars for every need.

DECREASING SPEED OF AUTOMOBILE TRAVEL

Almost every highway design standard in the federal and state systems focuses on the ease of vehicular traffic to ensure that it flows safely. Widening and straightening roads improves visibility, which, in theory, also increases automobile safety. In both cases, however, these measures often result in heightened speed. And, while increasing speed may be an important goal on freeways, it should be avoided in identifiable communities that aspire to convert streets to public places (see chap. 19, by R. K. Untermann).

Standards are pervasive. For example, the engineer of a small town in Washington discovered a state standard that prohibits parking within thirty feet of intersections. Interpreting the code liberally, he applied the rule to alleys and to some busy driveways and restriped the town's no-parking zones at a cost of about fifty parking places. The town, in consequence, may now be safer for cars, but it is definitely more dangerous for pedestrians. Increasing the visibility at

intersections encourages higher speeds, and cars can now dart faster than before. Yet, when people complained about the loss of parking, the engineer insisted that were the parking to be replaced and an accident to occur, the town would lose any subsequent lawsuit because of the failure to follow state rules.

Vehicular speed must be reduced if pedestrians and bicyclists are to be encouraged. More study is needed to determine the extent of reduction, which, moreover, varies from place to place (see chap. 19, by R. K. Untermann). However, I believe the optimum speed is far slower than most people realize, given especially that drivers tend to exceed the posted limit by 5 to 7 miles per hour. On streets alongside which pedestrians walk, I estimate the maximum safe speed to be 20 miles per hour. On neighborhood streets, it should be 15 miles per hour, with speeds posted at 10 miles per hour. Some drivers will inevitably be annoyed at first, but new speed limits may provoke them to switch, at least occasionally, to foot or bicycle travel. We have, after all, gotten used to reduced speeds on freeways. Education about road safety has also helped drivers understand the advantages of slow speeds in communities and much more can be done in this area.

IMPROVING PEDESTRIAN SAFETY

Lack of safety is a prime factor that decreases one's desire to walk and cycle. People simply will not take chances with themselves or with their children. Elderly people, aware of their reduced mobility and perception, are even more cautious. Roads with no sidewalks or with the walk adjacent to a busy street make many pedestrians and bicyclists feel vulnerable (figs. 8-2 through 8-5). Wide streets with large volumes of high-speed traffic are dangerous for pedestrians to

8-2. Complex intersection: dangerous for cars, murderous for pedestrians and bicyclists.

a.

b.

8-3. Free right-turn intersections compromise the pedestrian, especially where there is <u>a.</u> a discontinuous sidewalk, and <u>b.</u> no sidewalk. Note also the absence of sidewalks and the resulting islands, which offer little protection.

8-4. Parking in front of shops takes over the sidewalk.

cross, as are wide driveways that cross sidewalks and encourage high-speed auto entry or exit (fig. 8-6).

In most suburban communities, the *appearance* of pedestrian danger may be just as important as the reality. The sound of heavy trucks can make a street seem unsafe (fig. 8-7). Reducing auto speed is a critical part of the solution. How many times have you stopped at an intersection and waited for a relentless stream of cars to let you pass? All one can do is wait, because the driver of a car going 25 miles per hour is incapable of stopping abruptly. Only in those nervous moments when the traffic spacing seems adequate will one cross. Pedestrians will not use the streets until they are safe, yet streets will not be social spaces until pedestrians use them.

DESIGNING STREETS FOR PEOPLE, NOT CARS

Functional problems aside from safety decrease a street's pedestrian potential. Parking lots reduce pedestrian activity and destroy the vitality of a street (figs. 8-8, 8-9). Most shopping is not arranged for convenience on foot because of physical barriers, such as wide driveways, extensive parking lots, and incompatible shopping uses.

Parking lots need to include space for safe foot or bicycle access from the street (fig. 8-10). Stores need to be interconnected, even across wide, busy streets, so that several shopping stops can be made from one parking place.

There is a need for a variety of street furniture, including climate protection devices, seating, lighting, food services, and devices that reduce noise (fig. 8-11). With no heater or air conditioner and no locked doors, the world beyond one's car or dwelling can be uncomfortable. It needs to be tailored to offer some basic necessities.

REDUCING TRAVEL DISTANCE

Reducing travel distances is a key solution to improving pedestrian access in suburban communities. Distance is not much of a concern when one drives, and an extra few hundred feet, or even a mile, causes little trouble. Poor weather, too, is of less concern to the driver than to the pedestrian. Storeowners know that; with the exception of a few key outlets, most retail stores are not situated on the basis of precise ideal location. They do not have to be—one place is roughly as good as another for the purposes of attracting a driving clientele. However, for the pedestrian or cyclist, distance does matter; and an extra 500 feet may discourage a trip by foot.

The number and diversity of services in close proximity to residential quarters should be increased to minimize the travel distances between necessary

8-5. Bus stop at intersection endangers the transit rider.

8-8. Parked cars disrupt the meager pedestrian right-of-way.

8-6. Narrow sidewalk further interrupted by driveways offers little protection.

8-9. Pedestrian right-of-way is rudely discontinued at the entry of a parking lot.

8-7. This sidewalk is too narrow to protect pedestrians.

8-10. Locating the pedestrian zone next to shops in Bellevue, Washington.

8-11 <u>a.</u>, <u>b.</u>: Two views of Kirkland, Washington, street design for slow-moving cars. Note wide, protected sidewalk.

shopping stores. Stores, in other words, should be placed in patterns that allow fulfillment of today's complex shopping needs from one location. At present, however, retail merchandising patterns are geared to auto travel from store to store, which decreases the need for convenient intermixing of retail uses, except at shopping centers.

Reducing travel distances can be accomplished by land-use or transportation adjustments. Land-use solutions include increasing residential density in areas surrounding existing activities and services or increasing services near large residential developments. Such solutions might also involve the location of stores and offices near apartments or even the incorporation of schools and libraries in office or apartment complexes. Effective transportation changes would in-

clude removing barriers to foot or bicycle access, developing shortcuts, and adding sidewalks and curb cuts for wheelchairs.

CHANGING LAND USES

The separation of single-family developments from shopping and work areas has enabled suburbanites to live comfortably away from business and heavy traffic nuisances. At the same time, however, it has greatly increased our dependence on driving and raised the question of the value of mixing land uses. Single-family residents are concerned about the potential negative effects of nearby mixed-use developments because they fear that increased traffic will decrease property values and environmental quality. We need to know more about how to design each land use to yield the benefits, while minimizing the problems, of integrated shopping, working, and residential areas. Some of these problems could be actualized if projects are not designed carefully. However, property values and environmental quality may erode, with or without new projects, if automobile traffic continues to increase as it has in the past.

INCREASING THE LEVEL OF INTEREST

Pedestrians need a high level of visual stimulation to maintain their interest and encourage trip continuation. To use Richard Nelson's coinage in *The Selection of Retail Locations* (1958), "dead spots" are areas where shoppers lose interest in going farther. At a certain point, the landscape is simply too boring for most pedestrians to continue walking.

As discussed in chapter 5, by Amos Rapoport, drivers require exactly the opposite type of streetscape from pedestrians: they need simple scenes because too much visual stimulation creates confusion and can lead to accidents. At 35 miles an hour—a normal speed in suburban neighborhoods—drivers cannot comprehend many distinct elements at the same time. But, walking at three miles an hour, the pedestrian requires a high level of visual stimulation to reduce boredom. The exact nature of this conflict between pedestrians' and drivers' perceptual needs should be researched further to determine the type and amount of visual stimulation necessary to maintain interest for walkers, while not overstimulating drivers.

Supporting Bicycles

The most important immediate action may be to develop safe access for bicycles. The longer distances and large-scale roads that have to be traversed in suburban communities may require more effort than is likely on foot. However, most roads can be made to serve the bicycle's speed of 10 to 15 miles per hour and its 3 to 5 mile range.

Bicycle improvements should be made *at destinations* and work back toward residential communities. Bicycles and cars should be kept separate by using parallel, wide sidewalks or bicycle trails. That may be contrary to the advice of commuter cyclists, who often argue for integration of the bicycle and roadway. However, most suburbanites perceive arterials as dangerous and will not venture onto them on a bicycle. Because suburban blocks are long between cross streets, there will be few interruptions. Curb cuts should be added at each intersection to prevent bicyclists from having to stop at every corner.

Widening the curb traffic lane on main commuter routes helps skilled bicyclists to ride safely in the roadway. (However, the wider lane can also cause an increase in overall traffic speed.) Eliminating or narrowing wide driveways reduces confrontations between automobiles and bicycles. Adding special signs alerts motorists to the potential of bikers. Striping right-of-way options at intersections is a final safety precaution.

Single-Family Subdivisions

The environment *within* single-family neighborhoods can be improved to cater to pedestrians. The creation of shortcuts between cul-de-sacs to reduce the auto-dominated hierarchy, and the addition of an occasional sidewalk may be all that is needed in many places.

Apartment Complexes and Open Space

Apartment complexes now exist in almost all suburban communities; in fact, some communities have more apartment dwellers than single-family residents. As apartments are generally close to shopping centers, work places, public transit, and other facilities, they are prime candidates for pedestrian improvements.

Most apartment communities comprise individual developments located side by side over a large tract of land. Many of these developments are constructed on a traditional pattern, whereby buildings are surrounded by roadways and parking lots outside and feature a small open space inside. These interior open spaces should be the pedestrian link between projects. In practice, however, neither they nor even the private parking/road system is connected. Since there is no unified pedestrian system, residents cannot move safely on foot or bicycle through other apartment complexes to stores or workplaces.

In most apartment districts, a sense of neighborhood does not exist. However, by studying an aerial photo, one can pick out potential shortcuts and linkage patterns through parking lots and parts of open space that would foster resident interaction and, thus, a community spirit. (One must ensure, however, that routes do not compromise resident privacy or amenity.) Although it may be difficult to implement an entire system at one time, each link improves access to nearby facilities for a larger number of people.

Apartment Buildings on Arterials

The appropriateness of placing high-density apartments on busy roads should be addressed. Current planning practices use apartments as buffers between residential and business complexes. As a result, they are almost always located on busy arterials, which are, unfortunately, noisy, polluted, and unsafe for walking or for children's play. They may also possess a poor image that impels residents to move from apartment to apartment in search of a more attractive environment. In the longer term, it may be desirable to reclaim these residential arterials. Reduced speed limits and on-street parking could lower the volume of traffic, making some busy roads better places to live. Persons with homes on arterials should fight to convert the roadway, even if it means diverting some traffic to secondary roads and facing the resistance of residents burdened with the extra flow. One can also change arterials to enhance residential character. This measure would "squeeze" traffic as well, but the concepts presented here are not intended to maximize traffic flow; they are intended to encourage nonmotorized circulation to enhance streets as public places.

New, small-scale apartments should be located closer to single-family residential areas and combined with services such as stores and offices. If the size and density are not too high, they may be attractive for the abutting residential communities as well as for the apartment dwellers themselves.

Pedestrianizing Strip Developments

Even strip developments that feature poor pedestrian access, lack of walkways, heavy through traffic, and continuous curb cuts can be strengthened for pedestrian use. The negative aspects of wide driveways, deep setbacks, and linear shops could be eliminated slowly if each new development were designed and located properly. There are two conceptual options to consider in converting strip developments. The public street could contain a pedestrian area that interconnects all activities. This measure might require changing building setbacks, so that new structures would be built close to the roadway. Parking could be located in the rear or alongside the building, with driveways off cross streets. Conversely, the main pedestrian area could be separated from the street and run parallel to existing buildings, linking them along their fronts (fig. 8-12). Cooperation among merchants and property owners would be necessary to assure through-pedestrian circulation; merchants would have to share the parking area and reconnect their walkways to the intersections. This concept is thus somewhat akin to the shopping center in that management would have to deal with a number of individual property owners.

The conversion of strip developments to pedestrian usage may be best in areas near residential concentrations or near other neighborhood shopping facilities. There is the need, in the long run, to eliminate retail use along portions of strip developments and concentrate it around certain intersections. Many areas have overzoned commercial land, used-car lots, trailer storage, rusting machinery, and construction debris. Storage, although an interim land use, is detrimental to street quality and to the comfort of passing pedestrians. In many instances, development is a long way off, and downzoning might hasten concentrated retail development at nodes near residential neighborhoods. The space between the concentrated retail nodes could be used for offices or for apartments, if the road nuisances were reduced. Concentrating retail near residential neighborhoods increases foot or bike access and could reduce the amount of driving that typically occurs along strip developments.

I have proposed downzoning in several communities, which approved it more readily than I expected. Local speculators represent the biggest obstacle, for they believe that higher use zones create a better chance for making a profit. In reality, however, if there is not enough commercial development to fill the zoned land, development sprawls throughout the community, as developers search for the cheapest land, and everyone loses.

Drive-in establishments, such as banks, drugstores, fast-food stores, and laundries, should be banned from areas that service pedestrian needs. Drive-ins consume too much land, they are unsafe, they offer little or no aesthetic interest to pedestrians, and they discourage the driver from running other errands on foot. In addition, automobiles that stand at drive-ins waste fuel and pollute the air.

The typical land-use pattern, with its wide front and narrow depth, needs to be revised. Generated in part by high-speed car travel, it exists everywhere in the suburban areas—in retail, commercial, industrial and residential uses alike. For pedestrians, narrow-fronted, relatively deep lots encourage visual diversity along the walkway. As the designers of shopping malls recognize, narrow lots maximize activity within a concentrated area. Other small developments could, over time, be infilled to replicate the shopping center's success. New developments could be lotted to conform to this idea, and setbacks eliminated to force parking behind stores.

Neighborhood Shopping Centers

Neighborhood shopping centers are well suited for improved pedestrian development and could benefit from all of the urban pedestrian techniques, such as increasing shopping density and residential density, and adding secondary services and other activities that maximize what a shopper can accomplish once his or her car is parked. The trick is to reduce the number of short driving trips that are typical of a shopping expedition by providing more shopping

8-12. Examples of pleasant pedestrian "parkways" in Bellevue, Washington: <u>a.</u> between street and buildings; <u>b.</u> between street and parking lot adjacent to buildings.

a.

b.

opportunities within close range of the parked car. Covered walks, curb cuts, trees, benches, eating establishments, and other services would also enhance these options. The addition of a second floor for medical, dental, residential, or office uses further supports the pedestrian environment. Neighborhood shopping centers could offer complete retail services, allowing a variety of needs to be satisfied quickly near home and on foot.

Recentralizing the Suburbs

Many metropolitan communities have evolved from compact cities to streetcar cities to suburban communities. Each step erodes the focus or sense of community that previously existed. In the Northwest, we are lucky because many of the former "streetcar" neighborhoods remain vital commercial places where neighbors regularly shop. People identify their homes by these neighborhoods, even if, in reality, they live miles away. The affinity of Americans for small towns contributes to a sense of community in individual places. If we can recapture a community image, and recentralize a decentralized region, we may be able to enhance the street as a social, public place.

Strong, central cities could become more vital by developing their own images. Meanwhile, the remainder of the metropolitan area could evolve as a series of nodes, each with easy foot or bike access to those living nearby. Not only would people be able to identify the character of their city, but they could do so as a first step in using its manifold attributes. It could be a work place, shopping place, and recreation place. This type of suburban community has developed over centuries in Europe, and its bicycle and pedestrian scale has helped return the street to the broadest social definition of *public purpose*.

REFERENCE

Nelson, R. L. 1958. *The Selection of Retail Locations*. New York: F. W. Dodge.

9.
Grids Revisited

ANNE VERNEZ MOUDON AND
RICHARD K. UNTERMANN

However appealing and successful the recent street transformations in Europe, they are, in many ways, inadequate models for the future of American streets. Few "organic," medieval-type street layouts exist in North America, except in parts of Boston, New York, and Philadelphia. The typical narrow, skewed, and irregular streets that result from the incremental platting of European cities are not commonly found. Grids are the staple of American cities. Even the irregular, curved street layouts, which prevailed in most post–World War II urban and suburban development, bear little resemblance to the historic organic cities: romantic emulations of historic cities, they are but "pseudo-organic." Today, after a few decades of urban development with curved streets, the benefits of orthogonal grids once again seem to outweigh their drawbacks (Groth 1981; see also chap. 7, by C. R. Wolfe). But whether loved or hated, street grids are, for better or worse, here to stay in many American cities.

In an effort to highlight the special conditions of North American streets, we will first look at the differences between organic European street networks and American grids. Then we will explore the opportunities that grids appear to offer for serving transportation and open space needs. We look at grids with optimism, for their individual streets and networks alike provide magnificent opportunities to redesign our cities.

Anne Heasly acted as a Research Assistant on the San Francisco and the Laredo cases. Partial research support from the College of Architecture and Urban Planning, University of Washington, Seattle, is acknowledged. All photographs and graphics are by the authors unless otherwise noted.

THE NATURE OF AMERICAN STREETS
Grids versus Historic Organic Street Networks

Several structural differences between American gridirons and European organic streets go beyond their distinct geometric characteristics. For example, grid cities have proportionately more street area per square foot of private property than do organic cities; the network of street grids is more extensive and the streets themselves wider than in organic networks. In London's City of Westminster, 27 percent of the land is reserved for streets, versus 32 percent in San Francisco and Manhattan, 34 in Boston's Back Bay, 37 in Indianapolis, 36 in Vancouver's West End, 41 in downtown Portland, and 43 in Seattle's Denny Regrade area (Razak 1981: 1) (fig. 9-1). These differences greatly affect the potential for reusing the streets.

To comprehend this potential fully, one should understand the process by which street grids were created, or, their raison d'être as *networks*. Street grids were laid out in relatively large chunks (if not directly on the land, at least in the heads of developers) before construction took place. Organic streets, on the other hand, were laid out incrementally, often on a lot-by-lot basis, over the course of development. Street grids represent a principle of development: they organize the distribution of urban land both to public and private sectors and rationalize the transportation network at the city scale. The gridiron therefore follows a logic that synthesizes the demands of an orthogonal geometry with ideals of lot and street size. But in organic street networks, the logic of the network relates to two needs: (1) the connection of important nodes of activity (as, for example, roads first link one village to another, then one urban subcenter to another); and (2) access to private individual parcels (as provided,

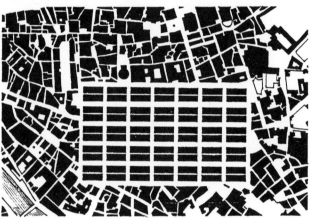

9-1. Figure ground of Seattle's Regrade grid inserted into <u>a.</u> London, and <u>b.</u> Rome. (Source: Razak 1981: 53)

for example, by subdivision development). Thus, while the organic street network is a tribute to the history of urban development, the gridiron actually *defines* (at least in part) that history. In other words, organic streets have always had a purpose and responded to a need, while grid streets have defined an intent.

These differences affect the characteristics of the streets themselves and hence their potential for reuse. The width of organic streets reflects their original function, and a hierarchy is built into their network: those connecting urban subcenters are generally wider and more traffic oriented than the streets that serve private parcels. In gridirons, on the other hand, streets widths are generic and often uniform, and hierarchies are embedded in the geometry of the network rather than in the actual transportation function of the individual street. For example, arterials occur every ten or twenty blocks, whether or not any perceived need for them existed.

The results are that most streets in organic networks tend to fit their basic function of access and

accommodation of through traffic. Their dimensions are commensurate with their expected, original transportation function. As traffic has increased exponentially in this century, street congestion has become the number-one problem in organic cities. In contrast, however, many of the streets of gridiron networks are begging for use because the principle of the gridiron has been applied indiscriminately through high- or low-density development. The standardized, uniform width of grid streets has yielded wide streets in the United States—especially in the Midwest and the West, where land was cheap and plentiful at first and where densities have remained relatively low due to the early use of the automobile. Thus, many fully developed and paved streets, which serve few properties, pedestrians, and drivers, are *underutilized* from the standpoint of transportation planning. Wide streets and low densities make for a marriage that is full of potential. Consider, for example, the opportunities possessed by residents of the Seattle neighborhood of Queen Anne, who each have 1,312 square feet of street area. In the North End of Boston, on the other hand, where no one has a private yard and public parks are scarce, there are only 73 square feet of street per inhabitant (Moudon 1984).

In addition, grids were stretched indiscriminately across hills whose slopes are often excessive for motorized traffic; others span bodies of water that necessarily discontinue the motorized movement network. Because many streets in these networks cannot be used by cars, they are "paper" streets that remain unimproved. On the books as public easements or rights-of-way, undeveloped paper streets are often left unmanaged or illegally assumed by owners of abutting land. In some cases, public pedestrian paths may exist informally as trails or stairways. Paper streets are also discontinuities in the grid network, where fully developed streets must end abruptly and serve only the immediate abutters. Whenever the gridiron meets a body of water, many street ends correspond to "waterways," which are rights-of-way related to water transportation. Because they are not needed for through traffic, street ends have a lot to offer to their community.

Finally, many of the older gridirons include alleys, which, in effect, double the circulation network and further the potential for streets to become open spaces. While this chapter will not address alleys, other works can serve as reference (Clay 1978, and chap. 23, by B. F. Ryan).

Pseudo-organic Networks

Although winding streets were used in laying out American neighborhoods as early as the end of the nineteenth century, planners' love affair with the grid actually ended sometime between the two World Wars (Wright 1935; Stein 1971). By the end of World War II, curved streets completely dominated suburban development. As Charles R. Wolfe observes (chap. 7), a second "street revolution" changed the character of American street layouts. Originating with the Garden City movement, which was based on the concept of neighborhood units, the postwar romantic layouts were meant to do more than just end the monotony of the grid; they introduced street hierarchies, thereby segregating traffic by speed and, typically, creating a network of arterials around each neighborhood. In contrast to grids, those street networks respected the irregularities of the terrain and responded to drainage requirements. As conflicts with topography were resolved and adjacencies to waterways considered in these layouts, street ends and paper streets were done away with. Yet, if much of the perceived "waste" and "ruthlessness" of grids was corrected, the geometry of curved street layouts remained, in the hands of land speculators, as arbitrary as the grids themselves. They were "reasoned" platting schemes, not organically grown settlements. As such, they too shaped the history of American urban form, but they were not shaped by it.

Furthermore, street widths, which by that time had been regulated, were exaggerated in anticipation of high volumes of automobile traffic. Hence, while grid cities have more streets that are unusable by vehicular traffic than their pseudo-organic counterparts, both offer generous rights-of-way that are not always strictly necessary for maintaining a steady flow of traffic. Both, therefore, presented unusual opportunities for the future.

FUTURE OPPORTUNITIES

Now that urban land is scarce, paved but underutilized streets, paper streets, and street ends can all be perceived as surplus streets available for purposes other than automobile transportation. Surplus streets are a resource not to be discarded, an unsuspected bonanza for cities. First, they provide an opportunity for innovative planners to do what hurried surveyors and developers failed to accomplish: to make places that offer a range of opportunities for public use. Also, they represent the land bank that no American city had the luxury to develop. They can be preserved or transformed into a tradable commodity to manage further and higher-quality development in cities.

American cities have good reasons to take a fresh look at the resource that their street networks represent. We do not know of any grid city that has taken a comprehensive approach to planning by using its streets as a resource. Many, however, have experimented or worked with some of the surplus aspects of their street networks. In most cases, the process has not been easy; often, special conditions require diverse approaches for implementing streets for public use. We will first discuss the transformations of individual streets—wide, underutilized streets. Then, we will turn to the reuse potential of entire street networks.

WIDE STREETS FOR PUBLIC USE

In the early part of this century, planners advocated not only wide streets but wide building setbacks in order to ensure the possibility of enlarging the roadway without disrupting the structures along it (Bassett 1940). Enlarging streets is still a common practice today, generally undertaken to improve *traffic* flow and thus representing a limited and outright biased approach. Now rights-of-way that are at least 60 feet are commonly required for roads with no sidewalks, or with single, minimum 5-foot sidewalks, in low-density, single-family neighborhoods (fig. 9-2). Not commensurate with the basic needs of automobile traffic in most neighborhoods, these road design standards are based on the untested belief that wide streets are safe streets. If perilous for pedestrians, such streets may not even be safe for vehicles because they make drivers feel at ease behind the wheel and facilitate higher speeds (see chap. 8, by R. K. Untermann). How much space is actually needed for vehicular traffic? And what can be done with surplus street width?

9-2. Maplebrook Lane, Redmond, Washington. Suburban street with single sidewalk and no curb.

Reduced Traffic Standards

Ironically, neither pedestrian nor driver's safety, but economy, is at the root of experimentation with new reduced standards for road design today! Carried out by municipalities, and often encouraged by the federal government, a few experimental housing projects display narrowed rights-of-way, in conjunction with narrow driveways and paired-up utility runs, to make single-family properties more affordable. For instance, standard local access streets in Sunridge, a planned residential community in Everett, Washington, have been reduced by more than 50 percent, from a standard 50 feet to 22 feet; collector streets in the same neighborhood have been reduced to 26 feet from 50 or 60 feet (figs. 9-3 through 9-5). T-turnarounds are used instead of cul-de-sacs. Sidewalks have been eliminated along small access drives. Single 5-foot-wide walkways have been provided on local access streets that connect to recreational areas. (To ensure pedestrian safety on the sidewalks, however, no driveways are permitted along those streets.) The reduced street standards, small lots (lowered from 7,000 to 4,500 square feet), and setbacks together have led to an increase in the number of units on the site from 56 to 81 (figs. 9-6, 9-7). The development also provides for small, collective open spaces, which would not have been possible under the traditional regulations (Planning and Community Affairs Agency 1984).

These trends show that reduced dimensions for rights-of-way are both possible and desirable. Indeed, narrowing the right-of-way for automobile circulation is becoming an alternative in many existing neighborhoods pressed for additional parking and plagued by high traffic speeds. In prewar neighborhoods, for instance, prevailing 60- or 70-foot rights-of-way include

9-3. Sunridge, planned residential community in Everett, Washington. Local access street (from a front yard).

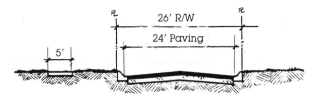

Sunridge Collector Street
• Reduced right-of-way width
• Reduced paving width
• Rolled curbs
• Single, detached, 5-foot sidewalk   a.

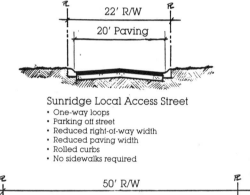

b.

9-4. Sunridge, Everett, Washington, collector street: a. reduced, and b. standard dimensions. (Source: Planning and Community Affairs Agency 1984: 107)

Sunridge Local Access Street
• One-way loops
• Parking off street
• Reduced right-of-way width
• Reduced paving width
• Rolled curbs
• No sidewalks required   a.

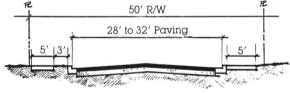

b.

9-5. Sunridge, Everett, Washington, local access street: a. reduced, and b. standard dimensions. (Source: Planning and Community Affairs Agency 1984: 106)

double sidewalks and planting strips as well as parallel parking on both sides of the street, which leaves space for two lanes of traffic. In those cases, it is possible to eliminate one traffic lane to accommodate diagonal parking on either side of the street—an option that many of the denser neighborhoods may consider since it will also ensure radically reduced traffic speeds (fig. 9-8).

But there are other possibilities. The city of Santa Monica (1973) has recently implemented street proj-

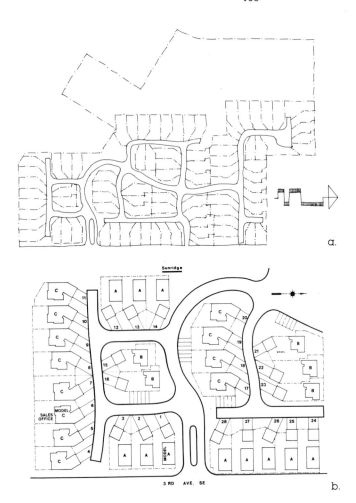

9-6. Sunridge, Everett, Washington: <u>a</u>. site plan under reduced standards (81 lots); <u>b</u>. detail from sales brochure. (<u>a</u>.: redrawn from Planning and Community Affairs Agency 1984: 104)

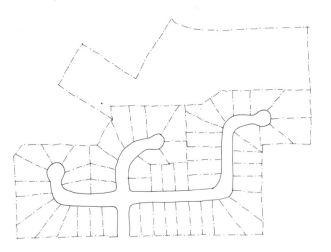

9-7. Sunridge, Everett, Washington, site plan under standard regulations (56 lots). (Redrawn from Planning and Community Affairs Agency 1984: 105)

ects on wide rights-of-way. Along the waterfront and near Palisades Park, Ocean Avenue has been reduced from a four-lane to a two-lane arterial, with additional parking and landscaping along it. Likewise, Fourth Street, transversing one of the city's neighborhoods, has been narrowed to two lanes with additional parking provided along as well as in the middle of the street (fig. 9-9). The band of space reserved for parking in the median strip is painted green and interrupted intermittently with potted trees. When funds become available, the city hopes to have a continuous park in the middle of the street with places for some parking. Both projects are the results of community pressures to control traffic as well as to increase amenities.

The reuse of excess street space is not always a pressing necessity: low densities, high amounts of private open space, and generous dimensions of overall neighborhood layouts may make reuse a luxury. However, median strips or sidewalks have been introduced in some places, along with additional greenery, to achieve a boulevard effect as well as to reduce the speed of traffic (fig. 9-10). With increased pressures for density in suburban areas, it will be wise to consider street space as a way to balance community wishes for the provision of generous open space with the demands for density. Much of the new parking required could, for instance, be accommodated on the streets. Also, the allowance of parking along business arterials will not only solve some parking problems but will also reduce the street width, thereby making sidewalks safer and increasing human activity along the street (see chap. 19, by R. K. Untermann). Because it requires no capital expenditure, this action would be easy to accomplish.

Higher Standards for the Public Use of Streets

To date, it appears that most efforts to take advantage of extreme street widths have consisted of single occurrences of street reuse rather than of deliberate attempts to use the untapped resource of wide streets. Often, too, the impetus for such projects has been more reactive than interactive: residents have sought measures that reduce traffic or discourage parking by outsiders rather than measures that improve pedestrian safety and increase the number of green, open spaces. Donald Appleyard's examples of Berkeley and Seattle, where several neighborhoods demanded traffic-restricting barriers, are especially illustrative (Appleyard 1981). Yet, contrary to their European counterparts, the wide streets of even the densest American neighborhoods provide opportunities for sharing space with cars, for increasing open green areas and recreational space, and for controlling noise and air pollution. These are all real and easily achiev-

9-8. Frederick Douglass Plaza, Pierce between Oak and Fell streets, San Francisco.

9-10. Winding street within grid in Santa Cruz, California.

a.

b.

9-9. Fourth Street in Santa Monica, California: a. parallel parking on the street and on the median strip; b. green strip next to parking in the median.

able possibilities that go well beyond traffic control.

Here and there we see hopeful signs. Already some homeowners are using the planting strips next to sidewalks creatively: there, they grow vegetables that would not fit or thrive in their backyards. (fig. 9-11). In Venice, California, some of the relatively narrow rights-of-way have been closed to vehicular traffic to create more generous front yards. Donald Appleyard and Peter Bosselmann showed how the 70-foot right-of-way of San Francisco streets could accommodate large front yards on one side without eliminating vehicular through circulation (Appleyard and Bosselmann 1982). A natural evolution of such ideas would be to systematically assess the potential for reuse of *all* city streets.

STREET ENDS

Street ends abound in older American cities. Again, however, little planning has been undertaken to exploit this resource positively. Examples in Seattle and San Francisco will show some of the possibilities, as well as some of the problems, involved with the reuse of street ends.

Seattle

A survey made in Seattle showed at least 500 street ends within the confines of the city, representing some 160 acres in combined area, or almost sixty city blocks (Untermann et al. 1980). These streets were originally platted irrespective of topography, water edge, or other barriers. When they eventually were constructed, often several years after platting had occurred, the portions that extended over steep topography, or those that ran into the water, were never completed, leaving hundreds of residue street ends.

a.

b.

c.

d.

9-11. Wide streets for public use: <u>a.</u> closing a street to automobile traffic in Venice, California; <u>b.</u> detail of private gardens and pedestrian paths in Venice, California; <u>c.</u> private garden on the planting strip in Wallingford, Seattle; <u>d.</u> gardening in the street space in San Francisco. (Source <u>d.</u>: Appleyard and Bosselmann 1982: 23)

In the street space, gardening provides urban dwellers with a chance to improve their home environment and engage in creative activity. Gardening requires soil in small or large plots close to home and can range from the planting and care of flowers, shrubs, and vegetables to the planting of larger trees. Gardens are most likely to be maintained if they are initiated by residents and are immediately adjacent to their homes. In Holland, residents can lease street garden space on nominal cost, long-term leases. These small plots can be in widened sidewalks or cul-de-sacs.

Commissioned by the Parks and Recreation Department, the survey was a part of background research for a bond proposal to determine whether low-cost parks could be developed in areas suffering from a lack of recreational space. Carried out by landscape architecture students from the University of Washington, the study rated all street ends according to those most likely to succeed as improved city parks and determined that street ends were attractive future park sites. Unfortunately, the bond proposal (which included some $200,000 for street-end reconstruction) was defeated, and more recent efforts of the Parks and Recreation Department have been directed toward maintenance, rather than new development, of parks.

Since that time, little has occurred at the city scale in the planning of future uses of these street ends. The city council has adopted legislation making it more difficult to close street ends, especially if they abut waterfronts. The city is also in the process of developing a street vacation policy, which, however, does not address issues specific to street ends (see chap. 23, by B. F. Ryan). The disposal of unused street space is still handled on a case-by-case basis. As a result, many street ends and alleys have already been vacated or sold in high-demand areas, while in less attractive areas, they remain underused and often uncared for.

Following pressures from abutters, most improvements have occurred along prized waterways, where developers see advantage, apartment dwellers seek access, and home owners vie to protect their seclusion. Several such street ends have been constructed as parks along the shores of Lake Union and they are enormously popular summer places. Recently, the Port Authority has agreed to develop several street ends in the Duwamish River delta for the benefit of the surrounding community and "in exchange" for further development of Port Authority facilities in the area. In other, less centrally located places, however, ongoing battles are waged among city officials, citizens, and street-end abutters regarding street ends that have been designated as public beach areas. Often in such places signs indicating public access have been taken down at night to keep the unwanted out, thick hedges planted, and threatening remarks made to a public who is largely uninformed of its rights to use this land.

There are reasons why street ends may not work as parks. Densities in many Seattle neighborhoods are so low that a street may remain vacant for years with few people recognizing that it is public. Public demand for recreational space is low because private yards and school grounds already provide adequate space. Some neighborhoods oppose using the street ends for public purposes because residents often feel a park will attract loiterers, vandals, and teenagers, with all their attendant problems.

Finally, ownership and maintenance responsibilities are complex, and city hall is often leery to get involved. Streets were originally deeded to the city for public access. If streets are not to serve that specific use, abutters have first option to purchase them. Yet *public access* can be difficult to define; in Seattle, it means that the Department of Engineering maintains control as the historically designated caretaker of streets. However, the department is more concerned with functional matters, such as moving cars, than with providing recreational space or space for pedestrians; only slowly is the department becoming interested in these "secondary," "soft" users. Street ends are low on the city's maintenance priority list; since they do not serve cars, they vanish from the minds of most people when they fall into disrepair.

This sleeper characteristic of many street ends—no one thinks about them until development pressures make them valuable—is the plight of many places that should be reserved for public use. By the time politicians, planners, and other decision makers discover a need for general recreation space, the land is valued for other purposes, and wresting it away from lucrative possibilities is difficult. On the positive side, however, planners in Seattle have used unimproved rights-of-way in green belts as a way to control development. Employing the so-called "Swiss-cheese" approach to land development, they can limit the size of private development to single city blocks by retaining the rights to all street space. Similarly, alleys in downtown blocks can be used to limit development to half blocks.

San Francisco

The San Francisco gridiron was laid out in the second half of the nineteenth century. Stretched over all of the city's hills except for the two tallest, Twin Peaks and Buena Vista Heights, the gridiron is responsible for the extremely steep streets that have been glorified in the car chases of many movies. Many of these streets, however, are impractical for cars and now represent opportunities for added community open space in the densely populated neighborhoods. This is especially true for those near the downtown.

San Francisco's high land values and tremendous pressures for development warrant aggressive planning for the use of street ends. Yet there are no comprehensive efforts to do so, just individual cases. For example, Lombard Street, now famous for its narrow, hairpin-shaped roadway and vibrant flowerbeds, is a special street within the ruthless gridiron. Formerly maintained by the Department of Public Works, the street is now in the hands of the neighborhood's association. Another example, Green Street, is interrupted at several points. At its intersection with Sansome Street, near the northern waterfront, the equivalent of a twelve-story change in grade has been developed as a neighborhood park, with additional parking accommodated on flat land at the top and base of the climb. Stairs and ivy cover a similar slope between Taylor and Jones streets. A special conditional use permit has been granted to a private developer building a condominium along Pfeiffer Street in the North Beach area. The Pfeiffer Street climb will be maintained by the abutters but open to the public. On the other hand, Kearny Street along Broadway, in the heart of the entertainment district, remains a sheet of asphalt flanked on both sides by ladder-type sidewalks (for a history of streets in the North Beach area, refer to Myrick 1972) (fig. 9-12). Numerous other street ends have simply not been considered useful beyond providing shortcuts for pedestrians (Moudon 1986). In fact, the number of undeveloped, city-owned rights-of-way is undetermined—a bizarre situation in a city where land is at such a premium (Shotland 1984).

With no overall city plan for the use of street ends, only independent concerns, such as neighborhood groups, seem to effect street transformation. The absence, moreover, of detailed plans for the neighborhoods results in piecemeal approaches to the process, despite the pressing need for open space. It is possible, but difficult, for individual communities to "take over" street ends. First, the Department of Public Works owns most of the street rights-of-way as the result of a land grant devised by the city's Spanish founders. If, however, a particular street end is developed as a park, then its ownership is transferred to the Parks and Recreation Department which, already burdened with more work than it can handle, is generally resistant to acquiring additional responsibilities that do not come with separate budgets.

The procedure for actually buying street land involves several time-consuming steps. First, a design proposal is reviewed by an interdepartmental commission. Second, if the proposal is approved, each line department reviews it independently. Third, the Department of Public Works has final review of the proposal and its implementation. And finally, the proposal must eventually be approved by the Board of Supervisors—San Francisco's equivalent of a city council.

If, as is more likely, a community does not want to buy the street but would rather use it to its specification, it must seek a right-of-encroachment permit, allowing it to build street furniture, plant trees, and so on. A proposal must be made to the Department of Public Works, which, upon conditional approval, sends it to the interdepartmental commission. The latter department has final review of the permit.

The case of Pfeiffer Street illustrates the complexities of taking over street space. Pfeiffer Street (a dead-end street also called Alcatraz Heights) used to have a few trees, stairs, paths, and rocks. People used it as a dog run, and one man actually lived there long ago. One of the abutters obtained a conditional-use permit in the 1970s to do some planting; he was in turn expected to maintain the right-of-way, for which he received some financial support from the Office of Community Development. More recently, the developer of a project along the street end obtained a right-of-encroachment permit to build a small part of his project on street property. In return, he was to build new stairs, benches, and a viewing platform; he was also to maintain the space (fig. 9-13). The Department of City Planning, in its review of the proposal, requested that the ownership of the street land be transferred from Public Works to the Department of Parks and Recreation, which was less than enthusiastic about the idea. The community, formally organized as the Telegraph Hill Dwellers, was generally in favor of the scheme, except for one citizen who deterred the process. Yet all were concerned that the street stub would become a tourist attraction. Labor unions made sure that they got their piece of the pie (Carter 1984; Rubin 1984). Everyone involved dealt with issues related to the number of cars parked in the area, including adjacent streets (before and after the new project), width of sidewalks, the design of the fountain, and elevation of the viewing platform (decided *in situ* with everyone present). The process took three years, with the developer's interests represented by a special consultant who oversaw every stage. The street end is now called Pfeiffer Park.

The Pfeiffer Park episode tells us that it takes a lot of energy and money to acquire even the right to use a street end. Paradoxically, this is especially true in areas where the demand for land is high (in those cases, however, a positive outcome is also much more appreciated!). More significantly, the episode shows that when the constituencies for street development are scattered throughout a city—even a city as sophisticated in environmental matters as San Francisco—no common lobby exists to force city governments to develop a coherent set of policies supporting the communities. Each neighborhood sees its problem as very specific and does not try to attract supporters from outside of its boundaries. Neither are public institutions likely to consider street ends as a citywide problem. They are overloaded with matters perceived to be more important—for example, downtown planning—and they must deal with warring factions from

9-12. Street ends in San Francisco: <u>a.</u> Green Street between Taylor and Jones; <u>b.</u> parking, stairs, and park at Montgomery Street in North Beach; <u>c.</u> sheet of asphalt at Kearny Street and Broadway.

9-13. Pfeiffer Park under construction, San Francisco.

the different line departments. Even engineering departments, which are good candidates for handling street ends, since they necessarily take a citywide approach to transportation issues, do not show much interest: traditionally, they have been inclined to deal with car rather than pedestrian movement.

Yet street ends potentially are a valuable asset. Ironically, tax surcharges have been proposed in San Francisco to generate money for the acquisition and maintenance of additional community open space—presumably on private land—as part of a minipark development program. It would then seem appropriate for planning authorities to facilitate carrying out local street-end improvement and maintenance programs. Street ends could become a citywide amenity, considered either as part of the transportation plan that communities do have (if only they would consider pedestrian traffic seriously) or as part of open space planning.

NETWORKS

Streets for recreation, for open space, and especially, for pedestrians make sense not as single occurrences, but as networks within a neighborhood or a city. These networks may not necessarily be apparent to the eye—for instance, they may not all be lined with the same trees or paved with the same materials—but they should be made to exist in the minds of the users. Good planning not only makes a city accessible to a variety of users, but it gives them ideas for creative use. We know of no city in the United States where an entire network of streets is considered for any purpose other than automobile transportation. But two near exceptions will be introduced here, Seattle,

Washington, and Laredo, Texas, to illustrate the potential of well-planned street networks.

The Hidden Pedestrian Grid in Queen Anne

The reuse potential of streets as networks is best investigated by first performing an inventory of what is there. In Queen Anne, one of Seattle's oldest neighborhoods, an inventory of unimproved streets, street ends, and stairs has pointed to the richness of spaces actually generated by the gridiron. It appears from this example that some grids were designed with the pedestrian in mind.

Queen Anne covers a substantial hill rising more than 400 feet above sea level. Arterials accommodating through traffic have, over time, separated the community from the shores of Lake Union on the east side, as well as from the adjacent hillside community, Magnolia, on the west. The grid in Queen Anne was laid out in a series of privately owned plats, which originated on the steep south slope, covered the flat hill top, and dribbled down the north side of the hill. Green belts of undeveloped land line the east and west sides; they too were gridded with streets that remained undeveloped because of severe slopes. Yet an impressive network of stairs and pedestrian paths exists on many of the grid's rights-of-way that are too steep for motorized traffic. We counted more than one hundred such paths linking the residential community to public transit, schools, commercial facilities, and community parks (Bicak 1986) (fig. 9-14).

This pedestrian network represents a resource that is only partly realized by the community. Some of the oldest stairs (dating from 1908), shortcuts, and related promenades on the southwest side have been made into historic landmarks. They are used extensively by strollers and joggers on weekends. On the west side of the hill, a small playground fits within the street right-of-way. Some of the abutting residents take it upon themselves to maintain the edges of the right-of-way, using them as extensions of their own yards. The publicly minded few provide delightful settings for everyone to enjoy, while others go as far as planting hedges to keep the public out (fig. 9-15).

Many of these street rights-of-way are in danger of disappearing as land becomes a premium and as individual property owners gradually seek to vacate street space for their own benefit. Preliminary studies show that stairs are often used by transit riders and young children on their way to and from nearby schools (Bicak 1986). Other rights-of-way, situated near commercial areas on the hill, serve as shortcuts for shoppers. Often, more remote rights-of-way, such as the ones located in the green belts, are used by teenagers and, in some cases, by vagrants.

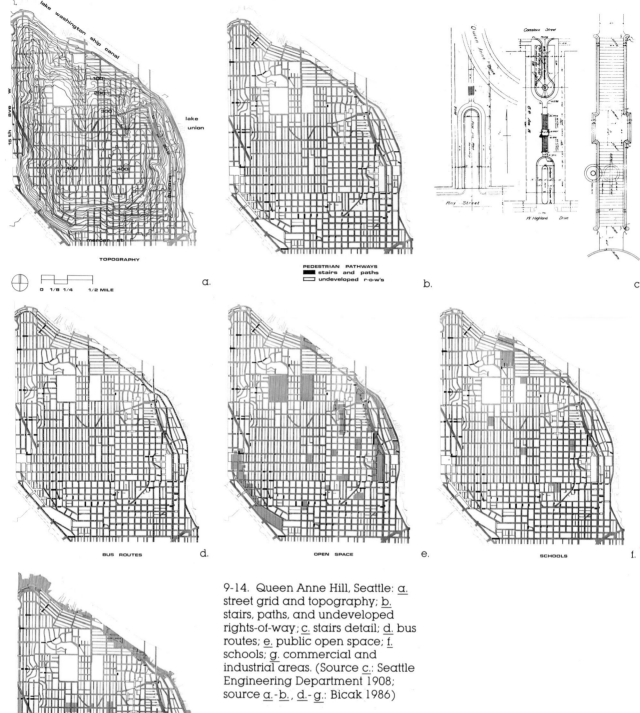

TOPOGRAPHY

0 1/8 1/4   1/2 MILE

a.

PEDESTRIAN PATHWAYS
▇ stairs and paths
▢ undeveloped r·o·w's

b.

c.

BUS ROUTES

d.

OPEN SPACE

e.

SCHOOLS

f.

COMMERCIAL/INDUSTRIAL AREAS

g.

9-14. Queen Anne Hill, Seattle: _a._ street grid and topography; _b._ stairs, paths, and undeveloped rights-of-way; _c._ stairs detail; _d._ bus routes; _e._ public open space; _f._ schools; _g._ commercial and industrial areas. (Source _c._: Seattle Engineering Department 1908; source _a._-_b._, _d._-_g._: Bicak 1986)

9-15. Queen Anne stairs: a. street end and crossing at Tenth Avenue; b. pedestrian path on reduced right-of-way.

Even the residents of these "leftover" streets do not readily perceive the richness of the pedestrian world hidden within. Neither does it get recorded by the Engineering Department's "car-counting boxes." By uncovering the impressive network of rights-of-way and open spaces, this inventory is intended to make people in the community, as well as the city staff, conscious of the wealth of alternatives for future use. One also hopes that it will guide future decisions regarding street vacation in the overall neighborhood; at present, decisions typically consider only the impact on the areas immediately adjacent to the vacation.

Streets for Sale in Laredo, Texas

In 1982, the City of Laredo, Texas, made national news with a newly initiated city-sponsored program of "streets for sale" (*Time* 1982). As in San Francisco,

Laredo's streets were originally given outright to the city through a Spanish land grant. Forming a regular pattern of blocks approximately 250 feet square, the streets are relatively narrow—between 55 and 65 feet in width—and represent some 35 percent of the land. Many have existed on paper as unpaved and unimproved rights-of-way because of the small size of the blocks, combined with many interruptions in their network. In the north-south orientation, these interruptions are caused by wide railroad and freeway easements and by the Zacate River Creek. South, the street grid meets the flood plain of the Rio Grande del Norte.

In the early 1980s, half of the streets in the city's 5,400 blocks needed paving, while the streets of some 2,000 blocks needed resurfacing. Under pressure to take care of its property, but in need of funds, the city designed a street-closing ordinance, which outlined a procedure for selling some of the surplus streets (fig. 9-16). Closing procedures, as specified in the ordinance, can be initiated by the street-closing city staff, by a city department, or by abutting land owners. If the city initiates the process, abutters have first option to buy; if they elect not to buy the property, it is then put out for bid to the general community. Street closing must be approved by abutters, by all city departments involved, such as fire and sanitation, and by utility companies. A public hearing is held as a preliminary procedure. Then the buyer must have the land appraised and cover the cost of surveys and title transfer (approximately $700). So far, one million dollars worth of streets have been sold, part of which is debt financed by the city.

Not all streets are for sale in Laredo, and some planning is involved in disposing of the properties. The city has formally closed street ends near the Zacate Creek, which planners hope to transform into a park. Other, smaller creeks will also eventually become public green spaces. Street closing was the vehicle for the construction of a "soft ball complex" on more than five city-owned blocks in South Laredo. Streets have also been donated to the Laredo Independent School District for the expansion of its facilities; the land will, however, revert to the city if the school district does not develop it within a designated period of time. The city and the school district are negotiating the development of sports complexes and dual-purpose parks near the schools, which are to be used by students during regular school hours but revert to community use at night and on weekends. On the west side of town, the city exchanged land with the Missouri Pacific Railroad in order to widen a truck route along which the railroad owned property. In return, the railroad company has been able to consolidate some sixteen blocks, making room for a future

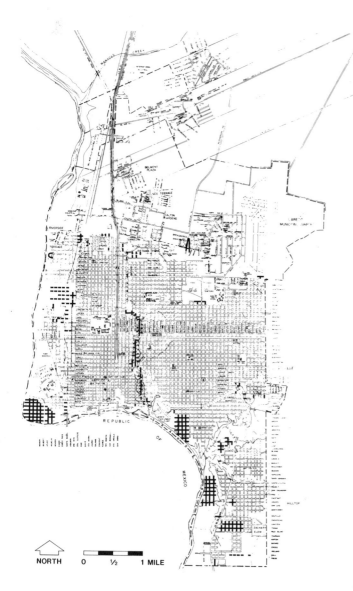

9-16. Map of Laredo, Texas, showing streets for sale. (Adapted from City Planning Dept., Laredo, Texas 1984)

industrial park, although parking seems to be the primary intended use for the near future. Finally, several individuals have consolidated properties for commercial and industrial purposes, with a few large tracts remaining in limbo owing to objections by abutters.

The consolidation of property is accompanied by replatting in order to ensure that residents can gain direct access to each lot from city-owned streets. In fact, the street-closing ordinance, which includes a long section showing alternative ways of replatting properties, proposed lots that were usually larger than the existing ones.

The Laredo example is limited in that it reflects the

policies of a city where demand for land is relatively low. Selling streets is not as good an idea in cities where land is scarce. In high-demand areas, the benefits derived from abutting "good" streets are substantial, and developers are often ready to improve streets that remain in the public domain (see chap. 16, by D. C. Miles and M. L. Hinshaw). From "carrots," streets can become "sticks": further development rights can be accorded only to projects that include street improvements.

In Laredo, however, low demand for street land limits the power of the city to piggyback improvements on street sales, even improvements restricted to transportation purposes. Hence, coordination with community needs and transportation planning does not have a high political profile. Yet the example can illustrate how the planning of street uses can take place at the city scale—an important concept worth applying in the politically difficult cases where pressures for development are high and where, so far, most street closings and vacations have proceeded in a piecemeal fashion (see, for instance, the discussion of the alley vacation for the TransAmerica building in San Francisco [Jacobs 1980], and chap. 23 by B. F. Ryan). What if cities began to seek actively to tighten the entire network of streets they own with the objective not only of saving money in upkeep, but of providing opportunities for additional parking, open space, and so forth?

The idea of planning street uses in communities that have both a surplus of streets and pressing needs for office or residential development is challenging. An essential task will be to define *surplus* within a comprehensive planning framework. Surplus streets may include those parts of streets and their networks that neither fulfill public transportation needs (including the needs of pedestrians, bicyclists, and emergency vehicles), nor supply such requirements as light, sun and air, views, active or passive open space, drainage, land banking, land-use control, or utility easements. Also, any street that cannot be maintained, either owing to a lack of funds or to the lack of supporting property owners, may be classified as surplus. A street-use plan can be derived from such definitions to include streets slated for vacation, for redevelopment and improvement, for preservation, and even for maintenance purposes. Any of these strategies can apply to either the entire right-of-way or to a part of it that maintains through passage for cars or pedestrians (see chap. 22, by R. B. Eichner and H. Tobey).

Communities can think of local surplus streets as privately owned and maintained by abutters. But even in the case of private streets, provisions need to be taken to ensure minimum easements for local

147

through traffic and access to the existing lots. The advantages for the communities buying the streets would be control over the use of a large portion of the right-of-way, including parking (for themselves or for outsiders), planting, paving materials, maintenance schedules, and so on (see chap. 20, by D. B. Lee).

CONCLUSION

Streets do not need to be no-man's-lands monopolized by drivers and cars. Considering the generous dimensions of American city streets and the expanse of urban street networks, it makes sense to start using street space to combat pervasive urban problems, ranging from overdevelopment, noise and air pollution, and parking to lack of green or recreational space and pedestrian safety. The same street space can be used to promote healthy communities, encourage pedestrian movement, foster the use of public transit, and create supportive public environments. Given the relative plethora of American streets, it should be neither difficult nor expensive to increase the public utility of streets by encouraging that the space be *shared* by several uses and users (fig. 9-17). In many cases, drivers and cars do not need the entire right-of-way. In fact, it is unsafe, and therefore ultimately expensive, to keep automobiles as sole right-of-way users.

Street improvements that respond to local neighborhood problems are only a fraction of the potential that cities can realize in planning. *The value of the entire street network needs to be assessed.* Street inventories, evaluated in terms of transportation, open space, pollution control, and land-use planning, will help identify the actual utility of the network. Inventories will also help rally constituencies for the future use of streets, making them aware of the potential, generating new ideas for new uses, and alerting them to "new" users. When the Queen Anne community is confronted with the costs of maintaining 1,312 square feet of street for each resident, it is likely to begin to think creatively.

a.

b.

9-17. Sharing the street space: <u>a.</u> snow-covered, 35-foot-wide street in the North End of Boston shows how tamed cars provide occasions for play; <u>b.</u> Dutch "lawn over canal" shows that green streets are possible.

The terms by which street standards are defined must be broadened to make streets responsive to the needs of the entire public, and constituencies must be brought into the process to represent the public interest. Private citizens are represented on "parks boards," yet few communities have advisory citizen "street boards." Citizen involvement will produce street classification systems that take into account users other than drivers (see chap. 12, by S. Dotterrer). Citizens may also support the development of special zones within land-use codes to govern the planning of future street space.

Finally, the processes by which the use of streets is opened up to pedestrians and residents must be simplified. Citizens interested in improving the right-of-way must not fall victim to interagency squabbles. Access to regulatory agencies must be improved, and the approval processes must be streamlined. It may be appropriate to have a socially minded agency, such as a parks department, manage the street space on a city-wide basis. Alternatively, a special street agency may be created to coordinate transportation, land use, and utility distribution, as well as to take care of maintenance problems related to a fully public use of the street network.

REFERENCES

Appleyard, D. 1981. *Livable Streets*. Berkeley: University of California Press.

Appleyard, D., and P. Bosselmann. 1982. "Urban Design Guidelines for Street Management." Working Paper No. 385. Berkeley: Institute of Urban and Regional Development, University of California.

Aquilar, Laura. 1984–86. Streets Coordinator, City of Laredo. Personal communications.

Bassett, E. M. 1940. *Zoning: The Laws, Administration, and Court Decisions during the First Twenty Years*. New York: Russell Sage Foundation.

Bicak, J. 1986. "The Pedestrian Network of Queen Anne." Master's thesis, Department of Architecture, University of Washington, Seattle.

Bray, Norman. 1984. Department of Public Works, City of San Francisco. Personal communication with authors.

Carter, Tom. 1984. A. Cal-Rossi Development Corporation, San Francisco. Personal communication.

City Planning Department. 1984. *Zoning and Street Name Map*. Laredo: City of Laredo, City Planning Department, August.

Clay, G. 1978. *Alleys: A Hidden Resource*. Louisville, Ky.: Grady Clay & Co.

Department of Community Development. 1982. *City of Laredo Street Closing/Sales Policy Handbook*. Laredo: City of Laredo, Department of Community Development, 8 March.

Fly, E., and L. Fly. (N.d.) "Black Settlements in America." Unpublished study of the dynamics of black communities (with some focus on life along alleys).

Groth, P. 1981. "Streetgrids as Frameworks for Urban Variety." *The Harvard Architectural Review* 2 (Spring): 68–75.

Liebermann, Eva. 1984. Department of City Planning, City of San Francisco. Personal communication with authors.

Lubliner, Alan. 1984. Mayor's Office, City of San Francisco. Personal communication.

Moudon, A. V. 1984. "Streets USA: Old and New." Paper presented at the meeting of the International Association for the Study of People and their Physical Surroundings, Berlin, July.

———. 1986. *Built for Change: Neighborhood Architecture in San Francisco*. Cambridge: MIT Press.

Myrick, D. F. 1972. *San Francisco's Telegraph Hill*. Berkeley: Howell-North.

Planning and Community Affairs Agency. 1984. *Affordable Housing*, Local Government Regulatory and Administrative Techniques. State of Washington, May.

Razak, A. J. 1981. "Redeveloping the Redevelopment: The Denny Regrade." Master's thesis, Department of Architecture, University of Washington, Seattle.

Rubin, Mary. 1984. Jack Scott Associates, San Francisco. Personal communication.

Shotland, Steve. 1984. Department of City Planning, City of San Francisco. Personal communication.

Stein, C. 1971. *Toward New Towns in America*. Reprint, Cambridge: MIT Press.

Time. "Gold Paving, Laredo Shows its Street Smarts." 8 March 1982.

Untermann, R. K. 1984. *Accommodating the Pedestrian*. New York: Van Nostrand Reinhold.

Untermann, R. K. et al. 1980. *Street Ends*. Seattle: City of Seattle, Department of Parks and Recreation, September.

Villarreal, Carlos R. 1984. Director, Community Development Agency, City of Laredo. Personal communication.

Winkler, B. 1984. "Streets for Sale." Student paper, St. Edward's University, Austin, Texas, 18 June.

Wright, H. 1935. *Rehousing Urban America*. New York: Columbia University Press.

PART THREE

Streets Reclaimed

10.
Cars and People in Stockholm

MARINA BOTTA

The high quality of the contemporary environment in Stockholm can be attributed to urban planning and design policies carried out in an extremely systematic manner over the past century. These policies have integrated several levels of concerns, from regional planning to residential design, with consideration for employment, services, and transportation. Comprehensive planning in the Swedish capital has also been greatly aided by municipal ownership of most of the lands used for expansion since the turn of the century, which is attributable to an aggressive land acquisition policy on the part of the public sector (fig. 10-1). Because most of the land is in the public domain, planners have been able to control and steer the shape and character of new development and to retain a sizable amount of land accessible to the public.

The design of the street network in the Stockholm area is an example of such coordinated efforts. The evolution of plans and policies that governed the development of this network is indicative of the planning and design principles that have been used in Swedish urban development in general. The planning of street networks has gone hand in hand with urban expansion and the development of the suburbs surrounding the historic city center.

Because urban expansion has been felt since the turn of the century, planners have had to develop a supportive public transportation network, which, originally, took priority over the road network serving private cars. At the end of the nineteenth century, for instance, the first ring of suburban development had occurred along railway lines. Djursholm and Saltsjöbaden are examples of such suburbs: located among attractive landscapes at the end of the two oldest ur-

ban railroads, they were originally places for second homes but then quickly became year-round residences for the more affluent classes.

By the 1940s, however, new suburban development was less the result of a search for amenable environments than a response to an acute housing shortage in the city. At that time, suburbs were planned as independent residential communities to be linked to the center city by rapid transit. Urban development proceeded along with the development of the subway network (fig. 10-2): for example, subway stations also served as centers for the new residential districts, and road access was considered only secondary to subway access. The separation of pedestrian and vehicular traffic was, nonetheless, considered important, and the 1952 Stockholm Master Plan proposed a citywide network of separate routes for vehicles, bicycles, and pedestrians (fig. 10-3).

The increasing importance of private cars, however, demanded more investment in the road network. The 1960 Stockholm Traffic Plan formalized a system of highways radiating from the center of the city, linked by one ring road. In addition, it proposed that two roads, running north-south and east-west respectively, cross the historic center. As enthusiasm for the car as a means of transportation continued to grow, the 1970 Greater Stockholm Regional Plan proposed the construction of additional highways for rapid connection between the various suburban districts (fig. 10-4). The objective was to enable people living anywhere within the boundaries of the metropolitan area to have good vehicular connections to workplaces. Along with the new roads, plans for increased parking facilities were made. In the inner city, particularly, on-street parking was to be eliminated in favor of parking garages.

But the expansion economy that was at the root of

All photographs are by the author.

151

10-1. Land owned by the
Stockholm Municipality. (Source:
Stockholm Town Planning Office
1964: 21)

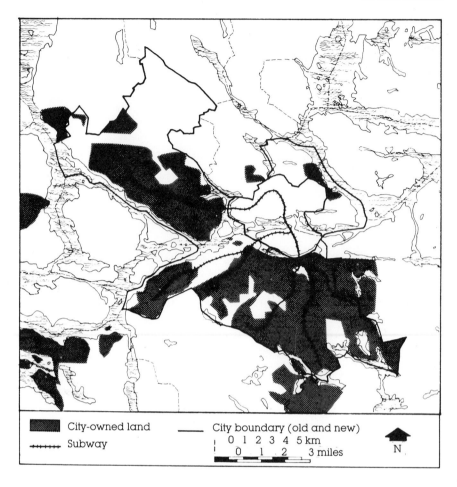

City-owned land   City boundary (old and new)

Subway

0 1 2 3 4 5 km

0   1   2   3 miles

N

10-2. Extension of the subway
systems related to the development
of the city. (Source: Stockholm Town
Planning Office 1972: 12–13)

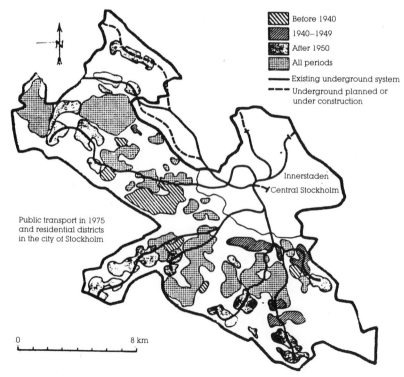

Before 1940

1940–1949

After 1950

All periods

Existing underground system

Underground planned or
under construction

Innerstaden
Central Stockholm

Public transport in 1975
and residential districts
in the city of Stockholm

0   8 km

10-3. Separating pedestrian and car traffic from subway system in Sergels Torg.

these plans came to an abrupt end in the early 1970s. The urban population stopped growing, the housing market reached saturation, and the health of the economy as a whole became questionable (fig. 10-5). For planners, it was a time of reflection, analysis, and criticism. Preoccupation with housing production changed to concerns for the quality of the environments created and, particularly, for their sociological and psychological effects on the residents. The provision of adequate services, from shopping to parks, became a central concern.

Priorities regarding transportation needs also changed from accommodating the growing number of automobiles to controlling the negative effects of cars on the urban environment and repairing the damages made earlier. Noise, pollution, and safety were part of the evaluation of public transit, automobile transportation, and pedestrian movement policies (fig. 10-6). Central planning issues revolved around street livability, the habitability of spaces along streets, and the

fragmentation of the urban areas due to traffic problems. Bicycling and walking took on increasing importance in policies for future transportation (fig. 10-7). Within this climate, not surprisingly, the construction of many of the new roads proposed in the 1960s was cancelled and traffic was relocated within the existing network (see fig. 10-4c and d). Improving the existing infrastructure had become a primary goal.

Suburban areas were replanned as small independent towns: safe and sociable areas, especially for children and others who did not have complete access to the environment (fig. 10-8). Cars were parked under the houses, and towns were transformed into pedestrian precincts with direct access on foot to open spaces. In the inner city, traffic planning, then renamed "traffic reorganization," became a central issue in urban revitalization schemes. Not only were buildings rehabilitated and services modernized, but new open spaces and traffic-free zones were created.

A new traffic plan, proposed in 1977, took into ac-

10-4. Reduction in the number of
arterials: <u>a.</u> main roads as per the
1960 Traffic Plan; <u>b.</u> main roads as
per the 1966 Regional Plan; <u>c.</u> main
roads as per the 1977 Traffic Plan;
<u>d.</u> main roads, 1980 (Source:
Stockholm City Streets and Traffic
Administration 1981: 15)

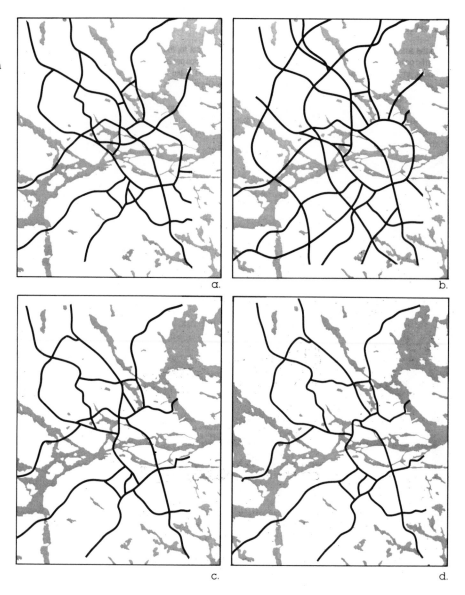

10-5. Population peaks in the 1960s. (Source: Stockholm
City Streets and Traffic Administration 1981: 4)

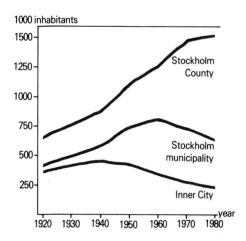

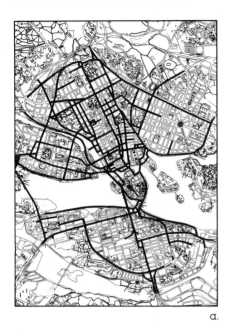 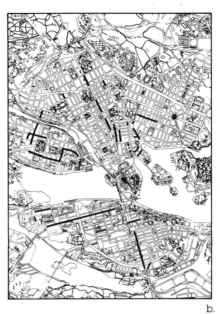

a.   b.

10-6. Noise and pollution as important aspects of traffic planning: <u>a.</u> streets in the inner city, with a noise level exceeding 70 dBA (mean energy level per 24 hours, with 70 dBA at a building facade being equivalent to 40 to 45 dBA inside an average building); <u>b.</u> streets with buildings on both sides, where the World Health Organization's recommended carbon monoxide levels are probably exceeded. (Source: Stockholm City Streets and Traffic Administration 1981: 11)

10-7. Nybrogatan planned for pedestrian and bicycle circulation.

10-8. The suburb of Kista, developed in the late 1970s, is a small pedestrian town where open spaces are designed for walking, cycling, and socializing and where cars remain at the periphery of the neighborhoods. (Source: Municipality of Stockholm 1983: 8)

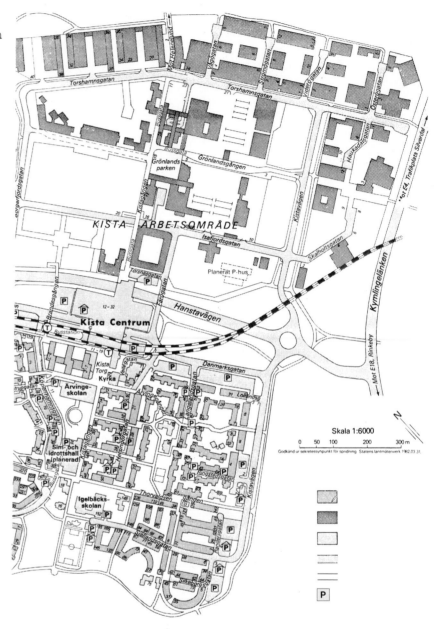

count the new concerns for the social and ecological impact of traffic on the environment. (Stockholm Town Planning Office 1977a). The goal was to reduce automobile traffic by 20 percent (or, to 125,000 car trips per 24 hours in the inner city) and to redirect it away from residential areas and from the city center. Other important elements of the plan dealt with improving road safety and air pollution, as well as with developing the public transportation network (there were 48 kilometers [29.8 miles] of bus lanes in 1980). Finally, it proposed that a reduction in parking capacities in the city center be accompanied by an increase in the cost of storing cars there. The plan is successfully being implemented. Most residential districts are

being divided into zones with a limited number of vehicular access points (fig. 10-9). Streets that transverse neighborhoods are usually narrow and one-way (fig. 10-10). Sound-insulating devices have been installed on buildings along streets with the most traffic. Within the pedestrian areas, special lanes are now reserved for public transit and bicycles.

Traffic reorganization has also supported urban revitalization, and a number of families now find the city center more desirable than the suburban areas farther away. As old buildings were cleaned up and apartments modernized, streets have been redesigned as public open spaces catering to pedestrian needs, children's play, and adult recreation. Now that many

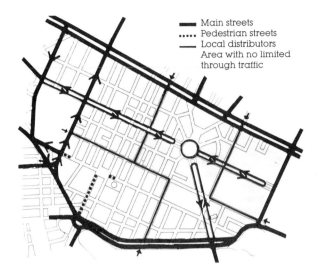

Main streets
Pedestrian streets
Local distributors
Area with no limited
through traffic

10-9. The Östermalm area is divided into zones with a limited number of access points for cars. (Source: Stockholm City Streets and Traffic Administration 1981: 13)

streets within the neighborhoods are dead ends (fig. 10-11), sidewalks take over most of the roadway (fig. 10-12), and paving, planting, and street furnishing programs have been implemented with the participation of residents (fig. 10-13). Finally, the system of street and traffic signs was redesigned to fit the policies.

Another important aspect of traffic reorganization has been the educational process introduced to make citizens aware of preferred roads, optimal driving speeds, and the best places for walking or bicycling. An all-media campaign was organized, which included articles in the daily papers, radio and television debates, and exhibitions, with the assumption that people would accept the necessary changes if they understood the intentions of the new policies. School programs also regularly addressed the issue of traffic and movement in the city.

Livable streets, reduced automobile access to roads, expanded public transit service, and increased opportunities for pedestrian and bicycle movement are not being achieved in some areas at the expense of others: both the inner city and the surrounding suburbs are benefitting from these policies. While in many other parts of the world such policies would entail interminable conflicts between automobilists and residents (Appleyard 1981), in Stockholm, the automobile is being tamed thanks to a broad educational process, which helped to change urban residents' attitudes toward the car and to develop a sense of responsibility for the maintenance and care given to the public right-of-way.

10-10. Limited car access in Karlavägen.

a.

10-11. Streets dead-end for car circulation at intersections: a. newly restored buildings along Sybillegatan, reclaimed as an open space; b. Smålandsgatan (note passage left for emergency vehicles).

b.

10-12. Median-strip crossing is prohibited for cars in Karlavägen.

10-13. Distinguishing between people and car spaces with paving, planting, and street furniture: <u>a</u> Strandvägen, <u>b.</u> Karlavägen, <u>c.</u> Grevgatan.

a.

b.

c.

REFERENCES

Appleyard, D. 1981. *Livable Streets*. Berkeley: University of California Press.

Municipality of Stockholm. 1983. *Kista Husby Akalla*. Stockholm: Municipality of Stockholm.

Ödman, E., and G. B. Dahlberg. 1970. *Urbanization in Sweden*. Stockholm: Allmänna Förlaget.

SL Trafikkontoret. 1979. *Trafikspolitiska åtgärder för bättre innerstadsmiljö*. Stockholm: SL Trafikkontoret.

Stockholm City Streets and Traffic Administration. 1981. *Traffic Planning in Stockholm*. Stockholm: Stockholm City Streets and Traffic Administration.

Stockholms Kommun. 1980. *Miljöpolitiskt handlingsprogram 1980*. Stockholm: Stockholms Kommun.

Stockholm Town Planning Office. 1964. *Stockholm: Regional and City Planning*. Stockholm: Stockholm Town Planning Office.

———. 1972. *Stockholm—Urban Environment*. Stockholm: Stockholm Town Planning Office.

———. 1977a. *Trafik Plan 1977*. Stockholm: Stockholm Town Planning Office.

———. 1977b. *Cityplan 1977*. Stockholm: Stockholm Town Planning Office.

11.
The Alaskan Opportunity

NEIL KLOPFENSTEIN
AND LINDA SNYDER

Located across the Wrangell Narrows in the southeast portion of the state, Kupreanof is one of Alaska's smallest cities (fig. 11-1). Many of its fifty residents work in nearby Petersburg (population 4,000), several are fisherman, some retired, most are white. The city is made up of single-family houses on several-acre lots, most of which have beach frontage. Kupreanof has no exclusively commercial uses, but several residents maintain home occupations, such as arts and crafts. Residents have their own sewer and water systems; only a few produce their own electricity with small, fuel-operated generators—the only means available.

There are no roads and, consequently, no wheeled vehicles in Kupreanof. Residents travel within the community sometimes by foot but primarily by shallow draft skiffs that can be beached or tied to small, floating docks (fig. 11-2). Boats take them to Petersburg, a half mile away, and to the outside world.

Settled since the early 1900s, Kupreanof did not incorporate until 1975, when residents felt obliged to protect what they saw as a special community. Kupreanof's 1984 Policy Plan (Klopfenstein and Winograd 1984) defines the community as a rural, sheltered, and low-density environment that has no taxes or urban services but has close affinities with the natural surroundings. The city's name comes from the island on which it is located, called Kupreanof after Captain Ivan Andreas Kupreanov, governor of the Russian-American Colonies from 1836 to 1840.

After the Alaska legislature passed the Municipal Entitlement Act of 1978, Kupreanof received title to 180 acres of state-owned land within its boundaries.[1] The city prepared a subdivision plan for the 180 acres with the intent of selling at least part to the private

All photographs are by Neil Klopfenstein.

11-1. Kupreanof is located midway between Seattle and Anchorage (Source: Klopfenstein and Winograd 1984: 11)

sector. Development pressures and the disposal of municipal land prompted the city to prepare a comprehensive policy plan, whose major purpose was to preserve the existing character and life-style of the community (fig. 11-3).

The "roadless" status of Kupreanof is seen by residents as an important element in preserving the community's uniqueness. The transportation section of the 1984 Kupreanof Policy Plan states that, "the City of Kupreanof shall oppose all road construction within its boundaries" (Klopfenstein and Winograd 1984). This policy has been implemented by the adoption of an ordinance that bans motor vehicles within the corporate limits. In addition, zoning and subdivision regulations prohibit any land use that requires the support of land-operated motor vehicles.

11-2. Roadless communities: boats and planes as primary means of transportation. (Source: Department of Community and Regional Affairs, State of Alaska 1984)

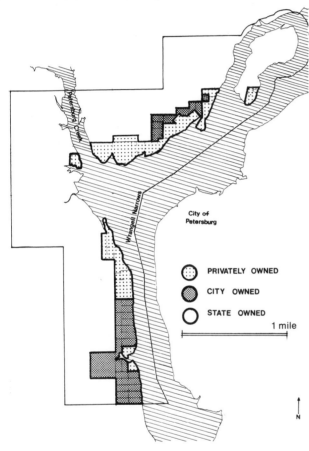

11-3. Kupreanof owns a large share of the coastal land which is considered well-suited for development. (Source: Klopfenstein and Winograd 1984: 30)

maintained as a walkway by adjacent owners" (Klopfenstein and Winograd 1984). Also, a shoreline setback requirement prohibits development near the water's edge. The beach is thus kept open for pedestrian travel and boat moorage.

With water as the primary medium for internal and external transportation, the city supports the development of a pedestrian trail system for recreational use. As formulated in the Kupreanof Plan, "the city shall develop a recreational-trails plan that includes trail routes, facilities, funding sources for construction and maintenance, labor sources, material sources, and construction priorities for each phase" (Klopfenstein and Winograd 1984). Although a physical plan has yet to be prepared, a map of trails has been developed (fig. 11-4).

Kupreanof is one of many Alaskan communities to receive title to considerable amounts of public land. So far, however, this community stands among only a few that have sought to preserve their unique characteristics through planning policies and land-use regulations. These policies and regulations will most profoundly affect the largest owner of developable land, the City of Kupreanof itself, as it prepares to subdivide and sell some of its municipal land holdings.

The remainder of this chapter moves from the case of Kupreanof to a more general discussion of how Alaskan communities recently gained title to public lands, what they are doing to plan for their use, and how both the development and use of these holdings can be improved.

The city further maintains its roadless status by accommodating boat transportation. Subdivision regulations require all lots to have beach frontage or to have access to an easement that provides direct access to the beach. The corresponding policy states that "all residential lots subdivided, by the City or by a private party, shall have access to beach frontage where a small boat can be beached or moored to a buoy. The access shall be held as public right-of-way that will be

AVAILABILITY OF STATE AND FEDERAL LANDS FOR MUNICIPALITIES

Although Alaska is the least populous state, its growth rate is among the highest in the nation. In 1960, a year after statehood, the population was approximately 200,000; by 1980, it had more than doubled, with most of the growth occurring in the Anchorage

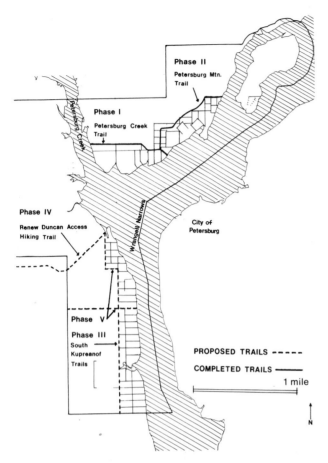

11-4. Kupreanof's trail plan. (Source: Klopfenstein and Winograd 1984: 36)

area. Fifty thousand in the mid-1960s, the greater Anchorage population today is about 240,000 (Sewell 1984).

Covering almost 590,000 square miles, Alaska represents one-fifth of the area of the continental United States. Although only a fraction of the state's land is developed, land available for private developments is scarce, especially in high-growth areas. This is partly due to the large federal and state land holdings. Any transfer of state and federal lands to local governments and thence to the private sector, is, therefore, significant.

Large amounts of undeveloped land have been transferred to Alaskan municipalities by two legislative acts, one at the state level and the other at the federal level. The first, enacted in 1963 and revised in 1970 and 1978 by the Alaska Legislature, is now known as the Municipal Entitlement Act. It established specific land entitlements for Alaska's eleven countylike boroughs and combined city/borough municipalities. A formula, provided to determine land entitlements in the remaining incorporated areas, also

offered communities planning to incorporate in the future "10 percent of the maximum total acreage of vacant, unappropriated, unreserved (state) land within the boundaries of each city" (State of Alaska [AS 29.18.202] 1978). For example, if the state owns 1,000 acres of land within a given community's boundaries, that community is entitled to 100 acres. The act, in effect, encourages incorporation by providing municipalities with a local revenue source (through land sales and subsequent taxation) as well as a community development tool.

The "10 percent formula" benefits large incorporated areas with large state holdings. For example, the Municipality of Anchorage was entitled to almost 45,000 acres of land, while the City and Borough of Juneau received over 19,000 acres of property. Skagway and Seward, communities with a population of about one thousand each, received about 500 acres of land under the act. Municipalities with small incorporated areas and small state holdings, however, received little land from this state provision. The act, moreover, was generally beneficial to predominately white communities.

The second piece of legislation affecting municipal land holdings is the Alaska Native Claims Settlement Act (ANCSA), passed by the U.S. Congress in 1971. This legislation provides small, predominantly native communities with relatively large amounts of municipal land; indeed, the ANCSA was designed to settle the land and resource claims of this population. The terms of the settlement included the transfer of land and resource rights from the federal government to locally based (village) and regionally based corporations of exclusive native membership.

A provision of the act, known as 14(c)(3), requires locally based village corporations to transfer no less that 1,280 acres of their acquired holdings to the city in which they are based.[2] The intent of the provision is to ensure that the communities have adequate land for future expansion, rights-of-way, and other community purposes. Not all Alaskan municipalities benefit from the ANCSA reconveyance provision. Only those with a village corporation, and therefore, a recognized local tribe, are entitled to 14(c)(3) lands. Yet, those that do benefit are richly rewarded: since almost all of Alaska's native communities have a developed area of less than 1,000 acres, the reconveyance acreage can often be two to three times the size of a community's developed area, or larger.

The selection of lands that should be transferred to a municipality, as well as the transfer timetable, is determined cooperatively by municipal and village corporation officials. These decisions are necessarily of a political nature and often controversial. No deadline for reconveyance is provided in the act, so municipal and corporation officials have moved slowly to complete land reconveyances. To date, only a handful of village corporations have completed the transfer of their 14(c)(3) lands to the entitled municipalities.

ISSUES RELATED TO LAND DISPOSITION

Because land disposition concerns vary among Alaskan communities, and especially between urban areas such as Anchorage and communities in rural Alaska, it is important to give a little background on both areas before addressing the major land-disposition issues.

More urban than most Alaskan communities, Anchorage is a sprawling city, whose population, since 1980, has grown by 39.9 percent. Smaller but nevertheless similar to Denver, Albuquerque, or Salt Lake City, Anchorage offers most urban amenities and suffers from many urban problems. Although expensive by "Lower 48" standards, the city's cost of living is relatively low for Alaska.

In Anchorage, the growth-related provision of roads, sewers, schools, and parks, and the growing shortage of land available for those purposes, have made the use of the newly acquired municipal land an issue of uppermost importance. Of a total land area of 1,955 square miles, only about 7,000 undeveloped acres remain in private ownership (Phelps 1984). Population increases, however, have yielded a demand for housing that is rapidly consuming this available land, while strong concerns for the preservation of natural woodlands and wilderness close to home serve to inhibit development.

Most rural Alaskan communities have fewer than 1,000 people and, unlike their Lower 48 counterparts, they serve no hinterland or nearby inhabited rural area. A village of 500 persons generally contains most of its population within its boundaries. Few such communities have access to the national road network; residents usually travel to the outside world by boat or plane. Communities with connecting roads are often more than an hour's drive from the next village and hundreds of miles away from large cities like Anchorage and Fairbanks. In communities with no road links, supplies and fuel are shipped in by barge or flown in by plane on a periodic, but often irregular, basis. In some western Alaskan communities, bulk commodities, such as fuel oil, are delivered only during the summer months, when the Bering Sea is ice-free. Transportation over long distances and population dispersal drive the costs of goods very high: for example, milk can reach $4.00 per gallon and a gallon of gasoline can cost over $2.00. Although state-supported construction projects and social service programs have created a few new jobs in rural communities, employment, especially for the unskilled, is difficult to find and often seasonal. Many families still depend on local game and fish for a substantial portion of their food supply. In general, most rural Alaskan communities can be characterized as poorer, more expensive, and more isolated than their Lower 48 counterparts.

As new municipal land is becoming available in these rural communities, local residents compete with other, wealthier Alaskans and develop the land for themselves. Housing is in short supply and expensive, and two or more families often share what in other areas would be single-family accommodations. Because private land is also in short supply and priced out of the reach of most families, communities were hard-pressed before ANCSA reconveyances. With the receipt of land from the state and the village native corporations, most rural municipalities now want to ease their housing shortage by selling inexpensive residential building lots to local residents.

PLANNING PROCESSES FOR LAND DISPOSITION IN URBAN ALASKA

In urban communities, the task of planning for the development and use of municipal lands has generally been undertaken by a professional municipal staff in conjunction with the local planning commission or, as in Anchorage's case, by a specially appointed commission. In most cases, municipal lands have been inventoried and then placed into "use" categories. Juneau is following a straightforward process that involves, first, the development of a land classification ordinance that identifies "use" categories and, second, the appropriate classification of all 19,900 acres of municipal lands, according to this scheme. A third, and yet to be completed, step will be to formulate a management plan for the lands. The final step will consist of the disposal of lands slated for private development.

The Heritage Land Bank

Anchorage has undertaken the most comprehensive municipal lands planning process in the state. Of the land entitlement of 44,093 acres, approximately 22,000 acres have been either patented (transferred from the state to the municipality) or approved to be patented. Some 12,600 acres have been committed to various public uses. Decisions were made by municipal officials under heavy pressure to acquire certain lands for recreation and school sites in new neighborhoods. For example, Pt. Campbell, a former military base in southwest Anchorage, is being developed as a cross-country ski headquarters.

The need for a process to dispose of the 9,415 remaining acres led to the creation of the Heritage Land Bank in August 1983 (Rue 1984). The Heritage Land Bank was established by municipal ordinance "to manage and dispose of land determined to be surplus to the Municipality of Anchorage's needs and to ensure that funds obtained therefrom, or funds obtained in lieu of land entitlement, are used for acquisition of future Municipal land needs, thereby promoting orderly development and achievement of the goals of the Comprehensive Plan" (City of Anchorage Muncipal Code [25.40.10]).

The Advisory Commission of the Heritage Land Bank is charged with advising the municipal staff, the mayor, and the assembly (the equivalent of a city council) on all matters of Heritage Land Bank activity, including the acquisition, disposal, and management of lands in its charge. The commission recently completed an inventory of the 9,415 acres, established its working procedures, and began to make parcel-level decisions. Members of the commission soon realized that assuring the protection of the public interest in parcels to be leased or sold went beyond negotiating advantageous prices and terms. Easements, open spaces, and road rights-of-way needed to be set aside. In some cases, the development options for the recipients of the land needed to be limited. Now, when preparing to dispose of a small parcel, the Land Bank staff notifies all relevant municipal and state agencies to inquire about utility easements, street rights-of-way, and pedestrian trail easements. In simple transactions, these and any other restrictions are drawn or written on the plat and subsequently recorded.

For larger parcels in which public interests are more complex, dedications for public purposes are tied to master-site development plans that are incorporated into lease or sale agreements. In one case, a 16-acre tract will be used to provide separate locations for new buildings, which will be constructed by several independent community service organizations. A master development plan will be prepared, dividing the tract into smaller parcels and reserving open space and road rights-of-way. When the plan is completed, each organization will execute a lease with the municipality for one of these parcels and will be required by provision of the lease to (1) reserve specific pedestrian and utility easements, road rights-of-way, and common open spaces; (2) locate buildings in a defined buildable zone most appropriate for construction; (3) maintain the reserved open spaces for public use; and

(4) submit building and site plans to the planning staff and the Planning and Zoning Commission for review.

The Heritage Land Bank has great potential to fundamentally alter Alaskans' attitudes toward the land. Much like the western United States in the last century, Alaska is the frontier, where land is wilderness to conquer and exploit. The Land Bank is now making it clear that public land is not free for the taking. In its short period of operation, major organizational problems have been solved. Anchorage's citizens are beginning to look to the Land Bank as a means to protect the Alaska they value in their own neighborhoods.

As the Land Bank commission and its staff make day-to-day decisions, numerous other issues arise that must be resolved. First, it is not yet clear how compliance with the development plan restrictions will be insured, beyond the simple cancellation of the transaction. Some of the enforcement methods under consideration are performance bonds, conditional release of the property pending the accomplishment of all requirements, and issuance of options to purchase the tract, which become effective only when the requirements are met. Responsibility for monitoring continued provision of services with public benefits, such as maintaining open space, must also be established.

Another issue to be resolved is the commission's need for increased budgetary autonomy from the city administration. Finally, the commission has yet to exert any level of design control over such issues as location of open space, wetland and woodland preservation, architectural character, and so on. The commission has so far preferred to require a Planning and Zoning Commission review of proposed site plans without specifying the standards to be met. This process has shortcomings, particularly because of the lack of certainty for the land recipient. Also, costs borne by the recipient for construction and administration are increased over a minimum period of six months during which the review occurs. In the case of a profit-making corporation, the viability of the project may be threatened. Nonprofit social or community service organizations are not typically skilled in managing such a process. Were the commission to state its design goals explicitly, they could act as criteria for reviewers and relieve the uncertainty.

Land and Transportation Planning

The municipality and the state are jointly responsible for planning Anchorage's street system. A computer model, which estimates present and projected trips based on zoning classifications, distributes the trips on the present road network and determines the size and location of major and minor arterials, collectors, and other types of streets. The entire system is approved by the municipal assembly following the Official Streets and Highways Plan, which also contains standards for right-of-way widths and cross sections. Construction projects to upgrade the roads are then listed in the Transportation Improvement Program, the capital budgeting document. Owners of properties adjacent to streets shown in the Transportation Improvement Program are required to dedicate the right-of-way for a street's eventual upgrading when the property is platted prior to sale or development.

Also considered are systems serving the nontraditional commuters who bike and ski the city's green belt and trail systems. Trail locations are mapped in the Areawide Trails Plan, which is also approved by the municipal assembly. Dedications of trail easements are required by the subdivision regulations when a property is platted or rezoned.

Pedestrians fare less well than cyclists or drivers. Neither the streets plan nor trails plan provides sufficiently for sidewalks, which public engineers have often eliminated to reduce road construction costs (see chap. 19, by R. K. Untermann). If required, sidewalks need be on only one side of residential streets. Consequently, when built, they are often too narrow and abut the curb. Not only do they fail to separate the pedestrian from traffic adequately, but they are often used as a dumping place for snow cleared from traffic lanes. Although, by ordinance, walks must be cleared of snow by abutting owners, most are impassable in winter because of heavy ice buildup.

As a landowner, the Heritage Land Bank is required to reserve street rights-of-way and trail easements. The extent of the Land Bank's holdings and its power to create lease provisions and deed restrictions give it the opportunity to go beyond the minimum transportation requirements. Streets, sidewalks, and trails could be integrated much more effectively by requiring master-site planning and the design of internal circulation systems. Rights-of-way that are wide enough to provide a buffer separating sidewalks from streets could be reserved for both internal and perimeter streets. Landscaped streets could be a model for private developers and public agencies alike. Maintenance requirements, such as snow storage areas, could be integrated into the design. Increasing the Land Bank commission's involvement with design will be the key to enhancing Anchorage's transportation system as public land assets are passed on to private control.

PLANNING PROCESSES FOR LAND DISPOSITION IN RURAL ALASKA

Few rural communities have undertaken comprehensive planning processes for their municipal lands. Some have developed policies for municipal land use during the preparation of local comprehensive plans and coastal management programs. Most, however, have only just begun to discuss how to proceed with the development of their lands. This low level of planning can generally be attributed to a lack of staff and resources.

The primary goal is to use at least part of the municipal land holdings to ease local housing shortages by subdividing them into inexpensive building lots for disposal to local residents. The disposal process, however, is lengthy and studded with problems. In many communities, several years can pass from the time the decision to subdivide land is made until the time the land sale is completed.

Once a community has determined what land to sell (which in itself can be a problem), several steps must be completed before disposal can take place. First, the community must decide what improvements should be made to properties and how they should be financed. The use of bonding to pay for local improvements is not always an option in rural Alaska: many native communities levy no property tax because most of the property within their corporate limits is restricted from taxation by deeds issued by the Bureau of Indian Affairs. Although it would be possible to include assessment in the lot price as a more expedient method to finance subdivision improvements, such a finance method would unduly increase the price of lots intended for an already disadvantaged population.

The second major step in the land disposal process is the determination of a property's terms of sale. The community must decide whether its land should be sold at market rate or at a price that is more affordable to people in the community, and whether or not restrictions should be placed on the property to prevent speculation and to encourage rapid development. Finally, a decision must be made whether to sell the land on contract or to require buyers to secure their own financing.

The most difficult step in this land disposal process is devising a method of getting land to those who require it most: local residents in need of building lots. Because private land is scarce, land speculation has been a problem in many rural Alaskan communities, especially in those that are attractive recreational areas for urban Alaskans. Many rural officials fear that an unrestricted land disposal would draw people from Anchorage and Juneau to buy land for recrea-

tional or investment purposes. Yet when one municipality decided to enact provisions for giving local
residents preference, the measures were struck down
by the Alaska Supreme Court. State officials are at
present working with attorneys and municipal officials
to develop acceptable legal solutions to this thorny
issue.

CONSIDERATIONS FOR IMPROVED DESIGN

As owners and developers of land, Alaskan municipalities are in a position to influence the design of their
community positively. The efficient placement of
infrastructure, the importance of climatic considerations, and the unique value of community characteristics, which together could provide the basis for good
subdivision layout and street design in Alaska, have
already been recognized by some municipal officials.

Local Transportation Plans

Rural land disposal processes can be directly influenced by local transportation plans to establish detailed street layouts. Because of the high cost of
infrastructure in rural Alaska, street layout and utility
placement are generally considered during the selection of land for municipal disposal. However, because
the extension of a rural community's street network
occurs when a new subdivision is developed, street
and utility plans are usually drawn up only *after* a
subdivision site has been selected. Combining street
and utility plans with the development of a comprehensive plan should, instead, lead the subdivision process.

Infrastructure

The cost of providing streets, sewers, and waterlines,
which can be twice as high as in the rest of the United
States, should and does influence subdivision layout
and street design in rural Alaska. A variety of factors
contribute to the high cost of construction. With the
exception of gravel, no construction materials are locally produced. Labor costs, often over half of a project's price, are high because of the cost of living.
Factors such as rough topography, poor soils, perma-
frost, and muskeg also contribute to the high costs.
Costs could be reduced by carefully considering infrastructure placement and use in subdivision design.
Subdivision regulations that allow clustering of dwelling units for the purpose of open space preservation
also promote efficient infrastructure design and should
be encouraged by cities and villages.

Climatic Conditions

Snow removal and storage should be major determinants of subdivision layout and street design. The
street cross sections now in use in Anchorage, which
reflect the need of more moderate climates, should be
made wider—with 5- to 10-foot buffers between the
cub and the sidewalk and wider travel lanes to allow
for snow storage and space for equipment maneuver-
ing. As sidewalks are often used for snow storage, winter walking is difficult and sometimes dangerous. Also
extensive use of de-icing agents and salts inhibits tree
growth on streets; alternative nontoxic agents, such as
sand, are preferable.

In northwestern Alaska, where the landscape is flat
and winter winds fierce, drifting snow can easily close
streets. Planners in the State Department of Community and Regional Affairs have helped some communities design subdivisions that minimize snow
drifting by aligning streets with prevailing winds (fig.
11-5). In southeast Alaska, the landscape is very hilly,
and precipitation can reach over 100 inches per year.

11-5. Drifting snow as a major design consideration.
(Source: Harrison et al. 1983: 58)

RIGHT-OF-WAY RULES TO FOLLOW

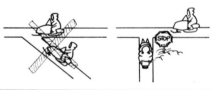

AVOID STEEP GRADES
Roads should not run
straight up steep hills.
Locate roads so the
grade is gradual. This
makes the road safer
and usable when it is
wet and icy.

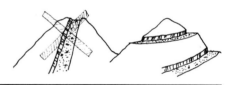

INTERSECTIONS
SHOULD BE AT 90°
Intersections with
sharp angles are dan-
gerous because vehi-
cles tend not to stop at
them.

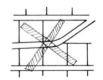

AVOID UNNECESSARY ROADS AND TRAILS
Usually, only one side
of a lot needs to be
next to a public road
or trail. Also, short cuts
that people use can
often be abandoned
without causing seri-
ous inconvenience to
villagers.

MINIMIZE DRIFTING
SNOW
In flat, windy country,
new roads and trails
can be lined up so the
wind blows the snow
from the streets.

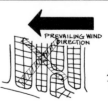
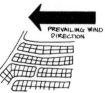

Deep snow and freezing rain can make steep streets impassable. In hilly downtown Juneau, many residents abandon their cars and use the publicly owned and maintained pedestrian walkways and hillside staircases when the weather turns nasty (fig. 11-6). Pedestrian alternatives to vehicle transportation, like those in Juneau, should be considered in subdivision layout and street design.

Downtown retail pedestrian improvements have been undertaken in Anchorage and Juneau. In both cities, design approaches used in other states have now been abandoned in favor of designs that reflect local conditions. Paving materials such as brick and tile have been replaced with fine aggregate concrete to reduce surface slipperiness. Visual interest has been maintained with lighting and graphics, both important during the long, dark Alaskan winters.

Short winter days should also be considered in street design and subdivision layout. At latitudes where daily winter sunshine lasts only a few hours (if at all), solar orientation is important. New private subdivisions in Alaska's cities generally have not been designed with climatic factors in mind. The sale of municipal land now offers planners the opportunity to improve conditions by carefully considering them.

Local Characteristics

Rural Alaskan communities have unique characteristics that set them apart from one another, as well as from communities in the Lower 48. Many native communities in southeast Alaska, for example, defy the grid and instead string themselves along one or two streets that parallel the coast (fig. 11-7). Predominantly white communities, however such as Petersburg and Skagway, are designed with the grid, like their small-town counterparts in the Midwest. In western Alaska, some communities are centered along a boardwalk with buildings densely settled beside it (fig. 11-8). The one or two roads that exist in those communities may connect to an outlying airstrip or a harbor but they clearly do not represent the "backbone" of the towns. As noted earlier, a few coastal communities like Kupreanof and Tenakee Springs are completely roadless. The latter is a densely built settlement that hugs the coast. Many of its buildings stand over the water on spruce pilings. As in Kupreanof, residents view roadlessness as a unique local characteristic contributing to a self-sufficient life-style that is "close to nature." In Tenakee Springs, new subdivisions will have no roads.

Municipal officials in other Alaskan communities are challenged to identify those local characteristics that are worth incorporating into the designs of their municipal subdivisions. By contrast, Anchorage, Fairbanks, and other towns linked by the state highway

11-6. In Juneau, the street network includes city-maintained stairs if the terrain becomes too steep to accommodate cars.

system find that the visual, social, and life-style oriented qualities desired by Alaskans have already been destroyed by arterials and strip commercial development. Northern Lights and Benson Boulevards in Anchorage are examples of the worst kind. Miles of unrelieved asphalt, gravel, and buildings with cheap construction materials create a desolate environment. Public concern over ugly roads, parking lots, and the intrusion of large-scale office buildings in residential neighborhoods has given rise to several efforts to correct the problems. Commercial zoning regulations are being revised to require landscaping and sign control. Tree plantings are now required by municipal regulations in all road construction projects, and design review is conducted by neighborhood committees.

IMPLEMENTING IMPROVED DESIGN

Infrastructure and utility placement, climate, and unique community characteristics are key factors that

11-7. Main Street in the native village of Hoonah. While many of the white villages in southeastern Alaska are laid out on a grid, the streets of native villages follow the coast.

11-8. Boardwalks constitute the primary street network in many Eskimo villages. Vehicular streets are located at the periphery of the villages.

should be considered in the design of subdivisions in Alaska's municipal lands. Because state planners, private consultants, and municipal planners will all be involved in the subdivision design process, each group needs to develop a competence to ensure that these key factors are considered.

State of Alaska planners, through the Department of Community and Regional Affairs, provide local planning assistance to rural communities on an as-needed basis. The subdivision and sale of municipal land is a major planning issue in many rural communities. As a result, state planners must be familiar with elements of good subdivision design to assist rural officials.

Private engineering firms are likely to be called on to design most subdivisions on municipal lands in both urban and rural Alaska. They need to develop an appreciation of Alaska's unique problems for the proper fulfillment of this task. The participation of landscape architects in subdivision design teams will help in solving design problems that engineers often consider peripheral, such as pedestrian and recreation circulation patterns and native plant landscaping.

Especially in urban Alaska, municipal planners will likely have to fulfill both design and review capacities. In Anchorage, responsibility for overseeing major arterial roads has recently been taken from civil engineers in the Municipal Public Works Department and given to planners in the mayor's capital projects office. An increasingly powerful review role is being adopted by neighborhood organizations. The city government hopes that with the involvement both of planners and neighborhood groups, more municipal land will be better designed through constructive review of the work of private consultants and incorporation of the neighborhood's sentiments into design plans.

NOTES

1. The city was actually not eligible to receive land under the Municipal Entitlement Act because of title restrictions on state land within its boundaries. However, 180 acres of state land were transferred to the city through other means, for which the Municipal Entitlement Act provided the impetus.
2. Village corporations consisting of exclusive native membership and limited to natives who are members of the local village tribe have been given land and resource rights near the village in which they are based. *City*, in this case, refers to the municipal government of a community, as defined by Alaska statutes.

REFERENCES

Ambio Magazine 13, no. 4 (1984): 256–57.

City of Anchorage. 1984. *Anchorage Municipal Code* 1984 Revision. Anchorage: City of Anchorage.

City and Borough of Juneau. 1984. *City and Borough of Juneau.* Press Release on Municipal Lands, May 25.

Department of Community and Regional Affairs, State of Alaska. 1984. *Southern Southeast Community Profiles.* Juneau: Department of Community and Regional Affairs.

Harrison, G., and Associates. 1983. *Community Planning for ANCSA 14 (c) Land Reconveyances.* Anchorage: Department of Community and Regional Affairs.

Klopfenstein, N., and I. Winograd. 1984. *Kupreanof Policy Plan.* Kupreanof, Alaska: City of Kupreanof.

Phelps, Bruce. 1984. Municipality of Anchorage. Personal communication with authors, October.

Rue, S. 1984. *Heritage Land Bank Inventory Study, a Report on Municipal Lands in Anchorage.* Anchorage: Municipality of Anchorage.

Scholes, Peter. 1984. Municipality of Anchorage. Personal communication with authors, October.

Sewell, Richard. 1984. Municipality of Anchorage. Personal communication with authors, October.

State of Alaska. 1961. *Alaska, State Statutes.* Title 29. Revised 1978. Juneau: State Capitol, State of Alaska.

Waring, K., and Associates. 1982. *Municipal Land Programs —State Conveyed Lands.* Anchorage: Department of Community and Regional Affairs.

12.
Portland's Arterial Streets Classification Policy

STEVE DOTTERRER

Portland, Oregon's Arterial Streets Classification Policy (ASCP) is the city's official set of guidelines for the use of streets. It is not a transportation plan in the traditional sense—that is, a list of transportation projects needed to meet current and future travel demands. Rather, the ASCP recognizes the street right-of-way as one of the most valuable resources controlled by the city and that, as such, it need not be used only for transportation purposes. The policy has the twin goals of providing efficient movement for people and goods and protecting the livability of Portland. These goals are in general accord with the traditional legal purposes of streets: the provision of access, light, and air.

The ASCP classifies all publicly owned or controlled rights-of-way, including arterial and local residential streets but excluding air, water, or railroad transportation routes. It is integrated with regional transportation planning through the Metropolitan Planning Organization, the transit agency, and the state Highway Department. Therefore, although it is called an arterial policy, the ASCP actually deals with

the entire vehicular traffic system, from the interstate freeways to local cul-de-sacs (fig. 12-1).

The ASCP divides the city into five transportation districts (excluding the downtown, which is governed by an entirely different policy) (fig. 12-2). These districts have been demarcated with regard to the major natural and man-made boundaries within the city as well as to the different age and development characteristics of the city's various areas.

As with most transportation policies or plans, the ASCP classifies or designates streets for certain functions. However, the ASCP classifies a street based on its *desired* future function (determined via an extensive citizen participation program, described below). This means that a number of streets are classified at "lower" designations than their current functional operations. In particular, a number of residential streets that currently have traffic controls to permit their operation as peak-hour commuter streets are designated as local streets in the policy.

Every street right-of-way is given at least two designations—one for its desired auto-traffic function and

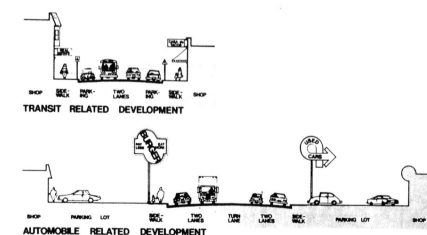

TRANSIT RELATED DEVELOPMENT

AUTOMOBILE RELATED DEVELOPMENT

12-1. Cross-sectional drawing contrasting transit- and auto-oriented commercial streets. (Source: City of Portland 1983: 4; drawing: Ernest Munch)

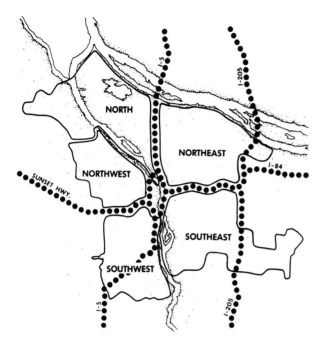

12-2. Transportation districts in Portland. (Source: City of Portland 1983: 27)

another for its public-transit function. The five auto-traffic classifications are Regional Trafficway, Major City Traffic Street, District Collector, Neighborhood Collector, and Local Service Street. The names are not those used by traffic engineering manuals, partially to emphasize the different purposes of the policy.

Because ASCP traffic designations are based only on desired function, expected street volumes are excluded as a criterion for classification. For example, although a "neighborhood collector" in a low-density, single-family residential area will have much lower volumes than a collector street in a high-density apartment area, the public will, for the most part, expect both streets to offer similar amenities: safety for pedestrians crossing the street, parking for guests or business customers, and a general feeling of "ownership" by the adjacent neighborhood.

Four public-transit designations follow a similar hierarchy, descending from Regional Transitway (regional express and limited service) to Major (limited and local) Transit Streets, Minor (local service) Transit Streets, and, finally, Local Service Transit (demand-responsive services only). In addition, a street may have designations for bicycles, special pedestrian concerns, truck usage, and beautification (figs. 12-3 through 12-6).

Most classification schemes identify each street type with a particular street cross section, indicating the number of lanes, sidewalks, and so on. Because

the ASCP's classification scheme is not volume-based, the ASCP substitutes for this approach one that defines each designation by four characteristics:

1. The street's functional purpose, identified by the primary type of trip for which the street will be designed. For example, a Major City Traffic Street will be built and managed for trips with one trip end within the transportation district.
2. Intersections, or traffic-control techniques that are used between streets of different classifications. For example, the intersections of a Major City Traffic Street and a Neighborhood Collector will provide all desired turning movements wihout requiring the use of a Local Service Street. But when the same Major City Traffic Street intersects with a Local Service Street, the latter will either yield right-of-way or be denied access to the former.
3. Land-use and development considerations related to the street classification, which guide the review of development proposals. For example, auto-oriented land uses will be encouraged along Major City Traffic Streets.
4. Specific design treatments as, for example, on-street parking in neighborhood commercial areas.

Finally, the ASCP document contains a chapter on implementation that lays out guidelines for the city staff regarding project development, funding eligibility, and public review and approval processes.

DEVELOPING THE POLICY

The ASCP was prepared over a three-year period (it was originally scheduled to take about eighteen months). Developed in response to the mayor's desire to redirect the city's (and the region's) transportation policies, the policy was to include a greater emphasis on transit service, the integration of transportation and land-use goals, and increased public involvement in decision making.

Initial studies began in 1974, and the policy was first adopted by the city council in 1977, with a five-year review and update. During this time, the city and region completely redirected their transportation program to strengthen the neighborhoods near the downtown area, while allowing continued central city employment growth. Turning away from an unfunded 1969 plan to build new freeways and numerous major arterial projects, city and regional officials sought to place equal emphasis on highways and transit, to which end they supported the construction of a light rail transit line. These land-use and development objectives were later embodied in the city's 1980 Comprehensive Plan.

12-3. Traffic streets in the northeast district.
(Source: City of Portland 1983: 34)

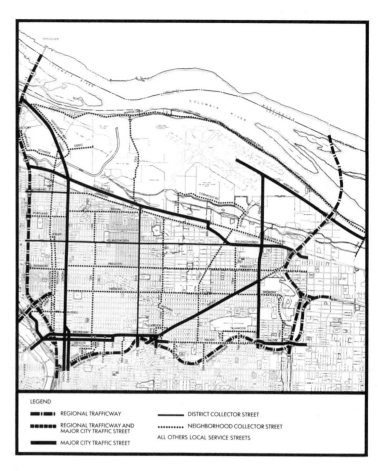

12-4. Transit streets in the northeast district.
(Source: City of Portland 1983: 34)

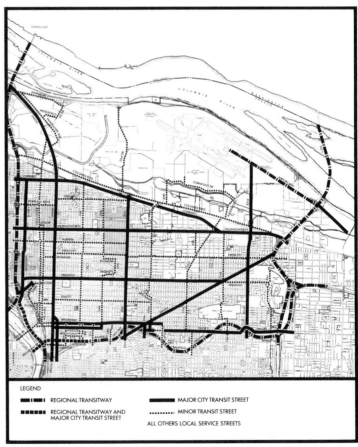

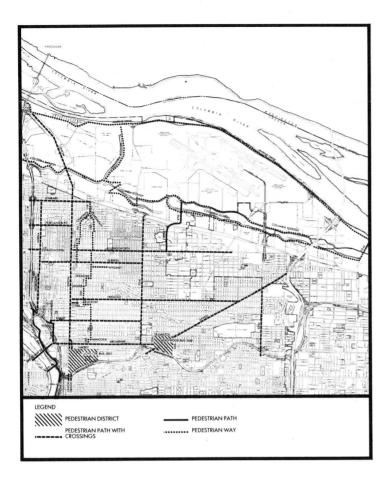

LEGEND

▨ PEDESTRIAN DISTRICT   ▬ PEDESTRIAN PATH

▬ PEDESTRIAN PATH WITH CROSSINGS   ••••• PEDESTRIAN WAY

12-5. Pedestrian designations in the northeast district. (Source: City of Portland 1983: 35)

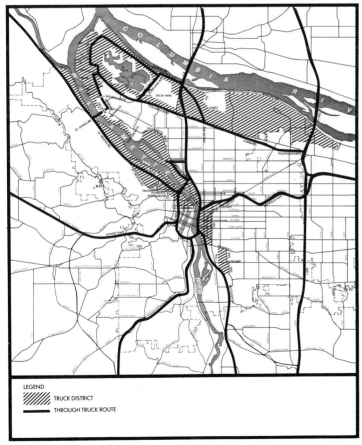

LEGEND

▨ TRUCK DISTRICT

▬ THROUGH TRUCK ROUTE

12-6. Truck routes as an example of citywide policies. (Source: City of Portland 1983: 23)

Strong leadership was key to Portland's policy changes. Neil Goldschmidt, then mayor of the city, not only oversaw ASCP development, but also led the removal of two nonessential interstate freeway segments from the highway construction program, transferring the funds to arterial and transit improvement projects. The availability of federal funds was critical, since it allowed the city to solve some of the problems identified during the development of the ASCP, thereby demonstrating the policy's usefulness.

The ASCP was also subject to major public review. The first element of the study was the preparation of background information, including the historical development of Portland's transportation system. This was presented in a slide show illustrating the city's growth, its dependence on transportation, and the importance of early decisions in shaping the city's basic character. Portland is old for a West Coast city: most of the basic development decisions and street platting activity occurred at a time when walking and transit were the dominant modes of transportation. The result is a small, central downtown area and a relatively weak system of arterials with many narrow streets that had formerly been streetcar routes. Even though much of the actual land development occurred when the auto first came into use, Portland's basic structure is characteristic of earlier periods, with a tight, relatively compact, "human-scaled" development, which most people find attractive. The challenge of the policy, therefore, was to build a working transportation network that retained the desirable characteristics of the existing system within the constraints of a budget that precluded extensive reconstruction.

IDENTIFYING THE ISSUES

The history slide show was presented at a first round of community meetings in ten subareas of the city where the policy development project was first introduced. More traditional background information on traffic volumes, accidents, and so on, accompanied the slide presentation, and a questionnaire was prepared to elicit specific details, such as those regarding home and work location and typical routes of travellers. Working committees met over a period of several months to help identify specific issues and develop proposals for each district. Emphasizing the public's point of view, the committees concluded that traffic movement was only one of several goals for the city's street system; the system also had to support residents' needs for clean air, available transportation, and quiet streets. Residents desired control over "their" streets to make physical improvements through trees and

plantings, as well as to broaden opportunities for play and recreation. In local commercial areas, they stressed the need for on-street parking, adequate sidewalks, and other uses of the street right-of-way. In the older-style, transit-era commercial neighborhoods (where stores were built right up to the sidewalk, so that pedestrians could see the merchandise), many residents expressed a strong desire to maintain the same character in new buildings, because it helped to identify the surrounding neighborhoods.

The first draft of a transportation concept and classification scheme embodied these recommendations. Alternatives were presented in a second round of community meetings. For example, in one area of the city, which had a complete grid of streets but a particularly weak arterial network, the community debated spreading traffic over several lower-order arterials versus designating one street as a major arterial. The neighborhood chose the "spread" solution. The information gathered and recommendations made in this process were used to prepare a staff-proposed policy. The Planning Commission held five public hearings on this policy in subareas of the city and then adopted it, with some modifications, followed by the city council's own hearings and adoption.

The slide show was the most effective element of the policy preparation because it brought information to the public and provided focus for discussion of the issues. An important by-product of the process was the identification of specific transportation problems in each district of the city. This became a work program for transportation studies in the following years, as funds were withdrawn from the freeway program and put into projects that met already-discussed public needs.

Weaknesses in the process occurred at the level of the technical staff. The Bureau of Planning clearly led the study, and traffic and street engineers never really accepted the basic concept. In fact, much of the extra year required to complete the policy was spent in trying to achieve acceptance from those groups. Many had difficulty accepting that a street's ideal engineering characteristics must often be sacrificed to other objectives. This difficulty not only had strong implications for project implementation, but it was critical for day-to-day operating procedures.

A WORD ABOUT DOWNTOWN

While the downtown street system is not classified in the ASCP, the basic transportation policies for downtown are key to achieving the ASCP's objectives. As the city's primary growth area, the downtown region cannot be expanded without adverse effect on the neighborhood arterial network unless traffic trips are controlled. Both the Downtown Plan and the Downtown Parking and Circulation Policy set a clear direction in support of transit and of an attractive pedestrian environment. As a result, federal air quality health standards are being met, and land areas turned over to the automobile, reduced (see chap. 13, by M. S. Harrison). These policies mean that downtown jobs have increased by one-third without any significant increase in traffic, because new job holders are being accommodated on the expanding transit system. (In the last ten years, the transit system has doubled its share of all work trips to downtown, now handling about 45 percent of the total.)

IMPACT ON PLANNING AND DEVELOPMENT

The ASCP has had its greatest impact on regional transportation planning, capital project design, and review of land-use and zoning cases. This is true because the Portland Bureau of Planning, as the originator of the policy, had either direct responsibility or substantial control in those areas. In preparing the policy, the bureau's staff became comfortable with the basic philosophy they were to carry out.

Regional Transportation Planning

The ASCP has reinforced the increasing importance of transit in the regional transportation system. The Metropolitan Planning Organization, the transit agency, and the state highway department all participated in the development of the ASCP and the Downtown Plan and benefitted from the city's general support of transit. Also important, however, was the mayor's ability to persuade the decision makers of these organizations to eventually implement plans that served ASCP objectives.

The ASCP policies have had direct impact on several regional corridor projects, as the case of the McLoughlin project illustrates. A four- to six-lane highway with limited local access and several very congested at-grade intersections, the McLoughlin corridor currently connects downtown Portland with the suburban communities of Milwaukie and Oregon City on the east side of the Willamette River (fig. 12-7). To avoid congestion, through traffic often uses adjacent residential streets. Because through traffic had overloaded both McLoughlin and Milwaukie Avenue, a neighborhood commercial spine, the city had

converted a local residential street (Southeast Seventeenth Avenue) to an arterial. Neighborhood residents argued for the removal of through traffic from this and other local streets in accord with the goal to maintain desirable family housing in the city.

In response, the city completed origin and destination studies to demonstrate the high percentage of through trips within the residential areas. It prepared two alternative neighborhood traffic plans, with through traffic greatly reduced on these streets. After substantial discussion, other city and regional agencies agreed to include this through traffic in the design assumptions for McLoughlin Boulevard. At the same time, the neighborhood supported some of the features of the McLoughlin project that were less advantageous to them (such as closure of convenient yet dangerous local street accesses to McLoughlin). In this case, the ASCP served to keep everyone mindful of the primary policy objectives.

Several lessons emerged from this process. First, a project's objectives determine the way data is collected to study a problem. Only if the objectives are recognized by all parties can the study process move smoothly. Second, trade-offs are necessary. If, for example, the policy objective is to protect residences on one street (or to preserve parking for neighborhood commercial uses on a local arterial), local access for businesses may need to be rearranged on the street designated for through traffic.

Capital Project Design

The Arterial Streets Study and ensuing policy were also intended to identify projects and guide their design. Several examples can be found in southeast Portland, the location of the previously proposed Mt. Hood Freeway. Plans for the construction of a freeway running through the district were cancelled during development of the ASCP in favor of rerouting regional travel around the district. As a result, the existing Banfield Freeway has now been widened, and a light rail transit (LRT) line built from downtown Portland to Gresham (a fifteen-mile stretch). Stations for the LRT are provided near commercial centers and areas of high-density zoning. At Hollywood, an older, transit/auto commercial center, changes in the street system improve area circulation and connect the new LRT/bus station, with widened sidewalks and street trees, to the historic core.

Additional improvements were planned for Powell Boulevard, an existing east-west arterial adjacent to the proposed Mt. Hood Freeway right-of-way (which had already been purchased in part by the state highway department) (fig. 12-8). As a "Major City Traffic

12-7. McLoughlin corridor project area (*detail at right*). (Source: City of Portland 1985: 2)

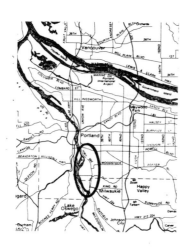

Street," Powell Boulevard's primary role is to serve trips with at least one destination within the southeast district. Left turns had been prohibited at signalized (arterial) cross streets to maintain through capacity, with the undesirable side effect of requiring drivers to use the local residential streets to get from one arterial to the other. The new guidelines permitted left turns on Powell through protected turn pockets, thus reducing neighborhood "infiltration" as well as improving the street's function (figs. 12-9 through 12-10). This may seem a simple decision, but it was not: traditional traffic engineering set smooth flow as the primary objective and thereby promoted the turn prohibitions. In this case, however, the policy showed that smooth flow for through traffic was not the only concern. In the end, the neighborhood sought to reduce the need for local arterials. It supported—and won—the accommodation of left turns, along with the removal of on-street parking. As Powell Boulevard has commercial uses and frequent bus service, designers responded to ASCP guidelines calling for safe pe-

destrian crossings by including pedestrian islands at nonsignalized intersections. Pedestrians now need to cross only half the street at a time, taking advantage of the traffic platooning that resulted from a timed signal system. Powell is classified as a Minor Transit Street as well, and bus bays or pullouts are provided at most transit stops to eliminate travel delays caused by buses blocking a traffic lane. Moreover, designated as a boulevard and an important visual focus for the city, Powell has a consistent street plan and landscaping.

Finally, Powell required an additional 30-foot right-of-way, which had major land-use implications. A standard highway project design would have left parcels with substandard depth, backyards exposed to traffic noise, and even, perhaps, a neighborhood without local commercial services. The project design team developed a sound wall/berm combination interrupted at several locations along the street by stretches of private commercial redevelopment. Recognizing that the shallow parcels were a deterrent to

12-8. Powell Boulevard, plan of segment showing traffic routes, proposed commercial areas, and parking. (Source: Oregon Department of Transportation 1979: 17)

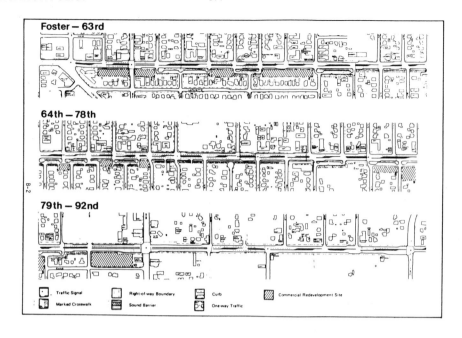

12-9. Powell Boulevard, cross section after reconstruction. (Source: Oregon Department of Transportation 1979: 16; drawing: Ernest Munch)

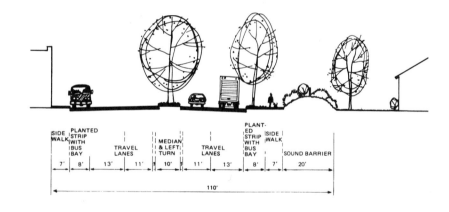

12-10. Powell Boulevard, perspective after reconstruction. (Source: Oregon Department of Transportation 1979: 60; drawing: Warner, Walker, and Macy, P. C., Landscape Architects)

redevelopment, particularly if on-site parking were required, the project provided on-street parking on short frontage roads. These roads also helped to increase safety by lining up local cross streets that were offset because of uncoordinated platting.

Powell Boulevard is only one example of an ASCP-influenced project. The ASCP also guided the rebuilding of Macadam Avenue, Union Avenue, and Beaverton-Hillsdale Highway, all of which have shown that new building activity along a street is important to the success of a project, especially where the project presumes a character or land-use change.

Land-Use Issues

As previously mentioned, each street classification has a land-use and related development component. Transportation planning staff reviews each zone change application for its impact on general transportation policy. The staff recommends specific actions, ranging from the denial of an auto-oriented drive-in restaurant in the center of ASCP "pedestrian districts" and neighborhood commercial areas, to the reduction in the number of driveway curb cuts on streets where through traffic has a higher priority than local access.

A major objective of these reviews is to minimize the impact of traffic arising from new development on adjacent residential areas. This has involved decisions as small as the location and angling of driveway entrances and exits to discourage the use of local streets. The most important cases have involved institutions, especially hospitals, within residential neighborhoods. An overall transportation management plan is usually requested to include transit and ridesharing incentive programs, which reduce both total traffic volumes and parking on adjacent residential streets. In two cases, an employee and visitor parking boundary was established that coincided with the institution's master plan or growth area. Institutions are responsible for achieving these goals through public information or manipulation of parking rates or through employee discipline. Annual reports, or status reports at the time of the next conditional-use permit application, are used to monitor the success of the plans, with future approval subject to compliance reviews.

CURRENT ISSUES

In 1982 and early 1983, the city staff conducted an update study of the ASCP, as called for in the original document. Several important events had occurred since the original study was completed. First, the city's Comprehensive Plan was adopted, and the zon-

ing code substantially revised. The plan essentially confirmed the land-use patterns and general policies used in the ASCP. Second, Mayor Goldschmidt left Portland, and, since his successor focused less on transportation and policy issues, greater responsibility rested with the bureaucracy. The city has, as a result, a weaker position in regional transportation decisions. Third, a number of the major projects developed during the ASCP's first planning program were under construction, and more attention was given to operating procedures and design details than to broad policy.

While the update process reconfirmed the basic policy structure, a number of changes were made. Some streets were reclassified to reflect conditions more accurately, and changes were made to respond to public criticism that the policy had not directly improved conditions on local neighborhood streets. While reduction in speed and through traffic on local streets had been a primary goal of the ASCP, the city had not been successful in actually implementing changes to meet this objective. In addition, a number of problems during the implementation of several projects resulted in a council decision to combine all transportation activities, from planning to maintenance, into a single administrative unit. These problems indicated a need to shift the focus from broad policy analysis to the development of effective implementation measures and operating policies. Recent actions to achieve this include:

1. A "Neighborhood Traffic Management Program" has established a procedure for testing policies and gaining public approval for the construction of traffic diverters and other control devices. Procedures are designed to ensure that these often controversial projects receive the broadest public consideration and that public actions, such as diverters, will not simply move a neighborhood traffic conflict from one residential street to another.

   Prepared jointly by planners and traffic engineers, the program is now operated under the jurisdiction of the latter group. This is appropriate, since the ASCP policies will only reach their full effectiveness when they affect the daily activities of the implementing agency.

2. The Bureau of Traffic Engineering was renamed the Bureau of Traffic Management to reflect its broader responsibilities. Traffic engineers have been reorganized, with one group concentrating on arterials and another focusing on local neighborhood streets.

3. A right-of-way encroachment policy was prepared

and adopted by the council. The most controversial aspect of this policy deals with the desirability of skybridges. Another feature recognizes the possibility of different encroachments (by columns, or other construction above and below grade, depending on the street's functional classification). Clearly, the more important the transportation function of a street, the less desirable are encroachments that might limit future transportation-carrying capacity. A similar policy has been prepared for access (driveway) review and approval.

4. Closer attention is being paid to basic maintenance because increasingly tight funds have necessitated the preservation of existing streets. At the same time, questions have been raised about the appropriateness of the single set of maintenance and construction standards covering the entire city. Some neighborhoods have expressed a wish to establish their own priorities. They have asked, for example, why one area could not adjust standardized priorities for expenditure, relegating more money to neighborhood traffic control and less to street repaving. Finally, the city's current program of annexing the eastern suburbs has raised the issue of uniform street standards from a financial point of view, because the streets in these suburbs were often built without the curbs or sidewalks now required by the city.

LESSONS

Portland's ten-year experience in developing and using the ASCP yields important lessons for others who plan to embark on a similar program. As a first lesson, two basic philosophical principles need to be accepted by those preparing a broad street policy based on extensive public input. One is that the street right-of-way should not be just a transportation movement and utility corridor. Streets set the tone and character for the entire city; they represent 30 to 40 percent of total urban land area, and offer the public its greatest opportunity to control the environment. This explains why people approach street issues with great passion and why public works departments often feel that everyone—public, planners, and development agency staff alike—want to invade "their" territory. Following from this principle, transportation investments should be a support or catalyst for other public policy goals, such as economic development, neighborhood housing improvement, or energy conservation, and not just a means to increase traffic capacity.

Second, as with most action in the public sphere, strong political leadership that can envision the relationship between streets and other public resources is necessary to develop comprehensive policies regarding city streets.

Third, the process of developing a policy or program with broad public involvement inevitably leads to high public expectations. Yet these may be easily shattered by the very slow process of public decision making. A basic acceptance of policy as the basis for decision making should help limit delays in the process. Open public explanations of technical and policy conflicts help people to understand why the process is slow.

Fourth, and related to the last two points, *everyone* within the bureaucracy who will be involved in the use of the policy should have a hand in its development. Those who will use the policy must understand how it will affect their work if they are to be convinced of its merits. The training of transportation technicians often emphasizes traffic movement as their only responsibility. With this background, the benefits of a street classification scheme based on function rather than volume is, at least initially, difficult to accept. They must understand the need to balance various objectives. At the same time, planners must recognize the need for specific operational decisions.

Fifth, the availability of substantial funds at the time of policy adoption allows the city to respond to the raised expectations that result from policy development. The ability (and willingness) to spread those funds over the widest range of projects and areas of the city will help to serve these expectations as well as basic equity.

Sixth, a transportation program based on a more effective use of existing rights-of-way means that construction may cause greater disruption than a program of building new roads (such as the freeways of the 1950s and 1960s). While not negating the broader public benefits, the reconstruction of existing streets presents its own set of problems—traffic delays, diversions, and the inconvenience of those who need local access—for which planners, engineers, and contractors have not yet developed effective responses.

Finally, an ASCP approach justifies the considerable difficulties involved because it gives the public an opportunity to manage more effectively its major resource—the right-of-way, which facilitates movement and provides light and air. It also establishes the ground rules for a policy direction that includes compromise, agreement, and decisions that can eventually lead to action. In the absence of such a framework, most transportation programs, like Portland's previous efforts, become bogged down in controversy.

REFERENCES

City of Portland. 1977. *Arterial Streets Classification Policy (ASCP)*. Vol. 1, *Policy* and Vol. 2, *Technical Appendix*. Portland, Oreg.: City of Portland.

City of Portland. 1983. *Arterial Streets Classification Policy (ASCP)*. Update. Portland, Oreg.: City of Portland.

City of Portland. 1985. *McLoughlin Corridor Improvement Program*. Portland, Oreg.: City of Portland. December.

Oregon Department of Transportation. 1979. *Powell Boulevard Environmental Impact Statement*. State of Oregon, September.

13.
Promoting the Urban Experience in Portland, Oregon

MICHAEL S. HARRISON

Of the many components of a successful environment for pedestrians, only the street furniture, benches, and bricks that highlight most pedestrian-oriented improvements ordinarily get close attention. Yet setting the stage for a pedestrian environment also involves dealing with issues of marketing and promotion. In Portland, festivals, celebrations, parades, and similar events have helped build and strengthen a constituency for pedestrian improvements. They have supported and reinforced the life-style changes necessary in shifting from an automobile-based to a pedestrian culture. Successful marketing must be broad in scope. It must convince people that values emphasizing pedestrianism are desirable for a community. Finally, it ought to build a positive image of the pedestrian or bicyclist without casting aspersions on the driver, for the automobile culture is strong and in control; it should not be unduly offended.

In Portland, we have learned that marketing is effective only when the spaces ultimately created are pleasant to use. Poorly designed and ill-planned locations will yield nothing but resentment about wasted public funds and reactions against further efforts to favor the pedestrian. Yet people want to take pride in their community, and pedestrian improvements can snowball if people perceive initial efforts as enviable aspects of their city or neighborhood.

Finally, philanthropy, especially the involvement of local benefactors with large and small contributions, is critical. Few jurisdictions are able to fund all necessary improvements exclusively through public resources. The ornamental drinking fountains in Portland are a small but significant example of the spirit of philanthropy that has typically occurred in the city. The one pictured in figure 13-1 (and twenty-three more like it) were donated in the 1880s and

All photographs are by the author except where noted.

13-1. Simon Benson drinking fountain in transit mall.

1890s by a Portland citizen, Simon Benson, who aspired to provide the numerous loggers and seamen who visited the city at the turn of the century with an alternative to drinking spirits. Today, we have more than forty sidewalk drinking fountains scattered throughout town. They are gracious touches.

A BIT OF HISTORY

Portland was one of several cities formed in the mid-nineteenth century at the confluence of the Willamette and Columbia Rivers, the upper reaches of deep-draft, ocean-going navigation. The city began as an inland port from which locally grown produce and other agricultural products were shipped to California gold miners. It soon became a prosperous, albeit small, agricultural community, competing for agricultural freight with nearby Oregon City, Milwaukie, St. Johns, Albina, East Portland, and Linnton and triumphing because of two advantages. A system of islands in the middle of the Willamette River, just south of the city, obstructed ships headed toward the competing cities upstream. Also, the so-called Great Plank Road, extending over the adjacent Tualatin mountains, provided direct access to shipping for Tualatin Valley farmers.

In 1940, Portland was still a small city (of about 250,000), with a few nearby suburban and farming communities. Today, the population is 420,000, and 1.1 million people live in the metropolitan area. By the year 2000, the metropolitan population is expected to increase by 400,000. This future growth is the subject of concern, especially for those who anticipate a corresponding decrease in the quality of the pedestrian environment. But because it will involve change, such growth can be a tremendous opportunity to rethink certain aspects of the city.

To understand the scale of Portland, one must understand the nature of its block structure. The city extends down a hillside to the west bank of the Willamette River, with streets laid out in a system of avenues running parallel to the river, approximately north-south. A second series of narrower streets, initially intended as service alleys, forms a grid with the avenues, which originally served pedestrian circulation. Together, streets and avenues form regular 200-by-200-foot blocks (fig. 13-2), which were divided in quarters, and each quarter divided in half. A benefit of the 200-by-200-foot block is a high air-to-building ratio and, consequently, large amounts of open space and light. Downtown Portland has 55 percent open space in its streets and parks, in contrast to 33 percent open space in downtown Seattle and New York.

One of the last cities built before the advent of extensive car and trolley use, Portland was ill-equipped to accommodate the automobile. By 1912, the city transportation network had broadened to a system of horse-drawn and electric trolleys and bicycle ways. As in most cities, bicycles were a prominent form of transportation, whereas the number of cars in 1912 amounted only to a few thousand. Not surprisingly, as the automobile's popularity soared, traffic conges-

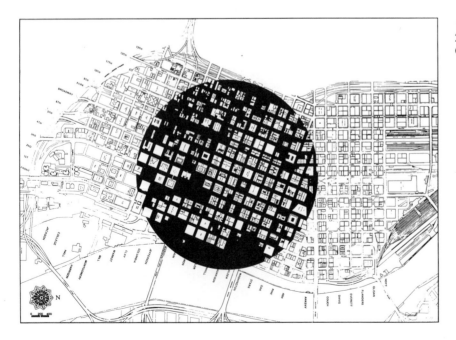

13-2. Downtown blocks are 200 by 200 feet. (Source: City of Portland, Oregon 1980: 13)

tion quickly became a major problem. In 1924, Portland gained more cars per capita than any other city in America. That year also, Edward Bennett, a planning consultant employed by the city, prepared what in essence was a transportation and urban design plan, which was adopted under the title of *The Greater Portland Plan*. Bennett's idea was to reconstruct Portland into a Paris of the Northwest, with broad boulevards, traffic circles, landmarks, and triumphal arches (fig. 13-3).

Since the 1920s, the history of Portland's planning has primarily been a history of trying to control the impact of the automobile—a task not altogether unlike fitting a square peg into a round hole. Interestingly, the first effort to salvage the integrity of the downtown as a people-oriented retail district was organized by local merchants as early as the late 1920s. At that time, the merchants paid for the construction of a cast-iron, lighted arcade on Third Avenue (fig. 13-4). An attempt to establish an identifiable shopping district through right-of-way improvements, this project represents a pivotal local precedent in the use of special street furnishings to enhance pedestrian activity.

Since then, planning in Portland has gained considerable sophistication. During the late 1970s, the city developed the Arterial Streets Classification Policy (ASCP), which documents a system of zoning by traffic type in the city's street network (see chap. 12, by S. Dotterer).

13-3. Bennett plan for west Portland showing redevelopment similar to that of early nineteenth-century Paris.

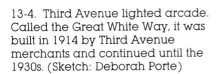

13-4. Third Avenue lighted arcade. Called the Great White Way, it was built in 1914 by Third Avenue merchants and continued until the 1930s. (Sketch: Deborah Porte)

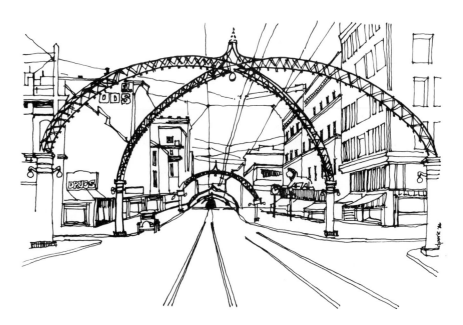

STREET AND WATERFRONT FESTIVALS

For many years now, Portland has been willing to temporarily close large segments of the downtown streets to vehicular use. Generally, the public reaction following each closure has been enthusiastic—so much so that a constituency eventually formed in support of permanent pedestrian areas. Now, nearly a mile of downtown streets has been closed to all motor vehicles, and the reclaimed space used for creating parks, parkways, and pedestrian malls. In addition, over a mile of exclusive transit streets features pedestrian amenities, such as widened sidewalks, special paving materials, trees, benches, fountains, and other street furniture.

Another of Portland's important successes to date has been the closure of a mile-long, six-lane highway adjacent to the west bank of the Willamette River, and the formation, in its stead, of a 50-acre park. To encourage use of the park and to create linkages to it, the city promotes major festivals twice a year. In fact, since the turn of the century, festivals have built a constituency for pedestrian use, without which other changes, such as mall treatments and even tree planting, would not have been possible. One such event, Neighborfair, occurs over a long weekend in July. It is a meeting of neighborhoods and ethnic groups, with each group sponsoring one or several booths (fig. 13-5). Typically, Neighborfair attracts about five hundred thousand people. Radio and television stations are actively involved, sending up hot-air balloons, broadcasting directly from the park, and sponsoring free concerts. A second event, the Rose Festival in Waterfront Park, has celebrated the rite of spring annually since the turn of the century. Combined with several other events, it, too, draws attention to the amenities of the Waterfront Park. But it is not restricted to that location; rather, it extends over all of the downtown, temporarily limiting the new transit mall to exclusive pedestrian use. Bands that come from as far away as Denver give street concerts in many of the special spots of the downtown plazas; they also march in one or more of the three parades. Up to a million people, many from eastern and southern Oregon, attend this two-week event.

Each fall, yet another event, ArtQuake, attracts crowds, builds constituents, and occasionally closes streets. ArtQuake is spread along the transit mall and in the atrium spaces of major buildings, which are given over for use as sculpture and painting courts. It is an opportunity for literally hundreds of major restaurants in the downtown area to advertise their products with food booths that line the temporarily traffic-free streets. ArtQuake draws an estimated two hundred thousand persons a day.

Downtown Portland is not just a city center but the heart of the region. Attendees of some of the downtown events can double the city's population. During the year, sections of the streets are closed for a variety of other events, as, for instance, when the international district, which includes twenty or so oriental restaurants, sponsors dragon parades on Chinese New Year. Again, the media are active in promoting festivals and in highlighting attendant pedestrian improvements.

Between annual events, park and street use is encouraged throughout the year. Every weekend from April through December, "Saturday Market," a crafts fair composed of some five hundred booths, draws about twenty thousand people. An entirely pedestrian experience, the market is located in Portland's "Old Town" historic district and is largely responsible for the economic vitality of that area (fig. 13-6). Thus, although the permanent merchants in Old Town offer comparable wares, they encourage the market to remain and grow in their area.

In the summer, the Parks Bureau provides live music. Several parks each host concerts on a particular day of the week, enabling residents in all city areas to have access to these free events, for which the Musicians Guild and other local musicians donate much of their time.

THE MAKING OF AN URBAN OASIS

Portland built a transit mall in the late 1970s with a $15 million federal grant. In part an attempt to control air quality, the project's other objective was to encourage transit ridership in and to the downtown (fig. 13-7). However, in a city that is developing as an automobile-oriented environment, a nonautomobile urban space finds itself at a competitive disadvantage. During the late 1960s, the city decided to stop trying to compete with every new suburban shopping center. Instead, it began to market what it could offer: an urban experience unique in the state of Oregon.

In another, rather radical, effort to achieve compliance with the Clean Air Act of 1972, Portland limited new parking downtown to 42,000 spaces. Despite the creation of ten thousand new jobs since 1975, only a negligible number of parking spaces has been added. Statistics show that more people are using alternatives to the car: the bulk of commuters use public transit, up to five thousand people ride bicycles each day, and many others walk.

The transit mall is a key component in the strategy of marketing the urban experience. The mall's sidewalks have been widened to 24 feet, and the width of

13-5. Neighborfair in Waterfront Park. (Photo: John V. A. F. Neal)

13-6. Saturday Market closes S.W. First Street for three blocks.

13-7. Transit mall. Transit ridership has increased by over 10,000 trips per day since the mall opened.

its streets limited to two bus lanes. The mall runs along downtown Fifth and Sixth avenues, an active space, two-thirds of a mile long, that has, if anything, been overdesigned. The street furniture is a uniform blue, and brick is heavily used on sidewalks, with the paving pattern extending across each street intersection. These extensions are intended to make the crosswalks more inviting and to demarcate clearly pedestrian from motor vehicle space. A wide curb gives pedestrians room for passing and buffers encroaching bus traffic.

Such changes can cause problems. Portland's engineering staff insists that every time sidewalks are widened, the full width of the street right-of-way has to be rebuilt—at great cost—to lower the crown of the street. In Seattle, Boston, and Philadelphia, a more flexible attitude has allowed sidewalks to extend to the existing crown of the street, with a covered gutter system at the old curb line. This approach costs about one-tenth that of rebuilding the entire street.

Downtown Portland's mounted police are more accessible and give a better sense of protection to pedestrians than do police cruising in cars. The area has occasional problems, usually conflicts between downtown workers and transients, and mounted police provide a comforting presence to people who feel threatened by transients.

PEDESTRIAN NETWORKS

If every other street in downtown Portland were closed to cars, auto movement would still be on a grid of streets spaced less than 500 feet apart. Such a grid would still offer ready vehicular access throughout the downtown. Accordingly, the street closures that are being implemented through the Arterial Streets Classification Policy and the Downtown Parking and Circulation Policy establish a natural system of pedestrian ways, yet not at the expense of automobile traffic.

Portland is also blessed with park blocks. When A. L. Lovejoy and F. W. Pettygrove originally laid out the city, they realized that only a certain number of streets would have a commercial market. Many streets were residential, with areas developed around established parks. A pedestrian promenade at the south end of the downtown, the South Park Blocks extend for two-thirds of a mile (fig. 13-8). North of the downtown, the North Park Blocks constitute another half mile. In between, a promenade lined with rows of trees is surrounded by historic structures. These park blocks form a major pedestrian route through the city's center, linking it to Portland State University at

13-8. South Park blocks established in 1851.

the south end. The university is a destination point where vehicular streets have been replaced by wide pedestrian walkways, fostering a campus atmosphere.

Skybridges between buildings are other, now common, pedestrian routes. Because the city blocks are small, many large corporations own more than one block and, often, they wish to connect activities that are functionally related. Portland has recently experienced a rash of requests for second- and third-story retail skybridges connecting multistory buildings either with one another or with parking structures. These bridges are subject to special regulations; for example, the city requires that ground-level pedestrian improvements equal or exceed those implemented at the skybridge level.

Finally, to protect and enhance further the environment for pedestrians, street furniture is located at the curb edge of streets that have several lanes of moving traffic. By keeping the building wall free, this approach also benefits window shoppers.

STOPPING PLACES

Places to relax encourage pedestrianism. The urban core is characterized by a constant moving, pushing, and shoving that is not conducive to an interesting and enjoyable environment. Facilities such as drinking fountains and retail shops can add to the richness of the downtown only if pedestrians are provided with safe places for relaxing over the course of shopping or after a hard day's work.

Street furniture can be arranged to create places where one can step out of the flow of street life for a few moment's rest. Fixed objects act as magnets; people collect around them, claiming the space. Given a choice, people will locate next to passive street furniture, such as a bench or a tree, rather than next to active objects, like a telephone booth or a mailbox. In the absence of street furniture, people will collect along built edges, trying to find safe "cover." Shade, shelter, and convenience combine to create attractive places that can easily be appropriated and emphasized with permanent street furniture. Resting places are ringside seats on the life of the downtown.

Although people can create stopping places for themselves, a city is more engaging if it provides some. Stopping places require a strong demarcation, best handled by simple, clear, geometrically regular shapes or by their installation at a level higher than the pedestrian way. They are marked by a clear sense of enclosure and by refreshment in the form of shade, water, or both.

Portland's main library has a sitting wall with benches along it, which sets the stage for an intensely used series of stopping places (fig. 13-9). Similarly, one of downtown Portland's better plazas opens off to the transit mall and actually goes underneath the building, providing many places to step out of the pedestrian flow and watch the crowd.

Recently, the city has been licensing the use of street rights-of-way for sidewalk cafés, which are permitted if the pedestrian count is low enough to be accommodated in a 5- or 6-foot sidewalk space. Although rain is commonplace in Portland, these businesses are active for about five months of the year. Permits are also given to many corner stands offering food or flowers (fig. 13-10). Vendors who locate in a park relate back to the tradition of the old produce market area of downtown Portland, where people sold merchandise from the curb and from within the property line.

13-9. Multnomah County Library. Sitting wall offers stopping places, which compensate for the lack of sidewalk-supporting activities related to institutional use.

13-10. Sidewalk vendor.

CIVIC PRIDE

Building design review is required throughout downtown Portland. Design guidelines and standards emphasize the pedestrian. For instance, one guideline calls for retail entrances to be located at corners of blocks, where two pedestrians ways intersect. Another calls for upper-level office development to have mid-block exit locations, so that the two types of entrances do not conflict and pedestrian loading is dispersed along the sidewalk. In the 1960s, many empty plazas and blank walls were built. In 1979, however, the city adopted regulations to prohibit blank walls. Public review now requires private development to complement public improvements taking place in pedestrian spaces. The constituency behind these measures was engendered by a fifteen-year effort to increase civic pride in the city and, particularly, in the downtown.

Among successful examples of this effort is the recent groundbreaking of Pioneer Square in the heart of the downtown. Conceived as Portland's principal public space, Pioneer Square exists on the site of a former parking lot that was acquired several years ago. A competition for its design was held, and the winning entry selected in 1980 (fig. 13-11). Initially, the downtown business community wanted a conservatory and not a square. They were slow to finance the project. Citizens raised the funds for the square themselves by organizing a sale of brick pavers. For fifteen dollars, each purchaser had his or her name pressed into a brick to be fired and installed in the square. More than sixty thousand bricks have been sold and nearly a million dollars raised. Completed in 1984, the square is a permanent monument to the deep pride Portlanders take in their city.

REFERENCE

City of Portland. 1980. *Downtown Design Guidelines*. Portland, Oreg.: City of Portland.

13-11. a. and b. Pioneer Square.

a.

b.

14.
Toronto: Streets Revived

KENNETH GREENBERG

As in most North American cities, postwar city planners in Toronto ignored the street as a public place,
adopting instead the precepts of the modern movement in architecture, which had long encouraged a
new kind of streetless environment. These precepts
were most clearly articulated in *The Plan for Downtown Toronto*, published in 1963 by the Planning
Board. Through a series of visionary sketches and
study models, its authors sought to convey what
downtown Toronto could become through redevelopment faithful to the new principles. A variety of
boldly conceived networks of pedestrian decks and
plazas were superimposed on the existing downtown
within a new fabric of clean-lined towers, while the
vehicular functions of streets were demoted to subter-
ranean service tunnels (fig. 14-1).

This vision was no doubt attractive at the time. The
separation of functions seemed to be a modern and
effective way to cope with volumes of movement in
a world infatuated with technological advances and
the growth ethic. However, when the public began
to experience some actual examples of high-density
"tower-in-the-plaza" and "tower-in-the-park" environments, their admiration for the clarity of the ideas
turned to alarm at the results (figs. 14-2, 14-3). Wind
velocities increased and shadows deepened at the base
of tall new buildings in the heart of the Financial
District at King and Bay Streets. Convenient shopping and interesting sights that had previously graced
the older city fabric were missing in St. Jamestown,
the first major downtown high-rise apartment district.
And the results of new development seemed to fall far
short of the promises.

All graphics are courtesy of the Toronto Department of Planning
and Development.

14-1. Radical alterations of streets proposed in the *Plan
for Downtown Toronto* (1963): <u>a.</u> street before the plan;
<u>b.</u> as proposed by the plan.

a.

b.

14-2. Towers in the Plaza, King and Bay streets.

14-3. Towers in the Park, St. Jamestown.

Worse still, people began to realize that the implementation of these visions would require serious incursions into existing neighborhoods—both rich and poor—through speculation and expropriation. When "redevelopment" began to threaten well-defended enclaves and a series of beloved historic structures in the downtown—for example, the Old City Hall dating from the turn of the century; the St. Lawrence Market, which contained a former City Hall; and the grand beaux arts Union Station on Front Street—the alarm turned into widespread resistance.

The first impulse of the myriad rate-payers and citizens' groups that emerged at the time was to stop unwelcome interventions. Community-based groups were formed to protect specific neighborhoods and buildings and to block highways (such as the Spadina Expressway) by writing briefs, lobbying politicians, and demonstrating in the streets. They began to realize that a common thread underlay their defensive actions and that it had to do with the vision of what the city should be.

A second reaction, when the imminent danger was forestalled, was to formulate alternative strategies, or "counterplans." The models for such proposals, not surprisingly, came from an intensive evaluation of the actual workings of the traditional neighborhoods. As organizations, neighborhoods were not found to be as unworkable or obsolete as the modernists had claimed. In fact, painstaking observation of these neighborhoods led to the reformulation of some compelling ideas that a few iconoclastic critics like Jane Jacobs, William H. Whyte, and Bernard Rudofsky had already put forward—ideas such as the virtues of a mix of land uses, of a careful blending of old and new, and of an attention to context and scale. The sympathetic reassessment of the older city inevitably led back to the rediscovery of the street itself.

At that point, Toronto had relatively little trouble changing its policies concerning the general thrust of redevelopment and the particular issue of street uses. From the beginning, the city had been reticent about implementing the bold plans that had been published, because of the absence of a major federal highway program and of inexpensive mortgages as enticements to move out to suburbia, the relative lack of racial strife within the city, and the inherent conservatism of the body politic. As a result, Toronto had fewer expressways and less abandonment of inner-city neighborhoods by the middle class than did cities in the United States. In the 1970s, it still had streetcars, old shopping streets, and many relatively intact neighborhoods that were street-oriented. The strong tendency of the community to move slowly and cautiously, inherited from the population's United Empire Loyalist forebears, caused those things to be preserved longer, while other cities, such as New York and Chicago, had moved more boldly into the modernist future.

Second, a tremendous number of people immigrated to Toronto from a great variety of cultures, especially after World War II. People who were accustomed to public life in streets quite unselfconsciously began to utilize Toronto's nineteenth- and early-twentieth-century streets, parks, and houses. They infused this fabric with new vitality, and, through their involvement in municipal politics, resisted attempts to do away with it.

Finally, the heady influence of a new ideology of grass-roots involvement, spilling across the borders from the United States and Western Europe in the late 1960s, provided the seemingly inexhaustible number of community-based groups with a legitimacy and a vocabulary for extensive participation in planning. These groups sprang up in defense of their communities and demanded a new approach to planning. They encountered a municipal body politic based on a ward system that was vulnerable to their pressure, and a municipal civil service that was honest and capable of changing.

In the municipal elections of 1968 and 1970, a reform movement gathered momentum. By 1972, it had elected a majority of the city council, as well as the mayor, former history professor David Crombie, who was committed to overhauling the city's plan. From 1974 through 1975, a moratorium on downtown development was imposed through a bylaw restricting the height of all new buildings to 45 feet; the objective was to buy time for the formulation of a new approach.

After extensive study, community consultation, and political soul-searching, a group of newly hired young, radical planners drafted the *Central Area Plan* in the mid-1970s. They espoused policies for downzoning the city's central core, and for mixed-use zoning that would provide housing suitable to a variety of income levels and family sizes. Also advocated were the preservation of historic buildings; improved amenities for pedestrians at street level; an emphasis on public transit; a halt to new expressway construction (some of which was well underway); and a limitation on growth by tying it to transit capacity.

The ideas behind this plan were not as much new as they were a restatement of some of the much older guiding principles embodied in the part of the existing city fabric that predated postwar redevelopment. In essence, the plan proposed to fill in the holes in the fabric rather than to continue to tear it asunder. Streets, of course, formed the matrix. If the first step was to stop unwanted expressways, road widenings, and demolitions, the second was to put forward positive strategies for redefining the role of streets.

The changing approach to streets can be clearly seen in a comparison of two documents published by the Toronto Planning Board before and after the election of the reform council. *On Foot Downtown*, first published in 1970, urged the city to participate financially in the creation of an integrated below-grade mall system for pedestrians. Modelled on such precedents as Place Ville Marie in Montreal, the idea was to encourage each major downtown project to provide a basement-level shopping concourse, and then to have the city assist in providing "tunnels" to link them below the street. This strategy did produce results. In fact, a very extensive network of interconnected below-grade pedestrian routes runs some 4.5 km (2.8 miles) throughout the downtown core and contains over one thousand shops (fig. 14-4). This system provides a very convenient and agreeable form of escape from cold and wet weather yet it also caused great concern initially because of its tendency to rob the city sidewalks of their vitality.

On Building Downtown was a consultant study commissioned by the reform council and published in 1974 as one of the background reports to support the proposals of the new plan and to serve as a guide in discussions of building form. In contrast with *On Foot Downtown*, it laid great stress on the older Toronto tradition of mixing vehicles and pedestrians in the same street space and it expressed concern about just how "public" the new underground malls were. *On Building Downtown* proposed the establishment of a clear hierarchy of street types, from major avenues to

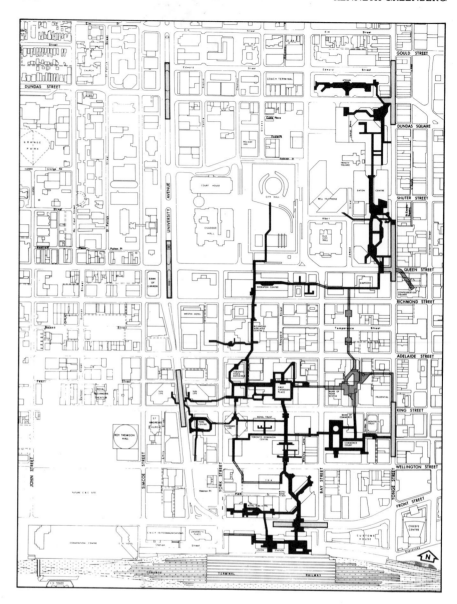

14-4. The emergence of the underground concourse network.

EXISTING ⎤ PEDESTRIAN MALL AND/OR WALKWAY
FUTURE ⎦
SUBWAY STATION

DOWNTOWN UNDERGROUND PEDESTRIAN MALL SYSTEM
REVISED: NOV. 1984   SCALE 1: 2400
CITY OF TORONTO PLANNING AND DEVELOPMENT DEPARTMENT
STEPHEN G. McLAUGHLIN, COMMISSIONER   DECEMBER 1983

small pedestrian lanes; the readjustment of the balance of space for vehicles and for pedestrians on existing city streets; the use of new buildings to define street walls; and the introduction of new streets subdividing large-scale development sites where streets did not already exist.

The changed attitude to streets was also evident in the new city government's major initiative to encourage people of a variety of income levels and family types to live downtown. "Cityhome," a nonprofit city housing corporation set up in the mid-1970s, began to plan the St. Lawrence project, a neighborhood designed for 10,000 residents on 44 acres of vacant and marginally used industrial lands the city had assembled adjacent to the core. Designers sought to knit this site into the surrounding fabric by extending existing streets and introducing new ones to form a tight

network of city blocks. This strategy, coupled with input from a great variety of architects and developers, produced a form of urban housing that does not look or feel like a housing project. As time goes by, one will be less and less able to distinguish its boundaries within the surrounding environment.

In the late 1970s, the city's Department of Planning and Development (an amalgamation of the Planning Board and former Development Department) began, through a newly formed Urban Design Group, to explore possibilities for altering the design of existing downtown streets to further the objectives of the city's plan. This work started in 1978 in two specific areas, the Yonge Street Corridor and the St. Lawrence Historic District (see appendixes 1 and 2 to this chapter). Each case was distinguished by unique problems, especially those regarding political climate and funding opportunities. Since 1978, however, a program benefitting from the Yonge and St. Lawrence experiences has evolved with broad applicability to streets throughout the city, including those in areas that fall under the traditional purview of the city's community renewal programs.

THE PROGRAM OF PUBLIC IMPROVEMENTS

The premise of the program is very simple: to build into the normal processes for city renewal the incremental improvement of public spaces, including streets, parks, and squares. The *Central Area Plan* (drafted in 1974 and finally approved in 1980) had envisaged a city where private developments were organized to enhance and support this traditional urban structure. The plan also anticipated that the city itself would upgrade the public spaces. Insofar as streets are concerned, the city could accomplish this as part of the normal cycle of reconstruction in the public rights-of-way, effected either through the annual programs of the Department of Public Works or as a result of reconstruction necessitated by private redevelopment. In both cases, the opportunity could be seized over time to emphasize amenities for pedestrians.

An annual capital budget administered by the Department of Planning and Development (a highly unusual responsibility in North America) is used to augment the base budget of the line departments and agencies responsible for the functional aspects of streets and utilities (primarily the Department of Public Works, although occasionally the Department of Parks and Recreation or of City Property). Each spring, when budgets are being prepared, intensive consultation occurs among these departments. Opportunities for joint projects and coordination are identified, resulting in a list of particular streets for which the Urban Design Group will prepare conceptual design plans in that year.

In the fall, estimates are prepared and budgetary approvals sought as part of the city's overall capital-budget cycle. Detailed design and contract documents for approved projects are jointly prepared by Urban Design and Public Works staff, who also draw on skills in a number of other departments, often including Parks and Recreation and Toronto Hydro, the electric utility company. Implementation of the work is, of necessity, highly seasonal. Most of the construction is carried out between May and October while the next round of projects is being conceived. By "piggybacking" onto the budgets for already-slated reconstruction, the annual capital budget for urban design and community renewal work ($2.5 million to $3 mil-

lion [Canadian]) is able to accomplish a great deal. Key to the success of this approach is the collaboration between departments, in particular the intensively cooperative relationship with the Department of Public Works.

Although experimentation continues in this program, there is now an emerging consensus about a repertory of workable construction details and suitable materials (available in a booklet called *Details for Downtown Streetscapes*; see appendix 3 to this chapter). Further policy consensus is emerging with respect to where these details can be properly used. There are, of course, limitations regarding the amount of work that can be accomplished on an annual basis, especially those relating to the priority assigned to this kind of work in the city's overall range of capital programs, the ability of the staff to handle the work load, and the capacity of the local contractors to carry out work in the field. These constraints have begun to define the rough parameters of the public program.

In addition to this publicly funded program of works, the city is able to enter into agreements with private developers and to commit them, for any significant project, to rebuild the public sidewalks on their frontage in accordance with the new city standards. The developers, moreover, must finance the undertaking. For each project, the details of such improvements must be negotiated with the staff of the departments of planning and public works alike. Ultimately, they must be reported to the city council for approval along with the review of the public aspects of the architectural solution, street-related uses, facade treatments, landscaping, location of entrances, and so on (fig. 14-5).

14-5. Typical site plan and sidewalk treatment presented at development reviews.

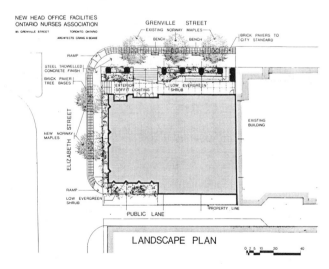

The publicly funded improvements stand as examples of the city's commitment to good street design. Through a combination of public and private efforts on adjoining segments of each street, an overall concept for the street is being realized, and the financial participation by developers is becoming readily accepted. On the average, every public dollar spent on street improvements in the past few years has been more than matched by a private dollar. This is especially important for Toronto because there are virtually no funds available from the federal and provincial levels of government for such work.

Developers are offered the option of paying the city to design and execute the agreed-on works or of designing and building to city standards themselves. Both options have proven to be workable.

LESSONS LEARNED

Out of the experiences of the past few years, one can now draw some conclusions and define an approach to the planning and design of effective streets for Toronto:

1. Good streets require:
   · community consensus about the role of streets;
   · plans that call for uses of an appropriate intensity and scale on the street frontages;
   · public and private developers who have confidence in the street environment;
   · architects who design buildings that respond to and enhance the street as a public space; and
   · traffic engineers who acknowledge the use of streets by pedestrians.
2. One should not construct stark categories of street types, differentiating streets that should be improved exclusively for pedestrians from those that should be left exclusively for vehicles. As part of an intensive network, almost any street can, to some extent, play both roles.

   The vitality of the city as a whole requires a conscious effort to maintain a balance between well-established and emerging development areas. In other words, street improvements ought to occur gradually over a broad range of locations, so that one area is not starved (or overfed) at the expense of another.
3. The car is not the enemy; overspecialization of the street space for the car is. Traffic can contribute to the year-round life, vitality, and publicness of the street. There are, obviously, some special exceptions of streets that benefit from being traffic free, for example, summer or weekend malls. Yet the creation of extensive and permanent auto-restricted zones to protect pedestrians does not seem necessary or desirable in Toronto.
4. It is not possible, necessary, or desirable to achieve total design consistency among all of the objects that appear in the public street. While coordination and the establishment of some basic themes can go a long way toward improving the quality and coherence of street spaces, one must also recognize that the street is not a shopping center (where such consistency may not be desirable either). Public facilities above and below grade in the street are the responsibility of a great variety of public and private agencies over time, and a certain amount of autonomy is inevitable.

   By the same token, in dealing with individual developments occurring along the street, one need not strictly adhere to common detailing, as long as the general thematic continuity of the public elements overrides the particularity of an individual project. The ability to tolerate a certain amount of variety within a clear common theme adds to the richness of the street.
5. Streets have to be rebuilt from time to time, either because of the cyclical need for replacement of public facilities or because of the special needs of private development. That is the sensible time to introduce alterations or improvements. To avoid wasteful renewal projects, the city ought to monitor ongoing private construction activity and to intervene at the appropriate time.
6. It is much more effective to produce conceptual plans for discussion purposes than to attempt to legislate recipes for all situations and enforce compliance with detailed guidelines. Face-to-face negotiations between actors in the public and private sectors allow for more subtle responses to the unpredictable variety of real problems and are much more likely to elicit support from all sides. Conceptual plans that do not have to be given the force of law can also go much farther in suggesting possibilities and encouraging a creative dialogue between players.
7. Work in an area is greatly advantaged by a number of small, phased interventions over time, as opposed to a single, large intervention. In the former procedure, one has the opportunity to learn as one goes, to respond, and to make changes where necessary. This procedure also allows time for the evolution of new relationships between a street that is changing and the buildings and uses that front on it. Finally, it avoids the necessity of large infusions of capital over short-term periods.
8. Publicly sponsored street improvements act as a stimulus for the private sector to upgrade adjacent properties. Not only do such improvements encourage privately sponsored improvements to private premises and their adjacent sidewalks, but they create a climate that encourages benefactors

to come forward with special projects for public spaces, which could not be paid for out of the public purse.

Historically, Toronto developed on a quasi grid based on concession roads that were further subdivided by individual owners and eventually linked. Most of the streets are relatively narrow (one railway chain, or 66 feet in width). They have now been accepted as the primary units that structure the urban environment. Slowly but surely, the program of public improvements is altering their character by reconstituting their qualities as a cohesive urban landscape and by introducing, through redevelopment, a complementary network of relatively small new parks and squares.

Because this process is now becoming integrated with routine construction in the public realm, one hopes that it will continue indefinitely (though it can obviously be scaled down as it achieves its goals). In the end, although the most extensively transformed sidewalks will compose only a fraction of the approximately 1,800 km (1,100 mile) total, they should be those that are most used by most people (fig. 14-6).

In areas where major changes in land use are anticipated, such as those occupied by obsolescent port, industrial, and rail facilities, the exercise is no longer one of improving existing streets but rather of introducing new streets where none exists (fig. 14-7).

APPENDIX 1
THE YONGE CORRIDOR: A CASE OF TRAUMATIC CHANGE

Extending 60 kilometers (37 miles) from Lake Ontario to Lake Simcoe, Yonge Street is Canada's longest and most famous street. Historically, it was the bustling center of downtown Toronto's shopping district. More recently, it has come to resemble New York City's Times Square in its glitter, excitement, and problems. But people keep coming to Yonge Street in enormous numbers to see and be seen. By day, the mood is pleasant and upbeat; at night, it takes on a slightly seedy edge in certain blocks where pimps, prostitutes, and their clientele congregate.

Yonge Street suffered two traumatic events from which it has not fully recovered. From 1949 to 1953, access to stores was obstructed during the installation of the subway in an open cut down the middle of the street (fig. 14-8). When this subway was completed it precipitated intensive redevelopment on lands adjacent to the stops, but tended not to support the continuous shopping strip (encouraged previously by the use of streetcars). A second trauma was the introduction of Eaton Centre, a massive commercial develop-

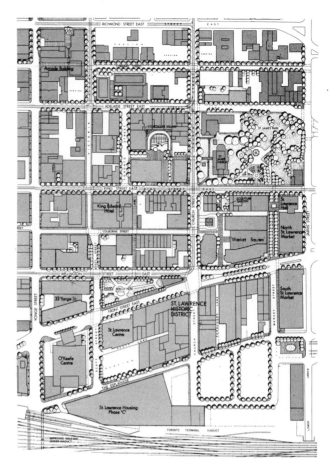

14-6. Urban design concepts and plan for the St. Lawrence Historic District.

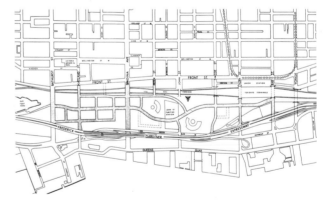

14-7. The introduction of new streets and blocks in the Railroad Lands.

ment, running parallel to the street for three blocks, with an interior mall system that plugs directly into two subway stops (fig. 14-9). Once again, the long period of land assembly and construction, combined with a new competing pattern, hurt the street.

By the mid-1970s, Yonge Street was clearly changing as massage parlors and trinket shops began to replace more traditional retail uses. A series of temporary pedestrian malls, set up for several weeks at a time in the summer, had, at first, a mixed success. Ultimately, however, they only amplified the problems of prostitution, panhandling, and drugs and

14-8. Excavation of the Yonge Street subway, circa 1950. (Photo: City of Toronto Archives)

14-9. Yonge Street, Eaton Centre.

created an atmosphere that was perceived to be unpleasant and out of control. In 1977, the issue of Yonge Street came to a head with the brutal murder of a young shoeshine boy in the back room of a massage parlor.

Having decided to take action, the city reviewed its options. Studies were done, and a special council committee appointed. It recommended an extensive program of remedial actions that combined intensive policing, by-law enforcement, social action, and physical changes to the street.

Policymakers felt that if the street could be made more attractive to a greater variety of people and to a better quality of business, it would deter further physical and social decay. The pedestrian environment became a high-profile political issue, as the city carefully considered installing a permanent full mall and a transit mall. In the end, however, the council decided that the most appropriate solution was simply to increase the proportion of 66-foot rights-of-way devoted to pedestrians by widening the sidewalks. Vehicles would continue to occupy the street, albeit in a narrower roadbed. This strategy allowed more room for tree planting, street furniture, and pedestrian scale streetlights. Proposals were made to erect at the intersections such amenities as transit shelters, canopies for vendors, and chess tables, thereby extending improvements into the sidestreets (fig. 14-10).

A modest approach toward revitalizing the street, the city's proposal did not seek to change the street radically, to remove its excitement, or to turn it into a tame and upscale shopping mall. The city council pledged $5 million for implementing the plan over an anticipated five-year period, the Urban Design Group was asked to coordinate the physical changes, and work was scheduled to begin in 1978.

Quickly, however, a serious impediment emerged to the implementation of the proposed sidewalk widenings. The metropolitan government, which had jurisdiction over Yonge Street as an "arterial," did not share in the new consensus regarding the role of streets. It continued to view Yonge as essentially a carrier of traffic, and, despite an extensive and expensive joint management study (which concluded that it was feasible to narrow the road pavement), Metro Toronto has steadfastly withheld its approval.

This political standoff necessitated a change in approach. Because the city government had jurisdiction over the side streets (of lesser importance in the traffic hierarchy) and because there was a perceived need to take some action, the program shifted its primary focus from Yonge Street (where only very limited work has occurred) to its perpendicular crossings for a block on either side. On many of those side streets, the sidewalks have been gradually widened, trees

14-10. Chess players and vendors on widened sidewalks at Yonge and Gould streets.

planted, pedestrian-scale lights installed, and special amenities introduced. While sidewalk widenings on Yonge Street itself are still a priority, the city has also realized that the side-street approach, although initially a second choice, has validity in its own right. Rather than lavishing all of the attention on a single linear element, the program has tended to enhance and animate a much larger area by encouraging local businesses to improve their own premises and to promote their efforts jointly.

APPENDIX 2
ST. LAWRENCE HISTORIC DISTRICT: FILLING IN THE HOLES IN THE NINETEENTH-CENTURY FABRIC

The St. Lawrence Historic District is an area to the east of the downtown core (and immediately adjacent to the emerging St. Lawrence Neighbourhood, which took its name). It contains a substantial number of nineteenth-century buildings in what was once the heart of the city, the old St. Lawrence Ward. Residential use of this area virtually ceased in the aftermath of the railway era, and it was used largely for marginal warehousing and industry.

In the heyday of urban renewal, large portions of the building stock had been demolished through public expropriation and private assembly, giving the area a gap-tooth appearance. Parking lots occupied the voids awaiting large-scale redevelopment. The *Central Area Plan*, in an abrupt reversal of policy in the 1970s, called for the retention of the remaining building stock and for the insertion of new mixed-use (including residential) development that was compatible in scale with the historic structures. It was apparent that if the plan worked, it would unleash a great deal of development activity in this potentially interesting setting.

Also clear were the virtues of reshaping the area's rather bleak and dreary public spaces to enhance its historic value and livability. In combination with the new St. Lawrence Neighbourhood, which also focuses on the historic market, the St. Lawrence Historic District offers the potential for a range of apartment types and tenure options provided by the private market and the nonprofit sector.

These considerations led the Urban Design Group to put together a conceptual plan in 1978 to improve and tie together the area's diverse street and park spaces. As in the case of Yonge Street, the work was phased over a number of years. Public funding for the program came from city funds and, initially, from provincial and federal programs. As the program gained momentum, its impact was substantially increased by close coordination with private development, which created the opportunity for privately funded public improvements.

With its rich history, old structures, and preserved open spaces, the St. Lawrence Historic District offered an unusual opportunity to develop connections with the city's past. Yet this program of public improvements clearly did not aspire to areawide "restoration" or the return to a particular historical moment. Rather, it was an attempt to make the continuous "layering" of new uses and new buildings work together with the old, thereby emphasizing and reinterpreting the historic forms at an urban scale.

In the 1850s the railways, in need of space for track-age, took over a waterfront area intended for use as a pedestrian promenade (fig. 14-11). The 100-foot-wide Esplanade (so named in the early nineteenth century) retained both its name and revised form until the 1970s, although the trackage was no longer used. As a result of the new St. Lawrence project, one section was turned into a linear park (fig. 14-12). By shifting

14-11. The Esplanade during the railway era, late nineteenth century. Development at the left of the tracks occurred on landfill.

14-12. Axonometric of the St. Lawrence Neighborhood.

the roadbed, planners transformed another section into. an extremely wide, tree-lined sidewalk suitable for outdoor cafés. Although no longer on the water's edge because of extensive landfill, the Esplanade has become a major pedestrian thoroughfare, with echoes of the use originally implied by its name.

The character of the new Esplanade has conditioned development along its spine. New buildings must respect the scale and importance of the street, whereas remaining structures preserve historical details that can be exploited—for example, traces of the hoists and carriageways that served the original wharves. Development along the Esplanade, as in most of the St. Lawrence area, is still progressing. Yet, as the pieces fill in, one may see the reemergence of a coherent whole.

One block north of and parallel to the Esplanade, Front Street was originally a very important east-west artery. Over time, however, its prominence and architectural distinction were eroded by the out-migration of important commercial enterprises, which left major holes in fabric (now used as parking lots), and by a heavy emphasis on the street's traffic function (fig. 14-13).

As an initial step in revitalizing Front Street, public improvements were used to break down the scale of

14-13. Front Street and the Flatiron Building: a. before, and b. after redesign.

a.

b.

the wide, open thoroughfare by introducing a tree-lined median boulevard in some places and by widening the sidewalks in others. Where the original surveyed grid departed from the irregular shoreline, Front Street splits at an acute angle, forming a triangular block whose apex is the site of Toronto's Flatiron Building. Behind the building, a pie-shaped open space, enlarged by the removal of one lane of traffic, was turned into Berczy Park, named for one of the early settlers. It is now framed at one end by a new atrium-type office building whose shape is a clear visual extension of the sides of the Flatiron Building (fig. 14-14). At the other end, a large public mural at the rear of the Flatiron Building is dedicated to an architectural theme. Now that all the vacant lots on the periphery of the park have been filled in, it is becoming a strongly defined and memorable urban room.

A third opportunity arose in relation to the very substantial St. James Anglican Cathedral, one block to the north on King Street. Although the cathedral had been rebuilt three times in its present location, it had never had any form of entry on axis with its prominent landmark spire. By utilizing vacant parcels (also the result of urban renewal) a walkway was created that now dramatically defines this vista (fig. 14-15). The walkway contains a public sculpture garden, the result of a generous private donation, and an easement, obtained through a private development that has preserved the opening.

14-14. Berczy Park: <u>a.</u> before, and <u>b.</u> after redesign. Mural by Derek Besant.

a.

b.

As new people and uses are introduced, and as contextual associations develop between the old and the new St. Lawrence, the area is beginning to offer the richness, complexity, and choice that are the true tests of urbanity. Although the transformation of the district cannot be exclusively attributed to the improvement of the public spaces, the latter has been an essential catalyst.

APPENDIX 3
TYPICAL PHYSICAL IMPROVEMENTS TO STREETS

PAVING

Sidewalks are widened, where possible, by the readjustment of traffic lanes; the minor setback of new buildings; and the use of colonnades, where appropriate. Concrete crosswalks emphasize pedestrian crossings.

Improved sidewalks often feature unit pavers set in a band parallel to the curbside, 1.6 to 2.0 meters (5.25–6.5 feet) in width and within which trees, street lamps, and furniture are placed. Located on streets that are especially important for pedestrians, these bands were originally made of a local clay brick in a double or square format. They were laid up in mortar bed on a concrete slab, the remainder of the sidewalk being concrete. In part an economy measure both for initial cost and long-term maintenance, the curbside band (as opposed to a full brick or stone sidewalk) has worked well as a unifying device.

In the initial stages of the street improvement programs, the Urban Design Group took great pains to apply these details uniformly throughout. Now, however, considerable liberties are being taken to enrich the idea of a common motif. For example, natural stone pavers such as limestone, sandstone, and granite have been used in different areas. Also permitted are occasional special modifications, such as breaks in

14-15. King Street East: <u>a.</u> before redesign; <u>b.</u> with sculpture garden after redesign.

a.

b.

the pattern at entrances and column lines, which emphasize the specific characteristics of individual buildings.

There is a recognized need to correlate the amount and quality of rich materials and the public significance of their location. Thus, a full granite band would appear only at extremely important public locations, a secondary street would merit a more sparing use of stone or brick, and a small residential street would require only a concrete sidewalk.

STREET TREES

Street trees are generally acknowledged to be the single most powerful device in defining and humanizing the street space; certainly, they offer the greatest visible impact. The program has emphasized the planting of large-caliper (8–10 cm [3–4 inch]) trees inground at relatively close centers in a line approximately 1 meter (3.2 feet) from the curb, so as to form a canopy, and in double rows on very wide sidewalks. This is not a rigid formula, however, and some flexibility is almost always required to relate to architectural elements and other objects in the street, and to avoid existing underground utilities.

There is, however, an ongoing dispute on this latter point. In the interests of flexibility for utilities, the metropolitan government insists that trees on roads under its jurisdiction be placed in concrete containers, a practice that is not favored by the city because the containers stunt tree growth, create unnecessary obstacles on the sidewalk, and seem to offer few practical advantages.

A great deal of attention has been devoted, in fact, to the details at the tree base. Because Toronto's sidewalks are generally narrow, it is not desirable to sacrifice this tree pit as walkable space. On the other hand, the roots, which need to breathe and receive water, must not be severely compacted. Both objectives are fulfilled by pavers that are laid up dry over a filter cloth on a steel grate supported by a lip at the opening of the pit.

Unfortunately, pollution and winter salting prevent all but a limited number of tree species from thriving on city streets. Those that do best in Toronto are Honey Locust, Green Ash, Norway Maple, and Little Leaf Linden, although on occasion, others have been tried.

In addition to the actual street trees, varied tree plantings have been added to the street edge where parks and open space abut the sidewalk. Planters, however, are not encouraged on streets (except where adjacent owners agree to look after them) because of the high maintenance costs.

LIGHTING

Here the effort has been to provide street lighting using post-top luminaires of a scale suited to pedestrians. Work with Toronto Hydro prompted the realization that operating costs precluded having both pedestrian-scale lights and conventional high-masted cobrahead street lights as a rule. An extensive search turned up a high-pressure sodium luminaire that could serve both purposes without excessive glare, while providing reasonable color rendition.

Several variants of pole and luminaire have been developed and are being installed on rebuilt sidewalks. Also, conduits are buried where feasible, although special conditions, such as the need for overhead streetcar electrical feeds, require other solutions, for example, bracket mountings or a mix of high and low poles.

STREET FURNITURE

The first projects reflected a natural tendency to overdesign and overfurnish the street space with coordinated objects—perhaps out of a desire to compensate for a lack of real activity. Experience has suggested much greater restraint.

The most useful items have proven to be benches, chess tables, information kiosks (maintained by a private company), and, in some special circumstances, canopies to provide weather protection. More and more, however, the tendency is to keep the street space simple. For props, it makes more sense to rely on facilities in adjacent buildings or temporary (and movable) facilities provided by others. People themselves are relied on to provide the animation.

REFERENCES

Commissioner of Public Works, Chief Planner, Commissioner of Development, and City Solicitor. 1970. *On Foot Downtown*. Toronto: City of Toronto, December.

Abram, Nowski, and McLaughlin et al. 1974. *On Building Downtown: Design Guidelines for the Core Area*. Toronto: Design Guidelines Study Group, June.

Planning Board. 1963. *Plan for Downtown Toronto*. Toronto: City of Toronto, Planning Board.

———. 1975a. *Proposals, Central Area Plan Review. Part 1, General Plan*. Toronto: City of Toronto, Planning Board, October.

———. 1975b. *Proposals, Central Area Plan Review. Part 2, Plan for Downtown*. Toronto: City of Toronto, Planning Board, October.

Urban Design Group, Department of Planning and Development. 1980. *Details for Downtown Streetscapes*. Toronto: City of Toronto, Urban Design Group, August.

15.
Experiencing Downtown Streets in San Francisco

PETER BOSSELMANN

TALL BUILDINGS AND THE QUALITY OF THE URBAN ENVIRONMENT

What in the eyes of the public appears to be a dramatic change in building form away from the glass box to buildings reminiscent of the 1920s is, in the eyes of many professionals, a revitalization of an American art form. In fact, few topics are discussed among architects with more passion than the new styles of tall downtown office buildings. Stunning examples have been built in recent years. Yet the discussion of style takes on a far more pragmatic tone in the corporate boardroom of the architect's client. There, the artistic qualities of a tall building will probably always be described as "prominent profile," or "institutional, timeless character."

Already, a trace of fear can be discerned concerning the future of the tall office building in general. For example, Skidmore, Owings and Merrill, the nation's largest designer of downtown buildings, has completed a 2,000-foot-long building in a suburban location near San Francisco, instead of a more conventional 400- to 700-foot-high downtown structure. Not only does this design represent a changing aesthetic, but it also addresses an important socioeconomic trend, namely, that the vacancy rate for office space has grown in many downtowns, while less expensive development sites are available in suburban locations. Such shifts in the style and location of office buildings has led a prominent San Francisco attorney with many developer clients to refer to tall buildings as "dying dinosaurs." But his talk might be premature: a "super high rise" of 130 floors is currently proposed at the Coliseum site in Manhattan,

and whether or not it is built, other cities will continue the competition for the tallest building (fig. 15-1). As before, engineers will tackle the project without technical difficulty. However, as Faslur Khan, engineer of Chicago's Sears Tower and Hancock Center, said fifteen years ago, "whether we will build such a building and how the city will handle it is not an engineering question, it is a social question" (Appleyard and Fishman 1979). We will see that, in San Francisco, it is also a political question.

Indeed, political controversies about the social and environmental impact of tall buildings are everywhere. Newspaper coverage of proposed buildings near Times Square in Manhattan have aroused New Yorkers. Now that One Hotel Tower has gone up where five theaters once stood, opposition is growing against this way of "cleaning up" the entertainment district. "Keep Times Square Alive" is an alternative goal suggested by community groups and newspaper articles (Goldberger 1985). A few blocks to the east, on Fifth Avenue, there is distress over the future of one of America's most famous shopping streets. Since the completion of the 60-story Trump Tower, citizens groups perceive the street space and the fine stores on Fifth Avenue as vulnerable. At election time, leaflets were sent to city officials that pictured Mayor Edward Koch participating in an outdoor parade and included the caption: "Do you want to continue to parade in the sun?"

San Francisco's height and bulk controls were legislated in response to tall structures built on the edge of the existing downtown, particularly the Bank of America Tower and the Transamerica Pyramid. The shape of those buildings may be less controversial today than it was twenty years ago, when they were first built; however, their location at the edge of the financial district is seen as being just as inappropriate today as it was when buildings first appeared on the

All photographs are by the Environmental Simulation Laboratory, Kevin Gilson, unless otherwise credited.

a.

b.

c.

d.

e.

15-1. Scale-model views of five of the invited entries in the Coliseum competition in New York, all viewed from Fifth Avenue looking west on Fifty-ninth Street: a. Donald Trump's 130-story building, designed by Eli Attiz; b. Murphy/Jahn's entry; c. Michael Graves's entry; d. Cesar Pelli's entry; e. the winning entry by Moshe Safdie. (Photos: Peter Bosselmann, taken for the Municipal Art Society of New York)

skyline. In San Francisco, people on both sides of the downtown controversy now agree on precise limits to downtown highrise expansion toward neighborhoods to the north and the west.

NEED FOR APPROPRIATE TOOLS

In San Francisco, as in several other cities, community groups are resisting the environmental impact of tall buildings and arguing their negative effects on the quality of the urban environment. Yet the ability to describe those experiential effects is a rarely found skill among professionals. Words and knowledge fall short of the environmental qualities that are experienced once places are built. There are few accurate techniques for explaining the experience a new development or plan will evoke. The experiential media of the twentieth century—film and video—have little importance in the planning and design professions (Appleyard 1979). Instead, architects' renderings of future buildings, while graphically elegant, convey little of the buildings' contribution to the street, neighborhood, or city. Philip Johnson was right when he said that the controversial top of the AT&T building is unimportant. The top cannot be seen at street level. However, Johnson failed to explain how the building destroys the scale of the narrow streets below. The renderings that were published showed views of the building that are unobtainable in the real world of the pedestrian. Furthermore, renderings for Johnson's round building on California Street in San Francisco show a sunny plaza with umbrellas and a gigantic, sunny glass lobby underneath the cylindrical tower. Yet only for one month in midsummer, at 8:30 AM, does the plaza receive sunlight. Most of the year, it is cold and windy.

Rather than admitting their inability to forecast future experiences accurately, designers have taken the liberty of construing a reality that will not come true. If, in many places, designers have been able to get away with it, in San Francisco, the public has insisted on more accurate and comprehensive ways of explaining the effects of proposed developments. By addressing these issues and developing tools to communicate about them, the environmental design profession has earned more credibility and promises to yield better environments.

SAN FRANCISCO'S DOWNTOWN PLAN

Continuing public concern with San Francisco's Downtown Plan led to new and innovative approaches in assessing the everyday experiential character of new development. Since the mid-sixties, citizens have mobilized to speak out at election time against what is locally called the "Manhattanization" of the city. The fight began over view blockage. Controversies continued when well-known old structures were replaced by monotonous, monolithic facades, oppressive in scale and incompatible with the surrounding architecture. Many also felt, and rightly so, that the new, taller buildings worsened the microclimate, producing additional shadows and making streets and open spaces cold and windy.

Four times in the past fifteen years, enough signatures have been gathered to qualify anti-high-rise initiatives for election ballots. Although all four initiatives were defeated, the last, in November 1983, failed to pass by only 1,919 votes, representing one-fifth of one percent of the voters. This sent a clear signal to politicians, planners, and developers, and their architects: the new plan had to address these issues.

Work on the new plan started in 1980, with growth projections made for the next twenty years of development. Existing height and density controls for downtown districts allowed significant development, which, early visual studies showed, would change the scale and character of several downtown districts. Most affected were the retail district around Union Square, the hotel distict in the Tenderloin, historic Chinatown, and Market Street. Studies of view blockage were done on the scale model of downtown San Francisco housed at the Environmental Simulation Laboratory in Berkeley (fig. 15-2). Views were taken from all directions, including those obtained by commuters travelling across the Bay Bridge, as well as those most San Franciscans are familiar with. Future development under existing controls was modeled, and slides were produced to show the before-and-after conditions. The views were tested against general master-plan policies that called for a skyline shaped in the form of a "downtown hill" (fig. 15-3). Although it was established that future views from Telegraph Hill would not change radically, views from Nob Hill and from other elevated points to the south of downtown showed an abruptly rising plateau instead of the gentle slopes expected of the "downtown hill."

"Middle-range views," or views taken from publicly accessible points in the vicinity of downtown, were also studied (fig. 15-4). They included Chinatown's Portsmouth Square, Union Square, the Convention Center, the Transbay Bus Terminal, and the Embar-

15-2. Scale model of San Francisco. Donald Appleyard (right) and William H. Whyte (sitting, center), with the author (sitting, left) and urban design students from the College of Enviromental Design at Berkeley. (Photo: Environmental Simulation Laboratory, Pechard 1980)

15-3. Model studies of downtown height zones.

15-4. Typical middle-range views of development at the edge of San Francisco's financial district: <u>a.</u> existing conditions; <u>b.</u> model of proposed 40-story building montaged into existing conditions; <u>c.</u> model of the building, which violates the Urban Design Plan requiring new buildings to step down gradually to the heights of existing ones.

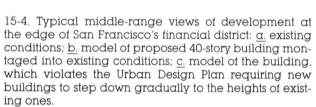

b.

a.

c.

cadero. With one exception, all showed a nonconformance with the urban design policy requiring
downtown development gradually to step down in
height to equal that of existing buildings in the neighborhoods surrounding the viewer.

Most telling were the comparisons of existing and
future views taken on downtown streets in areas heavily impacted by future development. For example,
streets in the retail district, currently lined with buildings 70 to 100 feet in height, were to be changed dramatically by the tower walls of new office and hotel
structures. The before-and-after eye-level views of
those streets were stunning (fig. 15-5) The San Francisco Urban Design Master Plan (City of San Francisco 1971) did not provide sufficient guidance in that
instance. The plan and subsequent legislation concerned themselves with the city as a whole, and their
policies were too general to reduce the impact of new
development on scale and to ensure the compatibility
of new with old at street level. But a new approach,
which accurately measured loss of sunlight and the
decrease of overhead sky above a street, made a con-
vincing case for new building height and setback rules
(fig. 15-6).

SUNLIGHT, CLIMATE, AND COMFORT

For almost a century, American zoning has responded to the need for sun and light on inner-city
streets. Indeed, New York's recent development controls for midtown Manhattan reintroduced the 1916
standards for adequate daylight and openness of a
street to the sky (see chap. 25, by H. Bryan and
S. Stuebing) (fig. 15-7). These revised standards compare the light conditions along avenues and streets
of Manhattan's historic development to conditions
expected under new development. Building forms,
setbacks, and height limits are all calculated for anticipated light levels (City of New York 1981). Planners,
at the incipient stages of San Francisco's new Downtown Plan, carefully studied the New York method
but regarded it as too complicated for the city's purposes.

San Francisco's winds, which blow from the ocean,
are strong and constant. As tourists (including Mark
Twain) know, the city's summers are cold and foggy.
As a result, sunlight is imperative for outdoor comfort, especially for people sitting on benches or walking on sidewalks (fig. 15-8). Existing sun, wind, and
outdoor conditions, as well as future conditions to be
created at specific downtown streets under alternative
growth strategies, were measured by a team of urban
designers from the University of California at Berkeley. Large models were made and measurements

15-5. Typical street view: <u>a.</u> existing conditions; <u>b.</u> proposed 40-story development.

a.

b.

a.

c.

15-6. Fish-eye view: <u>a.</u> existing conditions; <u>b.</u> 40-story development without setback beyond the height of the established street wall; <u>c.</u> same development with setback. The grid is superimposed to measure the openness of the street to the sky. (Photo: Peter Bosselmann)

b.

taken in the Simulation Laboratory and Boundary Layer Wind Tunnel at the College of Environmental Design (fig. 15-9). Tested with actual weather data in San Francisco, the initial observations of the Berkeley team were confirmed: sunlight is essential and shelter from winds is desired for a comfortable outdoor environment (fig. 15-10).

But research had only begun when the San Francisco Department of City Planning requested results. In the fall of 1981, a proposed 132-foot-high condominium project was threatening to shade a small playground in Chinatown, a place swarming with kids after school. The hours between 2:00 and 4:00 PM were prime time on the small square because many of the children left in the late afternoon to attend Chinese school (Bosselmann 1983a).

To evaluate the situation, researchers photomontaged possible building envelopes reaching the allowable building height of 160 feet into pictures of the playground taken with a fish-eye lens. These studies revealed the sky exposure afforded by new develop-

15-7. New York zoning, 1916: <u>a.</u>
Hugh Ferriss' rendering of
prototypical high-rise buildings; <u>b.</u>
street sections.

a.

b.

15-8. The preservation of sun
access to streets, parks, and squares
consists of a combination of height
limits, bulk controls, Floor Area
Ratio, and cutoff planes.

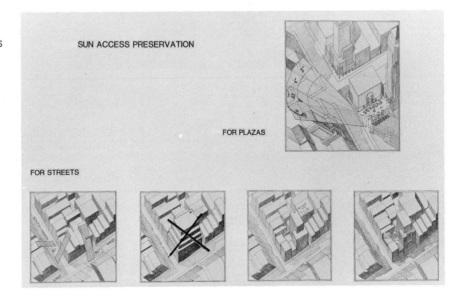

SUN ACCESS PRESERVATION

FOR PLAZAS

FOR STREETS

15-9. San Francisco planners watch a demonstration at the Berkeley Wind Tunnel. (Photo: Environmental Simulation Laboratory, Gray)

15-10. Wind effects and tall buildings.

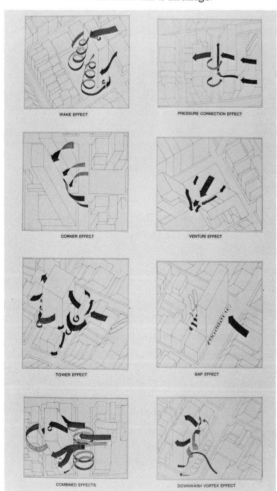

ment. By superimposing sun-path diagrams, they could measure the hours of sunlight that new development might take away from the playground (fig. 15-11). The studies showed that sunlight during afternoon hours would be diminished. In response, the Planning Commission quickly passed a resolution to lower the building heights. The Board of Supervisors (San Francisco's city council) upheld the resolution one year later, and the allowable building heights surrounding the playground were reduced from 160 feet to 50 feet. This resolution marked a departure from the traditional way of defining building heights according to contour lines. Instead, building heights were to follow "cut-off" planes based on the path of the sun and called "solar fans" (Bosselmann et al. 1983) (fig. 15-12).

The Planning Commission then ordered solar fans for all open spaces in downtown San Francisco. Although the mayor and several politicians tried to interfere, "Sun for Open Spaces" was, by then, a movement that had received such publicity that the momentum was hard to stop. As policies were made based on people's need for comfort, research had to continue. The Department of City Planning began conducting a user survey of twelve downtown open spaces. Questioned about qualities that attracted downtown office workers to open space, responders mentioned sunlight most frequently (Liebermann 1983). Yet the limited survey was not sufficient ammunition against developers who might have rejected the need to lower building heights in the vicinity of a public open space. One had to contrive a systematic study of the relationship betwen building form and the four important variables of the human thermoregulatory system: sun, wind, humidity, and temperature (Berglund and Stolwijk 1978). These variables were to be analyzed for all seasons in San Francisco.

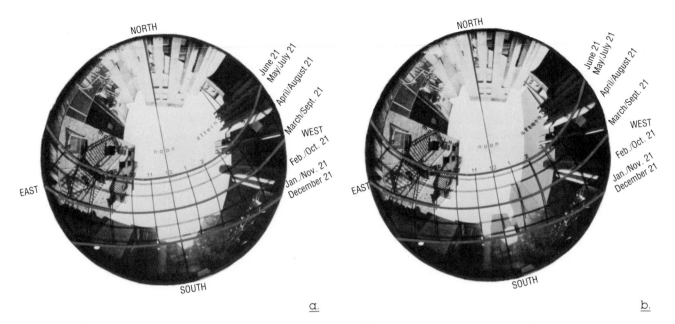

a.   b.

15-11. Amount of sky above the small children's area of the Chinese playground: a. fish-eye picture of existing conditions; b. photomontage of possible building envelopes reaching the 160-foot allowable building height. The amount of sunlight taken away can be measured with the superimposed sun path diagram. The same measurements were taken from the center of all play areas within the playground. (Photo: Peter Bosselmann)

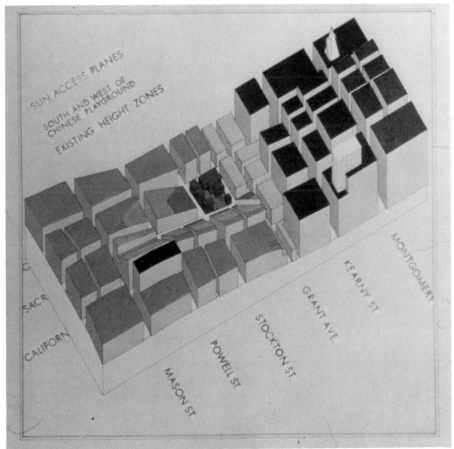

15-12. "Solar fans" for the Chinese playground.

Additional large models of four downtown areas were constructed to measure existing and future sun and wind conditions. The resulting data were related to a computerized comfort model for San Francisco's climate (fig. 15-13). Seasonal maps confirmed the initial hypothesis: areas that receive direct solar radiation are comfortable more than 50 percent of the year, while places in shade are rarely comfortable. Although shady places that are windy are especially uncomfortable, reducing high wind speeds is usually not enough to offer relief (fig. 15-14).

The team also verified that abrupt changes in building heights cause significant impact on wind velocities in adjacent streets and parks. This is particularly important along the edge of the city exposed to prevailing west and northwest winds. Zoning height changes should therefore be done gradually, in increments of less than 100 percent of the adjacent height zones (fig. 15-15). For similar reasons, height-zone changes should not be drawn along streets but in the middle of blocks.

When the results were published (Bosselmann et al. 1984), work on the Downtown Plan had entered into a critical stage. Citizens' groups and members of the Board of Supervisors viewed the new plan as too development-friendly; others, including the mayor, were concerned about too many restrictions on downtown development. Environmental groups decided to take the issue a step farther and to make sunlight on public open space an initiative in the 1983 primary election ballot and a proposed amendment to the City Charter (fig. 15-16). Seven months after the narrow defeat of the previous referendum, a majority (64 percent) voted to preserve sunlight in parks and squares. This, many voters knew, limited high-rise development in major sections of downtown San Francisco, a not-so-small victory after a decade-long fight (Bosselmann et al. 1984).

VISUAL QUALITIES

As the preservation of sunlight had become a political issue, the value of "visual continuity" in the city, undisrupted by major new development, received public support as well. But the *amount* of disruption was subject to a good deal of discussion.

A building's contribution to the visual quality of a street or of a skyline can be measured just as well as its contribution to the climate. In fact, the public is extremely sensitive to the visual environment for its symbolic attributes. Matters of scale, color, shape street character, and view affect a population's image of its city and of itself (Appleyard and Fishman 1979).

15-13. Seasonal comfort maps of a downtown street under alternative planning controls. The darker the large dot, the less comfortable the particular portion of the sidewalk.

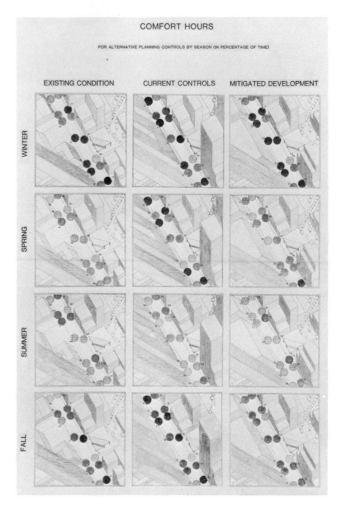

Visual qualities convey powerful emotional messages as to who dominates the city's environment.

Many planners, however, consider the visual aspects of the environment as trivial in comparison to the economic, fiscal, and social issues. When it came to deciding on height zones for the new downtown plan, planners never questioned the general policies in the Urban Design Plan. Discussion focused on maximum building heights and on heights in the south of Market portion of the financial district.

Naturally, groups in opposition to downtown development quickly blamed the city's permissive attitude for the degree of change to the skyline, middle-range views, and street views. In contrast, the development community frequently argued for higher buildings in certain locations to enhance the skyline. In such a politicized debate, clear methods of showing the visual and experiential impact of new development can

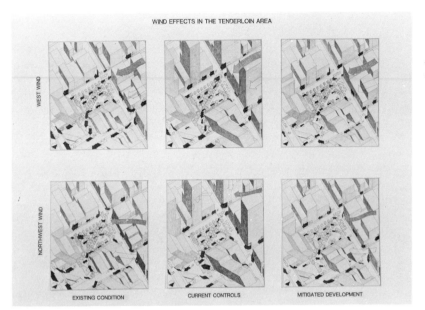

WIND EFFECTS IN THE TENDERLOIN AREA

WEST WIND

NORTHWEST WIND

EXISTING CONDITION   CURRENT CONTROLS   MITIGATED DEVELOPMENT

15-14. Wind effects in the vicinity of a downtown open space under alternative planning controls.

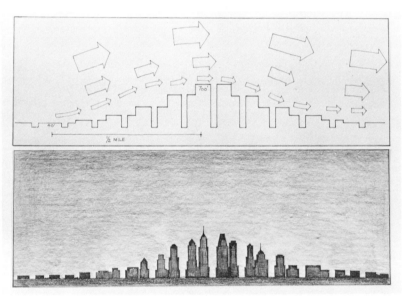

½ MILE

15-15. Gradually sloping "Downtown Hill."

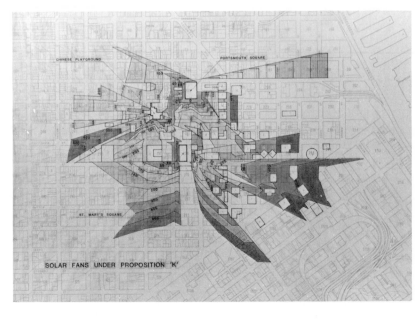

CHINESE PLAYGROUND   PORTSMOUTH SQUARE

ST. MARY'S SQUARE

SOLAR FANS UNDER PROPOSITION 'K'

15-16. Allowable building heights near three open spaces *after* the passage of Proposition K, the "sunlight ordinance."

only aid in reaching compromises. To this effect, the team at the Environmental Simulation Laboratory prepared models of towers of various heights, ranging from 200 to 600 feet, to be inserted into the downtown model at locations with high-development potential. These simulations showed the impact of development on both the skyline (figs. 15-17, 15-18) and the street-scape, thus guiding discussions between various interest groups and, eventually, helping to reach a consensus.

The Urban Design Committee of the local chapter of the American Institute of Architects convened a meeting around the model for discussion with planners and members of the Planning Commission. Prior to the meeting, the architects had argued for higher buildings in specific locations. But after studying the model, the architects and the city's staff surprisingly reached a consensus regarding specific building heights. The planners were well prepared for this discussion. They had frequently discussed proposed

height and bulk regulations, and alternative controls were modelled, tested, and remodelled. Opponents to downtown development requested to see the scale-model studies as well, which helped them realize that views of the future impact on the skyline were exaggerated. All parties frequently challenged the assumptions made in the modelling before they voiced their agreement.

It was interesting to see how, during the course of the planning process, changing political pressures influenced many people's assessment of the impact of development. After seeing film clips of the model, a high planning official decided that several buildings made possible under the new plan were too high. Previously, however, he had strongly defended the appropriateness of the height and bulk controls. His change of opinion did not correspond to changes made in the modelling technique or in the heights of the buildings modelled; rather, the plan had entered another critical stage in the political process. Simi-

15-17. Sequence of existing (1985) skyline views of San Francisco taken from publicly accessible locations: a. Treasure Island; b. Bay Bridge; c. Potrero Hill; d. Dolores Park; e. Buena Vista Park. (Photos: Environmental Simulation Laboratory, Gray)

a.

b.

larly, several supervisors openly opposed to the plan made no reference to building heights as symbols of permissive growth after they saw the film.

Because the effects of development on street-level views can be more significant than those on the sky-line, large models of typical street sections were con-structed to measure primarily two factors: first, the impact of new development on the scale of city streets and, second, its compatibility with the surrounding architecture. The public frequently describes new buildings as monolithic, monotonous, and dull. The words *scale* and *compatibility* are rarely used. The ideas these words express need to be explained, since they encompass not only the visual impact of individ-ual buildings, but the cumulative effect that several new constructions can have on the streetscape. Mea-surements therefore needed to take both phenomena into consideration.

The Downtown Plan defines goals to preserve visual continuity of street facades and to provide a visually interesting experience along the sidewalks. Yet it gives no standards to help measure those qualities. Empiri-cal data shows, for example, that in streets between 60 and 80 feet in width a pedestrian most clearly per-ceives up to the first six stories from 200 feet away (Blumenfeld 1953). The difference of one story or so will not be perceived as a disruption of the street fa-cade if most buildings maintain a height of six stories along the street. Even an additional two stories will not unduly disrupt the visual continuity of a street. The greater the height of the street facade, the wider the range of differences in height that will be invisible to the pedestrian. If the prevailing height of surround-ing buildings is ten stories, then the acceptable range of additional facade height is two to four stories (Bos-selmann et al. 1983).

If, however, a significantly taller building is built in the context of six-story facades, the base of the build-ing ought to be visually separated from its upper sto-ries. This can be achieved by setting the upper stories

15-18. Sequence of skyline views from the locations indicated in figure 15-17, showing development possible in the year 2000 under the 1985 Downtown Plan. (Photos: Environmental Simulation Laboratory, Gray)

a.

b.

c.

d.

Figure 15-17. (continued).   e.

216

c.

d.

e.

Figure 15-18. (continued).

in a tower, back 14 to 20 feet from the base facade (Bosselmann et al. 1983) (fig. 15-19). Our three-dimensional model studies also repeatedly showed that, contrary to common belief, changes in facade materials do not provide the necessary visual separation; for example, the change from one shade of granite to another will not make a tall facade less looming.

As studies like these were conducted by the Berkeley team, results were made available at public presentations to the Planning Commission. Ranges of acceptable dimensions for setbacks, facade length of individual buildings in special districts, and street-wall heights have found their way into the new plan (City of San Francisco 1985).

In September 1985, a new downtown plan was approved, addressing most of the issues raised by San Franciscans over the years. Planners have called it bold and trendsetting. The *New York Times* found the proposals intelligent and sensitive and called them "one of the most complete prescriptions of growth" bestowed on an American downtown. But local opposition to the plan remains. Many San Franciscans say that it allows too much growth; that it will not preserve the character of the city; that coldness and monotony will spread into an increasing number of downtown streets; that housing will become even more scarce; and that roads and transit conditions will eventually become unbearable.

Only at the national level are the provisions of this plan seen as progressive; locally, the plan's image is, for the most part, conservative. This was not always so. Initially the plan was viewed as too restrictive, catering to the left of the political spectrum represented by the Board of Supervisors. Then came the very narrowly defeated high-rise initiative of November 1983 and the success of the "Sunlight Initiative" of June 1984. In the light of intense public pressure, the plan became politically acceptable for most supervisors, because any plan less restrictive would have had no chance for public approval.

PUBLIC STREETS—PUBLIC INTEREST

The issues raised by the public, and particularly the users of downtown streets, make it clear to planners and designers that considerations of stylistic qualities of high-rise buildings are not sufficient and are often meaningless. Environmental impact statements could, but unfortunately do not, yield adequate information on the experiential impact of new buildings. Since the National Environmental Policy Act of 1969, all significant structures are subject to an environmental impact study, where disclosure of all possible effects on the environment and on the community is mandatory. However, good portions of impact statements of individual buildings remain best guesses. Even where methods of measuring impact are available, the information presented is frequently faulty and erroneous.

In 1982, out of twelve environmental impact reports of downtown building in San Francisco, ten showed misleading or incorrect information on the shadows projected by future buildings. Since 1985, however, all environmental impact reports have very accurate shadow-impact analyses. Also, environmental impact report firms used to print shadow diagrams for three times of day, 9:00 AM, noon, and 4:00 PM, on three days of the year. The same firms have now demonstrated their ability to print shadow diagrams at any hour and minute on any date desired. One can be accurate; one only needs a strong public interest in the work.

Wind studies used to be done in a similarly cavalier manner. In May 1983, it was discovered that the weather station's records for northwest winds in San Francisco wrongly showed consistently calm readings. (The weather station's anemometer, located on the top of a downtown building, had been sheltered from northwest winds by a penthouse.) As a result, all wind-tunnel studies performed on tall buildings to that date used a calm baseline for northwest winds, although, as anyone who has sailed across the bay can confirm, northwest winds are not only the strongest winds in San Francisco, but also the most frequent. Thus, ten years of wind-tunnel tests became irrelevant.

Currently, six environmental impact reports on downtown buildings in San Francisco are in court for various reasons. Suits have been brought by citizens' groups. In San Francisco, these groups have proven to be the real hope for change.

The public accountability of planners and designers needs to be taken more seriously. New York's planning commissioners are now working on detailed specifications for those who make presentations of proposed buildings and plans. San Francisco's new Downtown Plan requires developers to construct scale models of proposed projects that fit into the large model of San Francisco housed at the Environmental Simulation Laboratory. Photographs are taken of the new building in the model from a variety of angles, with three criteria in mind. First, the presentation has to be tested for accuracy. Proponents as well as opponents have access to the facility, where they can check dimensions of the proposed building as well as those of surrounding buildings. Second, the model has to be realistic: color, shape, texture, detail, and light have to be as close to reality as possible. Third,

15-19. Eye-level views from a 600-foot and a 400-foot distance of: <u>a.</u> and <u>c.</u> existing conditions; <u>b.</u> and <u>d.</u> new development. The design of the building's upper stories was changed following presentation of these studies at the design review meeting.

a.

c.

b.

d.

the photographic presentation has to be objective. The new development is not only viewed from one angle (the most glamorous view or the most devastating, depending on who tries to make the point), but from as many angles as possible. Ideally, all views that can be obtained in the real world are matched.

With respect to urban environments, San Francisco is ahead of other cities because citizens have taken a great interest in the politics of downtown development. Innovative and useful, the ordinance that requires developers to give previews of their proposed structures is the result of a continuous concern by citizens and environmental groups for new development that is compatible with the city's character. The public has, with good reason, questioned the predictions advanced by planners and architects and it is now demanding (and will continue to demand) complete information and full disclosure regarding the impact of proposed projects.

REFERENCES

Appleyard, D. 1979. "Understanding Professional Media: Issues, Theory, and a Research Agenda." In *Human Behavior and Environment*, edited by I. Altman and J. F. Wohlwill. New York: Plenum Press.
———. *Identity, Power, and Place.* 1982. Unfinished manuscript. Berkeley: University of California, Institute of Urban and Regional Development.
Appleyard, D., and K. H. Craik. 1974. "The Berkeley Environmental Simulation Project: Its Use in Environmental Impact Assessment." In *Environmental Impact Assessment: Guidelines and Commentary*, edited by T. G. Dickert and K. R. Domeny. Berkeley: University of California Extension.
———. 1978. "The Berkeley Environmental Simulation Laboratory and Its Research Programme." *International Review of Applied Psychology* 27: 53–55.
Appleyard, D., and L. Fishman. 1979. "High-rise Buildings versus San Francisco: Measuring the Visual and Symbolic Impacts." In *Behavioral Response to Tall Buildings*, edited by D. Conway. Stroudsburg, Pa.: Dowden, Hutchinson, and Ross.
Appleyard, D., P. Bosselmann, E. Klock, and A. Schmidt. 1979. "Periscoping Future Scenes: How to Use an Environmental Simulation Laboratory." *Landscape Architecture* 69: 487–88, 508–10.

Arens, E. 1981. "Designing for an Acceptable Wind Environment." *Transportation Engineering Journal* (American Society of Civil Engineers) 107 (March): Technical Report No. 2.
Berglund, L. G., and J. A. J. Stolwijk. 1978. "Use of Simulation Models of Human Thermoregulation in Assessing Acceptability of Complex Dynamic Thermal Environments." *Energy Conservation Strategies in Buildings*, edited by J.A.J. Stolwijk. New Haven: John B. Pierce Foundation, Yale University.
Blumenfeld, H. 1953. "Scale in Civic Design." *Town Planning Review* 24 (April): 1.
Bosselmann, P. 1983a. "Shadowboxing: Keeping Sunlight on Chinatown's Kids." *Landscape Architecture* 73: 74–76.
———. 1983b. "Visual Impact Assessment at Berkeley." *Urban Design International* 7: 34–37.
Bosselmann, P., and H. Gerdes. 1980. "Film and Video in the Planning Process." *American Planning Journal* 46: 12–14.
Bosselmann, P., J. Flores, and T. O'Hare. 1983. *Sun and Light for Downtown San Francisco.* Monograph No. 34. Berkeley: University of California, Institute of Urban and Regional Development.
Bosselmann, P., J. Flores, T. Priestley, and W. Gray. 1984. *Sun, Wind, and Comfort.* Berkeley: University of California, Institute of Urban and Regional Development.
Bosselmann, P., and K. H. Craik. 1987. "Perceptual Simulations of Environments." In *Behavior Research Methods in Environmental Design*, edited by R. B. Bechtel, R. W. Marans, and W. Michelson. New York: Van Nostrand Reinhold.
City of New York, Department of City Planning. 1981. *Midtown Zoning.* New York: Department of City Planning.
City of San Francisco, Department of City Planning. 1971. *San Francisco Urban Design Plan.* San Francisco: Department of City Planning.
———. 1985. *Downtown Plan.* San Francisco: Department of City Planning, October.
Goldberger, P. 1985. "Will Times Square Become a Grand Canyon?" *New York Times*, October 6.
Huxtable, A. L. 1982. "The Tall Building Artistically Reconsidered: The Search for a Skyscraper Style." *New Criterion* 1, no. 3 (Nov.): 63–75.
———. 1984. *The Tall Building Artistically Reconsidered: The Search for a New Skyscraper Style.* New York: Pantheon.
Knowles, R. L. 1981. *Sun Rhythm Form.* Cambridge: MIT Press.
Lieberman, E. 1983. "Downtown Open Space Use Survey." Paper presented at the *Boulder Pedestrian Conference*, September 23.

16.
Bellevue's New Approach to Pedestrian Planning and Design

DON C. MILES AND MARK L. HINSHAW

Plans to curb urban sprawl often call for the intensification of suburban centers to create medium-sized cities with many of the urban amenities of their larger cousins. Bellevue, Washington, a city of 80,000 near Seattle, is exemplary. Since its incorporation in the 1950s, Bellevue has rapidly grown from a suburb to become Washington's fourth-largest city.

An innovative element of Bellevue's downtown plan is the public/private partnership being used to develop a downtown pedestrian area known as the Sixth Street Pedestrian Corridor (City of Bellevue 1985b). Over 2,000 feet in length, with three major public open spaces situated along its alignment, the pedestrian corridor is the focus of the downtown "core," which calls for a diversity of uses built at a higher intensity (City of Bellevue 1983). Funding for the design, construction, and maintenance is provided by adjacent property owners. The corridor connects the retail hub and regional shopping center with high-rise office development, additional retail development, and transit facilities.

This chapter describes the objectives, planning process, and design features of the Sixth Street pedestrian corridor and their relevance to development in other communities.

BACKGROUND

Until the late 1970s, Bellevue's downtown area had consisted of a collection of low-rise commercial structures, with a sprinkling of six- to thirteen-story office buildings, a sprawling regional shopping center, and

All photographs and graphics are by DMA/PPS unless otherwise noted.

strip commercial development. The 400-acre downtown had been totally oriented to the automobile, with about half of its area devoted to parking. Today, a skyline of 4.5 million square feet of high rises has emerged and is being tied into a pedestrian-oriented street network. Another 1.5 million square feet is under construction and will contribute further to the variety and intensity of the downtown (fig. 16-1).

In 1978, the City of Bellevue initiated the preparation of a plan that would provide an entirely new direction for the future growth and development of the

16-1. Map of downtown Bellevue, Washington. (Source: City of Bellevue Planning Dept.)

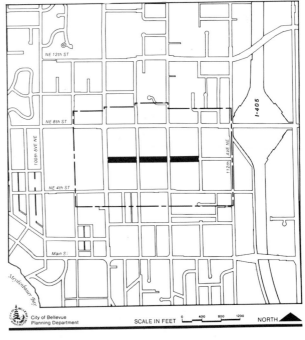

■ **Pedestrian Corridor**

downtown. Completed in 1979, the plan included a number of policies intended to bring about a greater level of intensity, variety, and amenity, particularly for people on foot. Other policies called for concentrating new commercial and high-density residential development in the downtown, with particular areas of the community being designated for development of lesser intensity. These policies contributed to the rejection of a major regional shopping center that had been proposed for a site on the edge of the city.

Approximately two years later, the city council adopted a radically new land-use code, now in effect. The plan contains a number of provisions intended for the downtown area, including dramatically lower parking requirements, an incentive zoning system that allows buildings to have heights of 300 feet or more in the core in return for street level amenities, and a requirement for detailed design review of all development proposals.

The centerpiece of the new code is a requirement that private developers individually construct portions of a pedestrian corridor, running through the middle of the downtown, as they incrementally construct buildings on their own properties (fig. 16-2). In return for this feature, developers receive not only floor-area bonuses, but also the right to exceed the maximum height limit.

The pedestrian corridor is but one of a group of public programs and policies designed to reinforce Bellevue. Another, which involves an agreement with Metro, the regional transit authority, calls for increasing transit service concurrent with increases in downtown employment. The focal point of transit service

is a $5 million "timed-transfer" center in the heart of the core area, which will provide half-hourly connections to other major communities in the region (fig. 16-3). Closely related is the construction of a new freeway interchange that will provide a direct connection to the downtown for buses and car pools. Finally, another public sector project that will add to the downtown's intensity and diversity is the development of a park on a 17-acre tract of land situated within two blocks of the pedestrian corridor. Awarded to the firm of Beckley/Myers of Milwaukee, Wisconsin, following a national competition, the park design will consist of a large meadow surrounded by a tree-lined gravel walk and a shallow canal that discards into a pool. Classical details unify the design. Built on city land, the park is now in its first phase of development, supported by a consortium of citizens and property owners.

The pedestrian corridor development in Bellevue has benefitted from a number of earlier projects elsewhere in the country.

In the 1970s, incentive zoning in special New York districts encouraged the creation of interconnecting midblock plazas and galleries. Located on private property, spaces such as the Olympic Tower Galleria, the Graduate Center, and various linear plazas near the Exxon Building provide alternate routes for pedestrians negotiating the long blocks and crowded avenues of Manhattan. These spaces, however, lacked sufficient continuity to become a pedestrian street system, and street crossings were not specially treated. Other projects that allowed public pedestrian ways on private property are a single block in length (for instance, Shubert Alley and Channel Gardens at

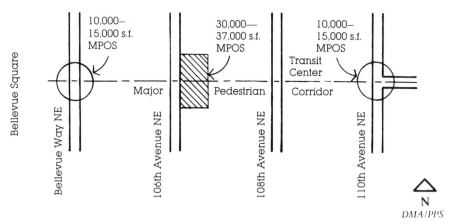

16-2. Bellevue pedestrian corridor plan showing development through the three 600-foot superblocks, including major public open spaces and transit center.

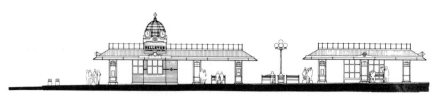

16-3. Partial elevation showing the Bellevue transit center. (Source: HNTB & ZGF & DMA/PPS)

Rockefeller Center) or they are enclosed as an arcade or galleria (for instance, the IBM building, the AT&T building, and so on).

The Loring Greenway in Minneapolis, a four-block extension of the Nicollet Mall, is the central focus of parcels within a redevelopment district. Its formerly private land was purchased by the city and cleared and replatted to create the pedestrian way. The Nicollet Mall, for which the business community pays a majority of maintenance costs, illustrates the more common case of a publicly owned street that has been redesigned for the exclusive use of pedestrians and transit riders. Similar transit malls have been built in Denver, Colorado, and Portland, Oregon. Minneapolis and Baltimore, among other cities, have extensive second-level pedestrian ways connecting private development parcels. However, none of these examples demonstrates the magnitude of private participation found in the Bellevue pedestrian corridor. Every major property owner along the corridor is obligated to participate in its design, construction, and maintenance and to orient and shape their buildings specifically to fit the corridor network.

DEVELOPMENT PROCESS

The Sixth Street pedestrian corridor development process is unusual with respect to the following four characteristics:

Private ownership and funding. The corridor is to be designed, constructed, owned, and maintained largely by the private sector. Existing public street rights-of-way and street crossings comprise approximately 30 percent of the area of the corridor and major public open space, while private property accounts for the remaining 70 percent. These figures contrast sharply with more typical streetscape improvement projects involving public streets and some amount of public funds (or at least lower interest rates through a local improvement district).

Phased development. The corridor will be developed over roughly ten to fifteen years, in marked difference from most "malls," which are short-term public works projects. The incremental development process will cause the finished product to seem less dated and more natural, with some portions having an older appearance or patina than others. One hopes this process will produce greater diversity as well.

New urban context. The corridor and the abutting development are being developed concurrently. Thus, unlike virtually all other street improvement projects, which require the transformation of a defined urban streetscape, the corridor demands that an entirely new series of public and semipublic spaces be created together with their context.

Private initiative. Leadership and vision in the Bellevue community are two important keys to the success of the pedestrian corridor. The business community, to a great extent brought together by the Bellevue Downtown Association (BDA), provides critical guidance in the planning process. The BDA has sponsored workshops on downtown planning and has organized various committees, including the Pedestrian Corridor Committee, which oversees the program's design and development and coordinates with various city agencies.

One example of the strength of private-sector commitment to the project occurred in response to the Bellevue land-use code (City of Bellevue 1985a). This code specifies that corridor property owners are required to develop general design guidelines both for the corridor and for the adjoining public open spaces. The Pedestrian Corridor Committee was originally organized to finance and oversee the preparation of these guidelines. Yet, after completing them, the committee voluntarily sought the city's adoption of additional guidelines that are even more specific about certain design features.

OBJECTIVES

General objectives for the pedestrian corridor include positive economic impact and high quality. Achieving high quality means going beyond the land-use code and specifying design principles that involve the following:

Flexibility
- to allow for individual design expression
- to allow for further development over time as needed by various parties
- to assure equal development rights among property owners

Continuity
- among various projects over time
- to make the pedestrian corridor and major public open spaces appear as a single entity; in other words, as a pedestrian street with activity nodes, not as a series of interconnected plazas.

Urbanity
- to create a pedestrian street, rather than a typical mall, by incorporating and emphasizing traditional movement patterns and spatial relationships.

Numerous questions guided the formulation of objectives. For instance, some debated the creation of an auto-free zone, while others hesitated about the addition of plazas. These questions were asked prior to the completion of design guidelines and they led to some soul-searching. Nationally, pedestrian malls have had mixed reviews. Often mall treatments have offered too little or appeared too late to revive a failing downtown retail district. Many design concepts have been simplistic and cosmetic: new street furniture and landscaping often have not sufficiently addressed economic issues. Planning trends seemed to be moving away from streets for exclusive pedestrian use. Plazas were publicly criticized for being barren, windswept spaces that eroded storefront continuity.

In Bellevue, however, the pedestrian corridor alignment is, at present, bordered primarily by parking lots and undeveloped land. Thus, the situation is entirely different from that of an existing street lined with retail facilities; in planning terms, it means that the preferred environment had to be determined. Planners could begin from scratch, working without the usual constraints, such as existing businesses, garages, utilities, traffic patterns, and landmarks. Several factors further supported the eventual decision to build a pedestrian street:

· Freedom exists to create a unique type of pedestrian corridor with all of the advantages of a pedestrian mall (such as separation from vehicles and pedestrian amenities) and none of the liabilities (namely, excessive width and lack of activity).
· Vehicular service is not a problem because space below grade can accommodate parking. Consequently, numerous opportunities exist to service retail facilities from below, and emergency vehicles can gain access to the corridor from the perimeter of the blocks.
· The corridor creates an opportunity for grade-level separation of vehicles and pedestrians and for a direct pedestrian path from the transit center to the regional retail shopping center.
· Much of downtown Bellevue is visually dominated by the automobile, whose presence is encouraged by wide streets and surface parking. The pedestrian corridor is an opportunity to create a haven and activity center for people on foot.

· The creation of a desirable pedestrian environment suggests a narrow corridor width, which would eliminate automobiles and service and transit vehicles at street level.
· Over ten million square feet of commercial space will eventually be developed around the pedestrian corridor. Many properties are being "master-planned" and developed in superblock-sized segments (300 by 600 feet). Development is being tailored to take advantage of the pedestrian corridor's retailing and activity focuses.

DESIGN

The design process involved three steps. First, a survey of over 1,200 employees and their spouses revealed the attitudes and preferences of potential users. Second, a set of general design principles were drafted and thoroughly reviewed. Finally, detailed guidelines were written and refined.

The issues that surfaced during the preparation of the design guidelines centered on two related ideas: pedestrian streetscape and concepts of classic civic design.

Pedestrian Streetscape

The pedestrian corridor Design Guidelines respond both to large- and small-scale considerations (fig. 16-4). Height and bulk provisions address solar access and sense of streetwall enclosure (fig. 16-5). Streetwall guidelines are concerned with pedestrian orientation and visual interest. The corridor itself consists of five zones (fig. 16-6). A horizontal zone adjacent to the buildings, ranging from 1.5 to 10 feet in width (25 feet for the major public open spaces), is designated as a pedestrian-oriented sector. This zone features sidewalk cafés and greenhouse-type structures projecting into the pedestrian corridor and major public open spaces (fig. 16-7). The sector in the middle of the corridor is reserved for planting, seating, kiosks, and

16-4. Pedestrian corridor section.

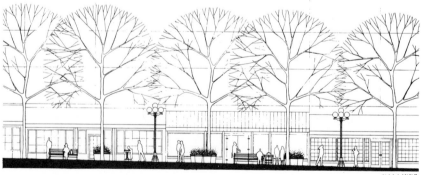

DMA/PPS

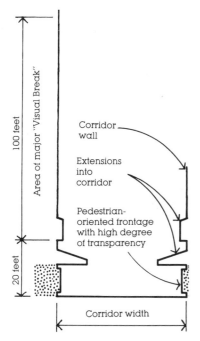

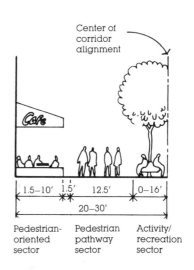

16.5. Pedestrian corridor "wall."
(Source: DMA/PPS & TRA)

16-6. Pedestrian corridor "floor."
(Source: DMA/PPS & TRA)

16-7. Sidewalk café seating on the pedestrian corridor.

16-8. Pedestrian corridor
streetscape elements.

DMA/PPS

other furniture and ranges from 12 to 32 feet in width. Between these sectors are two pedestrian pathways with a constant width of 12.5 feet. By providing these sectors in varying widths and designs, any individual development will produce a unique solution within an overall framework.

Street furniture is designed to relate to the scale of a street rather than to that of a mall (fig. 16-8). For example, many mall projects typically have light fixtures in the height range of 12 to 14 feet. Light fixtures on the pedestrian corridor are 15 to 16 feet high, which is nearer the scale of traditional street lighting.

The design guidelines intentionally offer some breadth of interpretation. Rigid, prescriptive standards are considered to be undesirable, except for certain streetscape elements necessary to provide a sense of overall continuity. Since the guidelines are administered by city staff through a process of project review, some latitude is necessary.

Concepts of Classic Civic Design

The desired image for the pedestrian corridor, transit center, and major public open space necessitated a recall of the best traditions of civic design. Although identified with "slick" high rises, and other expressions of high technology, Bellevue was searching for its soul in the design of the pedestrian corridor. Prevention of the sterility found in most contemporary public spaces required the selection and design of architectural and street furniture elements with historical references and classic lines that would survive the test of time. Light fixtures incorporate a fruit motif commemorating Bellevue's origins as a fruit farming region (fig. 16-9). Globe light forms were found in both "period" and "contemporary" fixtures and were therefore selected for their timeless qualities. Globes specified for the corridor are clear, etched acrylic to avoid an antiquated look and to allow refractors to be used to direct light patterns. Drinking fountains, litter receptacles, and bollards are also custom-designed (figs. 16-10, 16-11).

Particular types of benches, planting tubs, tree grates, and paving bricks are all selected for their "classic" qualities.

Further, the architecture of the transit center carries on the tradition of public transportation facilities serving as prominent civic design landmarks. A clock tower, dome, brick and metal materials, and traditional detailing contribute to the visual interest and landmark (eastern terminus of the corridor) function of the transit center.

IMPLEMENTATION

Already, much has been accomplished in the realization of the Bellevue pedestrian corridor. A one-block "interim" corridor has been established and a master plan developed for a central segment of the corridor. The western end has been constructed, including an active major public open space at Bellevue Square and a major street crossing (fig. 16-12). Final designs for the transit center block have been completed (fig.

16-9. Pedestrian corridor light fixture base with historic fruit motif and planter fence.

16-10. Pedestrian corridor median with lighted bollards, pedestrian-scaled light fixtures, and brick paving.

16-11. Pedestrian corridor bollard (unlighted).

16-12. Pedestrian corridor, looking east, with completed portion of project in the foreground. (Photo: Plaza: Charles Kober Associates/Seattle)

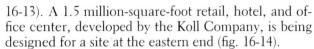

16-13. Eastern terminus of pedestrian corridor illustrating the Bellevue transit center. (Source: HNTB & ZGF & DMA/PPS)

16-13). A 1.5 million-square-foot retail, hotel, and office center, developed by the Koll Company, is being designed for a site at the eastern end (fig. 16-14).

What will be the future development pattern? Several possibilities for the short term (five to ten years) exist. At worst, only those projects now underway may develop. Possibly, development will occur only around the perimeter of blocks, postponing the corridor's construction. Development may, on the other hand, focus on short-term completion. Finally, a hybrid pattern of development may occur, whereby the corridor would be constructed in segments.

For many reasons, the third scenario seems most likely to occur. First, several property owners hold large land parcels and wish to retain ownership. When development proceeds, they will be required by code to build the pedestrian corridor (or to effectuate an "intermediate" improvement) along their entire corridor frontage rather than merely in that portion abutting a partial development. Second, the corridor is viewed as an amenity that will contribute to the successful leasing of perimeter high-rise office development. Third, public attention is focused on the pedestrian corridor. This affords an opportunity for good public relations if developers choose to build the corridor. On the other hand, it is a source of potential

16-14. The Koll Company's multiphased development containing 1.5 million square feet of office space, street-level retail, and, potentially, a hotel. The site abuts the east end of the pedestrian corridor. The base of the building steps out to contain and frame the corridor in compliance with adopted design guidelines. (Photo: The Callison Partnership)

criticism if progress on the corridor is not made. Fourth, master planning is being done by single developers of projects involving multiple ownership, which results in coordinated development of major portions of the corridor. Finally, the construction costs and difficulties inherent in building half of the corridor (out to the centerline) encourages coordinated development.

EVALUATION

What are the potential pitfalls of the Bellevue pedestrian corridor development and design process? As with any innovative planning approach, foreseeable problems must be resolved over time. Some of these issues have been identified, as follow:

· As a result of special pedestrian corridor and major public open space floor-area bonuses, which allow building heights above the 300-foot height ceiling, building heights may become excessive and diminish the attractiveness of pedestrian areas.
· The transfer of bonus floor area to other properties at the perimeter of superblocks may result in too much building and development too far from the pedestrian corridor.
· As bonuses are calculated on the square footage of the pedestrian corridor or major public open spaces, the intended variety in the width of the corridor may be difficult to achieve, with each property owner maximizing his or her bonus.
· Deeding the city-owned right-of-way back to adjacent property owners eliminates the potential to use local improvement district funding mechanisms, which impose development if the majority of property owners support it.
· The city council might at any time reduce bonuses, discouraging corridor development.

The Bellevue approach maintains, however, distinctly positive attributes. One of its primary advantages is that virtually no public funds are involved. In a period when municipal budgets are shrinking and voters are reluctant to approve bond issues, major public amenities are increasingly difficult to provide. In a very general sense, the City of Bellevue, in approving the pedestrian corridor scheme, has "sold" development rights for the price of a coordinated downtown public open space system.

Savings also were made in the time allotted to planning: for example, the design guidelines were completed within one-third to one-half of the time normally consumed by public sector projects of similar scope.

Also contributing to the success of the project was an intensive short course in urban design that was offered to property owners and developers. Issues were presented in an informative manner through slides and descriptions of related national examples. At the beginning of the process, a time-lapse film analysis communicated the point that, contrary to popular belief, a substantial number of pedestrians were indeed using Bellevue's streets. Each proposed guideline involved a period of consensus-building. If no consensus was achieved, the guideline was dropped. Participants felt they had a hand in the final project. After a period of regular meetings, property owners used terms and concepts usually found only in the urban designer's lexicon. In fact, they became so well versed in the subject that they are now applying some of the same notions to other projects.

Finally, private-sector leadership involved additional private contributions. A survey of downtown employees and spouses brought public opinion into the process. Survey results were tabulated with computers contributed by several businesses. Property owners funded the camera-ready art and typesetting for a public information document printed by the city, which describes the corridor design guidelines. Each work element of the pedestrian corridor and major public open space design plan, as it was completed, became a section of that booklet. Now, all the relevant design guidelines are under one cover, helping to market and coordinate the project.

APPLICATIONS

The approach taken in the development of the Bellevue pedestrian corridor may be worth emulating in other communities. Following is a checklist of conditions that may contribute to a successful project:

· The project should involve a major portion of the downtown and include all of the street network.
· There should be a strong market for retail and office uses to take full advantage of the bonus "incentive" system.
· A comprehensive plan must be in place that includes a variety of mutually supportive policies and programs.
· Public and private sectors should share a vision of the future.
· Strong continuous leadership must exist both in the private and public sectors.
· People must be willing and able to spend money voluntarily as an extension of business activity rather than as a city-imposed tax or similar obligation.

CONCLUSIONS

One could compare the transformation of downtown Bellevue to that of a "new town." Both share several contemporary urban planning and design concepts: a small, dense core; a linear "spine" structure; an emphasis on pedestrian movement; an emphasis on public transportation; and so forth. However, many new towns have had a subtle, but nonetheless pervasive, anti-urban bias, with an excessive emphasis on the picturesque and a romantic notion of small-town folksiness. Downtown Bellevue, in contrast, will be intense, urban, and varied.

Virtually every major property owner in the downtown is actively exploring development alternatives. Conservative estimates by the city anticipate a doubling of office space over the next decade. Forecasts for the mid-1990s indicate a daytime employment population of 30,000 and roughly 1,200 households. This represents a dramatic shift toward an urban downtown.

Bellevue is in the position, through its strong policies and codes and resulting public/private partnership, to direct otherwise-disparate development forces to create more than merely a collection of buildings. The intent is to produce a true sense of place: a setting for a wide range of human activities, which is, after all, what cities at their best are all about.

REFERENCES

City of Bellevue. 1983. *Design Guidelines for Building/Sidewalk Relationships, Central Business District*. Bellevue, Wash.: City of Bellevue.

———. 1985a. *Bellevue Land Use Code*. Bellevue, Wash.: City of Bellevue, December.

———. 1985b. *Design Guidelines for the Pedestrian Corridor and Major Public Open Spaces*. Bellevue, Wash.: City of Bellevue.

Cook, R. S. 1980. *Zoning for Downtown Urban Design*. Lexington, Mass.: D. C. Heath.

Hinshaw, M. 1983. "The Private Sector Builds a Public Place: Sixth Street Pedestrian Corridor, Bellevue, Washington." *Urban Design Review* 6, no. 4 (Urban Design Division, American Planning Association): 6–8.

Miles, D. C. 1985. "Using a Public/Private Partnership for Pedestrian Planning and Design." *Urban Design Review* 8, nos. 1–2 (Urban Design Division, American Planning Association): 14–17.

Miles, D. C., with R. S. Cook, and C. B. Roberts. 1978. *Plazas for People*. New York: Project for Public Spaces.

Project for Public Spaces. 1981. *Designing Effective Pedestrian Improvements in Business Districts*. Planning Advisory Service Report No. 368, American Planning Association.

Whyte, W. H. 1980. *The Social Life of Small Urban Spaces*. Washington, D.C.: The Conservation Foundation.

17.
Conservation and Pedestrianization in Plaka, Athens

DONALD APPLEYARD AND MANIA SEFERI.[1]

The three locations selected by Greece for the Urban Renaissance Program—Plaka (in Athens), the central area of Athens, and the old town in Thessaloniki—are all areas where historic conservation is the primary concern. In the spring of 1981, the conservation plans for Plaka were finally implemented after fifteen years of study. Streets have now been pedestrianized and new planning controls are being carried out.

Planning in Greece may be entering a new era, now that the nation has joined the Organization for Economic Cooperation and Development (OECD). The OECD is in the course of reviewing the Greek environment, and a first planning step, the development of new plans for Athens and the various Greek regions, is almost complete.

The case of Plaka is interesting because plans have been implemented in a context totally different from that found in northern Europe. Over the course of three decades, Athens grew from a city of 1.8 million (1950) to 3.6 million (1980). It now represents 37 percent of the country's population and an extreme example of urban centralization. In 1970, about 74 percent of dwellings with three or more units had been built after World War II. Amazingly then, with the exception of a few neighborhoods, Athens is as new as Los Angeles. The main reason for this complete transformation of the old city is a development device called *antiparochi*.

This paper consists of excerpts from "The Urban Renaissance in Southern Europe," a report comparing the progress of Urban Renaissance programs in Venice, Italy, and Athens, Greece. The analysis of design and development in Plaka included in this chapter was presented at the *Streets as Public Property* conference, held at the University of Washington in May 1982, and published in the conference proceedings (A. V. Moudon and P. Laconte, eds., 1983). This work was interrupted by the authors' tragic death. The text was lightly edited and illustrations added for this book.—ED.

Through the workings of Greece's *antiparochi* law, any individual owner can have a developer tear down his old house and rebuild to substantially higher densities—thereby affording original owners two or three additional apartments without further expense. Since land and buildings are the only secure investments, virtually every property owner in Athens is taking advantage of the device. Only houses whose owners are too affluent to be swayed by economic motives, or where ownership deeds are still unresolved, remain unchanged. The result is a new city of six- to eight-story apartment buildings (fig. 17-1).

General planning opinion condemns the *antiparochi* law for allowing increased densities that erode living conditions. To make things worse, it contributes to the congestion of an already-narrow street system. The law, however, has enabled housing to be provided to fulfill the needs created by unprecedented inmigration. It has also allowed the retention of a social mix of residents throughout Athens and has maintained a quality of mixed uses and street life that have enlivened the city. But, given the dramatic picture of urban transformation, one cannot help wondering what conservation has to do with Athens. The answer, until now, has been "not very much." Plaka is now the only extensive area of nineteenth-century building left in the entire city.

WHAT IS PLAKA?

Plaka lies to the north and west of the Acropolis, spreading out in a 350-meter-wide (1,145-foot) semicircular band over a distance of about one kilometer (.62 miles) (fig. 17-2). It climbs the slopes of the Acropolis to a mere 50 meters (197 feet) below the level of the Parthenon. At its southern edge, the ancient

17-1. View of Athens's Likavittos, looking east. In the foreground, the maze of *antiparochi* structures built over the past fifteen years. The two large buildings in the background are special zones. (Photo: Anne Vernez Moudon)

17-2. Map of downtown Athens, with Plaka's blocks shown in black. (Map: Deborah Porte)

Greek and later Roman agoras have been excavated. Underneath the neighborhood lie the foundations of various other Greek and Roman public buildings, including the Gymnasium of Ptolemy and Diogenes; the Panathenaic Way, which circled the Acropolis to the theater of Dionysos on its southeastern flank; and the streets and houses of the ancient city's slave quarters. After the fall of the Roman Empire, Athens became a relatively unimportant city of the Byzantine Empire, which left Plaka dotted with tiny Byzantine churches.

The Acropolis was recaptured from the Turks by Greek revolutionaries in 1822, and Athens was finally declared capital of the new Greek nation in 1834. The city then had a mere 4,000 people. Legend has it that the revolutionary leaders told their chief followers to throw stones from the top of the Acropolis and to claim the land bounded by the fallen stones. Subsequently, Plaka played a central role in the formation of modern Greece. Many of its elite built classical houses there, and the neighborhood contained many cultural facilities. Also, during the 1830s, islanders from Anafi who were working on the new king's palace stealthily built squatter housing in their vernacular style on the upper slopes of Plaka, an area to be called Anafiotika (fig. 17-3).

But the picturesque quality of Plaka was not especially valued in the nineteenth (or twentieth centuries.) In the 1830s, German planners, enamored of all things classical, were called in to plan the new Athens as a system of three main boulevards and squares axially based on the Acropolis, to which end they wanted to tear down the Byzantine churches. A century later, in 1930, the first large-scale demolition of houses was carried out to allow the American Archaeological School to excavate the Greek agora.

Plaka today is interesting to the tourist for its picturesque winding streets and staircases that climb the slopes of the Acropolis. It contains a mélange of buildings and artifacts dating from Ancient Greek, Roman, Byzantine, Turkish, and Venetian times, as well as from the nineteenth century, incorporating everything from Roman latrines (were they worth tearing down houses for?) to a clock donated by Lord Elgin, who took the Parthenon statues to London.

To contemporary Athenians, Plaka symbolizes the beginning of modern Greece. A sizable number of the Athenian elite were either reared or educated in Plaka and speak lovingly of it. For them, the old quarter holds important meanings. Plaka epitomizes the community of premodern Greece, still typified in many of the Greek islands. According to George and Vasso Vassiliou, who have made a lifelong study of the Greek national character in their institute of Anthro-

17-3. Villagelike street in Anafiotika. (Photo: Deborah Porte)

pos, this life was, and still is, one that centers on the idea of cooperation rather than competition. Plaka, with its healthy mixture of all social classes and its classical nineteenth-century villas and small single-story island houses, still symbolizes this world (fig. 17-4).

Only twenty-five years ago, Plaka was serviced by some thirty tree-shaded *tavernas* lined with huge *retsina* barrels and offering *mezedes* (appetizers) at modest prices and serenades played by guitar trios. It was a much sought after living place, an attraction for writers, painters, and philosophers. Even a recent president of the Greek republic, Constantine Tsatsos, took up residence there. Vestiges of the old community life remain. Two or three traditional *tavernas* are still patronized by Athenians. Some of the merchants and *taverna* owners live in the area and contribute to the improvement of the local squares and churches. Members of social groups, like the old Picturesque Plaka Association, can be found singing authentic old songs from Plaka, while the discos drum out their

17-4. Shop in Plaka. (Photo: Deborah Porte)

blasting rhythms on the street below. For all these and other reasons, many Athenians, who either still live in Plaka or are "alumni" living elsewhere, wish to retain this last remnant of the origins of modern Greece.

Residents of Plaka

The average household size in Plaka in 1974 was 2.4 persons. Single-person households there tend to comprise younger people either working or studying. Two-person households consist mostly of the elderly. Compared to the city of Athens, Plaka has fewer children and more persons over the age of fifty; but compared with the greater Athens area, a relatively large number of persons below the age of twenty-five live in Plaka.

Of the population, 40 percent is employed, 12 percent unemployed, and the rest comprises pensioned persons and housewives. Women in the labor force tend both to work and live in the neighborhood, whereas a large percentage of working men have jobs outside of it. Plaka can be characterized as a mixed neighborhood, with 17 percent of the heads of household categorized as upper class, 45 percent middle class, and 38 percent working class. In 1974, 41 percent of the households earned less than $166 per month; 32 percent between $167 and $333; 19 percent between $334 and $666; and 8 percent more than $667. Of the heads of households, 30 percent were

born in Athens (with 14 percent in Plaka itself), 61 percent came from the provinces, and 9 percent from abroad.

Three Areas within Plaka

Plaka has traditionally been divided into three areas: Lower Plaka, the Upper Plaka, and Anafiotika. West Lower Plaka, next to the Athens commercial center, is itself almost completely commercialized, with the *Monastiraki* (flea market) at its southern end and tourist shops in the center. This area contains the cordoned-off Hadrian's Library. North Lower Plaka, near the downtown office district, is one of the areas of greatest conflict because it contains several higher-income residences and conventional tourist shops, together with cheap student hostels and ever-encroaching office and commercial development.

West Upper Plaka contains the Roman Agora, above which is a residential area; to the north lies the main entertainment center, with its *tavernas*, night clubs, bars, and tourist shops. The northern part of the Upper Plaka is mostly residential and of a somewhat lower income than the Lower Plaka, because of its smaller houses and less interesting views.

Anafiotika contains about 100 families, including a few foreigners. Although the houses are somewhat dilapidated and lack some of the essential infrastructure services, such as sewage, they have pleasant patios, several trees (a rarity in Athens), and excellent views. The feeling of community is high among the remaining residents of Anafiotika.

PRESSURES ON PLAKA

The Archaeological Agency

Preservation of Plaka is a story filled with irony, for it has been the continuing target of the Greek Archaeological Agency, whose archaeologists, supported by their international friends, have aspired to uncover there the whole of ancient Athens. When it had financial resources, the Archaeological Agency would acquire available buildings in the area and, if necessary, tear them down. Anyone wishing to reconstruct his house was forced to allow the agency to inspect the foundations for significant archaeological remains. If they existed, the agency would acquire the building or threaten to take it over under eminent domain. Frequently, the issuance of building permits would be stalled until financing for expropriation was available. Fear of such actions virtually paralyzed development in Plaka, in contrast with the rest of Athens, which was being almost completely transformed. Many houses fell into dilapidation, and although some have been saved from destruction, the Archaeological Agency has managed to acquire over 100 of the 1,000 buildings, most of which now house cultural facilities or lie empty, since the Agency does not want to manage housing.

In 1970, the Archaeological Agency expropriated all the houses of Anafiotika in order to build a walkway around the Acropolis. In the long legal battle that followed, most of the residents refused to leave. At present, even though Anafiotika is owned by the Archaeological Agency, hard-core residents remain in their homes, refusing to collect the money from the expropriation.

Tourism

Situated as it is below the Acropolis, Plaka is the next stop for many tourists who have completed their pilgrimage to the Parthenon. There, boutiques sell souvenirs and folk products of all kinds. Restaurants and *tavernas* open at about seven at night. Most are located in the open air, sometimes on converted roof terraces; they stage folk dances and play very loud Greek music well past midnight. Added to this, there are a number of discotheques. These facilities mostly serve the conventional tourists. But another kind of tourist, the *alitotouristes*, or vagabonds, terrify older local residents, who feel their influence is morally threatening to their children. Indeed, half of the sur-

veyed high school students of Plaka in 1974 were found to admire these tourists for their "realism" and lack of conformity. *Alitotouristes* stroll nonchalantly around the northern part of Plaka, sit on residents' front doorsteps, strum intensely on guitars, beg, sit at coffee tables, and sleep on benches. They are part of an international network of persons for whom cheap intercontinental bus rides are advertised at local laundromats and student hostels.

The impact of tourism has been felt mostly through the intolerable noise levels late into the night that are a primary source of resident complaints. Also, former housing is being overtaken by the ever-expanding number of *tavernas*, restaurants, and boutiques. Finally, the sailors' bars, which were traditionally housed in the Troumba quarter of Piraeus, were moved out by an aggressive mayor during the Junta era (1967–74). In search of a new location, they ended up in Plaka. So now, beneath the surface of conventional and vagabond tourism lies yet another kind of night life, and, from the thirty *tavernas* of twenty-five years ago, there are now reportedly 700 nights spots of various kinds.

Downtown Commercial Expansion

Less dramatic, but perhaps more powerful, are the commercial pressures on property in Plaka stemming from its adjacency to the central business district of Athens. Already, the northwest zone contains as much office as residential space (33 percent), and several 4- to 5-story office buildings are being constructed. As we shall see, since few properties are owner-occupied, and as buildings to be conserved make up only 40 percent of Plaka, the neighborhood is quite vulnerable to further office and commercial development.

Traffic and Parking

Plaka has been used as a shortcut for traffic that must negotiate the obstacle of the Acropolis and other archaeological sites. Since average traffic speeds in Athens have been reduced to 7 kilometers (4.3 miles) per hour, efforts to circumvent the main streets are ubiquitous. Since there are few sidewalks, and streets are lined with parked cars, pedestrians must walk in the streets, competing with the congestion of moving vehicles (fig. 17-5). Besides, traffic is noisy and disturbing, especially on hot summer nights when bedroom windows must be open. Parking space is a rarity, so a few buildings in Plaka have been torn down for parking lots. All these aspects of traffic and parking have detracted from the livability of the neighborhood and are a source of constant complaints on the part of residents.

17-5. Perikleou Street, a typical street in downtown Athens. (Photo: Deborah Porte)

THE CONSERVATION PLAN

In response to these problems and pressures, staff members of the Ministry of Housing and Planning, in consultation with Professor Dionysos Zivas, an architectural historian, have developed a physical conservation plan for the area. This is unusual for Greece, where all planning is generally carried out by the central government ministry or assigned to consultants. Also, most is of the master-plan variety, usually used for whole cities. The Plaka plan is a neighborhood plan with specific and detailed kinds of actions and controls, similar to those being used in Britain.

The planners want to keep and enhance Plaka's residential character, to conserve older buildings, and (although this last goal does not correlate with specific actions) to restore the feeling and character of the old neighborhood, so that it becomes a pleasant place for middle-class Athenians to live in and visit. With this in mind, the reduction of noise and the control or elimination of the offending *tavernas*, bars, and traffic become essential elements of planning policy. The plan has four components: pedestrianization, conservation of historic buildings, sign controls, and building code and land-use controls. Professor Zivas calls this approach "a tolerant strategy," or one that does not explicitly try to eliminate such undesirable elements as vagabond tourists, bars, or noise, but hopes they will disperse naturally as a result of the policy.

Pedestrianization

The major strategy, already partially implemented in Plaka, is the pedestrianization of the northern part of the neighborhood. This was carried out in the winter and spring of 1981, principally along Kythathineon Street. Selected streets have been paved with stone to the same level as the sidewalks, new channels for services have been provided at each side, and a television cable is being installed, ultimately to eliminate the forest of television aerials on roofs. Work for the first phase cost $800,000 and, by time of its completion, the scheme will exact another $1.6 million.

Change so far has been dramatic. From a street jammed with parked cars and sometimes fast-moving traffic, Kythathineon Street has been transformed into a quiet pedestrian way. Small plazas have been tastefully refurbished with benches (figs. 17-6, 17-7). Restaurant and store owners, initially disturbed by the construction, are now pleased with the absence of cars, and business has improved. Of course, the open street has also allowed the vagabond tourists to come out in force. Yet, whereas there were only a few places for them to sit, now they have ample room to spread out on the safe and sunny streets.

Traffic has been reduced to one-third of its original volume, while the speeds on the surrounding arterials have risen 5 kilometers (3.1 miles) per hour. There seem to be no major complaints from drivers. The parking situation, especially for people working in the area, is more problematic, but there is no apparent effort to manage it.

Conservation of Buildings

An ordinance to preserve designated historic buildings (about 40 percent of those in the area) has been enacted. No external alterations, "dilution," or additions to the original structures are allowed unless they are approved by a five-person Committee on Architectural Control, which represents the Technical Chamber of Greece (equivalent to the American Institute of Architects), the Archaeological Agency, the Ministry of Housing and Planning, and representatives

designated by the minister. Restoration, internal rehabilitation, and modernization are allowed so long
as the general architectural character of buildings is
not altered. The Ministry of Culture is also restoring
a number of prominent buildings. Some taken by the
Archaeological Agency are now made available to
local and citywide organizations, provided that they
undertake the restoration and maintenance.

Two million dollars were allocated for rehabilitation
loans in 1981, at interest rates of 11 percent over
twenty years, and $1 million for the more common
18-percent loans. Since the earthquake of early 1981,
3-percent loans to repair earthquake damage have
also been available. The number of people likely to
take advantage of these loans was difficult to predict
after only three months of operation, although it was
estimated that between ten and twenty properties
would be affected. Loans will be used for structural
restoration, internal and external rehabilitation, installation of water supply, addition of kitchens, and
subdivision into smaller apartments. Only 40 percent
of the total number of buildings are covered by the
conservation ordinance, and this excludes the Anafiotika area.

Sign Controls

The Alcazar Music Hall billboard stands behind an
old Byzantine church. Pappas Rent-a-Car, Peter's
Pub, McDaniel's Pub, and the Pinocchio Disco are
merely a few establishments whose signs and billboards dominate Plaka with moving lights and garish
colors. They have little relation to the place and convey a tawdry, commercial-strip character. A few old
signs in Greek have survived, the new ones being almost entirely oriented to the tourist.

A strict sign-control ordinance has now been enacted. Signs must not be erected over architectural
elements, such as balconies, doors, windows, or roofs;
lighted, protruding, and vertical signs must be eliminated; none can appear on trees or posts in public
open spaces. This ordinance went into effect in the
spring of 1981, with heavy fines (ten times the cost of
the sign) for nonconformance. Although the earthquake of 1981 delayed these changes, some are already visible. The huge, pink Pinocchio sign has been
replaced by a modest brown one of a more traditional
style. Others are now appearing, giving Plaka a more
dignified character.

Building Code and Land-Use Controls

For years Plaka has been under strict building height
controls in order to protect view blockage to and from
the Acropolis. In Upper Plaka, allowable building
heights are two stories, whereas in Lower Plaka, they

17-6. Agias Eleftheros in Plaka. Note that the Byzantine
church is sunken below street level. (Photo: Deborah
Porte)

are between three and four stories. As development
pressures from the central business district increased,
high-rise office buildings have been constructed on the
edges of Lower Plaka, ironically blocking more of the
view of the Acropolis from the rest of the city. Even
with lower building coefficients, Plaka is not built to
capacity, mainly because of the small existing lot sizes
and protests by the Archaeological Agency.

The plan now proposes the reduction of building
coefficients, and, because there are currently no land-
use controls in Plaka, it stipulates that the neighborhood be designated as a "general residential quarter,"
placing an emphasis on housing. Only stores catering
to neighborhood needs will be allowed to locate freely
in the area. Other commercial uses (such as tourist
shops) will be limited to certain areas to avoid spreading. Such special-use elements as guest houses, restaurants, and cultural buildings will be allowed in the
entire area, but only if they serve primarily the "needs
of Plaka." Despite their lack of specificity, these con-

17-7. A new pedestrian area, Metropolis Square, in front of Agias Eleftheros. (Photo: Deborah Porte)

trols could help in enhancing the residential character of the neighborhood. Unfortunately, however, they are still in the proposal stage and specific ordinances have yet to be formulated.

COMMUNITY REACTION TO THE PLAN

Seven years have passed since efforts to save Plaka were initiated: streets are being repaved and turned into pedestrian ways, some prominent nineteenth-century buildings are being restored, offensive signs are coming down, and ordinances for land-use controls are being prepared. Does this all mean that Plaka has been saved? Feelings on the subject are mixed, both on the part of the residents and of the Plaka alumni, who live in other areas of Athens but are still emotionally and, in some cases, economically, connected to the neighborhood.

First, one should realize that few citizens are directly involved in the development and implementation of the conservation plan. The community groups that have remained active have pursued their own goals, which include organizing cultural activities for their members as well as revitalizing some of the old neighborhood traditions, such as the communal roasting of lambs on Easter Sunday. In addition, these groups have tended to concentrate on improvements for which the plan made no provision, such as the reduction of noise, the closing of offending bars, and the acquisition of a five-man patrol to police the streets every evening at eleven.

Residents have a wait-and-see attitude regarding the plan. Although they are in favor of pedestrianiza-

tion, and the resulting drastic reduction of traffic, they are concerned about the increased use of the streets by vagabond tourists. Some property owners feel that the assistance they are offered in the form of loans is too little and, ultimately, too expensive, because strict development controls limit their return on the land. But merchants in general are pleased with the changes, even though petty crime is on the increase.

Because organized committees seem to be most concerned with supporting a given political party line, they tend to be competitive rather than cooperative. In fact, no effective coordinating committee has appeared whose issue orientation transcends party affiliation. This is especially unfortunate because conservation efforts have also encouraged development and helped to intensify pressures on Plaka. Without a clearly articulated set of goals for the physical as well as the sociocultural restoration of Plaka, backed by active citizen involvement, the physical conservation efforts may only further erode the residential character of the area.

LESSONS FROM PLAKA

The conservation plan for Plaka raises issues about Greek planning in general that are of interest to American planners:

1. The plan has already had some visible impact. In particular, pedestrianization has completely changed the area's character. It shows that a profound transformation can take place merely by keeping traffic out and opening up public space for

pedestrians. For the United States, where pedestrianization in conservation and tourist areas is still rare, Plaka's example is worth emulating.

2. The conservation ordinance is aimed at preventing the final destruction of Plaka, but its effectiveness in fulfilling that goal is still uncertain. While the conservation plan may protect the area from the threat of the Archaeological Agency, it may not be powerful enough to withstand pressures from downtown commerce, which may now move in and build to the maximum allowable envelopes. Since only 40 percent of the buildings in Plaka are designated for conservation, other buildings can be replaced in modern or pseudotraditional style. Were this to occur on a large scale via the assembly of existing small lots, the quarter could be substantially altered. In addition, the availability of loans may be insufficient to stimulate much conservation. Loans may, however, attract private gentrification of the area if prospective buyers are assured that its physical character will be improved and social problems eliminated. This can be both an opportunity to revitalize the area and a problem, because too much revitalization may displace low-income residents. Despite these reservations, the first signs of change and the spots of rehabilitation hold a promise that Plaka may ultimately be turned from an anathema to a source of pride for Athenians.

3. Plaka sets an important precedent for a style of planning hitherto unknown in Greece. Elsewhere in the country, plans are usually long term, large scale, and indivisible, whereas the planning of Plaka is small scale, incremental, and free of theoretical and ideological overtones. By concentrating on environmental details and the conservation of individual buildings, it resembles much of what is going on in northern Europe. Moreover, although one could accuse Plaka's planning efforts of naivete, they have unquestionably led to action.

4. As with all conservation efforts focusing on physical planning, the program has its limitations, its unknowns, and its potential losers. For example, of all the groups who currently occupy Plaka, who has the most right to be there? Should "troublemakers" be controlled or eliminated? If eliminated, where would they go? And will those who can currently afford its more dilapidated housing survive if the aims of the plan are achieved? These are difficult questions that a "tolerant strategy" does not address.

Also, in order for low-income residents to remain in Anafiotika, they will need better water supply and sewage systems, rent controls, and other aids. Perhaps service agencies should take some responsibility for the care of vagabond tourists. Perhaps the countries of origin should provide some support. Most of those young people simply want to gain new experiences without getting into dangerous and harmful situations. They should not be seen merely as an undesirable group to be dealt with by the police. In short, planners must look at the social problems as well as the physical ones if Plaka is to become a healthy place.

5. Citizen participation, a major feature of the more progressive northern European conservation efforts, is not well developed in Greece. Yet the citizen groups that actively lobby to save Plaka represent a new and spreading trend of public concern over environmental issues and quality of life. Although the Ministry and several of the citizen groups communicate to some extent, the plan in its present form does not provide for organized citizen participation. But Plaka could become something of a model for this kind of planning, since it is the focus of considerable attention. Its area is small enough for organized community groups to be effective, and residents have ample reasons to wish to save the neighborhood. All in all, Plaka has great charm and it can become a model of conditions for good urban living.

NOTE

1. We would like to thank the following persons for supplying us with information and insights about Plaka: Mr. Brachos, Mr. Nicolas Faraclas, Ms. Ketty Garzou, Mr. Kyriakides, Ms. Despina Mylona, the Papadepoulou Family, Mr. Nikos Psarras, and Professor Dionysos Zivas.

18.
Graveyards into Gardens:
Public Open Spaces in Nineteenth- and Twentieth-Century London

ELIZABETH RIVERS AND
DAVID STREATFIELD

The preservation of public open space and the conversion of space to new purposes are critical issues currently faced by many cities. The issues were, however, addressed in London in the middle of the nineteenth century. Since that time, London has enjoyed a reputation for the great diversity and quality of its private residential squares and its system of public open spaces (Eliot 1902). Indeed, the city set an important precedent for the formation of the Metropolitan Park System created in Boston, perhaps the finest example of nineteenth-century American open-space planning. Further inspiration and direction in planning for today's cities may be derived from a fresh examination of how London's open spaces evolved and how they are used today.

London's open spaces make a significant contribution to the city's quality of life and have done so since the eighteenth century, when private builders began to create speculative developments that featured residences surrounding large, tree-filled gardens. These spaces in Mayfair, Bloomsbury, Kensington, Belgravia and Pimlico were privately owned and used, yet they were public elements in the landscape of the street. Publicly owned open spaces range from the relatively wild Hampstead Heath to the Royal Parks in the West End (such as Hyde Park, Kensington Gardens, Green Park, and St. James's Park), the large outlying parks (such as Battersea Park and Victoria Park), and a series of tiny public gardens all over central London that were created from former graveyards.

These reclaimed graveyards are of great importance today because they are often the only open spaces in the dense and crowded parts of the City and the East

All graphics are by the authors.

End that can be enjoyed by the public. The gardens are elements in an extensive network of open spaces, and their small size belies their importance in providing space and visual relief. Furthermore, they were part of one of the earliest conceptual programs of open-space planning at a regional scale.

The graveyards from which these gardens were created had become a severe public health hazard by the nineteenth century. Their conversion was an important element in a concerted attack on health problems by doctors and social workers. Gardens of this scale and nature exist in cities throughout England. In the twentieth century, provincial city and town graveyards were also converted into gardens, not because of health problems, but because of a decline in the churchgoing population and a desire to reduce the cost of maintenance.

London, the source and greatest beneficiary of the conversion program, has been selected for case studies of this little-known episode in the historiography of open-space planning. It will be argued that these examples are of more than historical interest; rather, they can serve as critical models for the preservation of urban open space and its conversion to new and more appropriate uses. A typology has been developed to demonstrate the range of spatial uses and the way in which the gardens relate to public streets.

In England, under Common Law, rights of burial in the churchyard had been granted to anyone who lived in the parish or to strangers who happened to die there (with the exception of Dissenters, who, in any case, generally had no desire to be buried in Anglican churchyards). In the Middle Ages, graveyards were not only burial grounds, but were also used for a variety of secular activities, such as meetings, games, dancing, and singing. Those communal activities were remarkably similar to uses that evolved in these spaces in the latter part of the nineteenth century.

By the seventeenth century, churchyards in towns —and especially those in London—had become grossly overcrowded. Mass burials in large graves and the vertical stacking of individual coffins were common practices. John Evelyn, the seventeenth-century diarist, described these graveyards as being "filled up with earth, or rather the congestion of dead bodies one above the other, to the very top of the walls, and some above the walls, so that the churches seemed to be built in pits" (Curl 1972: 33).

Following the Great Plague and the fire in the City of London, Evelyn campaigned for the formation of cemeteries outside the City. This had been done once before when the Dissenters created their own burial ground at Bunhill Fields (Curl 1972). The practice of inner-city, or "metropolitan burials," continued, however, and by the 1840s, the situation had reached a critical stage. Under the Common Interments system, many bodies were buried together until it was necessary to remove them for replacement by the next group. In 1843, the space allotted for burials was about half of the 110 burials per acre then estimated to have been needed. The situation was even worse in certain churchyards; St. Olave, Hart Street, averaged about 1,200 burials per acre, and the number in Bunhill Fields was about twice that (Curl 1972). A contemporary report of the day described the Drury Lane Churchyard as "an admirable specimen of the art of packing, on a large scale—of compressing the greatest possible quantity into the smallest possible space" (Anon. 1840: 829).

The issues of sanitation and open space were linked by Dr. Edwin Chadwick, who advocated the creation of public parks as one means of solving the problems of the overcrowded industrial cities. In 1843, Dr. Chadwick published a report that dealt specifically with the health problems associated with the overcrowded burial grounds. This report, which was considered radical at the time, was a supplement to the *Report on the Sanitary Condition of the Labouring Population of Great Britain*, a comprehensive study of health problems resulting from the rapid urbanization that occurred in Britain at the end of the eighteenth and in the early nineteenth century. Problems of inadequate housing, polluted water, and almost nonexistent sewage systems were further complicated by polluted air and the lack of open space. The outbreak of epidemics, however, beginning with the cholera epidemic of 1832, finally drew attention to the severe sanitary problems.

Typhus was essentially a disease of the poor. Cholera epidemics, however, touched people at all levels of society, resulting in more serious consideration of the reports issued by Chadwick, and those of his colleague, Dr. Southwood-Smith. Ultimately, they resulted in the passage of the Public Health Act of 1848. One of Chadwick's more controversial suggestions was that churchyards in towns were a cause of cholera and should no longer be used for burials (Morley 1971).

The problem of overcrowded burial grounds was not peculiar to Britain. By the early nineteenth century it had been faced in one form or another by every urban center in Europe. Having prevented burials within church grounds, Sweden, in the eighteenth century, promoted the idea of cemeteries outside towns. The Père Lachaise Cemetery was formed in Paris in 1804, and cemeteries were created in several German cities, such as Karlsruhe and Munich. John Claudius Loudon, who had visited those German cemeteries, was one of the earliest figures in Britain to realize the potential of cemeteries built outside cities as a form of open space. On May 14, 1830, he wrote a letter to the *Morning Advertiser* in which he argued the case for cemeteries "regularly laid out and planted with every sort of hardy tree and shrub." He felt that "the burial places for the metropolis ought to be made sufficiently large to serve at the same time as breathing places." (Curl 1972: 55–56).

An Act of Parliament, passed in 1832, enabled the creation of the first cemetery outside London. This was operated by a private company at Kensal Green. Other private cemeteries were built at Norwood in 1837, Highgate in 1839, and Nunhead in 1840. While these new suburban cemeteries appeared to be an ideal solution to the overcrowded, older central graveyards, they were by no means universally popular. In 1854, however, opposition was overcome and the Metropolitan Burial Act was passed, which eventually remedied the situation by forbidding further burials in the City.

While the problems of basic health were being addressed, sanitary reformers joined those who were promoting an equally important, but less obvious, concern, the need for open space. Commercial development was rapidly absorbing what little open space remained in the City, and in the most crowded areas, where the need was greatest, little land was left. The now disused burial grounds were especially susceptible to development by private builders or by the expanding railroad system. The railroads were a particular threat, since they tended to acquire undeveloped land aggressively. Moreover, they were politically powerful and difficult to stop. Green open spaces were important to Victorian reformers because, as recreation places, they provided a morally superior alternative to the "degrading pastimes" enjoyed by the poor at the gin palace, pub, skittle-alley, and dancing houses (Chadwick 1966). John Loudon has suggested that open spaces acted as "breathing places," exuding "bad" for "good" air (Simo 1981: 187).

Just as the developers coveted the unbuilt space of the churchyards, so too did those who recognized the need to preserve those spaces. John Loudon and Dr. Chadwick had both advocated converting churchyards to gardens and had suggested that they be used for recreational purposes. Bunhill Fields, the Dissenters' cemetery since the seventeenth century, was preserved by an Act of Parliament in 1867, which also sought to permit public access. The initial agitation for that Act had been based not only on religious factors (since the Dissenters had been denied burial in Anglican cemeteries) but also because it was a "singularly rich burial ground," with particularly "fine monuments and sculptures" (Curl 1972: 37). Ironically, several years later, the Society of Friends decided to build on an adjacent portion of the burial ground. No amount of pleading by influential figures would persuade them to relent, and the open space was lost (Bell 1942). This action so incensed those who had been fighting to obtain additional open space, that an organized movement, the Kyrle Society, was founded in 1876 by Miss Miranda Hill under the patronage of Her Royal Highness, Princess Louise. This organization was named after Pope's "Man of Ross," John Kyrle, who had expended most of his small fortune on public beautification improvements in the town of Ross-on-Wye, where he laid out walks, prospects, and elm-lined roads (Erskine-Hill 1975). The Kyrle Society was devoted to "the diffusion of beauty" (Bell 1942: 151), and it established a committee with the specific purpose of securing urban open spaces, including burial grounds.

The Metropolitan Public Gardens Association, formed in 1883 under the chairmanship of the Earl of Meath, also influenced the designation of churchyards as public open spaces. The work of these two organizations finally resulted in the Disused Burial Grounds Act of 1884, which forbade the construction of any building other than an extension of the church on land originally set aside for burials (Binney and Burman 1977). Thus the threat of development was alleviated and the remaining churchyards were preserved. Another Act of Parliament, the Open Spaces Act of 1887, permitted the graveyards to be made into public parks and gardens (Curl 1980). The individuals and organizations involved in that effort managed to marshal public opinion behind them, so that by 1895, ninety burial grounds were open to the public as recreation areas within London (Holmes 1896).

The significant work of the Open Spaces Committee of the Kyrle Society owed much to the direction of Miss Octavia Hill, the society's treasurer and younger sister of Miranda Hill. Octavia Hill had already acquired a reputation as a housing reformer through the enlightened and humane management of housing for the poor, which was to influence housing policy in other European cities and in the United States. Octavia and Miranda Hill were the daughters of James and Caroline Hill, who were interested in education reform; they were also the granddaughters of the aforementioned Dr. Southwood-Smith, one of the most ardent leaders of health reform, who had served on London's first Board of Health with Dr. Edwin Chadwick. The sisters, therefore, came from a background of enlightened concern for improving the lot of the poor. Octavia Hill's work as a housing reformer and her advocacy of the need for the preservation of open space, which culminated in her role in the foundation of the National Trust, was based on a firsthand acquaintance with the medical and psychological problems of the poor. She advocated a conceptual hierarchy of open spaces ascending from the private garden to a large-scale metropolitan/regional open space. In a paper written in 1905, she argued that, "The natural complement of the house is the garden. The more difficult it becomes to provide the separate garden, the more urgently is the public garden needed" (Hill 1905: 937). She felt that each neighborhood should contain "as many public gardens, within near reach of the people's homes, as can be secured. It is most important for them to be near enough to be used by infants and mothers; also if they are scattered, they have the added advantage of opening out breathing spaces, most valuable as giving air to the blocks within" (Hill 1899: 28). She proposed three levels of public open spaces: (1) the small, centrally located urban garden or playground; (2) the park, common, or field in or near large towns; and (3) the country common, or woods and roadside wasteland. She further suggested that these three types of open spaces be linked by an already existing public walks and footpaths system (Hill 1899). Her primary work in converting churchyards into small public gardens, her contribution toward the acquisition of Hampstead Heath, and the foundation of the National Trust show that she was active at each of these levels.

Octavia Hill envisaged the small urban garden as a daytime place for mothers with their children and for the aged; people with more mobility were to use it in the evenings and on the weekends. Churchyards fulfilled these needs admirably: "Public open spaces must, in cities, replace the separate garden" (Hill 1905: 937). The communal nature of these gardens was emphasized by her advocacy of games, drills, outdoor processions, festivals, and gardening. In one small garden in Southwark, the churchyard was divided into little plots that were tended by Sunday scholars, "each plot bright with its special flowers" (Hill 1899: 29). Octavia Hill's idea of small gardens was based somewhat on the model of the exclusive and fenced private gardens in the residential squares of London's West End, which she fought unsuccessfully to have opened once a month to the public. Although smaller than the residential squares, churchyard gardens were public: they were accessible to a much larger number of people and became gathering places in a way that recalls the medieval use of the space. In this respect they may be considered among the major achievements of nineteenth-century open-space planning.

Since the close of the nineteenth century, the population of parishes in the City of London has dwindled to the extent that small public gardens no longer serve the needs of the weary housewife and small children. They have, however, become a valuable resource for office workers in the middle of the day.

New gardens that closely follow the nineteenth-century graveyard model were created after several churches were irreparably damaged during World War II. The properties became public open spaces with, in many cases, the original church structures partially preserved (see, for example, figure 18-11b; only the walls of the old church have been restored). This practice has spread to provincial towns throughout England, where the old churchyard has often been cleared of gravestones to create a quiet garden space. The appropriateness of moving tombstones and using consecrated ground for recreational purposes in rural graveyards, where the need for space is not as critical as in urban areas, has been questioned. Within the City of London, however, the need for open space overrides the issue. Also, the small gardens fit easily into the medieval character and human scale of their surroundings. These spaces have evolved as part of the urban fabric of the City, but at the same time they provide relief from its complexity.

The public gardens frequently lie in the center of large blocks surrounded by tall buildings and they can be reached either by narrow passages that tunnel through the surrounding buildings or by narrow streets, which carry little traffic. Throughout the nineteenth century, homes were built along the edges of the churchyards—sometimes even hanging over them—supported by poles and inadvertently forming "cloisters." Today, the tall office buildings often have replaced those dwellings, transforming the gardens into quiet courts that muffle traffic noises. These spaces are either paved or planted and have small benches placed at their edges. Some are completely covered by a canopy of foliage from large trees that reach up toward the light; they have become part of

the pedestrian network of the city. Functionally and perceptually, however, they are retreats from the street and form a transition between the public street space and the surrounding private areas.

Churchyard gardens outside the City, where the population is less dense, do serve as extensions of the street, linking it with the community. They are reminiscent of places in medieval towns where major streets intersected or widened to provide areas for business transactions, markets, or social meeting places. The visibility of the neighborhood from the park reinforces the interweaving of public space, garden, and streets with private space, homes, and businesses.

The particular character of the urban texture of London suggests that the example of these public gardens can be replicated elsewhere only in a very general way. The differences in physical configuration reflect both the history of the sites and the existing patterns of surrounding uses. Most of the street system in the City is medieval in origin. What are today narrow pedestrian alleys with an occasional use by service vehicles were, in the Middle Ages, busy streets used by pedestrians and vehicles alike. Major road improvements were introduced in the nineteenth century in the form of broad, straight streets that cut through the winding medieval streets, much as Haussmann's boulevards cut through Paris. These wider streets (as, for example, Queen Victoria Street) quickly become the principal arterial roads that frequently bear heavy traffic volumes.

The location of the former graveyards within this street network has established three basic classes of open space. In the first, the gardens are not visible from the street and are approached by pedestrian passages. Indeed, one frequently walks past the entrances to these spaces without being aware of their presence (fig. 18-1). Gardens of the second class are open to or made visible from the street, and in some cases, they intrude into the street space itself. The character of the street is thus changed by the presence of trees and other plants (fig. 18-2). In the third class, one can see a combination of enclosed and open space, often with a clearly defined distinction between the two types (fig. 18-3).

On the busy street of Cornhill, St. Peter-upon-Cornhill and St. Michael Cornhill are separated by one building. While they are both good examples of the first class of gardens, they demonstrate a markedly different pattern of use. In both cases the former churchyards have been converted into quiet gardens. Approached by tunnels through buildings or from intersecting alleys, they are a welcome relief from the unpleasant street outside. One enters St. Peter-upon-Cornhill through arched, open doorways that pierce

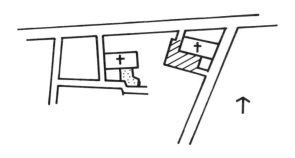

a.

18-1. Small urban garden of the first class. St. Peter-upon-Cornhill, Cornhill, City of London: <u>a</u>. plan; <u>b</u>. photograph.

b.

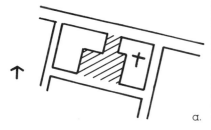

a.

18-2. Small urban garden of the second class. St. Mary-le-Bow, Cheapside, City of London: <u>a</u>. plan; <u>b</u>. photograph.

b.

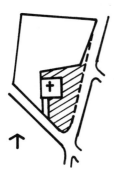

a.

18-3. Small urban garden of the third class. St. Anne and St. Agnes, Gresham Street, City of London: a. plan; b. photograph.

b.

the surrounding buildings. The space is filled with magnificent plane trees, which are as tall as the buildings and whose canopies filter the light onto the paved floor (fig. 18-4). This space, with its strong sense of enclosure, promotes relaxation and quiet contemplation.

By contrast, St. Michael Cornhill has a more open and spacious character. Because the surrounding buildings are not as tall, more light enters this space, especially in the central area, which is a luxurious, green lawn. The space can be entered either from the main street through a tunnel or from intersecting alleys, which provide service vehicle access to several adjacent shops and a pub. Office workers can purchase food there at lunchtime and eat either on the lawn or on benches. The pedestrian traffic and noontime visitors give this space a higher degree of activity

than many other similar enclosed areas (fig. 18-5).

Another enclosed space can be found at the Church of St. Olave, Hart Street (fig. 18-6). The churchyard garden there, which is surrounded by a very high wall, offers privacy from the street. Privacy within the space is afforded as well by the garden's winding paths and mature vegetation.

Gardens of the second class have a greater number of variations. One of these, St. Mary Abchurch, lies in the center of a large block between two major roads. It is approached by narrow alleyways that widen out into a paved space in front of the church and form both a forecourt to the building and a place to sit. The hard surfaces, walls, floor, and potted plants help to integrate it functionally and visually with the street space (fig. 18-7).

At Postman's Park, the former graveyards of three

18-4. St. Peter-upon-Cornhill, Cornhill, City of London.

18-5. St. Michael Cornhill, Cornhill, City of London.

churches have been amalgamated into a large, irregularly shaped garden behind the large office building that was, until recently, the headquarters of the Post Office. Heavily used and lavishly planted with shrubs and trees, this garden is not a part of the street. Its trees, however, can be seen at the break in the plane of the buildings, which define the interior space (fig. 18-8).

At St. Mary-le-Bow, the entrance to the church is on Cheapside Street. It is bordered on the far side by another street, which runs parallel and provides a large volume of foot traffic through the space. A flower vendor positioned at one entry to the space provides color and heightens the activity level (fig. 18-9).

The third class of spaces is characterized by a strong, simultaneous feeling of enclosure and openness. One example, the Church of St. Anne and St. Agnes, is situated at the corner of Gresham, a broad street, and Foster Lane, a narrow side street. The graveyard, which surrounded the church at one time on these two street frontages, has been converted into a small garden defined by low walls and plantings of high shrubs (fig. 18-10). The garden has been extended across the sidewalk that runs along Foster Lane, giving the impression that it merges with the

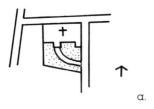

a.

18-6. St. Olave, Hart Street, City of London: a. plan; b. photograph.

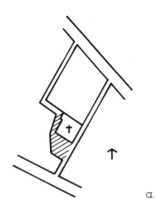

a.

18-7. St. Mary Abchurch, Abchurch Lane, City of London: a. plan; b. photograph.

b.

18-8. Postman's Park, St. Martin's-le-Grand Street, City of London.

18-9. St. Mary-le-Bow, Cheapside, City of London.

18-10. St. Anne and St. Agnes,
Gresham Street, City of London.

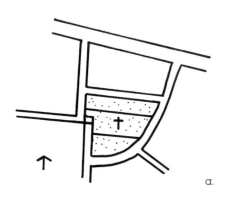

a.

18-11. St. Dunstan's-in-the-East, St.
Dunstan's Hill, City of London: a.
plan; b. photograph.

b.

18-12. St. James's, Piccadilly, Piccadilly, City of Westminster: a. plan; b. photograph.

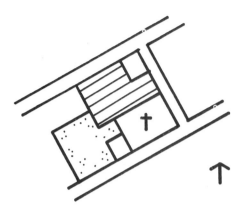

a.

street. The entrance is clearly defined, however, and it is distinct from the sitting areas, which are more private.

At St. Dunstan's-in-the-East, the churchyard garden is visible from the street but, resting on a somewhat higher level, it is not functionally a part of it. Lush vegetation brings relief to an area otherwise entirely paved and built on. A second garden lies within the walls of the church itself (fig. 18-11). This more private, enclosed space is surrounded by the remains of the church. Only the walls and the Gothic-style steeple by Sir Christopher Wren survived the blitz of World War II.

At St. James's, Piccadilly, the church is approached from the very busy Picadilly thoroughfare through a large, open paved courtyard. This space is used for a variety of church-related and secular activities (fig. 18-12). Against the wall of the church, a small caravan provides a place to receive spiritual advice, while a

b.

small outdoor café has been created in the space between the church and its upper garden. From there, one ascends a short flight of stairs to the upper-level garden. Trees, flowers, and sculpture add to the more passive nature of this space. Jermyn Street, which runs parallel to Picadilly and borders the space, is approximately one flight of stairs lower than Picadilly, the paved courtyard, and the main floor of the church. This elevation change ensures that views into the café area are restricted and enhances its use as a quiet sitting place.

These small English public gardens are important for two reasons. They are a hitherto undocumented incident in the history of open space planning. More important, they are a classic example of the transformation of a problem into an asset. While the precedent that they represent may not be directly applicable to American cities, they demonstrate that the scale of transformation of the urban fabric does not have to be large to result in substantial benefits. Octavia Hill believed that the transformed churchyard gardens made the lives of the people who lived close to them much more pleasant: the local air was purified by the presence of trees, and the space enabled all members of the family to engage in a variety of safe activities. The specific nature of these transformations does suggest a set of planning principles that have a broad applicability.

The three classes of public gardens confirm three entirely different relationships to the street. In instances where the street completely and unavoidably overwhelms pedestrian use, the garden that is invisible from the street is a place of refuge. On quieter and less hostile streets, the relationship of the garden space can range from visibility from the street to different levels of intrusion into the street space.

One hopes these examples suggest solutions to those who are concerned with the formulation of policy and design proposals for streets in contemporary American cities. The problems are not substantially different from those of nineteenth-century London, for which traffic congestion, air pollution, and the lack of open space was inimical. Since the street is the principal open space in the American city, the re-examination of its functions and nature is a matter of paramount importance. The precedent of London's small public gardens and their relationship to the street could provide a conceptual answer to some of these issues.

REFERENCES

Anonymous. 1840. "Post-Mortem Musings." *Blackwood's Edinburgh Magazine* 48: 829–34.

Bell, E. M. 1942. *Octavia Hill*. London: Constable.

Binney, M., and P. Burman. 1977. *Change and Decay: The Future of Our Churches*. London: Studio Vista.

Chadwick, G. F. 1966. *The Park and the Town: Public Landscape in the Nineteenth and Twentieth Centuries*. New York: Praeger.

Curl, J. 1972. *Victorian Celebration of Death*. Newton Abbot, Devon: David and Charles.

———. 1980. *A Celebration of Death*. New York: Charles Scribner's Sons.

Eliot, C. W. 1902. *Charles Eliot, Landscape Architect*. Boston: Houghton-Mifflin.

Erskine-Hill, H. 1975. *The Social Milieu of Alexander Pope*. New Haven: Yale University Press.

Hill, O. 1899. "The Open Spaces of the Future." *The Nineteenth Century* 46 (July): 26–35.

———. 1905. "Natural Beauty as a National Asset." *The Nineteenth Century* 58 (December): 935–41.

Holmes, I. (Mrs. Basil). 1896. *The London Burial Grounds*. London: T. Fisher Unwin.

Morley, J. 1971. *Death, Heaven and the Victorians*. London: Studio Vista.

Simo, M. L. 1981. "John Claudius Loudon: On Planning and Design for the Garden Metropolis." *Journal of Garden History* 9: 184–201.

PART FOUR
Considering the Future

19.
Changing Design Standards for Streets and Roads

RICHARD K. UNTERMANN

For at least twenty-five years, street design has been an almost mechanical process of reaching for the *Design Standards* and choosing a standard road section. Most of this work has been carried out by civil engineers, and it hardly can be called *design* in the sense of exploring different options, needs, and approaches in search of the best solution. Current design standards by and large cater to the private automobile and are formulated on the basis of two criteria: safety and elimination of congestion. Yet measures taken to fulfill either criterion almost always result in more cars travelling at faster speeds.

Although safety is an underlying motive of street design standards, the safety of drivers rather than of all potential road users is the fundamental consideration. Yet pedestrians and cyclists have rights to safe and functional use of the road, and residents who live along heavily trafficked streets equally deserve a reasonable amount of security and quiet. The encroachment of auto uses has, in most places, precluded balanced or *public* use.

In seeking to provide the safest route for the most cars capable of travelling at the highest possible "safe" speed, street standards have fostered wider, smoother, and straighter roads without questioning the conventional belief that those attributes indeed contribute to safety. Wide and straight roads may improve driver visibility but they also encourage vehicles to travel at increased and *unsafe* speeds, thereby possibly offsetting much of the safety advantage accrued to cars. Although research has not been conducted to substantiate the degree to which a wide, smooth road undermines its intended safety purpose, we do know that fast-moving traffic threatens pedestrians and cyclists. Drivers have less time to notice persons crossing the street, walking to a parked car, or traversing a driveway. Moreover, engineers seeking to alleviate vehicle congestion have constructed smooth and efficient motorways that permit increasing traffic density, volume, and speed. All of these characteristics, in spite of the ends for which they were originally designed, ultimately limit public use of the street.

The prevalence of standards in road design has been motivated in large part by fear of liability. Road-building agencies accept certain responsibilities for vehicular safety, and design standards help absolve culpability when an accident occurs: if a road is up to the standards, the agency may more easily defend itself in a lawsuit. The liability issue surfaced in the late 1950s and early 1960s, when motorists who were injured in accidents went to court if they believed the roads were inadequately designed or constructed. Liability has been further exaggerated by fire marshals, who declare that if roads are not sufficiently wide, their equipment cannot reach the fire or accident in time. This argument is powerful but not unassailable. No one wants to accept responsibility for loss of life because equipment was blocked by narrow roads. Yet East Coast cities with minimal road widths have had no more accident- or fire-related casualities than newer cities with wide roads. Moreover, fire vehicles can now be much smaller than in the past.

SCOPE AND NATURE OF ROAD STANDARDS

The development of road standards has been influenced by a consortium of road-related interest groups and organizations that benefit from increasing road width, size, and shape. The increased size of roads is, therefore, not surprising. For instance, in 1950, federal standards required highway lane widths to be 10 feet. By 1980, they had been expanded to a minimum of 12 feet. For road shoulders, standards required an 8-foot width; now 10 feet is the minimum. Parallel parking spaces (when allowed) were at least 8 feet wide; now they are 10 to 12 feet wide before engineers enlarge them even further to allow for normal risk factors.

The increase in widths stipulated by road standards is supported by a number of government collaborators. For instance, the early Federal Housing Administration (FHA) standards required wide roads as well as deep setbacks for buildings in housing subdivisions. While setbacks put some distance between buildings, people, and fast-moving vehicles, and thereby offered a degree of protection, they were originally required in the event of even further increases in road width. Since then, virtually every municipality across America has adopted FHA road standards in their subdivision ordinances. It is not unusual for a cul-de-sac serving ten houses to have a 40-foot-wide road, when in practice a 20-foot-wide road would suffice. Sidewalks that were installed on only one side of the road or directly adjacent to the roadway adequately fulfilled FHA requirements. Yet they are neither comfortable nor safe for pedestrians, and by widening the road perceptibly, they may even encourage car use and high-speed travel. Wide roads also increase the cost of housing and can mar natural landscapes.

Road standards are set by the appointed road-building agency of a city, county, state, or federal government. But they are affected by many special-interest groups. For instance, the cement, sand, and gravel industry or heavy equipment manufacturers, will often support enlarged road standards to benefit from the increased cost of construction. Automobile clubs and insurance companies support standards that enhance auto safety and usage. Auto manufacturers lobby to lengthen and to improve the road network, and the trucking industry argues for wider and more sturdy roads.

These lobbies were responsible for devising the method of financing the interstate highway system developed in 1956. President Eisenhower appointed a citizens committee to work out an acceptable way to finance this massive road-building effort. Yet the committee's "citizens" were not ordinary. Rather, it was chaired by General Lucius Clay and included the president of Bechtel Corporation (one of the nation's largest road contractors), the president of the International Brotherhood of Teamsters, the president of Allis-Chalmers (a large construction machinery producer), the secretary of the American Association of State Highway Officials, the president of Bankers Trust, and the commissioner of public roads. No representatives of the public-at-large were included to

balance the other members' single-purpose development emphasis. Following development of a proposal for a dedicated gas tax fund to finance road building, each lobby mustered its supporters and hounded Congress until, eventually, the Highway Trust Fund was passed.

New standards are very slow to develop, and, generally, they build on previous ones, especially those developed in the early days of the interstate highway project. At that time, road planners were considered infallible, and far-reaching "new" standards were readily adopted. Originally, the standards were influenced by the need to move heavy military equipment, which explains the increases in standard road dimensions. In fact, the interstate system was called the National System of Interstate and Defense Highways at its inception. Although the word *defense* was later dropped, the original purpose of the highway network remained.

Typically, local or state standards are adopted (or modified) from federal standards, because the latter are developed, at least theoretically, under the most scrutiny and because they are uniformly recognized. Also, since higher governmental agencies often fund the road construction of lesser agencies, their standards rule. For instance, many states finance portions of the cost to construct local roads, which usually have to match the standards of the "funding" agency. As a result, many local governments simply adopt the state or federal standards as their own.

Adopting federal standards can cause special problems to urban areas. For instance, state and federal transportation agencies have traditionally been responsible for intercity transportation. Trucks, however, represent a large part of highway vehicles, and as the trucking lobby grew in numbers (and political power), it pressed for wide road standards to meet perceived growth needs. Soon, the turning radius for trucks on highways became the minimum radius for intersections in small communities.

Several special interest groups have devised their own standards for adoption by local agencies. One example, the *Uniform Vehicle Code* (UVC), was first produced in 1926 by the National Conference on State and Highway Safety. This conference included representatives from state, federal, and local government, as well as legislators, police officers, highway and traffic engineers, motor vehicle administrators, judges, and prosecutors. In addition, the conference included motor vehicle equipment manufacturers and dealers, insurance companies, motor clubs, safety councils, and trade and transportation associations. An updated *Uniform Vehicle Code* is still in use today (NCUTLO 1968). Although attitudes and values toward the car have changed, the bias toward the car that ruled the conference continues to influence the physical design and management of highways.

In Section 11-502 on pedestrian street crossings, the UVC recommends that "vehicles . . . yield to pedestrians within the crosswalk when the pedestrian is on the half of the roadway upon which the vehicle is traveling, or when the pedestrian is approaching so closely from the opposite half of the roadway as to be endangered"(NCUTLO 1968). That sample provision makes it clear that in jurisdictions that have adopted the UVC (approximately 80 percent of states), the driver must yield only when there is danger of collision. It makes no mention that cars should stop, let alone for pedestrians who want to cross the street. Yet, often, yielding does not provide enough of a safety margin for older or younger pedestrians. That pedestrians have to put themselves in a dangerous situation before drivers have to yield is unacceptable, particularly in areas where enhancing pedestrian circulation is an objective.

Section 11-1004 of the UVC prohibits angled parking on federal and state highways. Angle parking has traditionally been used in small-town shopping areas to increase the number of parking spaces near stores and to slow down traffic, thereby resulting in increased pedestrian safety and usability. Yet, since many business districts are on state highways, this parking arrangement often has to be bypassed. Adoption of Section 11-1004 not only takes the control of the pedestrian shopping environment away from local jurisdictions, but places it in the hands of a jurisdiction (the state) whose primary objective is moving cars over long distances. The code also recommends that any adjustment to speed limits on state highways by local jurisdictions must be approved by the State Highway Commission—an additional bureaucratic step that usually discourages action.

The establishment of standards and guidelines was shaped in part by research carried out during the early highway era. Some of it was highly publicized, such as the research on the advantages of one-way streets. Studies showed that one-way roads could carry up to double the volume of cars at far higher speeds, leading many towns to convert some of their main streets to one-way couplets. However, it did not assess the reduction in street quality to abutting property owners or to pedestrians caused by increased traffic.

The UVC recommends speed limits that are too high for pedestrian use: 30 miles per hour in an urban district and 60 miles per hour in other locations (NCUTLO 1968: Section 11-801). As we will see later, streets suitable for public access should have speeds in the range of 15 to 20 miles per hour. Research by Appleyard and others suggests that most drivers travel up to 5 miles per hour faster than the posted speed limit; persons who drive beyond 20 miles per hour cannot see a pedestrian in time to stop at an intersection (see chap. 8, by R. K. Untermann). Furthermore, lower speed limits can encourage drivers to carry out activities and errands on foot, thereby reducing the amount of "stop-and-go" traffic. And lower speed limits encourage compatible shopping arrangements such as the clustering of drugstores, grocery stores, dry cleaners, banks, and so on.

The "free right turn on red" issue is another example of how seemingly unrelated standards impinge on pedestrian and bicycle safety. In the early 1970s, most states prohibited free right turns on red traffic lights. In 1975, however, Congress passed the Energy Policy and Conservation Act, which required each state to reverse its prohibition for the purpose of improving energy conservation. A cursory assessment of this measure showed no adverse effects. Yet several recent studies conducted outside the Federal Highway Administration have revealed that the new law dramatically increases the accident rate at intersections and that the pedestrian is likely to suffer the most. For instance, Zador et al. (1982) tallied the accident rate at intersections before and after conversion to free right turns. They found a 20 percent overall increase in the frequency of automobile accidents following adoption of a permissive right turn on red. In urban areas, the increase was 25 percent for automobile accidents and 79 percent for overall pedestrian accidents (specifically, 30 percent for pedestrian accidents involving children, 100 percent involving adult pedestrians, and 110 percent involving elderly pedestrians). Preusser and Leif (1982) found a 48 percent increase in pedestrian accidents and an 82 percent increase in bicycle accidents related to free right turns on red. They calculated that this change has led to a 1 to 3 percent increase in total bicycle and pedestrian accidents. One interesting point they make is that drivers look the wrong way, toward oncoming traffic to the left, and ignore the pedestrian or bicycle trying to cross from the right.

Finally, the actual increase in energy savings provided by free right turns is now questionable because of new fuel-efficient cars. Thus little rationale remains for the current law, whereas reimposition of a full stop until the red light changes would reduce the number of accidents at intersections and generally make the intersection a more comfortable place for pedestrians.

STREETS FOR PUBLIC USE

As discussed, *wider, smoother,* and *straighter* are key concepts in road design standards. Yet they are anathema to pedestrians, bicyclists, and road abutters, because they decrease the public-use potential of streets.

The first (and perhaps the easiest) way to increase this potential is to reduce the ironically large "minimums" required in all road standards. For instance, standard minimum intersection curb radii might be 35 feet, whereas, in fact, the actual minimum curb radius is about 5 feet—the radius of thousands of urban street corners across America. Similar issues exist concerning road width. Minimums should be lower, leaving the opportunity to increase them depending on the conditions. That would allow, for instance, a 5-foot curb radius on an intersection between two one-way streets (where no right turn is allowed), a 20-foot-wide roadway on a street serving, say, ten houses, or a road with tight vertical curves posted at 15 miles per hour.

Arterial Road Width

Vehicles can travel safely in lanes as narrow as 9 feet, but 14 feet are required on highways and 13 feet, on many arterials. Wide shoulders and acceleration lanes along arterials further increase the streets' effective width, but narrow lanes induce slower speeds and careful driving. Moreover, slower driving reduces noise levels and allows people (particularly the elderly and the young) to feel safer near the street.

Because arterial improvements have been funded by state gas taxes for more than twenty years, many communities have designated streets as arterials in order to qualify for state funds. Many arterials today are abutted by land uses that are threatened by "efficient" roads; the latter attract additional vehicles and eventually decrease pedestrian safety. Street standards that encourage narrower streets, sidewalks with planter strips, small intersection radii, on-street parking, and tree planting would slow traffic and could increase pedestrian safety and usage.

Speed of Travel

Reducing the speed of vehicular traffic reduces the severity of pedestrian accidents. For instance, it is generally agreed (Ashton and Mackay 1979; Jamieson 1971; Tharp and Tsongos 1976) that with current car designs, pedestrians struck at impact speeds of less than 15 miles per hour usually sustain minor injuries, but at speeds greater than 25 miles per hour, injuries are far more severe. At impact speeds of less than 30

miles per hour, injuries can be survived, while at speeds greater than 35 miles per hour, they most likely cannot. Although these figures ignore the ages of pedestrians and the variety of injuries at different speeds, they point up the importance of reducing speed to enhance pedestrian safety.

Many advocate higher speed limits under the assumption that swift travel reduces fuel consumption. However, cars achieve near-maximum efficiency at a very low speed. For instance, in most cars, fuel consumption reaches efficiency at speeds over 9 miles per hour; heavier trucks achieve maximum efficiency at 22 miles per hour. Hence, fuel efficiency is related to *minimum*, not maximum, speeds that are within pedestrian safety limits.

Intersection Radius

The larger the intersection radius, the faster vehicles can round a corner. But curb radii lengthen the distance pedestrians must travel in the street to cross it (some elderly people refuse to venture outdoors because they fear having to cross busy streets). The narrow curb radii found in older cities balance the needs of pedestrians and motorists: radii of 5 to 12 feet restrict the speed of right-turning autos, which allows safer pedestrian crossing. Also, the narrower the radius, the shorter the distance to cross a street and the more crossing opportunities for slow-moving pedestrians. A 5-foot curb radius produces a maximum 35-foot crossing distance, whereas a 25-foot radius produces a maximum 75-foot crossing distance.

Urban curbs and sidewalks are now often extended into the street at the intersection, effectively reducing the curb radius, slowing traffic, and facilitating pedestrian crossing. Those additions usually occur on streets with parking, and the expanded sidewalk occupies the place at the corner where parking is not allowed. Unfortunately, these alternatives are not considered in suburban communities, where even parking is seldom allowed on busy streets.

Sidewalks

Sidewalks are the sine qua non of pedestrianism. The exact dimension of a safe sidewalk varies. On lightly travelled streets, it can be narrow, whereas on busy streets, it must be wider or separated from the traffic with a planter strip or on-street parking. Narrow sidewalks directly abutting a busy travel lane receive the brunt of dust, pollution, and winter splashes and produce unsafe and unattractive pedestrian environments.

Most contemporary road standards do not require sidewalks in residential areas, not even near bus stops.

Some standards require them on only one side of the street. Most recent standards allow sidewalks to be constructed *directly adjacent* to the street. This is a change from earlier times when a 3- to 7-foot planter was used automatically. Sidewalks adjacent to the roadway offer insufficient pedestrian protection until they become at least eight feet wide. Wide driveways on private land near sidewalks further increase the discomforts and dangers associated with inadequate sidewalks that are nothing more than isolated pedestrian islands.

Public use standards should make sidewalks on both sides of the street mandatory. They should require a continuous sidewalk network, just as a road network is required for cars. Buffers to separate traffic and parking lots from pedestrian areas (with planter strips or generous sidewalk widths) should likewise be considered essential.

Pedestrian Islands

Pedestrian islands are an opportunity to recoup portions of the street for public use. Every town has small, raised or painted areas on which pedestrians can wait. Yet they are generally poorly designed, left-over spaces in wide intersections. Well handled, they can increase the feeling that the street belongs to pedestrians.

Where free right turn lanes have been removed and pedestrian zones widened with "peninsulas" extended at corners, sidewalk use by pedestrians is favored.

Traffic Signals

Standards for signals have increased from four post-mounted lights (one on each corner) to a present minimum of eight lights per intersection. The diameters of lamp lenses have increased from 6 inches to 12 and, in some instances, 14 inches. These standards have improved a driver's ability to see the intersection condition. However, they again encourage travel at higher speeds, which in turn, reduces the public use potential of intersections. Furthermore, the increased size and number of lights require heavy supporting hardware (massive steel poles and cantilevered arms) that can overwhelm pedestrians with the sense that an intersection is the exclusive domain of the automobile.

Federal standard signal arrangements are expensive —almost $100,000 per intersection—and these high costs further jeopardize pedestrian safety. For example, most agencies will not install fewer than eight "walk" lights at an intersection, yet many cannot expend the requisite sums. Thus, the agencies indulge in a twisted logic whereby they cannot increase pedestrian safety because they have to follow federal standards, which they cannot afford.

Signal timers operated by pedestrians are set to move automobiles. Push a "walk" button and find out how long it takes for the light to change—at least thirty seconds, often longer, even if the opposing light has been green for as long as *five minutes*. Thirty seconds is long enough to encourage many pedestrians to cross illegally or to forgo walking and return to their cars.

Parking and Driveways

Most suburban communities do not allow parking on their through roads. By improving road visibility and reducing traffic conflict, the absence of parking also encourages higher speeds and increased traffic volume, further degrading the ability of the road to serve other uses. Not only does on-street parking improve sidewalk safety and comfort, but it also simplifies the transition from driver to pedestrian.

Many small communities have constructed loop (as opposed to through) roads in their new business sections. In Redmond, Washington, for instance, loop roads are 44 feet, or four lanes, wide and, according to state road standards, parking on them is prohibited. Forty-four feet is wider than the main through streets of many dense downtowns, where parking typically is allowed on both sides of the street. Also, no-parking zones are inefficient because curbside parking is bypassed. At the same time, however, parking standards could be reduced in public-use areas. According to the *Community Builder's Handbook* (McKeever 1968), the amount of parking needed for retail developments can include a redirection factor for the amount of walk-in trade generated by nearby areas.

Angled parking slows traffic even more than parallel parking because of the potential conflict of cars backing in or driving out. (It has been established that the back-in, drive-out pattern is safer than a drive-in, back-out one, which may help solve the safety concern on busy streets.) As one might expect, such parking is discouraged in most model standards because it potentially increases congestion. Yet angled parking can benefit public use, not only because it helps traffic move slowly, but because it provides more parking spaces per block. The feasibility and potential benefits of angled parking should be weighed by each jurisdiction.

Private parking lots need standards to enhance public use. Most suburban parking is located between the street and retail stores that are deeply set back from the street. Because adjacent parking lots are seldom connected the walk between stores can be risky. Moreover, a walk from the sidewalk to the shops through the parking lot is not only unpleasant, but potentially unsafe. Upon leaving the store, shoppers automatically get into their cars, because it is the most convenient thing to do. Covered walks that are protected from cars by curbs, planters, and so on, and that link shops across parking lots, would increase pedestrian activity.

Standards for the widths of driveways that provide access to parking lots have increased over time. In fact, driveway width standards are usually set to enable a car travelling at the arterial speed limit to slip into the driveway without interrupting the speed or flow of traffic, hence discouraging the driver from slowing down at the sidewalk. The allowable driveway width should be reduced and driveways relocated away from the main pedestrian streets onto side streets.

Driveway widths along public-use streets can be quite narrow—10 feet are sufficient for the entry of all cars and most delivery trucks. San Francisco limits curb cuts in residential areas to 10 feet, serving traffic travelling both ways. Occasional delays may occur if the driveway is blocked by a vehicle waiting for traffic, but for the many parking lots with ten to fifteen cars, the 10-foot driveway width is adequate. In general, driveways should not exceed a maximum width of 14 feet for lots that accommodate up to twenty cars and 18 feet for lots that accommodate more than twenty cars.

During the prewar years, most sidewalks were separated from the street by a planter strip. "Driveway aprons" allowed cars to move off the street and wait while the pedestrian crossed. Today, with no planter strip, the apron is sloped *across* the sidewalk, creating a discontinuity in the sidewalk surface. As a result, the sidewalk cross slopes may become too steep for wheelchairs to perform properly.

A return to prewar driveway apron standards with 4- to 6-foot planter strips would increase safety and security for pedestrians. In other situations, use of a rolled curb, which slows entering and exiting cars, would be preferable.

CONCLUSION

The list of standards that need to be revised goes on and on because we have allowed vehicles to invade every portion of our metropolitan community. In many places, this invasion has been so successful that pedestrians literally have been driven away. Unfortunately, those most seriously affected—the young and the elderly—are least likely to protest, and have little political clout. But they are only the most obvious victims: we all lose when one of the most productive arenas of social contact becomes increasingly less available to us. The revision of street and road standards is part of the solution.

REFERENCES

Ashton, S. J., and G. M. Mackay. 1979. "Pedestrian Injuries and the Car Exterior." *Society of Automotive Engineers Transactions*, Paper 770092. Warrendale, Pa.: Society of Automotive Engineers.

Jamieson, D. G. 1971. *Traffic Collisions in Brisbane*. Special Report No. 2. Canberra: Australian Road Research Report.

McKeever, J. R., ed. 1968. *Community Builder's Handbook.* Washington, D.C.: Urban Land Institute.

National Committee on Uniform Traffic Laws and Ordinances. 1968. *Uniform Vehicle Code*. Washington, D.C.: National Committee on Uniform Traffic Laws and Ordinances.

NCUTLO. *See* National Committee on Uniform Traffic Laws and Ordinances.

Preusser, D. F., and W. A. Leif. 1982. "Effect of Right Turn on Red on Pedestrian and Bicycle Accidents." *Journal of Safety Research.* 13, no. 2 (HS-034 117): 45–55

Tharp, K. J., and H. G. Tsongos. 1976. "Injury Factors in Pedestrian Collision." *Proceedings of the Conference on the Biomechanics of Injury to Pedestrians, Cyclists, and Motorists.* Lyon, France: International Research Committee on the Biokinetics of Impact.

Zador, Paul, J. Moshman, and L. Marcus. 1982. "Adoption of Right Turn on Red: Effects of Crashes at Signalized Intersections." *Accident Analysis and Prevention* 14, no. 3 (June): 219–34

20.
Streets as "Private" Goods

DOUGLASS B. LEE

Streets are public resources in at least two senses. First, they are (mostly) owned and operated by the public sector. Second, they are valuable assets that society has created and may use as it sees fit (by which definition houses and telephone lines are public resources as well, although they happen to be under private ownership).

Streets are also private goods, however, in that they possess characteristics that make street services amenable to private ownership and market allocation of use. This chapter will show how the management of streets as a public resource could be guided and improved by exploiting their private-goods characteristics. Whether streets ought to be actually transferred to private ownership is a related, but secondary, issue.

When demand for a highway segment exceeds its capacity, the result is congestion. When demand for a privately marketed good or service increases faster than the supply, the result is an increase in the market price. If the price (in dollars and cents) of street usage were escalated in times and places of congestion, all of the following would occur: the number of occupants per vehicle would increase, some travel would be redistributed from peak to off-peak hours, delay would be eliminated, use of high-capacity modes (bus and rail rapid transit) would be stimulated where demand warranted, and the service quality of bus transit would be improved.

Many persons regard those objectives as desirable. Many public agencies have made substantial efforts to achieve them through nonprice means, such as car-pool lanes, auto-restricted zones, special permits, parking restrictions, and regulatory devices. By and large, however, such efforts have had only small impact and, often, they have made things worse.

If we could look at a city where higher user charges

were imposed, the overall appearance of streets would not be much different from what we see now. Congestion would be largely eliminated, of course, but cars and trucks and buses and traffic would remain. Underneath, however, we would find that people would think differently about how they used the streets. A person might choose to go downtown during a time when charges were highest because the trip, although it cost more money, could be accomplished quickly. That person might also plan the trip for a less congested time or destination or might see if a friend were interested in making the same trip. Streets would be regarded as valuable and not to be used thoughtlessly or frivolously, in large part because the users would be paying in the form of money rather than in wasted time.

A FEW DEFINITIONS

The presentation and discussion of these issues will benefit from a short list of basic terms.

PUBLIC GOODS

Some goods and services have characteristics that make it difficult for private markets to supply the goods. The most important is "nonrival consumption," which means that the amount of the good or service consumed by one person does not affect that available for others. National defense is a typical example: the amount of protection enjoyed by one resident is not reduced by adding another. Air quality or peace and quiet are similar "goods" that everybody (or a community as a whole) consumes equally, with total "output" unaffected by adding another customer. Road space can be nonrival if the road is almost empty, but obviously the amount of road space occupied by one vehicle cannot be used by anyone else; otherwise, congestion would not occur.

Many neighborhood amenities are public goods in the technical sense, and thus they are hard to allocate in normal private markets. Yet they are easily destroyed by overconsumption or by production of negative externalities, such as pollution, noise, and unsightliness. Motor vehicles are major contributors to these undesirable effects, but little or no effort is made to charge the costs to highway users in a way that would cause drivers to consider the effects.

PRIVATE GOODS

Services that can be produced by individual firms and distributed to individual consumers on a selective basis (depending on whether or not the consumer has paid), are private goods. Many goods and services that are publicly provided are not necessarily public goods as described above. Nor are all public goods publicly provided. Broadcast television has public-goods characteristics in that if I turn on my television someone else's signal will not be reduced. Yet broadcast television is produced privately. Cable television, on the other hand, has private-goods characteristics which eliminate the need for advertising as a sole means for earning revenues. Garbage collection and fire protection are quasi-private services typically provided by the public sector. Streets belong to the same intermediate category.

PROPERTY RIGHTS

A property right enables the use of a piece of property for a period of time. Ownership normally conveys full property rights, but different aspects can be separated. An easement (for a sewer line or a right-of-way) transfers a restricted portion of property rights to another "owner." A registered vehicle and valid license give their possessor a right to use the highways under the conditions stated in the vehicle code. Yet another example is the right to store a properly parked vehicle on the street.

EFFICIENCY

Streets constitute a scarce—and valuable—resource. By *scarce* is meant that more of the resource would be desired if it could be obtained for free. A resource may be a naturally occurring substance (air), a constructed thing (a street), a service (labor), or anything else that has positive value. Parking space, street lanes, clean air, quietness, street trees, sidewalk space, lighting, and lack of danger are all scarce resources. Money—cash, credit cards, and so on—is not a resource in

itself but represents a claim on (unspecified) resources that the money holder can potentially exercise.

Allocation concerns the ways resources are used. Whether the streets are congested or free-flowing, whether they are filled with trucks or cars, buses or bicycles, commuters or children, whether they are clean or dirty, noisy or quiet, dangerous or safe, and whether I or you can drive down Broadway at 5 PM, are all results of allocation decisions. Almost all are made by individuals who consider only the tradeoffs in money or time to themselves, with little consciousness of the aggregate effects. This, of course, is the way markets operate. The buyer of a suit does not perceive the impact of that decision on the prices and styles of suits any more than the auto commuter considers how other travellers will be affected by his or her decision to drive during rush hour.

Some people feel that congestion is its own price, so there is no need to levy monetary tolls. In reality, delay consumes a valuable resource (time) whereas collecting a toll consumes only the resources necessary to collect it.[1] Delay time is a "deadweight loss," meaning that resources are used up with nothing to show for it. User charges, however, are simply "transfers"—exchanges of money without expenditure of real resources. Efficiency concerns the elimination of such deadweight losses.

EQUITY

The allocation of scarce resources has two parts. One, discussed above, concerns how to use each resource to maximize net benefits. The other part concerns the distribution of property rights, or who gains and who (if anyone) loses. Ideal equity, as represented, for instance, by the distribution of income among people or classes, cannot be determined on a purely objective or technical basis. We can go so far as to say, however, that the rich should not be made better off at the expense of the poor.

Actions taken to improve efficiency may have undesirable income redistribution consequences. Conversely, actions taken to improve equity may decrease efficiency, and affect everybody for the worse. The object is to improve both efficiency and equity, which is usually possible by using different instruments for different purposes. Increasing the price for street use would not have a regressive equity impact, so long as the revenues were used to generate progressively distributed benefits.

THE URBAN HIGHWAY SYSTEM

When one considers all urban streets as a system, patterns emerge from the numerous small-scale decisions that make up the whole. The patterns can be described in terms of vehicle volumes by time of day; the mix of vehicle types (autos, trucks, and buses); vehicle occupancies and weights; system capacities; expansion or contraction of capacity over time by location; air and water pollution; ambient noise levels by location; and additions to, as well as deterioration of, the stock of facilities. The shorter-run decisions are referred to as utilization, and the longer-run decisions are categorized as investment.

How High the Price?

According to theory, utilization of the available facilities is efficient if the price charged to the user is equal to the marginal cost of the usage. If congestion is treated as a cost (in time, fuel consumption, and accidents), then the theory calls for the addition of a money toll at times and places where demand exceeds supply without the toll. There is nothing wrong with the theory, but there are questions concerning the practical compromises necessary to apply it. Another pricing standard is that applied by the private firm, which says that revenues from operation of the system should pay the full long-run costs of capital and operation, including taxes and a return on investment at least as high as the prime borrowing rate.

Currently, user charges for highways cover about 60 percent of annual expenditures, and expenditures are estimated to be about half of the long-run capital and operating costs if the existing system were maintained in its present state.[2] These costs do not include the taxes a private firm would pay on its property or revenues, or a rate of return on investment. Marginal cost prices, alternatively, would also raise revenues several times the current levels.[3] Thus, by either standard, current user charges fall well short of being "high enough."

How Much to Build?

With users paying charges that relate directly to the costs of their usage, high demand (or the willingness to pay more than the current price) would imply a need for additional capacity. Correspondingly, if user charges were insufficient to support a particular segment, the road authority could defer maintenance on the segment until revenues balanced costs, or the segment could be sold for another purpose (agriculture, housing, and so on). Heavy-duty highways are justified if the scale economies of carrying larger loads in

a single vehicle exceed the additional capital costs of stronger pavements, whereas light-duty highways are adequate if they are not used by heavy trucks. Variations in geometric design (including turns and grades), pavement structure, safety features, alignment, and capacity allow a road to be precisely adapted to user demand over the road's lifetime. When the user benefits are tested in a properly functioning market, the signals transmitted to users about costs, and to the authority about demand, create strong incentives to build the right road in the right place.

Urban Form

Planners have long asserted the ability of transportation to shape urban form. Yet recent investments in high-capacity transit modes have not borne out the claims for indirect land use and development benefits. For example, many neighborhoods serviced by the Bay Area Rapid Transit in the San Francisco and East Bay areas successfully suppressed redevelopment around transit stations (they could do so because alternative modes of transportation were available, namely cars).

A far more powerful shaper of urban form would be marketlike highway user charges. Highways being the dominant mode, other modes respond to highway prices. If highways are underpriced, then demand for substitute modes will be lower than in an efficient equilibrium. Subsidizing competing modes only serves to underprice transportation as a whole, increasing (not decreasing) the degree to which cities spread out and populations disperse to suburbs, small towns, and the exurban fringe. Higher user charges will lead to more compact cities, and more nodal (concentrated as opposed to uniform) patterns of urban development.

Institutional Factors

Federal, state, county, and city governments are the major producers in the public highway enterprise. At present, the assignment of responsibilities is poorly articulated, especially in the design and implementation of user fees. Users, for example, pay federal fuel taxes whether they are travelling on an interstate highway (90 percent financed by the federal government), a state primary or secondary highway, an unpaved rural local road, a neighborhood street, or a toll road built by an independent authority. Political incentives reinforce this ambiguous management: it is preferable to get a higher level of government to raise the revenues and pass them back with few or no strings. Citizens often want state governments to protect them from local taxes, including highway fees. User charges are visible and hard to increase politically, while general fund borrowing and intergovernmental transfers are of far less concern to the narrow interest groups that pressure governments for favorable treatment.

Heavy-handed centralized management is not necessary to achieve coordination. If agencies were dependent on user revenues (rather than on political appropriations), consistent standards and pricing policies would be in the interest of all parts of the system. The highway network is at a mature state of development, and questions about building roads that do not connect or that carry different loads are no longer significant. A more important problem is getting rid of existing underutilized mileage that is not worth replacing when it wears out.[4] In turn, this requires the ability to design and implement user charges that will force highway agencies to make rational investment decisions based on users' willingness to pay.

LOCAL VERSUS THROUGH TRAFFIC

Similar resource allocation choices occur at lower levels of the street system. The problem here is the tradeoff between the demand for travel and the preservation of neighborhood qualities. Here two strategies can be used to reduce the impact of traffic: channeling and filtering. Channeling is the traffic engineering technique for routing through traffic onto main streets and arterials until it needs to be distributed back to local streets. Filtering is the opposite, in that it uses a light flow of through traffic on local streets as a substitute for collectors and some arterials.

Filtering can be controlled by physical means more readily than by user charges. Numerous devices, such as diverters, stop signs, chokers, cul-de-sacs, pavement markings, speed bumps, pedestrian markings, speed limits, and landscaping can be used to restrict the speed and volume of traffic (Laverty 1978; Simkowitz et al. 1979). An increase in the effective price of travel to the motorist would allow streets to be allocated to residents for open space and play purposes. Many of these devices are objectionable to motorists, and a strong neighborhood consensus is needed to obtain and support such controls.

The only justification for filtering is the lack of satisfactory higher-capacity streets and the belief that distributing the negative externalities of traffic equally throughout the neighborhood is more equitable than concentrating them on a few streets. A purely market process for seeking an efficient equilibrium might in-

volve a road enterprise that bought up portions of adjacent properties and acquired easements for noise, fumes, and other pollutants. Berms or landscaping could be constructed to mitigate some of the impacts. The road authority would then sell space to vehicles, setting the price according to the cost of acquiring the capacity and also according to the characteristics of the vehicle (size, noise and pollutant emissions, and so on). Especially heavy or loud vehicles would be effectively routed off of most residential streets, both because the price would be high and because much cheaper alternatives would be available.

Missing at present is any compensation to abutting owners for the intrusion on their property rights, with a corresponding lack of consideration for reducing the production of the negative impacts.

NEIGHBORHOOD PARKING

Parking becomes a problem when the number of cars seeking on-street spaces starts to approach the number of curb spaces available. Residents then complain that they have to walk too far or look too long.

Occupant Demand

By conventional wisdom, all residents have a right to park on the streets of their own neighborhood. Occasionally this right is articulated explicitly (as in Boston during the snow season, by marking a particular space with garbage cans or other delineators), implying a proprietary interest backed up by physical intimidation, if not by legal sanction. Residents less willing to assert themselves compete for the remaining spaces.

Allocation of this property right could be made both more explicit and more equitable in a variety of ways. Each space could be assigned according to some priority system; individuals not using their spaces for a brief or extended period of time could reallocate them in line with their own preferences. Or, the total number of spaces could be treated as a common resource, and permits issued for some fraction greater than the size of the pool to take advantage of absences on any given night. Or, the permits could be sold to eligible residents for a fee just high enough to drive away owners who had the least "need" (as expressed by willingness to pay) for a space. Persons owning several cars, or simply storing a car they never used, would most likely be among the first to be priced out. If some households had lots of cars (as in the case of shared apartments) while others had few, it might be thought more equitable to set a maximum on the number of permits issued per dwelling unit. Each suggestion constitutes a slightly different allocation of property rights. The particular method does not matter so much as the explicit ability to trade the rights for a price.

Nonresident Demand

When outsiders—visitors, commuters, shoppers—overload the parking supply, an increase in the price might result in commuters outbidding residents. The usual solution is to issue permits only to bona fide residents. Enforcement is then geared to the level of excess demand, increasing the expected price to the nonresidents (the cost of a parking ticket multiplied by the probability of getting one) so as to maintain an equilibrium.

This dual-price system (for residents and nonresidents) can be somewhat rationalized by installing a few meters for short-term parking or by selling permits to nonresidents at a higher price. So long as further allocation by market mechanisms were prevented, allocation of property rights would be the same as the allocation of use.

If, however, we imagine ways to facilitate transfer of the property rights (for a price), the actual market allocation more closely approximates the ideal. Suppose that an owner of a parking space could have the city install and operate a meter; suppose the owner sets the rates and leaves enforcement to the city. All meter and fine revenues, net of installation, rent, and enforcement costs would accrue to the owner. At this point the resident would also be a small capitalist, renting out a property right for whatever return it will yield.

Given that the resident has the choice of using the space or renting it, the decision to rent implies that the monetary income generated by the space is worth more than the value of parking to the owner. The space could also be rented out on a daily, weekly, annual, or other basis that might be more profitable. In this example, the allocation of property rights via parking permits does not prejudice the allocation of the resource (or, who uses the spaces). Efficiency matches that of the ideal market, while equity depends on who gets the permits.

One may with reason argue that since streets are built by the city they should not be given away for private profit. One ought to recognize, however, that the city is already giving away its resources. Moreover, the resources are inefficiently utilized because of the means by which they are dispensed. Allowing individuals to have explicit title to parking spaces would at least improve the utilization aspect. The city could, in principle, achieve the same results if it could determine the market price for each space.

Off-Street Parking

If street parking is priced at its economic value, landowners will have an incentive to use more nonstreet land for parking. Because this could generate negative effects on neighborhood quality, it would have to be controlled by regulation or some other means that would internalize the costs.

Achieving efficiency in off-street parking is more complicated because many of the resources that are affected have aesthetic or qualitative values. A carefully designed and landscaped driveway with a well-tended garage at the end is seldom a detriment to the neighborhood, whereas a front yard left as dirt used only for parking is a blight to its neighbors. It is also a blight to its owner, but the cost to the neighborhood is much greater. Thus, there is some benefit to off-street parking as a means for increasing supply (although curb cuts may remove more spaces than are added by driveways), but regulations should be aimed at limiting the amount of off-street parking as well as its negative impact.

Land-use controls that apply constraints to layout and design are very indirect mechanisms for allocating resources. They can be very inefficient if done poorly, but they can serve the purpose of protecting amenities. Restrictions may include requirements for paving, screening, landscaping, setbacks, and drainage, with limitations on the share of the site covered by building and parking or by parking only (Williams 1978). Exposed ground-level parking under the building may also be restricted. Whatever the form of restriction, it should reduce negative externalities across property lines to levels suitable to the character of the neighborhood, with the least amount of constraint to the property owner.

CONCLUSIONS

Making the best use of public streets requires taking some actions that emulate those of a private firm selling a private good. Other actions involve regulations that will ensure that consumers in the street "market" consider all the costs they create. Based on a review of current experience with highways, it can be noted that:

1. Streets are inefficiently utilized as a result of current management. For some (generally rural) streets, usage does not justify the costs of retaining the street, but for many streets the inefficiency takes the form of too many vehicles and too few occupants.

2. Negative externalities—noise, unsightliness, danger, and air and water pollution—are not included in the cost to the user and, hence, they are overproduced.
3. Charges for street use are too low by any reasonable normative standard. This applies as well to parking, including neighborhood on-street parking.
4. Because political institutions are reluctant to increase prices of basic goods and services, some form of privatization of public street rights might be considered as a means for rationalizing street utilization and investment.

There are many ways to improve efficiency and equity in the use of streets, but the most effective depend on recognizing their private-goods characteristics. This does not mean that streets should be entirely turned over to the private sector, but that public streets should not necessarily be "free" if we wish to obtain the most benefits from them.

NOTES

1. The cost of collection, which includes user time, collection facilities, and administration, is a real cost, but it can be small relative to the efficiency gains. The downtown cordon in Singapore uses barriers with toll booths, which is only one of many alternatives. For example, Hong Kong has successfully tested a direct method of collection, whereby road sensors automatically identify the time and location of vehicles and enable drivers to be billed on a monthly basis. At the other end of the scale, indirect methods, such as parking rates, area licenses, and illegal parking fines, can be used.
2. Data are published in the Federal Highway Administration series (1984). Additional analysis is contained in Lee (1985).
3. The definition of marginal-cost pricing for highways and the empirical estimation of the magnitudes and revenues were undertaken for the Federal Highway Administration (1982).
4. Both a review of the highway "needs" literature and an independent assessment are elaborated in Lee (1985).

REFERENCES

Charles River Associates. 1981. *The Transportation System Management Handbook*. Prepared for the Federal Highway Administration, Urban Mass Transit Association, and Transportation Systems Center. Boston: Charles River Associates, July.

————. 1984. *Madison Peak-Period Parking Pricing Demonstration Project*. Prepared for the Urban Mass Transit Association. Boston: Charles River Associates, May.

Federal Highway Administration. 1982. "Efficient Highway User Charges." Appendix E to the *Federal Highway Cost Allocation Study*. Washington, D.C.: U.S. Department of Transportation/Federal Highway Administration, May.

————. 1984. *Highway Statistics 1983*. Washington, D.C.: U.S. Department of Transportation/Federal Highway Administration.

Laverty, K. 1978. *Streets and Traffic*. North Side Neighborhood Preservation Study Report No. 5. Iowa City: City of Iowa City and University of Iowa, May.

Lee, D. 1985. "Assessing Highway Infrastructure Needs." Paper presented at meeting of the *Association of Collegiate Schools of Planning*. Cambridge, Mass.: U.S. Department of Transportation/Transportation Systems Center, November.

Rhyner, G. 1985. *A Preferential Parking Demonstration in Hermosa Beach, California*. Prepared for the Urban Mass Transit Association. Los Altos, Calif.: Crain and Associates, February.

Rhyner, G., and P. Webb. 1984. *Parking Permit Demonstration Project in Santa Cruz, California*. Prepared for the Urban Mass Transit Association. Los Altos, Calif.: Crain and Associates, April.

Shoup, D. C. 1984. "Cruising for Parking." Paper presented at the annual meeting of the *Association of Collegiate Schools of Planning*. Los Angeles: Graduate School of Architecture and Urban Planning, UCLA, October.

Simkowitz, H., L. Heder, and E. Barber. 1979. *The Restraint of the Automobile in American Residential Neighborhoods*. Prepared for the Urban Mass Transit Association. Cambridge, Mass.: Transportation Systems Center, June.

Weisbrod, G., and W. Loudon, et al. 1982. *Downtown Crossing: Auto Restricted Zone in Boston*. Prepared for the Urban Mass Transit Association. Cambridge, Mass.: Cambridge Systematics, July.

Williams, V. 1978. *Parking*. North Side Neighborhood Preservation Study Report No. 6. Iowa City: City of Iowa City and University of Iowa, May.

21.
A Successful Street Design Process

JOHN H. OWEN, JR.

Traditionally, streets have been considered chiefly as transportation conduits. In recent decades, however, the realization has grown that multi-objective street design is crucial for the support of a variety of public activities, commercial efforts, and residential conditions (see chap. 22, by R. B. Eichner and H. Tobey). Many cities have embarked on a series of public street improvement projects intended not only to ameliorate traffic conditions, but also to revitalize fading business and residential areas. Following the work of Rudofsky, Appleyard, Lynch, Jane Jacobs, and others, designers have emphasized the pedestrian life of the street and the visual and functional elements necessary to support that life. Many of these efforts have been successful, yet many badly needed street improvement plans were left on the drawing board unimplemented. So the questions arise: Why do some projects work while others do not? Are there key activities in the design process that increase chances for success?

During the past ten years our firm has participated in over fifteen street improvement projects in business and residential areas. In evaluating the results of these and other projects, we have found that the principal factor contributing to a project's success is a design process that has the following characteristics: it promotes cooperative efforts among all interested participant groups and it deals responsively with the project's objectives, opportunities, constraints, and context in developing an appropriate urban design expression.

Furthermore, a successful, multi-objective street improvement project requires a design process in which the interests of all the users can be articulated and their needs incorporated into the final design. Vital, pedestrian-oriented streets have the most complex activity patterns and user requirements of all common types of public spaces. The main streets of many small communities are good examples of this complexity. They must serve local traffic, through commuters, commercial transit, and service vehicles, as well as people strolling, shopping, or just relaxing. They also must fulfill the service needs of businesses, residents, and utility suppliers and meet the stringent safety and maintenance requirements of the local engineering department.

As a result, the diversity of technical, functional, and aesthetic issues encountered in street design requires a process that integrates the project's many objectives into a coherent concept. Developing this concept often involves solving several problems at the same time. Because a street is both metaphorically and physically a connecting element, the notion of a design solution "fitting" into a complex system of requirements and contextual factors is particularly applicable to street improvement projects.

CENTRAL ROLE OF THE URBAN DESIGNER

The salient aspect of a successful design process is the need for urban designers to assume a central role in the negotiation of engineering/design issues. To our mind, the training of an urban designer, whether as an architect, landscape architect, engineer, or planner, is less important than his qualifications, which include (1) an ability to recognize the various aspects of professional responsibility in the public decision-making process, (2) the necessary skills for considering both functional and aesthetic requirements in design, and (3) an understanding of policy planning or capital improvement implementation strategies.

All graphics are by MAKERS, Seattle.

When faced with their immediate concern for traffic safety, budget and maintenance operations, engineering departments and other public agencies too often will relegate the original community objectives, such as pedestrian access, parking, and design character, to secondary importance. In those cases, it is important to have an advocate for community concerns, and the urban designer can most easily assume that role. At the same time, however, the importance of engineering considerations must be explained to community and business groups. This brokering back and forth on issues such as funding priorities, street use, light standards, planting, and traffic signals is an extremely time-consuming, but critical, part of the process. In assuming the central, communicating role, the urban designer, trained to handle a broad range of issues and people, becomes a mediator in the design process, negotiating issues towards a mutually satisfactory solution.

In the Broadway Street Improvement project in Seattle, for instance, the community argued for decorative pedestrian lights to reinforce their shopping district's identity; yet engineering department policy only allowed the standard high-pressure sodium luminaires. Painting of the streetlight poles in a signature color, which is normally not acceptable to the engineering department, was finally accepted as a compromise. That compromise would probably not have been reached had the community and the designers not pushed for special lighting. Although a simple solution, the painting not only adhered to the engineering department's maintenance standards, but it also gave the community a unique design touch.

A similar confrontation occurred over the course of a downtown improvement project for Port Angeles, Washington. Funded by a federal Economic Development Act grant matched by local merchants' contributions, the project was intended to stimulate business. Naturally, the merchants wanted highly visible improvements that would attract people to the downtown area. The city's engineering department, on the other hand, wanted a large portion of the funds to go to street repairs, thus alleviating the burden of street maintenance on the city budget. Where and how much money was to be spent became a constantly debated issue during the design process. An informal compromise was finally reached. It involved implementing some engineering maintenance improvements, such as street paving and placing utilities underground, that directly reinforced the more visible streetscape elements.

FORMATION OF A PROJECT TASK FORCE

A community task force committee is extremely useful for involving the public in the design process. In addition to larger groups, such as the community council and the chamber of commerce, it is desirable to form a compact, ad hoc citizen's task force of six to twelve members to act as an advocate for the larger community. Not only is this group most effective in lobbying for community goals, but because of its direct involvement, and because its members' ideas are incorporated into the plan, the task force can be among the project's strongest proponents. People who ought to be involved in a task force include representatives from the city planning office, the merchants association, and the local press.

FOCUS ON PROJECT IMPETUS

Experience has taught us the importance of keeping in mind the fundamental public and economic impetus for design improvements. In many business improvement areas, the value of local property will be assessed to reflect a portion of the project's value. It is essential to relate this new expenditure to increased sales and property values. Residents and users need to be shown, and reminded, how they will benefit from the project in terms of increased convenience and community viability. If these groups lose sight of the project's value, they will lose interest and not participate, or worse, become opposed to its continuation. To highlight the economic relationship between project cost and long-term economic gain, our firm has worked with economic consultants and developed a set of techniques to project retail business growth over time as a result of a public improvement project.

We found that current average annual sales per square foot must be determined to establish a base line of commercial activity. The percentage gain in activity expected from a physical improvement program or cooperative marketing effort can be established from the relative saturation of the market and the extent of competition. Sometimes estimating commercial growth can be problematical, and the assistance of a market analysis will be required, especially if the market population is growing and there are competing commercial developments. However, the use of some conservative rules of thumb and adjustments for local conditions will generally result in reasonable estimates.

To date, this method for predicting increased retail sales has been successful, and we have been able to base project budgets on expected financial returns to merchants and property owners. On local improvement district projects, where the property owners are assessed the cost of the street improvements, for example, the project budget is set so that increased income to merchants and property owners is substantially more than their assessment payments. Depending on the specific situation and on the types of improvements made, retail sales usually increase from 10 to 15 percent above inflation.

CONCEPTUAL FRAMEWORK

Simple spatial concepts tied directly to project objectives are critical elements in successful street design. Active participants ought to understand these concepts because they will be the central rationale for later decisions regarding design features, improvement priorities, and development strategies. As a result, however, the concepts must remain *simple*, taking a few lines on a plan and a few sentences to explain.

A clear conceptual framework is also an especially useful sales tool in demonstrating a project's functional value. Street improvement projects featuring visual amenities often get labelled as "cosmetic" or "beautification schemes." A simple diagram illustrating the logic of traffic and pedestrian circulation patterns and parking access, for example, can convince concerned participants that the improvements will successfully respond to functional objectives. An example of such a conceptual diagram is shown in figure

21-1. Conceptual diagrams illustrating the Kent Downtown Improvements strategy of linking the two retail areas: <u>a.</u> the basic concept of a Z-shaped circulation spine; <u>b.</u> traffic movement and parking scheme; <u>c.</u> developed toward the end of the planning phase, this diagram fleshes out the concept with specific improvements.

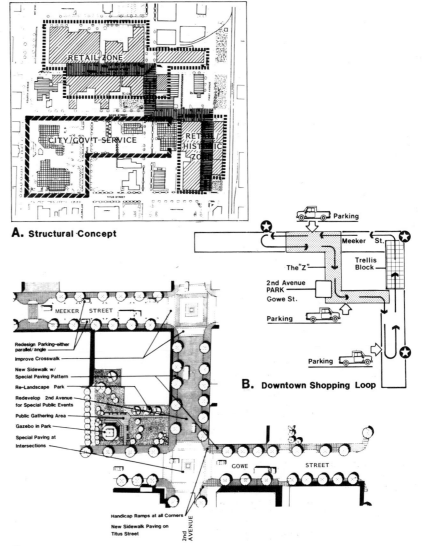

A. Structural Concept

B. Downtown Shopping Loop

C. The "Z", Second Avenue Park and First Avenue Trellis

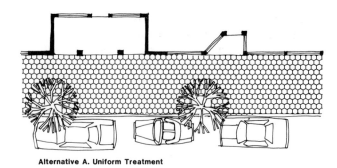

Alternative A. Uniform Treatment

21-1, which was developed for the City of Kent Downtown Improvements project. It illustrates how two disparate retail areas can be linked and points out the need for improvements along the pedestrian connection.

In a project for the town of Port Angeles, Washington, the objective was to attract visitors arriving into the central shopping district via either the ferry or the highway. Figure 21-2 was used to argue for concentrating improvements as a focal feature within the central core. This strategy resulted in the design and construction of a brightly lit, heavily landscaped fountain visible from the ferry dock.

In the Broadway Street Improvement project in Seattle, design issues dealt with individual pedestrian movement, placement of utilities, and visual emphasis. In this case, it was important to explain the concept of relating the pedestrian areas to the building faces, rather than placing visual emphasis near the curb line, as done in many other projects. The three diagrams of figure 21-3 were used to illustrate the options available to organize public improvements along Broadway. The project's steering committee selected the third option because it focused interest on the areas of heaviest pedestrian movement and emphasized business entries, window displays, and building features. This spatial concept later contributed to the idea of using a ceramic tile band as a unifying decorative feature.

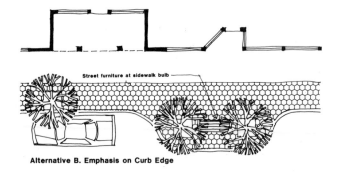

Alternative B. Emphasis on Curb Edge

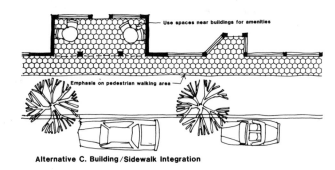

Alternative C. Building/Sidewalk Integration

21-3. Alternative sidewalk design conceived for the Broadway Street Improvement project.

21-2. Conceptual diagram illustrating the Port Angeles project's concentration of capital improvements in the core area.

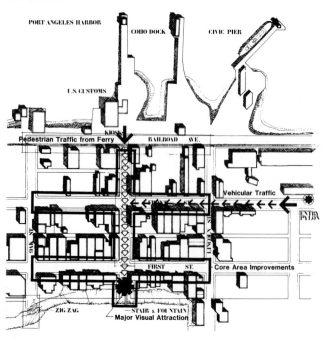

TECHNICAL STUDIES

A lesson learned on many occasions is the need for in-depth technical studies to deal with the engineering aspects of street design. Because city engineers are concerned with traffic safety issues and are responsible for the operation of complex, large-scale traffic systems and maintenance operations, they are often reluctant to deviate from standard design criteria. This is true even when a deviation would make engineering sense as well as support design objectives relating to pedestrian movement, landscaping, lighting, and other amenities. Justifying a departure from engineering standards takes rigorous analysis and research and points to the desirability of having a creative, experienced traffic engineer on the team.

The need for technical back-up occurred during the development of a neighborhood plan for a community in Spokane, Washington. At the request of the local community, we, as the consultant team, had recommended a traffic circle at the intersection of two wide residential streets. We were subsequently told by a city engineer that traffic circles were unsafe devices that no responsible professional would consider. In fact, they were categorically prohibited by the city's traffic department. Fortunately, we were able to argue the community's case, based on a recently completed, detailed study by the Seattle Engineering Department showing that traffic circles in similar applications resulted in significantly safer streets.

In Seattle's Broadway Street Improvement project, the consulting engineer found out that many of the elderly in the community took a much longer time to cross the street than the normal light signal sequence allowed. Only after he had carefully documented the pedestrians' needs and calculated a longer signal sequence that would not reduce the efficiency of traffic flow, was he able to convince the traffic section to increase the pedestrian walk time.

POSITIVE APPROACH TOWARD DESIGN CONSTRAINTS

In most successful projects, constraints are seen not as restrictions but as opportunities. Viewing stringent funding, as well as technical, physical, and administrative requirements, as opportunities may seem like a contradiction, or even more like an architectural cliché, but the notion is valid for three reasons. First, this attitude forces the designer to focus on what is really essential to the project and on what must happen to make the design work. Second, it helps to identify those existing conditions that are unique to a project and, therefore, to avoid "standard" solutions. Third, by limiting the design possibilities in some areas, the designer is directed to explore more fully the latitudes of freedom that do exist.

The notion that visually exciting designs can result from meeting several diverse requirements is illustrated by numerous, well-known historical examples. The spacious layout of Haussmann's Parisian boulevards, for instance, responded to pragmatic requirements for traffic circulation, troop movements, and provision of light and air. The boulevard system was an effective tool for organizing new urban development, clearing slums, and restructuring the urban core. Parisian officials also saw the new boulevards as a way to make their city the most beautiful and prestigious of all European capitals by introducing ribbons of greenery and providing a set of showcase promenades for the rising middle class. Economics, too, played an important role in shaping the Parisian streetscape. The regular rows of buildings, with their celebrated mansard roofs, stemmed from concurrent development standards and from tax laws, which disregarded the floor area added in the roof-enclosed attic. Thus, a major prototype for nineteenth-century streetscapes developed, not from a single-minded artistic concept, but rather out of a variety of functional requirements, economic conditions, and social values.

A more modest but contemporary example of designing to fit diverse requirements occurred with respect to the aforementioned Broadway Street Improvement project. The provision of physical support for the traffic signals was a particularly difficult problem. Neither the community nor the design team wanted the standard mast arms because of their bulky, highway-scaled appearance. Spanning wires from posts was the next obvious solution, but trolley wire clearance requirements, coupled with the maximum allowable signal head height, precluded the placement of a vertically hung signal head. Likewise, post-mounted lights did not fit within the cone of vision required by the traffic signal standards. The designers developed the pipe mast arm shown in figure 21-4. This solution satisfied the community because it was unique. The engineers were happy because it met clearance requirements and protected the signal head. And finally, the designers liked being given the opportunity to use similar pipe detailing on the street furniture.

Another feature of the Broadway project was the ceramic tile band in the sidewalk pavement (fig. 21-5, 21-6). The band was developed as a low-cost alternative to the brick paving that the community had originally requested. When they realized that the brick would consume all of the project's funds, the design team had to devise paving solutions that would meet both the community's budget and its desire for individuality. Budgetary limitation, combined with the spatial concept of emphasizing the area near the building facade, discussed earlier, ultimately led to this solution.

RESPONSIVENESS TO CONTEXT

Working with a street's existing character is a strategy that is too often overlooked, perhaps, ironically, because it is so obvious. Undoubtedly, most designers

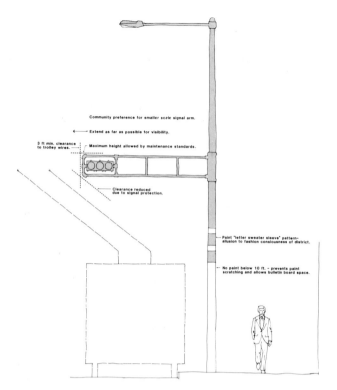

Community preference for smaller scale signal arm.

← Extend as far as possible for visibility.

3 ft min. clearance to trolley wires. Maximum height allowed by maintenance standards.

Clearance reduced due to signal protection.

Paint "letter sweater sleeve" pattern— allusion to fashion consciousness of district.

No paint below 10 ft. — prevents paint scratching and allows bulletin board space.

21-4. Light standard from Broadway Street Improvement project.

Tile Band
Light Standard

Bulletin Board

Handicapped Ramp

Crosswalk

21-5. Sidewalk pavement and fixture details from Broadway Street Improvement project.

21-6. Sidewalk details from Broadway Street Improvement project.

would agree that a contextual street-design approach emphasizes an area's uniqueness and utilizes existing features most effectively. Nevertheless, while street improvements in historic districts usually build on the character of existing structures, the standard design solution for retail business streets, no matter what their character of function, seems to be a landscaped "street as park" approach, with the ubiquitous street trees and unit paving symbolically indicating pedestrian-oriented areas.

Another common solution, especially for transit malls, is to repave the street in a striking pattern and furnish it with a uniform set of stylized pedestrian-oriented fixtures. Although useful in establishing a design identity, this "persian carpet" approach, to use a term coined by our colleague, Gerald Hansmire, can detract from the unique local conditions of an existing urban setting.

We have enjoyed more gratifying public response on projects that incorporate a street's particular scale and architecture into the design. On the Lake City Gateway project in Seattle, for example, the design approach built on a generally unpopular precedent: it recognized the street as it was, a highway developed in the 1950s, when America was in love with the automobile. Given the street's automobile scale and orientation, the team worked with a bold, racing-strip paving accent, utilitarian accessories, and a highway-scaled median. The project was well received by the community, and shortly after completion, Lake City became the region's favorite cruising center. If we cannot claim that this was a planned outcome of the street design, merchants, nevertheless, were pleased by the unexpected drawing power after the improvements.

A contextual approach is also fruitful in dealing with public artwork. Of the several works incorporated into street improvement projects, the Northwest's most successful is the Broadway dance footsteps by Seattle artist Jack Mackie (fig. 21-7). Unlike many public artists who bring a preconceived design to a site, Mackie worked directly as a part of the design team and spent weeks on the street talking to people and trying to define the district's essential image. Emphasizing pedestrian movement, this participatory art piece has been well received by young and old alike. The merchants are using the dance steps as the district's symbol and as a marketing tool: the project's ribbon-cutting ceremony featured a giant conga dance line meandering up the street, and when Carol Channing visited Seattle, the merchants persuaded her to give an informal dance performance on the street.

MAINTAINING AN ELEMENT OF FUN

Finally, fun is an important dimension of the design process. Good street designs are those that demonstrate a little serendipity and enthusiasm. Such an attitude quickly infects community participants, smoothing the design process and resulting in more creative expression.

If a strategic approach to planning and careful study of technical issues are critical to the process itself, in the end, the local communities hope to see one or more highly visible elements that represent their effort and commitment. Character-giving focal features, such as fountains, gateways, art pieces or signing, can serve an important image-building function. For example, the Port Angeles project's improvement strategy called for a major visual attraction to draw pedestrians to the center of town. A small existing fountain was "dressed up" with heavy landscaping, structural features, and neon lighting to provide a jukeboxlike element that could be seen for blocks and also serve as a festive backdrop for public functions (fig. 21-8).

In the same vein, refining the decorative tile patterns for the Broadway project became a rich and fascinating process of researching the historic role of decoration in pavement, developing patterns that would transform smoothly one into another, and selecting designs with various symbols and optical qualities. For example, a floral-pattern tile was located next to the street's florist shop. The second pattern, shown in figure 21-9, has been interpreted as a patchwork quilt design or a primitive fertility symbol, depending on the audience. Actually, both statements are correct. The tile patterns garnered community interest in the project, and people began asking questions and offering advice as the design developed.

CONCLUSION

Streets must be regarded as a vital public resource. Street improvement projects should not only increase traffic efficiency, but fulfill other objectives as well. It is especially important to seize the opportunities of street improvements to enhance environmental conditions, reinforce community identity, provide for a variety of pedestrian activities, and revitalize community business.

This extended view of street design calls for a corresponding expansion of the urban designer's role in a more complex and comprehensive design process.

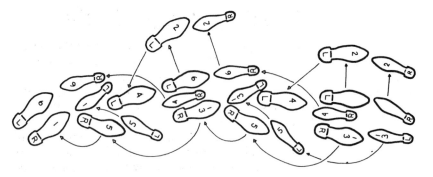

The Mambo   a.

21-7. Dance Steps, <u>a.</u> early sketch, and <u>b.</u> completed art work from Broadway Street Improvement project.

b.

21-8. Port Angeles Fountain.

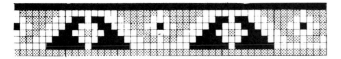

FLORAL WREATH
This pattern recalls the Victorian-era designer's practice of using elaborate naturalistic decoration to reintroduce an element of nature into the city.

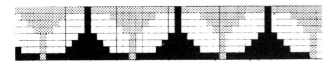

PATCHWORK
A field pattern combining motifs from traditional quilting designs and early fertility symbols. Chosen for its integration with other patterns.

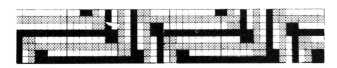

KNOTTED NET
This exemplifies an optically active pattern in that, when viewed at an angle down the sidewalk, the pattern dissolves into a herringbone texture, suggesting that it might be a small strip taken from a larger field. The net is a cross-cultural symbol for order and regulation, and knot designs have long been powerful symbols of human bonds and continuity of life.

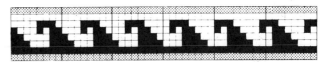

MONADIC WAVE
Aside from the obvious allusion to natural elements, the theme is a variation of the Yang-Yin circle, which symbolized the creation of the universe from opposing essences.

COILED SPIRAL/CROSS AND DIAGONAL
An example of a perceptually multistable design: Is the pattern a three-dimensional spiral or interlocked diagonals and crosses?

21-9. Tile band patterns selected to provide a variety of decorative allusions and optical qualities in the Broadway Street Improvement project.

The urban designer must balance an expanding spectrum of technical, administrative, economic, social, and aesthetic issues. He or she must skillfully manage a large design team consisting of technical specialists, public officials, artists, and community representatives.

Perhaps most important, the urban designer must assume the role of educator, helping local communities to visualize new ideas, to identify opportunities, to fulfill nontraffic objectives, and to understand implementation and funding techniques. More than any other design professional, the urban designer must advocate programmatic inclusion of environmental enhancement, pedestrian activity, and community development objectives within the context of street engineering projects.

Because streets play such an important role in our day-to-day activity, street improvement projects naturally generate a great deal of public interest. In our experience, urban design projects involving street improvement produce a higher level of community interest and a broader spectrum of goals, values, and opinions than any other design effort. Seen in this light, streets are not only conduits for the physical movement in our daily lives, but they also have the potential to be the conduits for community cooperation, organized public action, and civic pride.

22.
Beyond Zoning

RONALD B. EICHNER AND
HENRY TOBEY

Central to a comprehensive approach to the street-scape is the notion that the form and use of the street are linked intrinsically with most other urban design issues. Of all the designed elements of the urban environment, the street most reflects the quality of city life. It is the means by which we judge a city's prosperity, sense its grandeur or quaintness, review its history, count its opportunities, and determine its character. In short, from the street, we read the message of a city. Although streetscape design should be seen as an integral part of all decisions affecting the urban environment, in practice, it is too often conceived as a task wholly separate from, and less important than, issues such as building design, land-use zoning, or vehicular traffic circulation. Decisions are made in isolation, and the streetscape is treated as residual space. If, on the other hand, a comprehensive set of goals for the public environment—the street—can be established, and if other decisions can be guided by these goals for the public realm, then most elements of urban design will fall into place. In this view, streetscape design goals can become the unifying foundation for effective urban design.

This conceptual approach, which begins in the public space and works its way outward to private buildings, requires a redefinition of urban design goals regarding the street. Rather than treating the street simply as a path that serves primarily to transport people and goods, and therefore has little to do with questions of form or character, the street should be seen in light of its potential as a place of human activity and as an organizing element for the form of the city. Goals for streetscape design must look beyond the narrow issues of efficient circulation and address qualities more frequently used to discuss architecture—form, amenity, use, and character.

In this chapter we will discuss how issues of use and form can become a foundation for a comprehensive approach to the streetscape and can present a framework for design. Our context of reference is the commercial district or downtown. The emphasis is on pedestrians—a group to which each of us at one time or another belongs—but not to the exclusion of vehicles, since successful design must be highly contextual, founded on actualities rather than on formulations of a perfect world. The goal is to foster a comprehensive approach to streetscape design, one that reflects the public nature of streets and recognizes that our public spaces serve as our most visible reminder of why we have built cities, indeed, of who we think we are and what we expect of ourselves.

THE CONTEXT OF USE

Cities are composed of many uses characterized by a range of structures, from high-rise offices to factories to single-family houses. In most cities, zoning codes separate incompatible uses, for example, housing and heavy industry. Zoning also guides development by allowing certain uses in some areas and not in others. The resulting pattern of urbanization is an aggregate of districts, each with a different character. By looking at the broad land-use zoning classifications, including regulations concerning density of development, and applying trip-generation formulae, transportation planners can project the number of pedestrians and vehicles that any area can expect. With this information, the planners can determine the demand on a street and its sidewalks.

Transportation planning techniques do not, however, consider land-use and traffic impacts at perceptual and experiential levels, because they do not take into account small-scale issues related to ground-level forms, uses, and configurations, which, in fact, determine the character and success of the streetscape.

Many cities have districts whose streets display obvious special qualities—ethnic character (Chinatown, Little Italy), historically interesting uses (waterfronts, warehouse districts), or a concentration of institutional uses. Sometimes, though, the character created by use is more subtle. The ways shopkeepers display their wares, their signage, the use of awnings or color may be the unifying elements on a street. These characteristics will never appear on a zoning map. But it is crucial that streetscape design be guided by small-scale issues of local context. One must go beyond the broad categories of zoning codes to capture thoroughly the character of districts, their public space, and their streets. To do so, however, one must understand the fine-grained pattern of uses; the characteristic configuration and functional needs of each use; and the idiosyncratic variations that local tradition and context have created. "Local context" sometimes will be most meaningful at the neighborhood or district level, in other circumstances at the individual street level. No prescription defines the appropriate level of "localness." Yet, although difficult to formulate as an objective rule, it remains an important issue for sensitive, albeit subjective, observation and analysis.

Observing a downtown on shop-by-shop, facade-by-facade basis can reveal a concentraion of a particular type of retail or office use that has a major impact on streetscape design and on planning strategies that affect the streetscape. For example, where analysis shows a concentration of restaurants, streetscape designs should anticipate evening use that might warrant special festive lighting or sidewalk cafés.

Such analyses may also reveal opportunities for private-sector involvement in streetscape improvements. The presence of several florists or art galleries can set the character of a block if merchants agree to display some of their wares on the street. This fine-grained approach can also aid planning strategies for encouraging or restricting particular uses to reinforce microdistricts. The resulting enhancement (or creation) of a street's identity would enrich the pedestrian's experience, whereas merchants could profit financially from being part of an identifiable district and would need little public sector prodding to contribute to celebrations, improvements, and other cooperative activities.

The typical configuration of downtown has been determined by its predominant uses: ground-floor retail stores below offices create a continuous rhythm along the public street; the occasional institutional use (city hall or church) or business with institutional pretensions (banks or hotels) are made conspicuous by breaking the continuity of shop windows and entrances; the city hall or court buildings face a public open space. This pattern, with some variations, has been characteristic of cities for centuries. It applied to medieval, baroque, and nineteenth-century cities and to most American cities up to the middle of the twentieth century. Not surprisingly, this pattern of use was reflected in a formal structure that reinforced the figural quality of the public spaces and public buildings, emphasizing their importance as unifying elements in our perception of both the physical and social form of the city. Together, this distribution of uses and configuration of buildings, and the resulting form of the street, can still produce a lively, accessible, and easily understood mixed-use street-scape environment.

Unfortunately, in the last thirty years, the emphasis has shifted too often to multiuse *structures*, which do not necessarily result in lively, multiuse *streetscapes*. Often, large mixed-use structures that look good on zoning maps because they appear to bring a lively mix of activities to the city have a deadening effect on surrounding streetscapes. This happens where retail uses are located within private development, with shops oriented to an interior mall. Too often, the street edges of such buildings feature blank walls and one or two entrances to the interior shopping center. Major department stores are a precedent for this type of configuration, but the scale and frequency of the large new developments and of their smaller progeny, the mini-malls, raise serious questions about their cumulative effect on a downtown.

The actual effect of most inward-oriented, mixed-use developments is to diminish the multiple-use character of the surrounding streets. The streetscape is reduced to a simple path, and the shopping experience, now *inside* the building, becomes more like that of the suburban mall. The downtown internalized mall offers a competing street, which shoppers may prefer but others may be reluctant to enter because it is inconvenient to their destination or because it seems to be (and is) a private place.

The street's potential for lively character depends largely on a rich mix of people and uses—shoppers, strollers, people in a hurry, those merely waiting— and the opportunity to sit back and watch the "show." This mixture underscores the public character of the street. Although rules, unwritten as well as legal, regulate behavior, the street allows its users considerable latitude because it "belongs" to them. The shopping mall, on the other hand, is a private place. In short, the traditional configuration of building uses supports an active, public, and interesting streetscape, whereas the new configuration, which ignores the streetscape in favor of the exigencies of shopping malls, can result in impoverished environments in both street and mall —all in the name of "mixed-use."

The concern for building-use configurations that contribute positively to the streetscape is applicable to other types of development too. Convention centers and the hotels they generate should be carefully analyzed for impact on the streetscape. While these uses may bring economic help to the city, they also tend to present blank faces to the street. Convention centers, particularly, are behemoths. They rebuild many city blocks at once, in ways contrary to traditional urban growth—for cities grow in pieces, by accretion —giving streets a complex rhythm of use and form. The simple addition of street-oriented retail at ground level could mitigate an otherwise disastrous intrusion downtown.

Although mayors and other public officials will profess commitment to enlivening the downtown, they are generally ensnarled in a trap. Hotels and convention centers appear as perfect agents for bringing in outside money. Cities in need will do whatever they can to lure these bonanzas downtown, away from the competing suburbs (where convention centers and hotels also are seen as catalysts for development and especially for creating much-needed identity). The increments of gain and loss in street liveliness can never be precisely documented, and thus, expressed concerns for vitality joust poorly when decisions are made that shape the street.

Developers, for their part, are not opposed to vibrant street life—on the contrary, they often feel responsible for its presence—but they prefer and usually insist on control of their own environments. Control is a complex issue and includes concerns ranging from security to marketing. The answers will be found at the expense of the street unless the questions are put in a larger context, one in which individual development of the street and the district are intrinsically linked. Where regulation and planning strategies create an overall framework for lively streetscape design, the advantage of compliance will be made clear, and the result can be participation on the part of developers in the creation of a lively public environment.

In the design of large downtown developments, and in their review for impact on the streetscape, consideration of use should go beyond zoning categories, or even beyond building programs, to include a careful analysis of configuration. Office buildings and other new developments need not be designed as if they were public institutions; in fact, when carried to an extreme, the symbolic messages communicated by such treatments are arrogant and inappropriate for our society. Architect and planner Denise Scott

Brown has noted that "it is characteristic of good urban architecture that it has not one but many images and not one but many levels of meaning" (1981: 95). Buildings that simplify their facades by eliminating all "messy" uses and small-scale expression in favor of a single, unified form deny their urban, functional, and (arguably) cultural contexts.

This is not to say that retail uses can occur only at the street or that monumental forms of architecture are never appropriate; Milan's Galleria and many similar arcades show that it is possible to provide interior environments that enhance street use. In fact, in a city with a strong public streetscape, an occasional galleria can be a welcome change—a special place *because* it breaks the urban pattern. However, if the pattern is weak or not established, or if a downtown plans for so many galarias that the urban pattern is destroyed, the wisdom of the downtown interior mall should be seriously questioned. When provided, interior shopping malls should not result in the elimination of street retail uses. They should connect places where people want to go; the provision of a meaningful connection through a block will give a mall a public function. Finally, they should appear to be an extension of the public space and, wherever possible, doors between street and mall should be avoided: the opportunity for persons to wander in, simple as it may seem, is critical to the establishment of a public character.

The problem of defining land-use programs that will restore vitality to a downtown involves not merely the reinforcement or addition of certain uses, but the determination of a specific configuration of uses appropriate to the area. The imposition of a use configuration that may be suited to suburban sites (where the mall turns its blank back to parking lots) is disastrous downtown, because the mall cannot turn its back to what should be a people place, the street.

THE CONTEXT OF URBAN FORM

Besides facilitating the uses of the street space and its adjacent buildings, a comprehensive approach to the streetscape must also deal with street form. How do buildings shape the street space? What image do they give to the street? The district? The city? That in today's city planning and design process these questions are commonly considered quite apart from conventional streetscape issues of paving, trees, benches, and so on is indicative of the fragmented approach to streetscape design that has become prevalent. Unless the street is viewed as a three-dimensional space rather than as a two-dimensional path, streetscape issues will continue to be addressed in a piecemeal, ineffective manner. A comprehensive, interdisciplinary approach to the street would include, at a minimum, the coordination of design and use goals for these separate aspects.

What are the formal qualities that contribute to the character of a street? Although street form is but one of the determinants of character, it can be considered apart from, for instance, pedestrian and vehicular uses whose functional responses can occur within the context of a variety of street scales and forms. Critical formal elements of street character include small-scale items, street furniture, paving, and so on. At the larger scale, the spatial character of the street and the architecture of the defining buildings are significant. Given the complexity of the city, and of streetscape design in particular, there is much overlap and interaction between the two scales. This is especially true for elements such as trees and arcades, which can have a critical effect on both small-scale use and form. In streetscape design, it is the task of the urban designer to recognize the appropriate formal qualities and to coordinate the efforts of individual architects to achieve the desired character; it is the task of the architect to be aware of the overall formal character and then respond to it.

The formal qualities of the street can be identified by looking both at the space formed by the building walls and at the walls themselves. Although the complexity of the urban context puts all generalizations and checklists in danger of oversimplification, a street should be analyzed for its inherent qualities. This is essentially an exercise in contextual analysis, since most streetscape design is a matter of infill. What kind of enclosure or spaciousness exists? What are the elements of continuity or variety? Are there rhythms or styles that give the street walls character? Is there a characteristic scale to the street? Are there exceptions to the "rules" of the street? Why are they made? What is typical and what is special about the buildings on the street?

A contextual analysis will create a guide for the streetscape, identifying opportunities, problems, and pitfalls facing the designer. But successful infill design demands more than matching building heights or cornice lines: thorough contextual analysis may reveal that rhythm, scale, or texture can be achieved while allowing increased height or bulk (see chap. 15, by P. Bosselmann). However, these decisions cannot be made without a complete analysis of the context of form.

As noted earlier, the responsibility for street form is shared by the urban designer/planner and the architect. At the scale of the street, the planner can identify elements and qualities critical to reinforcing or establishing the form appropriate to the urban context. The controls that result should combine two seemingly incompatible qualities. They should be light (to encourage creative solutions from individual architects) but firm and precise (to achieve the goals for the public space).

The types of intervention associated with street form are familiar—urban design controls, zoning codes, design review procedures, and persuasion. These tools are applied to a variety of urban design goals, with varying degrees of success. Amenity-related goals, focusing on the social possibilities of the street, are the most problematic because of the difficulty in specifying quantifiable human performance requirements. Most form-related goals, however, are more easily set by urban design controls, which can be part of a downtown or development area plan or can be incorporated into zoning codes. Examples of common urban design controls include height, where maximums can be established to maintain spaciousness or out of deference to existing lower buildings. Variations include setting mandatory heights along a street to increase the sense of continuity or establishing height setbacks to minimize the appearance of the bulk of a building and to increase light on the street. On some streets, height setback requirements that have been in place for years may have created characteristic forms that can become a visual theme. Building setback lines are also regulated. Build-to lines can fix the location of street facades to achieve the desired sense of spaciousness or enclosure as well as continuity of street form. Even in areas of dense, high-rise development, build-to lines and minimum height requirements can generate low, street-defining elements while allowing towers to be set back, providing access to light, air, and view. Where the perception of the city's structure of streets—the rhythm of open space and built-up blocks—is endangered by the size of multiblock developments, view corridors (volumes of unobstructed space) are often established. They can also preserve visual access to natural features or urban design elements, such as monuments or landmark buildings.

Finally, the control of form often includes the specification of ground-floor retail or arcades. But merely permitting or requiring ground-floor retail can result in a plethora of unimagined responses. Acceptable height and width of entries, displays and signage, and so on, can become important in shaping the street's formal character. Other related questions are: Must shops present a uniform rhythm or proportion? Is diversity valued or something to be constrained? Much of the richness of the urban street can be found in the aggregation of different design decisions through the years.

Many formal goals are therefore relatively simple to achieve, and if the requirements are clearly stated in the controls, compliance will be easy to evaluate. But for such issues as scale, and continuity of architectural elements (for instance, color, character and rhythm of fenestration, style, building organization, and so on), strict criteria are difficult if not impossible to set. Where it is necessary to regulate these qualities, design review for compliance is necessary. Even where the final approval is left to the judgment of the reviewers, a detailed description of the desired goals should be provided.

THE STREET SPACE

Along with the analysis of the use and form of the street edges must come a similar investigation of the street space itself. How are its various uses to be accommodated? What are the formal consequences? How do all the pieces come together in a streetscape design?

When a street space is designed properly, many activities can occur simultaneously without conflicts among users. Avoiding spatial interference between activities is the key, and the major task of any analysis is to identify such dysfunctions as bus stops impeding the flow of pedestrian traffic; vendors obstructing access to and from the roadway; pedestrians denied adequate space at intersections to wait for traffic lights; drivers denied adequate space to drop off or pick up passengers without disrupting vehicular traffic; and so on. Insufficient use of facilities is a dysfunction of the street space that is more subtle but ultimately as insidious as conflict interference. Empty benches, the fountain that fails to attract people, the ignored mid-block pedestrian crossing signal—all such underused facilities indicate problems to be resolved.

Given the flexibility of pedestrian movement and the richness of a streetscape environment offering a variety of activities, it is clear that rigid categorical distinctions for pedestrian behavior are difficult to apply to street space uses. Rather, it is important to see the streetscape as a dynamic environment providing opportunities for many activities. Table 22-1 presents the major classifications of uses.

To respond to these uses, most streetscape plans employ a zone concept for the organization of the street space. This is a logical extension of existing use patterns in downtowns. A section across a typical downtown street reveals a building, a sidewalk with an agglomeration of street furniture elements, a roadway, and a sidewalk, and building on the other side; below the street surface is a maze of utilities, subways, and building vaults. This easily translates into more or

TABLE 22-1.
MAJOR STREET SPACE USES

FUNCTIONAL USES

VEHICULAR CIRCULATION
· through movement
· picking up/dropping off passengers
· curbside parking
· access to parking
· buses
· on-street service
· off-street service
· emergency vehicles

PEDESTRIAN CIRCULATION
· through movement
· waiting for, boarding, and alighting from vehicles (buses, taxis, cars)
· entering and leaving subways
· crossing street
· entering and leaving buildings

URBAN LIFE SUPPORT
· providing space and access for utilities
· controlling traffic
· providing for emergency services
· lighting the streetscape

SOCIAL/AMENITY USES
· strolling and window-shopping
· resting
· people-watching
· vendors
· telephones
· newspapers
· art works and banners
· "shmoozing"
· eating
· waiting
· orientation/information
· street performers
· drinking fountains
· fountains

less functional zones for building, pedestrian, and vehicular uses. In further detail, the areas adjacent to the building are broken down into a walking zone, buffer or collector strip for street furniture, and a lane-wide traffic area used for vehicles or for additional pedestrian space adjacent to the roadway. As a basic framework for street design, the zone concept seems workable. It is applicable to most streets, compatible with an efficient layout of utilities, and flexible enough to accommodate variations in use and configuration.

This zone concept is intended to make the traditional street section work within the context of our central cities. Neither the radical spatial separation schemes proposed by planners through the 1970s nor the equally utopian total integration schemes of the 1980s seems to offer much promise for widespread application. The total spatial separation schemes deny that vehicles are an inherent part of urban life contributing to its richness and convenience. Indeed, such schemes are rarely well integrated into existing urban patterns and structures and are typically wildly expensive proposals, with little chance of implementation.

Most schemes for spatial integration of pedestrians and cars are based on the notion that many pedestrians in the same space will overwhelm motorists, who will be ever mindful of people crossing. The applications of this idea are limited and restricted, at best, to those districts where pedestrians vastly outnumber vehicles and where through vehicular traffic can be rerouted outside the district. Further, few downtown commercial districts could function under such a restriction on vehicular traffic.

The zone concept seems best to accommodate the many demands on the street space. The major street zones and their predominant use characteristics are depicted in figure 22-1. The basic functional requirements of each zone are essentially those of its predominant use. The window-shopping zone, for instance, requires windows and space not necessary for walking and can be enhanced by overhead awnings for protection from the elements and for spatial definition. The functional, social, and amenity uses that are facilitated by the street furniture zone have their unique requirements but share the need for noninterference with pedestrian through traffic. This common need reinforces the zone idea. The overriding concern at intersections is adequate space for people turning the corner or waiting to cross and for the various equipment and activities that "want" to be located at the corner—"walk" lights, mail and newspaper boxes, vendors, and so on. These needs would seem easy to accommodate; at first glance, it might appear that the common design practices in cities would suffice. Unfortunately, a brief survey of several typical use conflicts illustrates that this is not the case.

Intersection and crosswalk problems typically include:

· Inadequate space for people to wait, due to proximity of other activities and obstructions, such as vendors, bus stops, shelters, or sidewalk cafés, which can force people into the roadway.
· Obstructed walking space due to the placement of traffic signals and lighting poles, traffic control boxes, newspaper vending machines chained to the poles, litter receptacles, or other elements of street furniture.

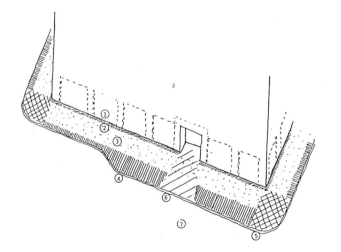

22-1. Streetscape zone concept.

- Zone 1: The Building proper, with commercial uses, entrances, lobbies, service access, and loading docks.
- Zone 2: Window-shopping is the primary activity in the 21- to 24-inch-wide space next to building walls. The zone is also used by leaners and by people taking a moment to orient themselves and to adjust clothing and packages before joining the pedestrian flow.
- Zone 3: Pedestrian traffic predominates in the enxt zone. The necessary width, 8 feet or more, is a function of needed capacity and desired density, as discussed earlier. Other activities, such as "shmoozing," waiting, crossing to and from the curb, and checking addresses, also occur in the walkway.
- Zone 4: Street furniture is located in a 4-foot or wider zone at the curb. This zone acts as a buffer between the walkway and the roadway, allowing seating, bus waiting, and vending to occur out of the walkway. Where this zone is wide enough, special amenity areas or vehicular drop-off areas may be created.
- Zone 5: Crosswalk areas are places with a high potential for use conflicts and are given special treatment.
- Zone 6: Major building entrances are another place with special requirements due to the intensity and variety of uses.
- Zone 7: Vehicular uses occur in the roadway. The near lanes may be used for parking or drop off.

Walkway problems typically include:
· Inadequate walkway space in locations where the effective walkway width or continuity is reduced by obstructions such as groups of people at building entrances, planters, or vending operations.
· Lack of space for amenities to serve the large number of pedestrians.
· Lack of protection from rain or sun.

Window-shopping conflicts typically include:
· Obstructions, such as advertising boards, vendors, and planters, which force window shoppers into the flow of pedestrian traffic.
· Ventilation grates that create a physical and psychological impediment, forcing people away from windows and into the flow.

These and other common dysfunctions could be remedied by the application of simple rules growing out of a zone approach:
· A crosswalk zone that is large enough to accommodate the waiting platoon and at least as wide as the crosswalk should be established. All facilitating equipment (poles, controllers, and so on) and other street furniture should be prohibited within the zone. Vendors, bus stops, and other activity-generating elements should be located outside the crosswalk zone, possibly some distance away from crowded intersections.
· The pedestrian traffic zone should not be obstructed by street furniture or other elements. Except in cases where the sidewalk is wide enough to provide an adequately sized, unobstructed pathway, all street furniture and other potential impediments should be located in a street furniture zone.
· At major building entrances, an area unobstructed by street furniture and vendors should extend to the curb to facilitate cross traffic between the building and curb and to widen the walkway effectively for easy bypassing of stationary groups of people.
· In the window-shopping zone, elements such as advertising boards, planters, and displays should not be allowed. However, where the sidewalk is sufficiently wide to allow a display area at the building, a window-shopping lane, and adequate space for other uses, a lively street market atmosphere can result.
· The zone approach can also help to redress the lack of space for pedestrian amenities. Where the curb lane of the roadway is not needed for vehicular through traffic, it could be converted to a wide amenity zone with the potential for facilitating both vehicular and pedestrian use. Amenities, in this case, could include parking, bus or car lay-byes, seating or vending areas, narrowed crosswalks, or

tree plantings. The result of such an approach might be the creation of a mixed-use zone, with some parts of it improving vehicular use, while other parts would offer additional space and activities for pedestrians.

The zone approach is adaptable to variations of street form. Where plazas or parks exist, their entrances can be treated like the major building entrance zone, providing an unobstructed space for people to pause before entering or leaving, or merely to stand and observe for a moment. The basic framework can be maintained for arcades although some redundancy would result from the provision of walkway space both inside and outside the structure. Most aspects of the zone concept also can be maintained in pedestrian malls. The window-shopping and walkway zones would remain essentially unaltered because the functional relationship to the buildings would be unchanged. The treatment of the street furniture zone, however, would be fundamentally changed where it extends across the middle of the street. In this case it could become a place for major amenity groupings or other activities. In transit malls, the roadway may be visually suppressed, but functionally, it still exists, so the zones would be basically unchanged, although the street furniture zone should be perceived as open and permeable, encouraging midblock crossings.

CONCLUSION

Synomorphism is a concept that refers to the fit between a physical environment and that environment's proposed purposes. A glove, for example, is synomorphic with a hand. Likewise, a baseball stadium is synomorphic with a baseball game. When the interest is the pedestrian environment, the question becomes: What are the uses of the street and the physical characteristics that fit them? *Fit*, in this sense, means, first, that certain desirable behavior is not precluded by the environment of the streetscape and, second, that the environment, to the extent possible, encourages such behavior. In an analysis of streetscape use, two fundamental and seemingly simple sets of questions arise: (1) How is the street currently used? In what ways does the existing street design support or discourage the various uses? (2) What would constitute necessary and desirable uses? How could the design of a new streetscape support or encourage these uses?

These questions are complex, subtle, and difficult to answer in definitive ways. Developing a functional street is not the problem: if one eliminates vehicular use, the cars will find another route; if one does not install benches or bus shelters, people will simply keep walking or will be reminded to bring their umbrellas next time. These are not great tragedies (although conflicts of use between pedestrians and vehicles can be); cities and their inhabitants are well-known for their ability to adapt to inconvenience. Far more difficult, however, is the resolution of potential conflicts among uses for the creation of a street that does not merely work but works well. This undertaking requires a thorough and comprehensive analysis of use, even for apparently simple situations.

Streetscape design, unlike building design, rarely has a single client, fixed schedule, finite budget, or easily identifiable user (see chap. 21, by J. H. Owen, Jr.). Unlike an architect, the urban designer seldom has direct control over more than a few of the aspects that constitute the streetscape. Rather, streetscape design is a matter of coordination and guidance and of the creation of a framework in which decisions by many will be made over time. Some decisions can result in immediately realized designs, but in many instances, the best a designer can do is to set the direction for future development.

To achieve a comprehensive streetscape plan one must consider a wide range of issues. Exclusive concentration on those elements that offer traditional design opportunities can lead to inappropriate, dysfunctional, or irrelevant proposals resulting from detachment from context or lack of control over critical aspects of the streetscape. To arbitrarily compartmentalize the various aspects of the streetscape—functional, circulation, spatial, social, and aesthetic—is to deny its complex, multiuse nature.

REFERENCE

Scott Brown, D. 1981. "Urban Design Plan: Hennepin Avenue Transit/Entertainment Study." Minneapolis: City of Minneapolis, June.

23.
Street Vacations

BEATRICE FARRAR RYAN

Through street vacations (also called street closures) a municipality sells or deeds to a private party either all or part of a street or the public easement over a street right-of-way. Street vacations are relatively common in newer American cities, which tend to follow a grid plan. The grid was usually platted with generous rights-of-way, reflecting the ample land supply and the desire to sell land efficiently and conveniently. The grid overlay often clashed with varied topographical conditions, resulting in discontinuities within the network of streets. In such cases, the street became a right-of-way "on paper," which remained undeveloped (see chap. 9, by A. V. Moudon and R. K. Untermann). These seemingly superfluous streets are often vacated when they appear to be better used by private development.

Vacations are not restricted to paper streets. Improved streets and alleys are also vacated, often in conjunction with redevelopment. Blocks are consolidated and alleys are removed to make room for larger development. Such vacations seem to occur more frequently in newer grid cities characterized by a high ratio of public rights-of-way to private land, but they have also occurred in cities with a fine-grained network of narrow streets and alleys. Now that most urban centers are feeling pressure to use land more efficiently, streets have become an untapped resource of increasing interest to developers and planners alike.

Street vacations span a wide range of situations. For example, a shoreline industry that wants to expand may request the city to vacate an adjacent street that ends in the water. Or a developer may recognize the economic benefits of constructing multifamily housing on a steep hillside site formerly passed over as too difficult to develop. To increase the size of a project and to make it economically feasible, a developer may

want the adjacent undeveloped street right-of-way. Or developers may seek to consolidate properties to make full-block developments on a prime downtown block bisected by an alley.

VACATION PROCEDURES

Public rights-of-way are not always owned by the public. Underlying fee title to the land often resides with the abutting property owners, and the public right to use the streets consists of easements. Streets and alleys provide the general public with circulation, access to abutting properties, light, air, unobstructed views, and open space. Likewise, they offer abutting property owners light, air, access, and views. Finally, they provide a location for utilities.

Street vacations are discretionary legislative actions that remove the public easement in the street and relieve the municipality of its responsibility for maintenance. Upon vacation, all rights to the land revert to the underlying fee owner.

Vacation applications may be initiated by abutting property owners, the city council, or any public agency, such as a port or redevelopment authority or a parks department. In cases of multiple abutting owners, local statutes usually require the approval of at least a majority of the owners to vacate a street.

Procedures for street vacation decisions begin with an application submitted to the board of public works, or similar local administrative body, usually composed of the directors of city departments, including departments of engineering, police, fire, water, city planning, and parks. Department staff members review the request and make recommendations to the board. The board then makes a recommendation to the legislative body, which, after public notice and a public hearing, decides whether to grant or deny the application. In cities with a city manager form of government and a part-time city council, the decision may be delegated by the legislative body to an administrator, frequently the city engineer.

The vacation procedure is time-consuming. In Seattle, street vacations in 1983 and 1984 took between seven and fifteen months, with an average of twelve months. In most cities, vacations can be requested in conjunction with other use and construction permits. Risk to the developer can be reduced by applying for the street vacation first and, if granted, proceeding with the other permits. In order to minimize time and costs in the early stages of projects, however, developers frequently make parallel applications for vacations and other permits.

LEGAL BASIS FOR GRANTING VACATIONS

The basis for granting street vacations is usually articulated in state legislation, developed over time through case law, and described in terms of weighing the potential public benefits of the vacation against the responsibility of the municipality to protect the public trust, as defined by public health and safety standards. If the right-of-way is not needed for access by vehicles, for utilities, or for light and air, the municipality may vacate it.

Public benefits resulting from vacations, while usually not specified in legislation, have come to be defined through practice and case law as: income from the sale of the property; return of the property to the tax rolls; employment generated both by construction and by the occupants of the newly developed property; elimination of the municipality's liability for the property; and reduction of public maintenance responsibilities. This list has grown over time to include secondary benefits, such as employment, and less tangible benefits, such as reduced public liability. As more cities are self-insured, liability is no small concern. Municipal claims officers view undeveloped streets as attractive nuisances for children. Undeveloped rights-of-way may cause drainage problems and hazardous soil conditions, which can threaten adjacent structures, and the municipality may be held responsible for damages.

The definition of the public trust has been broadened as well. Once narrowly construed in terms of the need for utilities, fire protection and transportation access, the public trust now also includes protection of light, air, open space, and views.

Vacations may be conditionally approved to specify acceptable ways to protect abutting properties (such as through appropriate setbacks for light and air and design continuity) or to protect public amenities, such as view corridors. Conditions may ride with the title to the land in the form of a property use and development agreement that is recorded with the deed. Or they may be attached to the land-use permit by the code administration agency. Sometimes conditions are imposed in both places, with those having to do with access and utilities riding with the land, and those specific to the proposed project design placed on the land-use permit.

State law usually specifies that disposition of public land be at fair market value. But in the case of streets and alleys, the fair market rule may be adjusted on account of their deviation in size and configuration from the standard lots. In Seattle, for example, vacated rights-of-way are sold for one-half of their fair market value (although when the city buys the right-of-way from a private owner, it pays full market value). Determining the market value of a right-of-way depends on practices and precedent in individual cities and states. A right-of-way has little or no value for development except when consolidated with adjacent property. Thus, some appraisers value street and alley rights-of-way based on what they would be worth were they joined with an adjacent parcel. Far more often, however, appraisals are determined solely on a square footage basis set by comparable values of standard-sized properties in the vicinity; they are not adjusted by the value added by the increased development potential of the vacated right-of-way plus the adjacent site. Where the latter appraisal practice occurs, and where rights-of-way are sold for less than fair market value, vacated streets can be bargains for developers.

Partial vacations increase the complexity of appraising value. The most common type is an easement left for emergency vehicle access or for utilities. Subsurface vacations are sometimes necessary for underground parking garages. Aerial vacations can be granted for architectural protrusions, but these features are more commonly handled through easements or street-use permits.

Street-use permits grant a private individual or organization the right to use the street or sidewalk temporarily. In contrast to street vacations, which are permanent, these permits are themselves temporary, but they may be renewed and are usually nominal. Push cart operators, flower stalls, and sidewalk cafés usually require them, as do street fairs and construction projects that close sidewalks.

HIGHER STAKES, MORE CONTROVERSY

Wholesale vacation of public rights-of-way was a common practice twenty or more years ago, when superblocks became fashionable here and in Europe during the heyday of urban renewal. Streets were vacated to remove cars and to create separate pedestrian walkway systems.

Public rights-of-way were also viewed as opportunities for development. If, for example, a public facility needed to expand, a street was the likely location for the addition. Opportunities for subsidized housing, encouraged by municipalities in the 1960s and 1970s, often included a public right-of-way for a sweetener. During that era, the majority of wholesale vacations occurred for publicly planned projects. These policies are now being questioned as discontinuities in grid layout tend to isolate communities by impeding local access (see chap. 7, by C. R. Wolfe).

Today, most vacations occur in conjunction with private development. Usually no more than a block long, vacations are sought for infill development on formerly passed-over sites and for redevelopment, which entails demolition and land assembly. Both types of projects look to street and alley vacations as a way to achieve density and design flexibility beyond that possible under the original platting.

While private requests for vacations are becoming more numerous, the stakes are becoming higher. Developers seeking vacations, as well as cities selling streets now have more to gain financially. Vacating a downtown alley, for instance, often makes the difference between a full-block or a half-block development. An analysis of a proposed vacation of an alley in downtown Seattle, for instance, revealed that while the vacation would increase the lot area by only 7 percent, it would increase the potential density of the new building by 20 percent, because the Floor Area Ratio (FAR) system favored large-site development. Similar incentives for enlarging sites through street vacations exist under most multifamily residential zoning.

Municipalities are also more conscious of the opportunities for increased revenues through the sale of streets (see chap. 9, by A. V. Moudon and R. K. Untermann). Yet, because vacations are becoming increasingly contentious, routine sales by a city council are unusual.

Citizen groups are too savvy to let vacations pass unnoticed and unquestioned. They ask about neighborhood gains and losses and about the impact of increasing development potential beyond that anticipated by the zoning. Even seemingly innocuous vacations in single-family areas are being questioned. Citizen groups are demanding that considerations

other than public access, safety, and utility service figure into the decision to give up the public street space; they are also concerned with light and air on the streets, with the preservation of views and open space, and with the scale of development made possible on parcels consolidated by street vacations.

City officials are becoming more aggressive in protecting the public trust. Not only do they ask about the financial profit from street sales and about the true financial value of a street after vacation has enlarged its development potential, but they consider the impact of increased development densities on utilities and public transit. In short, they ask whether vacating streets will cost more or less in the long run. A memorable example of this breed of public questioning occurred with respect to the TransAmerica tower in San Francisco: there, vacation of an alley allowed a much higher building than would have been possible had the alley been retained (Jacobs 1978).

The complexity of the factors involved in making vacation decisions, combined with the intensity of public debate, have sent some cities searching for better ways to guide the process. Following are several issues and procedures that facilitate the grant of street vacations.

GUIDING DECISIONS TO VACATE STREETS

The quality of street vacation decisions can be improved by clarifying priorities, considering broad planning objectives, and attending to procedural and timing factors.

Priorities

Which essential qualities of a street space should be considered first? Where do public benefits, such as increased employment and a raised tax base, fit in? Seattle's proposed policy for street vacations outlines a sequence of prioritized needs assessments (City of Seattle 1985). First, the street or alley is assessed for purposes of circulation, access, and utilities. If those needs are adequately met by current conditions or if they ultimately prove to be unneccessary, then the street is assessed for light, air, open space, and view. Further, a sufficient provision of those conditions leads to an evaluation of land-use effects. Finally, public benefits must be established for granting the vacation permit.

The logic behind Seattle's ranking proceeds from the basics—circulation and access—to secondary considerations of benefits, such as revenues. At each stage in the sequence, guidelines aid decision making. For example, to evaluate open space one must consider the extent to which an undeveloped street will contribute to a land bank for future greenbelts. A guideline for land use states that "no portion of any right-of-way which has been officially designated as a view corridor may be vacated" (City of Seattle 1985: 15). The first guideline under public benefit begins: "Only after the negative effects of the vacation have been adequately mitigated, will the issue of whether the vacation provides a public benefit be addressed" (City of Seattle 1985: 22). Economic development, provision of more housing units, and increases to the tax base are factors to be included in the appraisal of the public benefit. While ordering the evaluation process and clarifying priorities, the proposed policy leaves considerable room for the city council to exercise discretion.

Assessing Effects on Built Form and Land Use

Many cities evaluate the merits of proposed vacations solely on the basis of circulation, access, and utilities. Yet a comprehensive street vacation policy should cover land use and should specify what decision makers need to know about the long-term land-use effects of the vacation in order to determine whether it is in the public interest.

The information available for assessing land-use effects can vary. An actual project proposal will yield the most detailed information on the impact of the vacation. In the absence of a project proposal, however, one can describe the maximum development of a given site based on land-use regulations. Under maximum floor-area allowances, a series of assumptions can be used to derive a theoretical maximum building envelope and to generate the figures for traffic, parking, and housing demand that will follow.

In practice, the major difficulty with this theoretical approach is that Floor Area Ratios (FARs) in many larger American cities are only the starting point for determining maximum building envelopes. In such instances, the greatest development potential is achieved through complex bonuses, transfers of development rights, fees, contributions, and linked development agreements, the results of which cannot easily be predicted in the abstract and translated into maximum FARs and envelopes.

Use of maximum potential development in evaluating whether or not to vacate a street means that decisions are based not on the merits of proposed projects, but on the public use of the right-of-way and on the effects of a vacation on land-use objectives. One drawback of this approach is that it precludes the opportunity to tailor vacation conditions expressly for the project proposed. The details of specific projects can, however, be evaluated subsequently by the code administration agency when development permits are reviewed. Additional conditions can be imposed at the time of the review. However, if many conditions are imposed by the legislature when it grants the street vacation, it will be difficult to add more conditions later on: project proponents can claim that the elected officials considered and acted on all necessary conditions at the time they approved the vacation and that the land-use administration agency should not impose any more.

Finally, whenever project-specific information is available, and when a development proposal for a site has been publicly announced, it is unrealistic to expect decision makers not to consider maximum development potential in their decision to grant the vacation.

Frequently, however, developers assembling property may apply for a vacation on the basis of a very general design concept and an analysis of financial feasibility. Because they have no details to share with the public at the time of application, the maximum development potential is all that can be used.

Placing Conditions on Vacations

Hard-fought battles over street vacations often revolve around the conditions to be imposed. When the stakes are high, petitioners may offer public benefits unrelated to the negative effects of the vacation. For example, an impressively high proportion of women and minority contractors for constructing the project may be promised. Similarly, petitioners may pledge to provide low-income housing in excess of that demolished for the development.

Controversy can be minimized by deciding in advance whether or not a direct relationship must exist between the conditions of the vacation and the mitigation of negative impacts. Although potentially attractive offers are ruled out in the latter approach, it tends to keep the public debate focused on the issues most closely related to the vacation.

As explained, conditions can be tied either to the land title or to the development permit. Conditions are more permanent in the first case; if left to the code administration agency to attach to a permit, conditions may change with a change in administration. It is not unusual for a right-of-way to be vacated for a specific project and then to languish unbuilt. Or, it is sometimes acquired by another developer, who redesigns it and renegotiates the terms of the permit. In those cases, the conditions originally contemplated by the legislative body when it approved the vacation may be changed or lost in the process, if not filed with the deed. On the other hand, the flexibility to respond to new circumstances can be reduced if most of the conditions ride with the land.

Timing of Vacations in the Development Review Process

Vacations can be reviewed either before or along with the review of use and development permits. The former procedure offers the advantage of having elected officials take the lead in making a discretionary decision on issues that are strictly vacation-related and of providing greater predictability to the developers in the land-use review phase of the permit process.

However, if the vacation decision occurs late in the development process, for instance, when the decision on the use permit is about to be made, considerable funds and time may have already been invested in design work and options on the land. Applicants sometimes argue that the amount of this investment should be considered by the legislators in reaching a decision. Legislators may, therefore, feel constrained in requiring design alterations to mitigate the negative effects and may be reluctant to deny the application outright.

Yet legislators sometimes like to see what the code administration agency decides on a land-use application before they rule on the vacation. After obtaining as many details on the proposal as possible and sampling public sentiment, they feel better prepared to choose whether to reverse or modify the agency's decision.

While developers argue for increased predictability in the permit process, they also prefer to have the flexibility to file for a vacation application at any time in the development process. Sometimes, they prefer to get the use permit review underway before applying for the vacation. In other situations, they want a vacation decision from the legislative body at an early stage in order to minimize risk and front-end investment.

Seattle's proposed policy will not allow a decision on the use permit before the city council approves the vacation, although the two applications can be processed simultaneously. Council would grant a conceptual approval but stop short of actual vacation until the land-use review is completed and additional conditions, if any, are incorporated in the property use and development agreement. Currently in Seattle, applicants for street vacations may file at any time in the permit process, and the council decides whether to wait for a decision on the use permit based on each application. In recent major cases, the council has followed the procedure in the proposed policy. Of

course, if no use permit is pending, the council must act on the vacation petition.

Adoption of Seattle's proposed policy has been delayed because of this timing question. Several well-respected civic organizations are opposed to allowing simultaneous processing and prefer a sequential process beginning with the vacation decision. The Downtown Seattle Association, which represents the development community, would like timing to remain flexible at the option of the applicant and would prefer that the use permit not be held for preliminary approval of the council, pending review. The mayor has recommended concurrent filing and processing of vacation petitions and use permit applications. In addition, he has recommended that the city require petitioners with concurrent vacations and vacation-related projects to sign a waiver recognizing that any investment in a project prior to vacation approval is at the petitioner's risk and will not be a consideration in the vacation decision. He also recommended that the council's decision may include project-specific land-use considerations, and that the legislative vacation decision be separate from and subject to different criteria from the administrative land-use decision.

Clearly, the timing and procedural aspects of a policy on street vacations are complex, since sequencing, level of land-use information, and types of conditions are all interrelated. If the policy were to allow processing the applications sequentially with no overlap, for example, the proponent could not be expected to furnish details on land use, and assessment of the vacation would need to be based on maximum potential development. Also, conditions would be more general, but they would not need to be tied directly to mitigating negative effects. Mitigation measures would be part of the development permit reviewed after the street-vacation decision.

Relationship to Other Plans and Policies

A city's transportation plan and policies are essential documents to support a vacation policy. Citywide street classification systems are good references, too, particularly for maintaining the continuity of pedestrian bicycle networks. With respect to land-use issues, a general citywide plan will likely be of little help in making specific street vacation decisions. But detailed plans for downtown, for historic areas, and for specific neighborhoods will be useful.

In some cities, it may be sufficient to reference these documents in an appendix to the street vacation policy. But blanket referencing gives little specific guidance to decision makers. If folding these plans and policies into a street vacation policy is too large a task, it is possible to repeat only the relevant parts of each plan or document and to cite the appropriate maps as necessary.

For example, Seattle's proposed street vacation policy reiterates the city policy requiring parking in multifamily areas to be accessed through the rear alley where possible. Designed to encourage landscaped front yards, this policy is in keeping with the predominantly low-density character of many neighborhoods where apartments and town houses can be built. The street vacation policy discourages alley vacation in residential zones except where topography makes alley improvement impractical, or where alley functions can be maintained after vacation. In neighborhood commercial areas, land-use policies also support access to parking via alleys to maintain pedestrian precincts with continuous sidewalks and retail along the street. Alley vacations would also be discouraged there. Finally, Seattle's downtown plan designates pedestrian streets, view corridors, street parks, and other features that will influence decisions regarding vacations. Maps provide detailed guidance on alleys and streets that are needed for various functions.

Clearly, Seattle's example shows that the method of referencing other plans and policies adds substantive depth and area-specific details to what otherwise would be a very general set of vacation priorities and guidelines.

CONCLUSION

As the issues involving street vacation grow increasingly complex, cities need to define their priorities and systematize their review procedures for vacating rights-of-way. Policies developed in the public arena with opportunities for public review and revision can help guide decision makers who must exercise discretion in determining how best to use public rights-of-way.

The discretionary nature of street vacation decisions cannot be overemphasized. Good policies—those that thrive, are used, and are not easily tossed aside as inapplicable—rely on the judgment and intelligence both of the decision makers who apply them and of the public that continually brings to light their relevance to community needs.

REFERENCES

City of Seattle. 1985. "The Mayor's Recommended Street Vacation Policies." Seattle: Interdepartmental Street Vacation Policy Task Force, November.

Jacobs, A. B. 1978. *Making City Planning Work.* Chicago: American Society of Planning Officials.

24.
Including Transit

LORNE CAPPE

The intimate link that exists between street and city design has been the subject of many city plans throughout history. Pope Sixtus V's visionary designs for the streets of Rome changed the city's character during the sixteenth century (Bacon 1974). Similarly, Haussmann's redesign of Paris and L'Enfant's plan of Washington, D.C., created powerful networks of public spaces and buildings, connected by grand boulevards (Peets 1927, 1930). In North America, the City Beautiful Movement was another attempt to create sequences of formal public spaces and vistas through the design of city streets and networks. Although many of these schemes were initially aimed at facilitating military control of the urban "masses," their effect also was to enhance people's opportunities to experience the city as they moved through its streets. This experience remains strong today.

In the twentieth century, however, modern planners downplayed the qualitative aspects of street design to concentrate on efficient traffic movement. In the 1950s and 1960s, during the "golden age" of the automobile, most streets were transformed into channels for vehicular traffic, with increased amounts of street space and public resources set aside for cars.

Only gradually did the experiential qualities of moving through the city regain importance in planning circles. And when this occurred, the motorist was, not surprisingly, at the center of attention. In *The View from the Road* (1964), Donald Appleyard, Kevin Lynch, and John Myer introduced a revolutionary approach to highway design based on the perceptual experiences of driving. They were interested in "the aesthetics of highways: the way they look to the driver and his passengers, and what this implies for their design" (1964: 2). This approach was embraced by

All photographs are by the author unless otherwise noted.

highway engineers and their related public works departments, an unlikely group that has indirectly had a great influence on city design. Seeking to provide motorists with pleasant environments, they helped transform lush valleys, urban waterfronts, and city centers into high-speed transportation corridors. Unfortunately, however, the rich visual experiences that ensued benefitted motorists at the expense of pedestrians, bicyclists, and transit riders.

Bernard Rudofsky's *Streets for People: A Primer for Americans* (1969) was a plea to consider once again the quality of the pedestrian's environment. Since that time, planners and urban designers have increasingly linked the emphasis on pedestrian movement with improvements in the quality of urban living.

If, today, the environmental experiences and the well-being both of motorists and pedestrians are accepted element of transportation planning, the status of transit riders remains low in comparison. The focus of the relatively short history of urban public transportation has gradually been narrowed to an obsession with efficiency. Passengers on old cable cars and streetcars used to be an integral part of a city's street life. Today, transit riders are tightly packed in large numbers and moved briskly from one place to the other. Run as public utility companies, transit authorities in North America thrive on improving the speed and efficiency of their systems. Model transit designs further reinforce this attitude: advertising, logos, and car designs often resemble those of the aircraft industry, because air travel is the most glamorous and fastest type of mass transit. That car exteriors are especially inspired by airliners is evident from the diagonal cut windows and angular stripes of the 1970s generation of General Motors diesel buses (fig. 24-1). Even though the interiors of transit cars are tightly designed and sometimes even comfortable, little at-

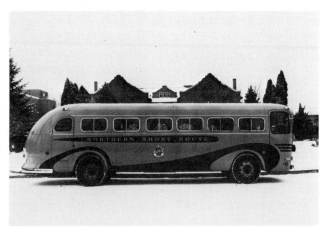

24-1. Transit vehicle design inspired by the airline industry. Gas bus "Northern Short Route" (Source: Special Collections, University of Washington Libraries, Seattle; photo: Warner #20 (n.d.))

24-2. View of College Street, Little Italy, Toronto. Serviced by surface mode of transit, College's small shops are spread evenly along the street.

24-3. View of Yonge Street, looking north toward Bloor Street, Toronto. Serviced by a subway, Yonge has high-density commercial developments located at major subway stops.

tention is paid to the way the cars "fit" in the street.

Yet well-conceived and -designed public transportation systems can contribute to the making of great cities. A well-developed network of transit routes can improve the form and land use of the city itself: transit-oriented urban centers (both in neighborhoods and downtowns) tend to be more compact and vital than their sprawling automobile-oriented counterparts. With the available alternative of transit, car usage may be reduced, thereby diminishing chaotic peak-hour congestion, parking needs, and air and noise pollution, while increasing pedestrian traffic.

The transit vehicle is itself a form of animation on the street. A sense of occasion is created when up to sixty people move past an area, some arriving, some departing, and some just moving through a place. The animation is experienced by pedestrians and bicyclists, as well as by people who look out of buildings that line the street. The stimulating array of colors, faces, and shapes adds interest to the street scene. In addition, citizens on buses and streetcars act as a form of surveillance, thus greatly contributing to a city's livability.

A well-designed transit system with frequent service is crucial for the economic viability of established commercial streets, whose form, moreover, is directly influenced by the mode of transportation that services them. Surface transit tends to spread commercial development over larger areas than do subways. Also, whereas shops are evenly distributed along streets with surface transit, subway stops tend to attract high-density commercial development (figs. 24-2, 24-3). (Note that land-use controls can eliminate this effect of transit on development. See chap. 20, by D. B. Lee). On the other hand, commercial streets serviced by the automobile can be as long as streets with surface transit, and, typically, their commercial buildings are deeply set back from the right-of-way to provide direct access to parking. They are, as a result, poor pedestrian environments (see chap. 19, by R. K. Untermann).

Transit networks feed and nurture a city by making urban centers accessible to many different kinds of people. Consideration of the aesthetic, environmental, and functional aspects of transit is a matter of equity in city design. While some people choose to ride transit instead of driving cars, those who cannot drive—the handicapped, children, and those who cannot afford to drive—have no alternative. Transit riders comprise a diverse group of people who are too often forgotten and disadvantaged. Those who elect to take transit have the benefit of being exposed to a true cross section of a city's population.

Finally, a good public transportation network can play an important role in the enjoyment of urban life. Riding San Francisco's cable cars, Venice's gondolas, and Vancouver's "Sea Bus" can add interest to the daily lives of citizens. Enjoying the journey is as important as arriving at the destination (fig. 24-4).

ELEMENTS OF THE TRANSIT EXPERIENCE

People's perception of the city while walking or driving has been a major focus of research in the past (Lynch 1960; Cullen 1961; Appleyard 1970; and see chap. 5, by A. Rapoport). However, the perceptions of public transportation users have not been examined.

24-4. Sunday drive in "Seeing Seattle Car." (Source: Special Collections, University of Washington Libraries, Seattle; photo: A. Curtis #4749 (n.d.))

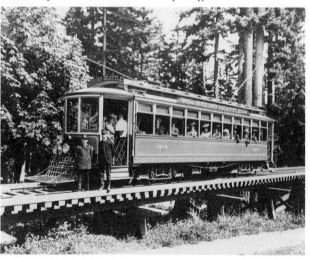

One gains satisfaction from a city by "comprehending" it (see chap. 1, by M. Francis). People interpret the sensory information they absorb from their environment to understand their surroundings and to feel a sense of belonging. Moreover, different persons interpret this information in a variety of ways in varied situations. According to Lynch (1981), a city is comprehensible when it is legible, imageable, and allows for easy orientation. Legibility denotes that a city's meanings, symbols, and cultural overlays can be easily uncovered. Imageability refers to the visual effects that the city leaves on people's minds, the unique character that creates vivid memories contributing to an individual's sense of satisfaction. Orientation is achieved when a person can clearly make his way around a city and easily understand where he is at any given time.

It is useful to compare the relative quality of experiencing the city on different modes of transportation. While transit unquestionably provides richer experiences than car travel, whether it offers less fulfillment than walking is debatable.

Walking versus Driving

Walking provides more opportunities to perceive and comprehend the details of the immediate environment than does any other form of movement. Slow speeds permit people to discern subtle and discrete elements that sustain interest. Central and peripheral vision is sharp, and complex street environments are more stimulating to the pedestrian than are simple ones (Rapaport 1983).

Fully mobile pedestrians can totally absorb the sensory world of the city because they are capable of perceiving easily through all senses and need not concentrate on creating their motion. Mere reflexes allow them to stop, change direction, adjust their pace, or focus attention on particular points of interest. Also, opportunities for face-to-face contact with others provide an important social function in city life.

Drivers experience the city in a radically different manner because the speed and enclosure of the automobile act as filters to perception. Drivers' perceptions are limited mostly to the visual field, and even vision is impaired owing to the speed of travel: peripheral vision narrows, the foreground tends to fade, and details become blurred. Environmental stimuli need to be grouped into larger segments in order for motorists to comprehend fully what is passing before their eyes. Distant views are more comprehensible than immediate surroundings. Subtle cues easily perceived by pedestrians tend to go undetected because motorists must concentrate on the act of driving. For reasons of safety, motorists have less freedom than pedestrians to select and focus on elements in their environment.

Appleyard, Lynch, and Myer (1964) noted that persons in a steadily moving car obtain only slight kinesthetic sensations. The driver uses the accelerator, brake, and steering wheel to control the automobile's engine and the tires to generate his movement. Except for abrupt changes in speed, direction, or incline, drivers must rely on vision to obtain a sense of motion. The pedestrian, however, because he or she is directly responsible for creating his or her movement, not only visually experiences motion, but feels every step, bump, and subtle change in incline and texture of surface.

Driving is an antisocial mode of urban travel. Isolated in their small private environment, motorists tend to interact negatively with one another. People are often more aggressive in the security of their vehicles than in less-protected situations.

Riding Transit

The perceptions of people riding transit differ greatly from those of either pedestrians or motorists. Transit requires low levels of concentration: passengers need not focus on their travel, except to ensure that they exit at their destination. Also, they need not worry about parking. Transit riders are therefore free to observe others, to look out the window, or to be totally oblivious to their surroundings, unlike pedestrians, who must at the very least watch where they are walking. The freedom to concentrate on activities visible from the transit window allows the rider more opportunities to experience the special characteristics of the city as he or she passes through it.

As an internal environment, mass transit provides an extra dimension to the urban dweller's perceptual and social world (fig. 24-5). Streetcars and buses all have large interior spaces with often lively, constantly changing environments. For the pedestrian, the street space *is* the environment. For the driver, the tight static interior space of a car is not stimulating. In transit vehicles, the coming and going of people inside the car competes with the passing streetscape for the rider's attention. The rider is therefore offered the choice of concentrating on interior or exterior situations.

The social dimension of transit can be enhanced by the design of the vehicle itself. Seating arrangements that E. T. Hall describes as "sociopetal" (1966: 101), in portions of buses, streetcars, and subways, are those conducive to conversing with others. Yet eye contact cannot be made when everyone faces forward, as in most vehicles. Sociability also depends on the nature of the transit route. In streetcars and buses that make frequent stops in inner-city neighborhoods,

a.

b.

24-5. Transit riders can opt to focus on the environment within the vehicle or on the street life outside: a. interior of Witt streetcar, Toronto, October 1928. Note the wood stove on the left side of the car; b. View from streetcar in Toronto today. (Photo a.: Toronto Transit Commission)

familiar faces are more likely to be seen (particularly on repeat trips) than on rides along downtown routes.

Perception of the street will vary depending on the person's location in the vehicle. For example, seats that are next to a window, facing forward or perpendicular to the direction travelled, all afford different perceptions. Perceptions also alter when one shares a seat or stands. Aisle seats emphasize views of the vehicle's interior, whereas window seats help to focus attention on the passing city. If driving limits views to the city as it unfolds directly in front of the car, riding transit provides the ability to experience the passing environment from a variety of vantage points: forward, backward, and sideways.

Perception also changes with eye level. Some

transit vehicles are raised well above the street, placing the passenger's eye level above that of the pedestrian. This affords a better view of buildings and activities on the street, but minimizes eye contact between people inside and outside of the vehicle.

Public transportation enables the tourist or resident to observe and comprehend a large portion of a city, far larger, of course, than would be perceived on foot. Signs above storefronts, the variety merchandise displayed in windows and on sidewalks, the manner and degree to which people maintain and "dress up" their properties, the amount of public expenditure on streetscape improvements (trees, street furniture, and so on) all provide insights into the nature and character of local residents and merchants.

Although they move relatively rapidly through the city, surface transit passengers observe and interact with other citizens. At any given place, they can learn something about local neighborhoods by the way people dress, by their manners, and by the languages they speak. Yet understanding the human characteristics of specific areas is an opportunity that is denied by modes of transit with their own rights-of-way (whether underground, above grade, or even at grade).

PRECEDENTS FOR GOOD TRANSIT

In the early phases of urban public transit development, the transit rider's experience was not considered apart from transit service efficiency. Stagecoaches, cable cars, and early models of streetcars were low to the ground and open to the outdoors; they moved along city streets at slow speeds, offering riders sensory experience of their surroundings. Transit riders were an integral part of a city's street life, sharing with other people the buildings, parks, shops, and activities. But now that transit planning focuses on moving greater numbers at higher speeds, special attention needs to be paid to the quality of the rider's experience.

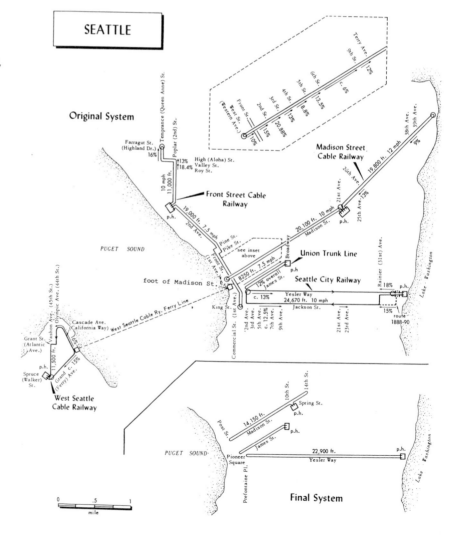

24-6. Seattle's cable car network, circa 1900. Note that changes in grade and speed of transit are indicated on the map. (Source: Hilton 1982: 390)

It is useful to study the early forms of public transit that often responded to the "genius loci" of a city. For instance, Seattle, at the turn of the century, possessed cable car networks of approximately twenty miles, running from the central waterfront to Queen Anne Hill, First Hill, and Madison and Leschi Parks (fig. 24-6). Transfers to ferries were possible at Lake Washington and Elliot Bay. Responding to the city's dramatic topography and spectacular views of the Pacific and the mountains, the network contributed to the rider's understanding of Seattle's uniqueness.

The design of the cable car itself contributed to the city's street life. Riders were able to hop on and off the low-lying, open cars as they slowly moved up and down the city's steep hills. The cars' open areas allowed riders to be in the same sensory world as those who walked and lived along city streets (fig. 24-7). Weather protection was provided through simple movable awnings. Some models had enclosed spaces and the capability of enclosing additional areas in winter. In some cities, convertible cars were used only during particular seasons (fig. 24-8).

Soon, however, the cable cars were perceived to be an outdated and inefficient means of transportation in most cities. Their cost, level of efficiency, and, especially, disruption to automobile flows were seen as drawbacks to continued use. From the 1930s on, transit took second place to the automobile. Streetcar tracks, overhead wires, and cable systems were removed and replaced by trolley buses. Yet, in most North American cities, the buses of the 1960s and 1970s were less energy efficient and comfortable and more noisy and polluting than their antecedents. Rapid-transit networks that operate on their own rights-of-way (particularly underground subway systems) have further removed the transit rider from city life. Sadly, Seattle is now proposing that a tunnel be built through the downtown core, thereby taking the bulk of commuter travel away from downtown streets.

Since World War II, attempts to consider the rider's experience have included the development of transit malls (such as those in downtown Minneapolis; Vancouver, British Columbia; and Portland, Oregon), which were conceived to balance an efficient traffic flow with an attractive pedestrian environment. Yet, because transit malls segregate pedestrians and buses from cars, which are a main source of street animation, they have not always been successful (see chap. 1, by M. Francis and chap. 22, by R. B. Eichner and H. Tobey). Despite landscaping, pedestrian amenities, and other streetscape improvements, segregated forms of travel remove users from full exposure to city life and tend to be less satisfying.

24-7. In old cable cars, passengers could experience the same sensory world as those who walked and lived along the city streets. (Source: Special Collections, University of Washington Libraries, Seattle; photo: UW #2061, circa 1901)

24-8. Car design for every season: a. closed and open cars, San Diego Electric Railway; b. convertible car, Toronto, circa 1905. (Source a.: Special Collections, University of Washington Libraries, Seattle; photo: UW #2062 (n.d.); photo b. Toronto Transit Commission)

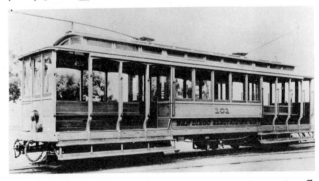

a.

b.

ENHANCING THE RIDER'S EXPERIENCE OF THE CITY

Transit planning and design can once again integrate transit into the fabric of cities by focusing on the design of vehicles themselves and on the characteristics and layout of their networks.

Vehicle Design

Comfort, sociability, accessibility, and views are important elements of transit vehicle design. The color, length, height, overall size, and fenestration of vehicles will affect the way they serve riders and street users alike and the way they will eventually fit into the city.

The specifics of vehicle design should relate to the characteristics of the city itself. For example, the "articulated" buses currently in use in Seattle are too long for much of the city's grid pattern. These buses are not compatible with the short downtown blocks and the odd geometry of the numerous intersections between different grids.

Contemporary vehicles should allow riders and pedestrians to interact. People are currently forced to file on and off through narrow doorways, which restrict and formalize access between the street and the vehicle. More attention should be given to designing

24-9. Toronto streetcar riders are given priority over motorists: a. Yonge and Queen streets, Toronto, 1923; b. College Street, Toronto, today. (Photo a.: Toronto Transit Commission)

a.

b.

vehicles that allow a freer flow of movement. The height of the vehicle, and particularly of its windows, should be carefully considered: often the pedestrian's eye level corresponds to the solid metal body of the vehicle, unnecessarily reducing the opportunities for visual and other kinds of contact between people inside and outside. Tinted glass windows and windows that open only slightly further separate the rider from the street, and vice versa. The pleasant sounds and smells from the street should be made accessible from inside the transit vehicle. At the same time, however, exhaust fumes and excessive noise from motors should be mitigated for the comfort both of riders and pedestrians.

Transit Network Design

Public transportation needs to be considered an integral part of urban design. Riders' experiences, as well as the experiences of those living and working along transit routes, are essential components of a transit network design that combines efficiency with experiential quality. How necessary is it to move quickly and undisturbed through a wonderful place rich with scenery? Isn't getting there half of the fun?

Toronto's extensive streetcar system allows riders excellent opportunities to perceive and understand their city. The classic PCC's (President's Council Cars, or "Red Rockets," as they are affectionately known locally) and the newer cars travel at a stately pace along major streets, offering glimpses of Toronto's diverse neighborhoods.

Transit riders on streetcar routes are given priority. Motorists are required by law to stop and allow people to move between vehicles and the sidewalk (fig. 24-9). Sharing the streets with cars and taking priority away from them has given the streetcar an importance beyond most modes of public transportation. Many of Toronto's rights-of-way serviced by streetcars are 66 feet wide with two lanes of parking, leaving no "through" lanes of traffic. Motorists have few opportunities to pass streetcars and are therefore forced to pause at transit stops along with the transit riders.

Over the years, streetcars have become a part of Toronto's street life. One expects to see the cars or to hear them rumbling past with their distinctive bells. Overhead wires and tracks give the system a strong presence, even when a car is not in view. If, as is commonly believed, the retail strips are the heart and soul of Toronto's ethnic neighborhoods, the streetcar can be considered the circulatory system that maintains the street's vitality. The streetcar's strong presence in Toronto has made the vehicle an integral part of Torontonians' image of their city, and local artists have often depicted streetcars in their work (fig. 24-10). Residents use them to go about their daily lives. Some people ride them along certain routes as a form of entertainment, comparable to "cruising" city streets in cars. For example, a trip on the "Queen Car" from the Humber River to the Beach provides an interesting glimpse of the socioeconomic and architectural cross section of Toronto.

Transit networks can be designed to heighten the joys of motion. Rem Koolhaus (1978) describes comparable pleasures of the amusement park at Coney

24-10. "Spring on King Street West," by Arto Yuzbasiyan (1983). (Courtesy Arto Yuzbasiyan and Kaspar Gallery, Toronto)

Island. Similar kinesthetic sensations can be generated by riding in and out of tunnels, moving past buildings on surface or elevated rights-of-way, watching as the city unfolds, and observing buildings appearing and disappearing. Appleyard examines how the "apparent motion of the city" (the feeling that the city is moving while, in fact, it is the person who actually moves) can be a source of delight in everyday urban life. He describes "towers dancing across roofs, circular objects rotating, buildings looming up, swinging, turning, shrinking and expanding, and the foreground blurring against the background" (1965: 166).

Transit designers need to take these sensations into account in laying out networks. Just as the design of buildings along city streets is controlled by city planning departments to enhance pedestrians' and motorists' views, so should views along transit rights-of-way be controlled and protected. The transit rider deserves equal consideration as he or she also contributes to urban livability.

The growing movement to consider the qualitative aspects of pedestrian and automobile travel must now include the transit rider. The time has come to convince transit authorities, city officials, and planners to recognize the importance of transit riders to the health of cities and to begin treating them with the sensitivity they deserve.

REFERENCES

Appleyard, D. 1965. "Motion, Sequence and the City." In *The Nature and Art of Motion*, edited by G. Kepes. New York: Brazilier.

———. 1970. *The Street Livability Study*. San Francisco: San Francisco Department of City Planning.

———. 1981. *Livable Streets*. Berkeley: University of California Press.

Appleyard, D., K. Lynch, and J. Myer. 1964. *The View from the Road*. Cambridge: MIT Press.

Bacon, E. 1974. *Design of Cities*. New York: Penguin Books.

Cappe, L., and A. Lehman. 1983. *Seattle: Expressions of Movement*. Student paper, College of Architecture and Urban Planning, University of Washington, Seattle.

Cullen, G. 1961. *The Concise Townscape*. London: Architectural Press.

Hall, E. T. 1966. *The Hidden Dimension*. Garden City, N.Y.: Doubleday.

Hilton, G. 1982. *The Cable Car in America*. San Diego: Howell-North Books.

Koolhaus, R. 1978. *Delirious New York: A Retroactive Manifesto for Manhattan*. New York: Oxford University Press.

Lynch, K. 1960. *The Image of the City*. Cambridge: MIT Press.

———. 1981. A *Theory of Good City Form*. Cambridge: MIT Press.

Peets, E. 1927. "Famous Town Planners I—Hausmann." *The Town Planning Review* (June): 180–90.

———. 1930. "Famous Town Planners III—L'Enfant." *The Town Planning Review* (July): 30–49.

Rapoport, A. 1983. "Pedestrian Street Use—Culture and Perception." In *Streets as Public Property*, edited by A. V. Moudon and P. Laconte. Seattle: University of Washington, College of Architecture and Urban Planning.

Rudofsky, B. 1969. *Streets for People: A Primer for Americans*. New York: Van Nostrand Reinhold.

25.
Natural Light and the Urban Environment

HARVEY BRYAN AND SUSAN STUEBING

The urban environment is a combination of many man-made and natural elements. Of the latter, natural light is one of the most important amenities to insure a vital, dynamic, and inhabitable city. High-rise building has increased the need to protect natural light to the street and to consider carefully the design of building bulk; in response, regulatory protections have taken many forms, the most common of which is the Floor Area Ratio (FAR). Unfortunately, FAR is an ineffectual device for environmental and aesthetic considerations and, in particular, for determining quantities of light, air, and wind. In fact, a building's blockage of light to the street is a function of the placement of building bulk in relation to the street, not of its FAR.

This chapter follows the historic development of building regulation for natural lighting concerns. It examines the differences between various regulatory methods that have been recently studied and implemented in New York City, San Francisco, and Boston. Finally, suggestions are made for the development of site-specific regulation, which will provide an overall qualitative analysis of the building's effect on the street environment. The qualitative approach proposed here may provide greater design flexibility as well as stimulate the designer toward a more environmentally pleasing aesthetic.

URBAN LIFE AND HIGH-RISE BUILDINGS

An urban street that is bright yet not heavily shadowed offers a pleasant experience to pedestrians. Imagine a city scene, a vibrant commercial area with a variety of storefronts that create a pastiche of architectural attitudes and historic eras. Some people hurry on their way to work, while others shop and stroll; perhaps a few indulge in a favorite pastime of many, watching other people.

This image is a positive view of the city, a sparkling street where light plays across the facades of buildings and highlights their architectural detail. The street is not windy or dusty, but crisp and alive. The brilliant natural illumination intensifies the faces of the passersby to make them recognizable and congenial. Many of these strangers are pleasantly enjoying the day as, for a few moments, they escape their office for some fresh air and natural light.

The assumption in this picture is environmental. Light and air are vital to the pedestrian's enjoyment. They not only influence the quality of street life, but reflect the ambience and livability of the city as a whole. Natural light enhances the usefulness of open spaces as well by increasing the enjoyment of squares, sitting areas, and parks. Even in cold weather, people may find the urban park a pleasant place to pause or to eat lunch, if it is warmed by the sun and sheltered from the wind.

Although architects and planners cannot control atmospheric conditions, they can do much to maximize and protect the natural resources of light and air, which highlight existing architecture as well as enhance the value of urban spaces.

Yet that valuable urban amenity, natural light, has been severely overlooked in the past thirty years, when increased density and high-rise development should have required especially careful study and planning. In comparison with the millions of dollars spent to create urban spaces for office and commercial facilities, very few resources have been expended for understanding natural light and protecting it. We have forgotten that the street represents a large portion of expensive urban land, of unbuilt public territory. This oversight has come to bear on the livability of the American city, where dark, shadowed, canyon-like streets have become the expectation, not the exception.

Natural light also increases the value of buildings. Real estate developers know that perimeter windowed spaces rent more easily and for more money than windowless spaces. Similarly, the value of a building cast in shadow is less than that of one highlighted by sun and sky. Imagine, for example, I. M. Pei's John Hancock Building in Boston crowded by buildings on all sides. The dramatic nature of that structure, its reflection of clouds, sunlight and, in particular, the sunset, which throws a shaft of color onto its bevelled facade, would be lost were the structure shadowed by neighboring buildings.

NATURAL LIGHT: SUNLIGHT VERSUS DAYLIGHT

With greater emphasis on the livability of cities in the 1980s, zoning guidelines and design review have become increasingly important. Yet these planning methods do not necessarily include considerations of natural light. As was stated, the Floor Area Ratio is an inadequate approach for guaranteeing natural light. Placement of building bulk on the site, setbacks, notching of corners, and reflectivity of the building facade all affect the amount of natural light that will reach the street.

Several steps are suggested to develop effective zoning guidelines or regulations for a particular urban environment. First, the type of natural light desired must be clearly defined. The methodology for assessing the impact of proposed development on specific urban streets and open spaces will differ based on whether the long-term goal is to obtain daylight, which emanates from the sky dome, or sunlight, which comes directly from the sun. Second, the existing context must be fully analyzed for current lighting levels and conditions. Third, based on the contextual study, realistic goals must be set for the type of light desired in various sections of the city. Flexible design guidelines may result that not only provide a positive urban environment for the pedestrian, but also offer architectural options for the designer.

Sunlight comes from sun rays, which follow a daily path; the angle of the rays varies depending on the season. In the summer the angle of the sun path to the earth is higher in the sky, while in the winter the sun is much lower. This difference affects the lengths of the shadows that are cast as well as the availability of sunlight during various seasons. Daylight, on the other hand, is diffused from the entire sky dome and can emanate from either an overcast or a clear sky. For this reason orientation is not as important a consideration as it is for sunlight.

While regulation for daylight can offer a wide range of loose parameters, regulation for sunlight, particularly in dense urban areas, typically must become specific and restrictive. The distinction between regulation for the two types of natural light is evident in the comparison of current proposals in New York City that regulate for daylight with those in San Francisco that propose to regulate for solar access.

HISTORICAL OVERVIEW OF NATURAL LIGHT REGULATION

Although the need for regulating urban development for daylight may be more pronounced today, public regulation of daylight and sunlight is not a modern invention. A long history of urban planning exists from which references can be drawn for contemporary planning.

The Ancient Greeks and Romans both mandated minimum lighting standards for their cities (Rodger 1972). The British Law of Ancient Lights, which dates back to 1189, was embodied into statute law in the Prescription Act of 1832. Under that act, buildings that had windows and had enjoyed uninterrupted access to natural light for at least a twenty-year period were protected from a new adjacent building encroaching upon that right.

In the United States, it was not until the turn of the century that daylight and sunlight problems in cities began to attract attention. In 1912, a Boston architect named William Atkinson developed a technique for quantifying how changes in orientation, shape, and building height affected natural light to the street (Atkinson 1912). This research helped him advocate the need for legislative control of building bulk and placement on urban sites. Boston's previous zoning law, dating from 1892, limited the height of buildings to two-and-one-half times the width of the street, with a maximum limit of 125 feet. In contrast, Atkinson's proposal used a sky exposure approach: a line was drawn from the opposite side of the street continuing through the edge of the street wall, which was one-and-one-quarter times the street width, forming the allowable envelope within which a proposed building had to be constructed (fig. 25-1).

Atkinson's work was influential in the development of modern zoning standards, which began to be drafted shortly after the publication of his work. In 1915, the New York Heights of Building Commission, established to study legislative controls in other cities,

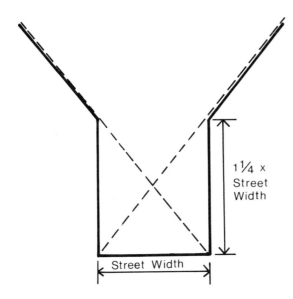

25-1. Atkinson's proposal for limiting building height.

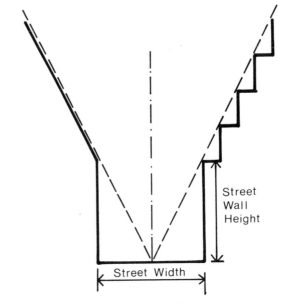

25-2. New York's 1916 street-wall and sky-exposure concept.

25-3. New York's 1916 height district map.

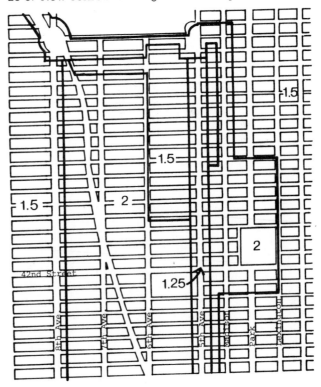

recommended that New York City be zoned on the German system, which divided cities into existing uses and building types and specified maximum building heights for each district (New York Heights of Building Commission 1915). Most of these recommendations were incorporated into the 1916 Zoning Ordinance for New York City (New York City Planning Commission 1945).

As the first comprehensive municipal attempt in the United States to guide and control physical form and function legally, the New York City 1916 Zoning Ordinance guaranteed minimum street-level standards of natural light and air. It incorporated Atkinson's two innovative approaches, the street wall and the sky-exposure plane (fig. 25-2). The street-wall approach related building-wall height to street width, based on five "height districts" related to perceived utility, neighborhood character, and the need for pedestrian amenity (fig. 25-3). For example, Fifth Avenue with its low-scale buildings and carriage-trade retail was designated a lower height district than surrounding streets and avenues.

The other approach, the sky-exposure plane, defined the amount of sky that could be seen from the center of the street, based again on street width and street-wall height. A lower height district yielded greater sky exposure, and thus, more light reached the street.

These regulations had major architectural and planning ramifications, limiting the allowable bulk of building bases as well as the total building bulk. The resulting buildings rose from the street to their allowable street-wall height, and then began a series of set-

backs to remain within the sky-exposure plane. When the floor area reached 25 percent of the site, a tower of unlimited height was allowed. The characteristic "ziggurat" or "wedding cake" buildings that later resulted from this ordinance may be attributed to the limitations of the design and development community rather than to the ordinance itself. Although often criticized for being too restrictive, the 1916 ordinance includes such diverse building designs as the Empire State, RCA, and Seagram buildings. In fact, architects such as Raymond Hood, chief designer of Rockefeller Center, found considerable inspiration in the 1916 ordinance. The numerous setbacks of the RCA tower were not required by the ordinance; rather, they celebrated the setback concept itself, much in the same manner as Hugh Ferriss did in his expressive drawings of an "imaginary metropolis" (1929).

For more than forty years, the 1916 ordinance remained the model zoning standard for many American cities. Even New York City did not substantially change it until 1961. Yet further work was being done, especially in England and Scandinavia, to refine methods of measuring daylight to the street and the effect of buildings on street daylight. George Ford, New York's regional planning director, in his posthumous book *Building Height, Bulk and Form*, added an economic analysis of daylight to his extensive review of planning attitudes and studies on this subject. He stated that, "Indeed, there is an almost universal feeling that light is one of the most important factors affecting the profitableness and permanence of larger bulk buildings" (1931: 7). The idea of linking profit to daylight, although based on common sense, has not been exploited expressly as a planning argument since then. Yet, of course, the real estate and development industry is fully aware of the relative value of buildings located on daylit streets, as compared with those that are shadowed throughout the day.

In the 1960s, most cities either had or were in the process of adopting a new type of zoning, usually based on the Floor Area Ratio. FAR is a convenient quantitative measure: it regulates the number of times the overall lot area can be multiplied, resulting in the total allowable floor area of a building. Yet FAR has not proved to be an effective method of controlling the *placement of building bulk on a site*. Its shortcomings were especially evident in the 1960s, when municipalities began to use FARs to encourage the inclusion of public amenities into proposed building projects. For example, an increase in building height or FAR was permitted only if plazas, lobbies, and retail spaces were included in the building design. This process, often based on discretionary review, frequently disregarded the traditional role of zoning to provide natural light and air to the street. It yielded buildings that rose sheer from the street or property line, creating the all-too-common "canyon effect" mentioned earlier.

ADVANCES IN DAYLIGHT ASSESSMENT

An alternative method of assessment to the FAR approach was used in the preliminary studies of existing conditions for Boston in 1984. It was adapted from a research methodology developed by the Swedish architect Gunnar Pleijel (1954), who designed a technique for measuring the percentage of unobstructed sky at any urban location. With this technique, existing conditions can be analyzed and the impact of proposed buildings in an existing context can be projected.

Pleijel used his invention, the globoscope (a device that was the forerunner of today's fish-eye lens), to photograph the sky dome. These photographs can document daylight at any desired location by recording a distorted, yet proportional, impression of the surrounding buildings on both sides of the street (fig. 25-4). Light to the street is measured by the amount of the sky dome that is obstructed by a building in the fish-eye photographs. The daylight cutoff angle created by the building's roof edge can easily be found and masked with a transparent overlay sized to the diameter of the fish-eye image. The overlay helps to measure the building's angle of elevation (the angle between the horizon and the roof edge). From the overlay, one can easily determine the amount of light to the street by extending the vertical edges of the street side property lines to the zenith and by subtracting the obstruction mask from the resulting pie-shaped form (fig. 25-5).

25-4. Typical fish-eye-lens photograph.

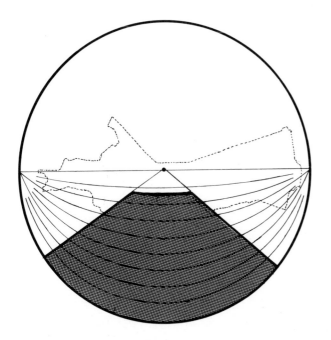

25-5. Obstructing mask subtracted from pie-shaped property envelope.

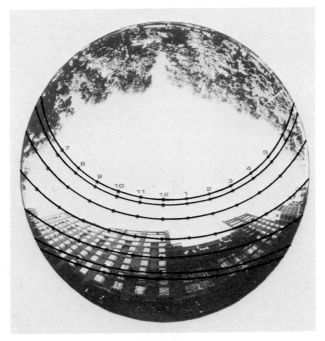

25-6. Sunpath overlay for block adjacent to the Boston Commons.

One can also use the fish-eye projection to determine the amount and duration of sunlight striking urban open spaces. This is done by using a sun-path transparency as an overlay on the fish-eye photograph taken from the open space (fig. 25-6). The number of hours per day of sunlight at any reference location

and at any particular time of the year can be easily gauged with sun-path overlay transparencies. This technique can be used to develop guidelines to guarantee solar access to open spaces during a specified portion of the day.

CONTEMPORARY PERSPECTIVE

Cities throughout the United States are placing greater emphasis on the livability of the urban environment by requiring downtown development to meet urban design criteria. Although the mistakes of the 1960s and 1970s cannot be reversed, cities can begin to look toward buildings that preserve the openness of streets and that protect the right of pedestrians to daylight. New York City initiated a zoning study for midtown Manhattan in 1980 (New York Department of City Planning 1980), San Francisco soon followed with a sun and light study for downtown in 1983 (Bosselmann et al. 1983, and see chap. 15), and Boston undertook a daylight study of Boylston Street and its financial district in 1984 (Bryan and Stuebing 1984). These studies find their roots in the early work of Atkinson and Pleijel and look toward more sensitive zoning methods.

Midtown Manhattan's New Ordinance

In midtown Manhattan's revised zoning ordinance, the placement of building bulk on the site and the admission of light to the street become, once again, key concerns. The design of new buildings must maintain the context of their surroundings based on pedestrian perception from the street, building mass, street-wall height and length, and the placement of building bulk on the site. These elements also predict the effective light to the street.

The performance approach of this ordinance involves a four-part test that evaluates a proposed building by a point system. The building must score 85 points out of a possible 100. The crucial test is for daylighting, which must be evaluated at a minimum 40 points and can represent as much as 60 percent of a proposed building's overall score. A modified version of a sky-vault diagram, called the Waldram Diagram, is used to measure the amount of daylight to the street for a given building (fig. 25-7). The chart is a grid that quantifies the daylight reaching the street from the top and around the sides of a building. As the proposed building is masked onto this grid, the grid's unobstructed blocks are multiplied by weighted values and then totalled, resulting in a daylight equivalency score. This score is obtained in each direction for

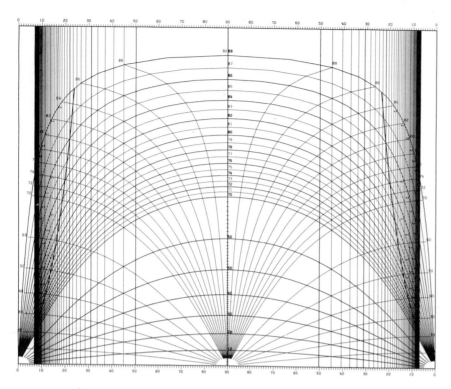

25-7. New York's daylight
evaluation chart for a 60-foot street.

each street on which a proposed building borders, evaluating the presence of the proposed structure as perceived from a point 250 feet away.

Although an important step to protect daylight, this approach has proven too complex to become an effective urban design tool. The New York City Planning Commission thus countered with an alternative prescriptive approach that was simpler yet architecturally more restrictive (New York Department of City Planning 1982). In theory, this prescriptive approach is similar to the sky-exposure planes of the 1916 ordinance. "Sky-exposure curves" are used, which define the allowable shape and bulk of proposed buildings (fig. 25-8).

San Francisco's New Ordinance

In 1983 the City of San Francisco commissioned a study to explore the effect of high-rise buildings on the quality of its urban environment. Although the evaluation of light to the street was similar to that of New York City, the resulting guidelines, based on the work of Ralph Knowles (1981) and the concept of a solar envelope, were more restrictive in an urban environment with existing high-rise buildings.

The study investigated a number of public open spaces and city streets for sun and light access during critical times of the day (from about 10:00 AM to 2:00 PM). Sunlight (as opposed to daylight) access during those hours was deemed necessary to ensure active

25-8. New York's alternative to the daylight evaluation chart: the sky-exposure curve.

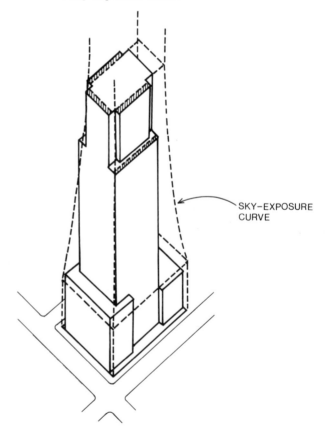

SKY–EXPOSURE
CURVE

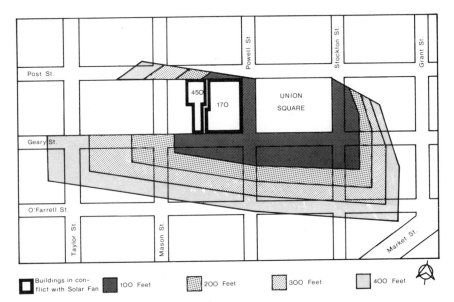

25-9. San Francisco's proposed height envelope around Union Square.

■ Buildings in con-
flict with Solar Fan ■ 100 Feet   ▨ 200 Feet   ▨ 300 Feet   ▨ 400 Feet

use, especially for outdoor lunch-hour activities. For each open space studied, solar access criteria were established and a sun profile plane was generated to shape the height envelope within which a new building would be required to conform. Thus, the envelope, as defined by the sun profile plane, set parameters of the shape and height of the largest possible building on a given site that would not shadow an adjacent open space (fig. 25-9).

Solar access criteria for San Francisco streets were developed in a similar manner as those for open spaces. Downtown San Francisco has four basic street orientations (north-south, east-west north of Market Street, northeast-southwest, and southeast-northwest south of Market Street). Along east-west streets north of Market Street, for example, solar access was allowed from March to September during the majority of the day. A sun profile plane was generated from the north sidewalk to establish an envelope within which proposed buildings on the south side of the street would have to be sited (fig. 25-10).

San Francisco's approach provides for selective solar access to public streets and open spaces (Bosselmann et al. 1983). Interestingly, however, it creates uneven allowable envelopes along downtown streets. For example, the heights of buildings along the south side of an east-west street will be less than those along the street's north side. Because much of San Francisco's existing downtown does not meet the proposed guidelines, widespread conformance to this approach may be difficult to achieve. However, San Francisco's use of solar access criteria to control development adjacent to public open space is a unique and useful model, although care must be taken to prevent such criteria from becoming overly restrictive.

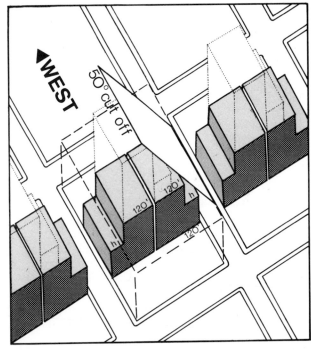

25-10. San Francisco's proposed zoning envelope for east-west streets north of Market Street.

The Boston Study

Both the New York and San Francisco studies laid the groundwork for the Boston study (Bryan and Stuebing 1984), whose goal was to develop daylighting guidelines that designers could easily address. Intended to predict the most positive attributes of proposed projects, the guidelines could not be overly prescriptive.

Unlike the gridirons of New York or San Francisco, Boston's historic narrow and curving streets have been continued by contemporary downtown development. As a result, however, these oddly sized streets and irregular patterns require more detailed analysis than was necessary in either New York or San Francisco.

Two areas were investigated: Boylston Street and the financial district. Assessments of fish-eye photographs resulted in values assigned to buildings based on the amount of daylight that was able to reach the street. The assigned numerical values accounted for site, design, setback, and notching of the building, which allow light to reach the street from the building's sides. Often, towers with high cutoff angles monopolized only part of the site and had lower values (because more light was reaching the street) than smaller buildings built to their property lines.

Boylston Street is a major entryway to Boston's downtown. Foresighted planning of the Back Bay area resulted in low cutoff angles and a general commonality in street-wall height. The low and consistent street wall, coupled with Boylston's generous width, offers a unique boulevard quality (fig. 25-11). For most of the length of the street, the cutoff angle remained below 65 percent, owing to both low building heights (maximum 70 feet) and the existence of setbacks at street level. However, several new structures violated the old established street wall, destroying vistas and creating shadowed pockets along the street. The need for sensitive regulation is demonstrated by such development, which, if continued, could threaten the openness of Boylston Street.

The level of daylight in the financial district is consistently lower than on Boylston Street (fig. 25-12). The majority of the streets there, particularly in the center of the district, have little light (above 80 percent cutoff) due primarily to the irregular street patterns, narrow street widths, and lack of setbacks. In addition, new office building construction during the last few years reaches building heights of up to 500 feet. A few nineteenth-century blocks are the only areas in this district that offer relief from the dark and shadowed street environment.

STATE-OF-THE-ART DAYLIGHT ASSESSMENT

Although high FARs often coincide with the loss of daylight to immediate surroundings, the Floor-to-Area Ratio is not the only factor to be considered. Buildings with similar FARs can result in very different amounts of light to the street, and buildings with low FARs can significantly reduce daylight, depending on the placement of bulk on the site.

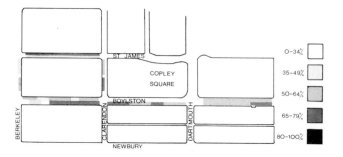

25-11. Daylight map of Boston's Boylston Street: percentage of sky obstructed.

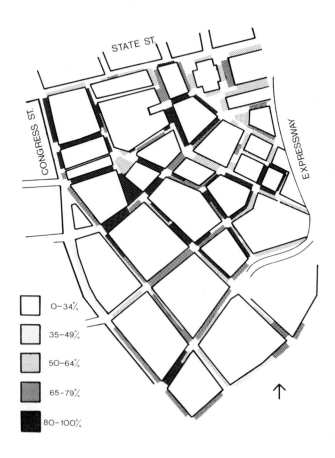

25-12. Daylight map of Boston's financial district: percentage of sky obstructed.

The following example illustrates the impact of a daylight analysis of a proposed building. Let us assume that two buildings that are to be constructed on the same site have identical FARs. Assume also that the buildings differ only in their design: the first (fig. 25-13a) is a large rectangular solid, while the second (fig. 25-14a) has several of its upper stories set back and its corners notched. One can compare the daylight impact of the buildings by constructing a projection that is identical to the fish-eye projection. The plan and the elevation of the buildings are drawn, with corners defining the shape of the building located in reference to the center of the street. Under the hypothetical conditions proposed, these corners are 40 feet from the buildings because the street is given to be 80 feet wide, with no initial setback from the property line in either case. By drawing lines to connect the center of the street to the critical corners

of the buildings, one can determine a series of angles and use them in conjunction with the angle of elevation overlay to mask the buildings onto the fish-eye projection (fig. 25-13b, and 25-14b). The percentage of light to the street is then calculated by dividing the pie-shaped property envelope into 100 units. This is accomplished by multiplying the ten equal angular increments that are on the angle of elevation overlay (which consists of ten fixed arcs of 9° each) by the ten equal angular increments (which vary depending on property and street dimensions) that have to be drawn within the angle of azimuth—the angle in plan that is formed between the reference point in the center of the street and the edges of the two streetside property lines. With the pie-shaped property envelope so divided, the number of units of unobstructed sky can then be subtracted from 100, resulting in the percentage of light to the street that is obstructed.

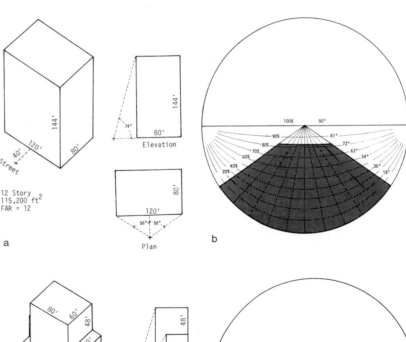

25-13. Proposed building designed as a rectangular solid: a. building bulk and relationship to the street; b. diagram showing 82 percent of the sky obstructed.

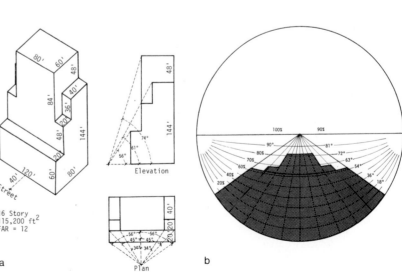

25-14. Proposed building designed to set back on the site: a. building bulk and relationship to the street; b. diagram showing 75 percent of the sky obstructed.

This hypothetical projection illustrates that although the FARs for both buildings are identical, the design of the second building accounts for 7 percent more daylight to the street. The placement of bulk to the back of the site, the street-wall (200-foot setback at 60 feet), and the notched corners are features that make the second building more sensitive to daylight, even though it is given to be 48 feet taller than the building illustrated in fig. 25-13.

Although the fish-eye projection is extremely useful for determining sky obstruction, the tediousness involved in its construction detracts from its use as a zoning evaluation tool. Through microcomputers, however, one can easily automate and graphically display the technique outlined in this chapter. In fact, a microcomputer program called BRADA was developed at the Massachusetts Institute of Technology for this purpose. BRADA will automatically construct a

25-15. Output from the BRADA program: a. daylight obstruction diagram for building shown in figure 25-13; b. same diagram for building in figure 25-14. Note the same results.

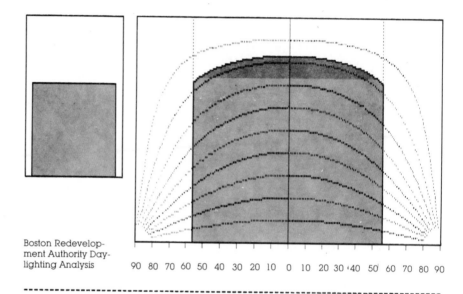

Boston Redevelopment Authority Daylighting Analysis

Daylight obstruction 82.7%

a.

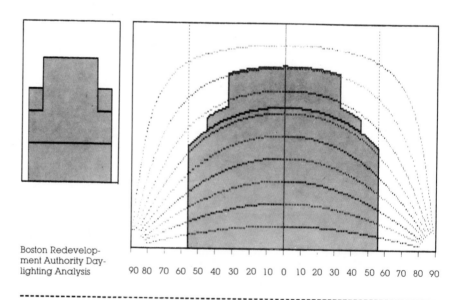

Boston Redevelopment Authority Daylighting Analysis

Daylight obstruction 74.5%

b.

rectangular projection of half the sky dome, plot the obstructing building, and compute the percentage of obstruction in approximately two minutes. The program also has a parametric run option, which allows the designer to quickly compare a new building configuration with previous analyses. Figure 25-15 presents BRADA output for the two previously discussed buildings (notice the same results as those generated in figures 25-13 and 25-14).

CONCLUSION

The designer need not be overly restricted by efforts to ensure the presence of daylight in the street environment. In this chapter, we have presented an alternative method to evaluate the design of buildings that involves a quantitative measure of a qualitative effect. It should be perceived as an example of methodology for considering daylight. Other methods may be developed that adapt this approach or that consider the same aspects from a different perspective and for particular circumstances.

In this methodology the following concerns are critical: (1) existing context, (2) building height to width of the street or street wall, (3) placement of building bulk, (4) type of light desired, specifically, sunlight or daylight, and (5) type of urban space, specifically, open space or park area. Additional considerations may include the type of material used on the building facade: light-reflective material may be considered as having a more positive effect on urban space than a dark absorptive material, such as dark tinted glass.

Each building must be considered individually. However, by standardizing the evaluation within the urban context, one can more easily establish a comparative basis between proposed and existing buildings. The method of evaluation need not be overly restrictive, even if it governs the design of the bulk of the building. For appropriate zoning, priority may be given to certain considerations, depending on the local context. For instance, if the street-wall relationship is considered the most important feature, it should not be altered for the purpose of daylighting without careful study.

Failure to ensure the presence of light and other environmental amenities threatens the livability of the urban environment. Clearly, the cost of increased density of development may be far greater than is measurable in economic terms. An urban environment may be compromised in such a way that a vital street can become dreary, dark, windy, and lifeless. Similarly, historic and renowned areas may be ruined if cast in the shadow of dense high-rise buildings that are erected without consideration of the context. The daylight assessment methodology presented in this chapter offers an approach that can both stimulate better design of buildings and protect urban environments.

REFERENCES

Atkinson, W. 1912. *The Orientation of Buildings, or Planning for Sunlight*. New York: John Wiley.

Bosselmann, P. et al. 1983. *Sunlight and Light for Downtown San Francisco*. Berkeley: Institute of Urban and Regional Development, University of California.

Bryan, H., and S. Stuebing. 1984. *Preliminary Report of the Feasibility of Incorporating Daylight and Sunlight Criteria into the City of Boston's Urban Design Guidelines*. Boston: Boston Redevelopment Authority.

Ferriss, H. 1929. *The Metropolis of Tomorrow*. New York: Washburn.

Ford, G. 1931. *Building Height, Bulk and Form*. Cambridge: Harvard University Press.

Knowles, R. 1981. *Sun Rhythm Form*. Cambridge: MIT Press.

New York City Planning Commission. 1945. *1916 Zoning Resolution* (amended to 1945). New York: New York City Planning Commission.

New York Department of City Planning. 1980. *Midtown Development Project*. Draft report. New York: New York Department of City Planning.

———. 1982. *Midtown Zoning*. New York: New York Department of City Planning.

New York Heights of Building Commission. 1915. *Commission Report*. New York: New York Heights of Building Commission.

Pleijel, G. 1954. "The Computation of Natural Radiation in Architecture and Town Planning." *Meddelande* (Bulletin) No. 25. Stockholm: Statens Nämnd för Byggnadsforskning.

Rodger, A. 1972. *Owners and Neighbors in Roman Law*. New York: Oxford University Press.

26.
Better Air Quality at Street Level:
Strategies for Urban Design

ANNE WHISTON SPIRN

The street is the busiest outdoor open space in the city. People who live and work in urban areas spend much of their time driving, walking, sitting, and playing outdoors. For policemen, street vendors, and taxi drivers, the street is itself a workplace. Unfortunately, however, the street is also the source for much of the city's air pollution. In Boston, for example, transportation accounts for 94 percent of the carbon monoxide emitted within the city. In certain street-side locales, carbon monoxide concentration may even exceed national safety standards for one-hour exposure, the length of a normal lunch break. Street-level air pollution can also contribute to poor air quality in building interiors; for example, when entrances to buildings or intake vents for ventilation systems are poorly located, they suck in air pollutants generated along the street (Godin et al. 1972). Improving air quality at street level must be an objective of any comprehensive street-improvement program.

The degree to which pollutants emitted at street level are concentrated or dispersed is greatly affected by the form of the city. To date, however, relatively few attempts have been made to enhance street-level air quality through the manipulation of urban form. Urban design, especially if integrated with other measures, could play an important role in dispersing street-level air pollutants, or at least in limiting human exposure in areas where pollutants are highly concentrated. Yet few urban designers understand

The work presented in this chapter was performed as part of research supported by the Boston Redevelopment Authority and the National Endowment for the Arts. The author was principal investigator for the project, and was assisted by research associate William George Batchelor. Drawings are by Raveevarn Choksombatchai and the author. Photographs are by the author except where noted.

the factors that affect the generation and dispersion of air pollution, and few air quality specialists appreciate the potential contribution of urban design to air quality.

This chapter presents a framework that bridges the fields of meteorology, air quality management, and urban design. The framework is based on the factors that determine how, when, and where air pollutants are likely to be concentrated or dispersed along the street and which human populations are most sensitive to them. In addition, the following pages briefly summarize the factors that influence air quality at street level, identify potential problem areas, describe urban design strategies to reduce either the level of air pollutants or human exposure to them, and classify design situations in terms of the opportunities and constraints they pose.

STREET-LEVEL AIR POLLUTION: PATTERNS OF DISTRIBUTION AND EXPOSURE

Transportation-related air pollutants and their spatial and temporal distribution differ greatly from spot to spot within a city. They are a function of commuting patterns, traffic volume and speed, meteorological conditions, the topography of urban form, and the material of which the city is composed. Pollution levels may be as much as six to ten times higher in one place than another. The application of effective measures to reduce exposure to street-level air pollution depends on an understanding of these factors, both individually and in combination.[1]

EMISSION LEVELS

The quantity of pollutants emitted by motor vehicles is directly proportional to traffic volume and speed. Vehicles emit fewer pollutants at steady speeds and greater quantities in stop-and-go traffic or while idling at stop lights.

PROXIMITY TO THE ROADWAY

In flat, open terrain under calm conditions, air pollution concentrations tend to be highest adjacent to the road and to decrease with distance from it (fig. 26-1).

AIR CIRCULATION: WINDS AND BREEZES

Wind patterns vary from city to city, influenced by regional climate and physiographic setting. The degree to which winds penetrate the city at street level is influenced by the orientation and continuity of open spaces, their dimension and shape, and the topography of buildings. Street canyons, for example, may channel winds or prevent them from reaching street level, depending on their shape, dimension, and orientation (fig. 26-2).

Within the city, wind speed and direction are altered as air flows around an obstacle (be it a building, a wall, or a grove of trees), creating zones of accelerated wind speeds and of reduced air circulation. Pollutants emitted within a well-ventilated situation may be quickly dispersed, whereas pollutants trapped within the wakes of buildings can become concentrated (fig. 26-3). Patterns of air movement around an obstacle are influenced by its dimensions, orientation, shape, porosity, and surface roughness. The higher and wider the obstacle, for example, the larger the wind shadow it casts.

26-1. In flat, open terrain under calm conditions, air pollution levels are highest adjacent to the road and decrease with distance from it. This diagram illustrates atmospheric levels of particulate lead generated by a traffic volume of 25,000 cars per day. (Adapted from Smith 1976)

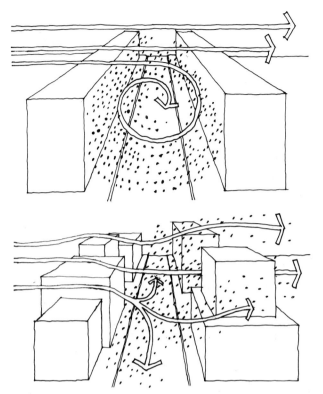

26-2. Street canyons lined with buildings of similar height, oriented perpendicular to the wind direction (top), tend to have poorer air circulation than street canyons that are lined with buildings of different heights and interspersed with open areas (bottom).

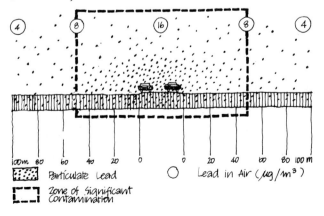

26-3. Wind shadows have reduced air circulation, and pollutants emitted with them may tend to build up.

AIR CIRCULATION: INVERSIONS

Inversions inhibit vertical mixing of air, thus slowing the dispersion of air pollutants. The frequency and duration of citywide inversions are influenced by regional weather patterns, but local, micro-inversions can also occur as a function of physiography. On calm, clear nights, cool air flows into valley bottoms where it may trap pollutants until the midmorning sun warms the air near the surface.

AIR CIRCULATION: SPATIAL CONFINEMENT

The more enclosed a space is by buildings, walls, embankments, or canopies adjacent to or over the roadway, the less opportunity pollutants within that space have to disperse (fig. 26-4).

SINKS

Under some conditions, plants may act as "sinks" for certain pollutants. Large, densely planted groves of

26-4. The more enclosed a space, the more likely the accumulation of pollutants. (Adapted from Kurtzweg 1973)

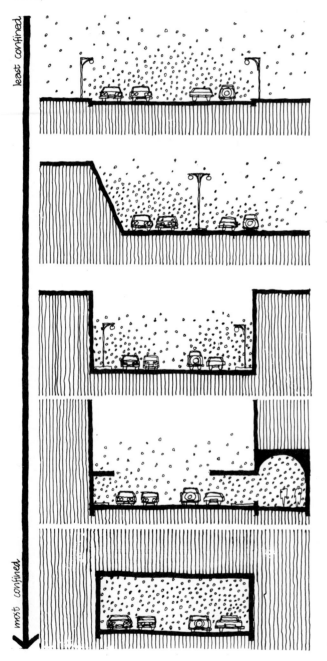

trees and shrubs, for example, may filter particulates (fig. 26-5).

POLLUTION-SENSITIVE USERS AND ACTIVITIES

Certain users, for example, young children and the elderly, are especially vulnerable to air pollution; the places they use are henceforth described as *pollution-sensitive*. Activities that entail frequent or prolonged use of a place are also described with this phrase.

TABLE 26-1.

PLACES PRONE OR SENSITIVE TO STREET-LEVEL AIR POLLUTION: A CHECKLIST

HIGH EMISSIONS

- Major street or highway (especially with parking lanes)
- Busy intersection
- Taxi stand
- Bus depot
- Parking garage entrance and exhaust vents
- Tunnel entrance and exhaust vents

PROXIMITY TO THE ROAD

- Median strip
- Traffic island
- Curbside
- Roadside strip

POOR AIR CIRCULATION

WINDS
- Wind shadows at leeward base of buildings
- Short street canyons blocked at both ends
- Long street canyons perpendicular to prevailing winds
- Urban districts with narrow, irregular street patterns

BREEZES
- Locations upwind of pollution source
- Windward base of obstruction to breeze

INVERSIONS
- Valley bottom
- Street canyon bottom

POOR AIR CIRCULATION

SPACIAL ENCLOSURE
- High, narrow street canyons
- Streetside arcade
- Bus shelter
- Interior atrium
- Tunnel
- Parking garage

POLLUTION-SENSITIVE USES

- Playgrounds and schoolyards
- Sports fields
- Sitting areas used either frequently or for a long period of time by same individuals
- Sitting areas used by elderly or convalescents
- Outdoor cafés
- Bus stops
- Building entrances, windows, and intake vents

Table 26-1 summarizes locations prone to air pollution as a function of the preceding factors. This checklist is both a descriptive and a prescriptive tool: it permits the analysis of a place in terms of factors that influence emissions, dispersion, and pollution-sensitivity and it enables one to predict where potential problems and opportunities resulting from certain combinations of factors are likely to arise. By tabulating the overlap of conditions in a single location, for example, one can identify, and then empirically evaluate, potential "hot spots." The checklist can also be employed to classify design situations, each of which represents a different combination of variables and

26-5. Plants as sinks for particulates. (Adapted from Smith and Staskawicz 1977)

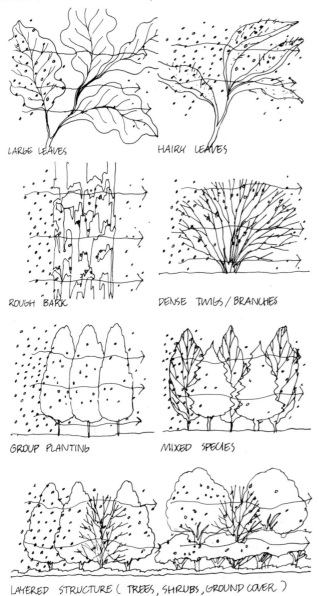

LARGE LEAVES   HAIRY LEAVES

ROUGH BARK   DENSE TWIGS / BRANCHES

GROUP PLANTING   MIXED SPECIES

LAYERED STRUCTURE (TREES, SHRUBS, GROUND COVER)

poses opportunities or constraints for urban design (see table 26-2). The design situations are ranked from one to six, where Class 1, with low or no emissions and with good air circulation, has the least potential for transportation-related air pollution, whereas Class 6, with high emissions and with poor air circulation, has the greatest potential. Each class entails a constellation of appropriate strategies for reducing human exposure to street-level air pollution.

URBAN DESIGN STRATEGIES

There are four basic strategies for addressing street-level air pollution: prevention or reduction of emissions; enhancement of air circulation; removal of pollutants from the air; and protection of pollution-sensitive uses (see table 26-3). Not all strategies are equally appropriate for every design situation; table 26-2 identifies those applicable to each class. For Class 2, for example, the concern is poor air circulation, and the strategy should be to improve air circulation. For Class 3, the main concern is proximity to the road, and the design strategy should therefore be aimed at filtering pollutants and separating pollution-sensitive uses from the road, either through distance or a barrier. All four design strategies are appropriate for Class 6, which is characterized by a combination of high emissions, proximity to the road, and poor air circulation.

Strategy 1: Preventing or Reducing Emissions

Various measures have been implemented to prevent or reduce emissions. Removing the source of emissions (whether it be the motor vehicle itself or a use like a taxi stand that may generate high emissions) is the most effective way to reduce or eliminate transportation-related air pollution in a particular location. Although elimination of the motor vehicle is rarely feasible, under certain circumstances it may be the most attractive option. Urban districts with narrow streets, relatively even building heights, and long blocks with few openings or with a highly irregular street pattern provide little opportunity for dispersion of street-level air pollutants and may be good candidates for conversion to pedestrian zones with restricted vehicular access. This was done in the center of Bologna, Italy, for example, where narrow streets lined by buildings with deep arcades trapped vehicle emissions. Bologna designated the core of this area as a pedestrian zone and a larger area as a zone with restricted vehicular access.

Pedestrian streets are another alternative. By linking a series of streets in dense urban districts, a convenient pedestrian route can be created through the

TABLE 26-2.
STREET-LEVEL AIR POLLUTION:
DESIGN SITUATIONS

	OPPORTUNITY FOR POLLUTION-SENSITIVE USES	CONSTRAINT FOR POLLUTION-SENSITIVE USES	APPROPRIATE DESIGN STRATEGIES (SEE TABLE 26-3)
CLASS 1 · Low or no emissions · Outside roadside zone · Good air circulation	■		
CLASS 2 · Low or no emissions · Outside roadside zone · Poor air circulation	■		2A–C 2D
CLASS 3 · Low-to-moderate emissions · Within roadside zone · Good air circulation		■	3A 4B–C
CLASS 4 · Low-to-moderate emissions · Within roadside zone · Poor air circulation		■	2A–D 3A 4A–D
CLASS 5 · High emissions · Within roadside zone · Good air circulation		■	1A 3A 4A–D
CLASS 6 · High emissions · Within roadside zone · Poor air circulation		■	1A 2A-D 3A 4A–D

city with minimal disruption to vehicular traffic. Even if the elimination of traffic from a district or street is not feasible, emissions at a particular spot may be substantially reduced by relocating high-emission uses, such as taxi stands, bus depots, loading zones, and parking garage entrances. Care should be taken to site such sources in well-ventilated locations, away from pollution-sensitive activities.

Strategy 2: Enhancing Air Circulation

Air circulation can be enhanced by promoting the penetration of winds and breezes, inhibiting the formation and duration of local inversions, and avoiding spatial confinement.

It is difficult, even impractical, to create a design or plan that responds equally well to all wind directions. One must therefore determine the most important wind directions in a given city and take note of the city's seasonal variations (if any). A maximally effective design to enhance air circulation at any given spot will be framed within the larger context of street, district, and city; failure to account for this larger context may nullify efforts at the local scale.[2]

Major open spaces can funnel winds into the city. Highways and parkways, as well as stream valleys and linear parks, are potential ground-level wind channels. Continuous corridors, oriented to channel winds from desired directions into and through the city, should be created. Large open areas may also bring winds to ground level in densely built districts.

Street canyons can be designed to promote ventilation through the use of the following strategies: widening the canyon; stepping buildings back from the street; increasing openings in the canyon; introducing uneven building heights or buildings of pyramidal or irregular shape; and designing intersections to deflect winds into the street canyon. Varying building setbacks to create a rough, irregular profile may have the additional benefit of reducing channelization of winds, a condition that might otherwise cause pedestrian discomfort (fig. 26-6).

One can promote air circulation around the base of buildings and other obstacles by orienting them to pose minimum surface area to the wind. This can be accomplished through the use of openings or porous building material to permit airflow, while reducing wind speeds, and through the placement of another obstacle nearby to deflect and direct winds into areas where air might otherwise be stagnant (fig. 26-7).

The duration of micro-inversions in enclosed low spots (called *radiation inversions*) can be shortened if early morning sun is permitted to penetrate at ground level and if the flow of breezes is maintained through the city. Street canyons, especially when located in a

TABLE 26-3.
STRATEGIES TO REDUCE HUMAN EXPOSURE

STRATEGY 1

PREVENTING OR REDUCING EMISSIONS
A. Remove source of emissions
  1. Designate pedestrian districts
  2. Designate pedestrian streets
  3. Remove high-emission uses
B. Prevent release of pollutants
C. Improve engine efficiency
D. Improve traffic flow
E. Reduce number of vehicles
F. Reduce peak emissions

STRATEGY 2

ENHANCING AIR CIRCULATION
A. Promote penetration of winds and breezes
  1. Design major open spaces to enhance the penetration of winds into the city
  2. Design street canyons to promote the penetration of winds
  3. Promote air circulation around the base of buildings and other obstacles
B. Inhibit inversions
  1. Design street canyons to enhance solar access
C. Avoid spatial confinement
  1. Design street canyons to reduce spatial confinement
  2. Design street-side shelters to reduce spatial confinement

STRATEGY 3

REMOVING POLLUTANTS FROM THE AIR
A. Plant landscape filters
  1. Design the landscape of major streets to filter particulate pollutants
  2. Design the landscape within highway rights-of-way to filter particulate pollutants

STRATEGY 4

PROTECTING POLLUTION-SENSITIVE USES
A. Locate pollution-sensitive uses outside high-pollution zones
  1. Locate pollution-sensitive uses in areas of good air circulation, with low to moderate emissions, upwind of major pollution sources
  2. Maintain distance between pollution-sensitive uses and major streets and highways
  3. Discourage the use of high-pollution zones for pollution-sensitive uses
B. Locate high-emission uses judiciously
  1. Site high-emission uses away from existing pollution-sensitive uses
  2. Site high-emission uses in areas with good air circulation
  3. Site high-emission uses downwind of existing pollution-sensitive uses
C. Buffer pollution-sensitive uses from high-emission uses
  1. Use barriers to separate pollution-sensitive and pollution-generating uses
D. Regulate time of use to separate pollution-sensitive and pollution-generating uses
  1. Establish vehicle-free time zones during intensive pedestrian use
  2. Limit traffic during times of limited air circulation

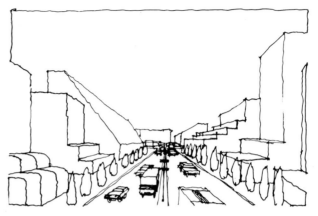

26-6. To promote air circulation in street canyons, step buildings back from the street, increase openings, and vary building heights.

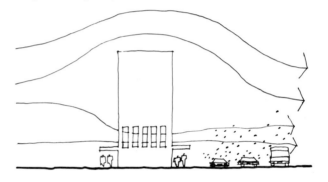

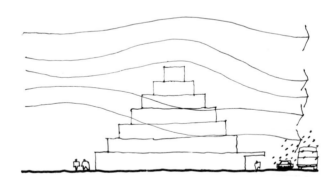

26-7. To reduce wind shadow at the base of a building *(top)*, design buildings with a pyramidal shape or with openings that permit air flow *(bottom)*.

topographic low spot, should be designed to permit sun to reach the ground relatively early in the morning. In streets oriented north-south, the street canyon can be widened, building heights lowered, and buildings either set back or stepped back from the east side of the street.

Spatial confinement should be avoided in locations with relatively high air pollution emissions, such as heavily travelled streets. The degree of spatial confinement in street canyons can be reduced through widening the canyon, increasing openings in the street canyon, lowering building heights, and setting or stepping buildings back from the street. Street-side shelters should be designed with open sides or high canopies to reduce spatial confinement (fig. 26-8).

Strategy 3: Removing Pollutants from the Air

Whenever possible, the roadside zone should be landscaped to filter the air. The effectiveness of such "filters" can be enhanced greatly by design. Major streets and highways should be accorded sufficient breadth to accommodate a dense, layered arrangement of plants (although street trees planted in a single row, or highway rights-of-way that consist of grassy meadows with scattered trees, will have an insignificant impact as filters). Highway rights-of-way with a sloped embankment covered by woodland (leaving a mowed strip adjacent to the road for safety) will not only filter the air, but will cost less to maintain than grass (fig. 26-9).

Strategy 4: Protecting Pollution-Sensitive Uses

Pollution-sensitive uses, such as playgrounds and schoolyards, sitting areas, outdoor cafés, and building entrances and intake vents, should be set back from the road in areas of good air circulation. New uses that may generate high emissions, such as parking garages and major streets, should be located downwind and away from existing pollution-sensitive uses in areas with good air circulation (fig. 26-10).

Pollution-sensitive uses must sometimes be located in zones of relatively high emissions; however, uses such as sitting areas and outdoor cafés can be protected through buffers, for example, walls, planters, and berms. Planted berms will not only provide a barrier, but can also be designed to filter particulate pollutants (fig. 26-11).

Occupation of the same space by pollution-sensitive and pollution-generating uses is sometimes unavoidable. In such cases, temporal separation may be the ideal way to reduce pedestrian exposure to air pollution. The midday lunch hour, for example, is a time of intensive pedestrian activity. By restricting or banning traffic during that time, pedestrian exposure to air pollutants could be substantially reduced.

COMPREHENSIVE APPROACH TO STREET-LEVEL AIR QUALITY

In the seventeenth century, the celebrated diarist John Evelyn proposed a comprehensive plan to alleviate air pollution in London. Evelyn's plan, outlined

26-8. To promote air circulation in streetside arcades, design them with high canopies.

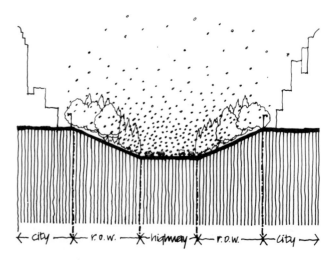

26-9. Sloped highway embankments and woodland growth help filter pollutants from the air.

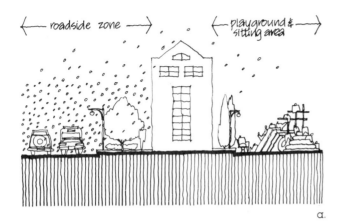

a.

26-10. Pollution-sensitive uses could be located away from high-emission zones: <u>a.</u> concept showing sitting areas and playground set apart from major street and highway; <u>b.</u> sidewalk along major street; <u>c.</u> protected courtyard garden in apartment complex; <u>d.</u> playground in protected courtyard garden; <u>e.</u> café and shops in interior courtyard (all photographs taken in Munich, Federal Republic of Germany).

b.

c.

d.

e.

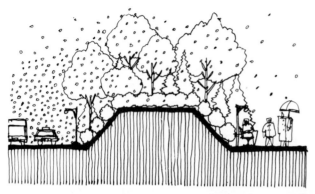

a.

26-11. Pollution-sensitive uses could be buffered from high-emission uses: <u>a.</u> concept showing uses separated by planted berm as a vertical and horizontal barrier; <u>b.</u> at Skyline Plaza in Denver, Colorado, the park is buffered from the major street by a planted berm; <u>c.</u> interior of Skyline Plaza, with the major street behind berm on the left. (Photo <u>c.</u>: Randy Palmer)

b.

c.

in *Fumifugium: Or the Inconvenience of the Aer and Smoake of London Dissipated* ([1661] 1930), employed the four basic urban design strategies described in the previous pages. Evelyn recommended the prohibition of high-sulphur coal, the relocation of such polluting land uses as tanneries from central London to outlying areas downwind, and the planting of entire square blocks with trees and flowers to sweeten the air. Rarely since that time has there been so comprehensive a proposal to improve urban air quality. Most programs in the United States today focus on reducing emissions and ignore the potential of other strategies.

If an air quality program is to be effective and efficient, it must integrate multiple strategies and coordinate efforts both at the citywide and street-corner scales (fig. 26-12). The specifics of such a program will vary from city to city, depending on climatic setting, transportation patterns, and existing urban form. What works in one city may be inappropriate or impractical in another. Whatever its particularities, however, a plan to address air pollution should always acknowledge the issues of energy conservation and climatic comfort. Increased air pollution is often the by-product of profligate energy use. The promotion of climatic comfort in outdoor spaces may contribute to decreased air circulation and an accretion of air pollutants; as, for example, when sidewalks and building entrances are protected by deep arcades with vehicular access, or when winds that might ventilate a space are deflected from it.

26-12. A comprehensive approach to improving air quality through urban design in Stuttgart. Federal Republic of Germany: a. aerial view of the city showing open space system designed to funnel cool, clean air into and through the city (the strip of park in the center is the Schlossgarten; see detail fig. 26-12c.); b. hillside canyon with public staircase designed to funnel air off the hillsides into downtown; c. Schlossgarten, the downtown park designed both for recreation and for improving the flow of air through the city; d. major downtown highway with pedestrian areas buffered by dense landscaping of trees and shrubs. (Photo d.: Jane S. Katz)

a.

c.

b.

d.

The framework outlined in this chapter can aid the formulation of a plan for improving street-level air quality at any scale. Rarely will a strategy be employed in isolation; more often, it will be integrated with others to address all factors contributing to air pollution concentrations in a given locale. These strategies have been based on experimental literature, including modelling studies of scaled or idealized urban conditions and measurements within actual urban settings. Further research is now needed to test, refine, and augment them through empirical studies. At the city-wide and district scales the effects of varying size, geometry, and arrangement of buildings, streets, and open areas should be tested and compared. At the project scale, the manipulation of landform, planted form, and building form should be studied. Wind tunnel experiments to test and refine the proposed strategies would be particularly valuable if related to actual development projects. Measurements taken before and after construction also could help verify these studies. The implementation of built models (or the identification of existing models) that incorporate the proposed design strategies would, moreover, afford the opportunity to assess their effectiveness through comparison with a control site. Such research efforts will entail collaboration among urban designers, wind engineers, and air pollution meteorologists, facilitated, one hopes, by the framework presented here.

NOTES

1. Dispersion models, both physical and mathematical, have been developed to predict where, when, and to what extent air pollution concentrations will occur. Many, but not all, of the variables described in this chapter are incorporated into most mathematical and physical models.
2. The most reliable way to predict airflow through the complex aerodynamic surface of a city is to test a scale model in a wind tunnel, manipulating the form of buildings and open areas to achieve adequate air circulation. The following recommendations are based on wind tunnel experiments.

REFERENCES

Bosselmann, P., J. Flores, W. Gray, T. Priestley, R. Anderson, E. Arens, P. Dowty, S. So, and J. Kim. 1984. *Sun,* *Wind, and Comfort: A Study of Open Spaces and Sidewalks in Four Downtown Areas.* Berkeley: Institute of Urban and Regional Development, University of California.

DeSanto, R. S., R. A. Glaser, W. P. McMillen, K. A. McGregor, and J. A. Miller. 1976. *Open Space as an Air Resource Management Measure.* Vol. 2, *Design Criteria.* Research Triangle Park, N.C.: Environmental Protection Agency, October.

Evelyn, J. [1661] 1930. *Fumifugium: Or the Inconvenience of the Aer and Smoke of London Dissipated.* Reprint, Oxford: Old Ashmolean.

Everett, M. D. "Roadside Air Pollution Hazards in Recreational Land Use Planning." 1974. *AIP Journal* 40 (March): 83–89.

Gandemer, J., and A. Guyot, 1976. *Integration du phénomène vent dans la conception du milieu bâti.* Paris: Ministère de la Qualité de la Vie.

Godin, G., G. Wright, and R. J. Shepard. 1972. "Urban Exposure to Carbon Monoxide." *Archives of Environmental Health* (November): 305–13.

Haagen-Smit, A. J. 1966. "Carbon Monoxide Levels in City Driving." *Archives of Environmental Health* 12 (1966): 548–51.

Horowitz, J. L. 1982. *Air Quality Analysis for Urban Transportation Planning.* Cambridge: MIT Press.

Kurtzweg. J. A. 1973. "Urban Planning and Air Pollution Control: A Review of Selected Recent Research." *AIP Journal* 39, no. 2 (March): 82–92.

Landsberg. H. E. 1981. *The Urban Climate.* New York: Academic Press.

Rydell, C. P., and G. Schwarz. 1968. "Air Pollution and Urban Form: A Review of Current Literature." *AIP Journal* 34, no. 1 (January): 115–20.

Smith, W. H. 1976. "Lead Contamination of the Roadside Ecosystem." *Journal of the Air Pollution Control Association* 26: 753–66.

———. 1980. "Urban Vegetation and Air Quality." In *Proceedings of the National Urban Forestry Conference, November 13–16, 1978,* edited by G. Hopkins. Syracuse: State University of New York, College of Environmental Science and Forestry.

Smith, W. H., and B. J. Staskawicz. 1977. "Removal of Atmospheric Particles by Leaves and Twigs of Urban Trees: Some Preliminary Observations and Assessment of Research Needs." *Environmental Management* 1: 317–30.

Spirn, A. W. 1984. *The Granite Garden: Urban Nature and Human Design.* New York: Basic Books.

———. 1986. *Air Quality at Street-Level: Strategies for Urban Design.* Cambridge: Harvard Graduate School of Design.

Spirn, A. W., and W. G. Batchelor. 1985. *Street-Level Air Pollution and Urban Form: A Review of Recent Literature.* Cambridge: Harvard Graduate School of Design.

Wedding, J. B., D. J. Lombardi, and J. E. Cermak. 1977. "A Wind Tunnel Study of Gaseous Pollutants in City Street Canyons." *Journal of the Air Pollution Control Association* 27: 557–66.

27.
Redesigning Residential Streets

PETER BOSSELMANN

Because street design standards and classification systems serve only to accommodate the movement of cars and to provide access to properties, up to one-third of the surface areas in our cities are rendered unavailable to other users. Even when cars are infrequent, their speed and unpredictable presence manage to dominate the street space. Moreover, traffic volumes, noise, and emissions have suppressed other activities that could take place on streets if the automobile were bridled.

In light of the automobile's deleterious effects, this chapter proposes ways to redesign residential streets to reflect the needs and values of nonmotorized street users, such as pedestrians, transit riders, bicyclists, the handicapped, the elderly, and children at play.

TAMING CAR TRAFFIC

That residents in urban and suburban neighborhoods are concerned about the effect of car traffic on the livability of their streets was confirmed by Donald Appleyard in his empirical research during the preparation of the San Francisco Urban Design Plan (City and County of San Francisco 1971). Furthermore, his studies showed that such concern was well warranted: lower traffic volumes proportionally yielded higher livability for residents (Appleyard 1980). Although Appleyard's findings may seem obvious, the research was important enough to have been repeated in Oakland, Berkeley, and Santa Cruz, California, as well as in London, England. Generally, studies in all areas confirmed the correlation.

The results contributed to policy changes in many

All graphics are by the author.

cities. Officials in San Francisco, for example, who supported ideas first advocated by Colin Buchanan in Britain (1963), proposed that defined areas be protected from through traffic by (1) improved public transit, (2) the concentration of traffic on the city's main arteries, and (3) the blocking of through traffic by devices such as rough pavement surfaces, "necked down" entrances, bent alignments, landscaping, lighting and sidewalk treatment, and so on. Traffic would thereby be slowed to a pace appropriate for residential areas. Other means to ameliorate conditions were proposed for streets where traffic could not be reduced.

Many cities in North America have helped to mitigate traffic volumes by installing diverters and similar control devices that filter out nonresidential traffic. Such devices as street bumps have successfully slowed the speed of car drivers (Appleyard and Smith 1981). Yet, in spite of these constructive measures, the Federal Highway Administration has in recent years withdrawn all support for the improvement of residential streets, and most states have not filled the economic void. As a result, the care of residential streets is left with municipalities, where budgets rarely allow for extensive improvements.

In Europe, by contrast, federal governments have supplied the impetus and means for street renovation programs designed specifically for enhanced residential use. The exemplary Dutch *Woonerven* and West German *Verkehrsberuhigung* provide American planners with models that can be—and, to a limited extent, have been—adopted in this country. Moreover, research following the implementation of these programs offers useful information regarding their impact (see chap. 4, by B. Eubank-Ahrens).

For example, the popularity of Dutch *Woonerven* was confirmed in a 1981 survey of residents of the redesigned streets: 70 percent of respondents considered the *Woonerf* desirable or very desirable; 16 percent were indifferent; and 25 percent disliked the new design. Those who favored the *Woonerf* cited safety, the quiet atmosphere, and play areas for children as primary benefits. However, residents complained (and speed checks and measurements confirmed) that speeding moped users continued to be a problem (Vissers 1982). Not all streets would profit from redesign as *Woonerven*, but the concept has proven appropriate for local residential streets, especially because designers have sought to achieve a balance of power among all users.

Although redesigned, protected areas are still a novelty in America, the idea has spread throughout Europe to neighborhoods in West Germany, Denmark, Sweden, and the United Kingdom. West Germany, in particular, has made street renovation a municipal priority. There, 200 cities have introduced government-monitored *Verkehrsberuhigung*, or traffic-restraint, programs, which comprise adaptions of the Dutch *Woonerf* as well as designs for collector and arterial streets in residential areas.

Research conducted in six such cities shows that although the number of accidents before and after renovation remained fairly constant, the severity of accidents declined significantly. In Berlin, for example, researchers found a 60 percent reduction in accidents involving injuries that had occurred on streets where the traffic-restraint program had been implemented. Research also confirmed a reduction in the level of noise caused by automobile traffic: comparison studies of thirteen streets showed an average decline of 3 to 5 dcb and a maximum decline of 9 dcb on streets under the *Verkehrsberuhigung* program. Finally, a 10 percent reduction in automobile speeds was measured on redesigned streets, as compared with 5 percent on streets where only speed signs were posted (Keller 1985).

GUIDELINES FOR DESIGN

Not all residential streets are the same. Some serve high-density inner-city neighborhoods, others suburban or rural districts. Many streets in older cities were laid out prior to the invention of the automobile and are often narrow and congested. Others were installed after the automobile became the dominant mode of transportation and are frequently too wide in relation both to the densities they serve and to appropriate traffic speeds. Furthermore, in each setting, individual streets can have different traffic volumes, ranging

from those with only an occasional car to collector streets and traffic arteries.

Street design needs to respond both to traffic volumes and to the character of the neighborhood. All designs, however, should be guided by a common objective, namely, a balance of power between nonmotorized and motorized users, which is essential in making residential streets truly public places.

Figures 27-1 through 27-3 illustrate the redesign of six residential streets that have been selected in three different contexts: a pre-automobile city street laid out before the turn of the century in San Francisco; one developed in the first quarter of this century in the "streetcar suburb" of Berkeley; and, finally, a street in a 1950 "automobile suburb." Redesign for each of these streets considers both low and high traffic volumes. All figures are drawn to the same scale.

PRE-AUTOMOBILE CITY

Because residents of high-density inner-city neighborhoods frequently have little access to private open space, streets in those areas can be shared equally by cars and pedestrians (fig. 27-1a). Ideally, the street would have to serve a dual set of corresponding needs: playing, relaxing, and socializing, as well as driving, parking, and delivering goods and services. To that end, a raised intersection or an adapted Dutch *Woonerf* is an appropriate design solution by which car drivers would enter a street space whose design, paving, and alignment would all signal the need for greater caution.

Naturally, all design changes would take into account access for emergency vehicles and garbage trucks, as well as for delivery vans to stores, restaurants, and other commercially used properties. In general, designs need to allow for the turning radius of fire engines, and pavings would have to be designed to bear the weight of garbage trucks. However, it can be a serious design limitation if these dimensions are taken too much for granted. Small emergency equipment is available. Communities in hilly areas with steep and winding roads have always had a need for small fire trucks. If many streets in inner-city neighborhoods are converted, fire and public works departments can acquire more suitable equipment.

It is far easier to improve the livability of streets with low rather than high traffic volumes. Figure 27-1b illustrates a situation where residents typically would be concerned about the continuous noise, visual presence, and perceived and real dangers of the many cars moving by. The concerns of elderly and disabled persons would be especially acute. Indeed, higher percentages of less-mobile population groups live on heavily trafficked streets than on streets with low traffic volumes in the same neighborhood (Appleyard 1981). The livability of residential streets, however, should be enhanced for all users, and several measures would go far in achieving that objective.

First, moving lanes could be narrowed to a maximum width of 11 feet, or even, in some cases, 9 or 10 feet. Traffic flow and noise levels could be reduced further if intercity truck traffic were routed onto nonresidential streets and if delivery by trucks were permitted only at restricted hours.

Widened sidewalks and tall trees (whose heights were selected proportionally to street widths) would offset some of the negative effects of remaining traffic. Generous sidewalks could accommodate separate bicycle lanes, low light fixtures, and bus shelters. Trees would screen the street from the view of residents, who would otherwise gaze from their windows onto a vista of cars and asphalt.

Finally, where space permits, a double row of trees could be planted at intersections. By suggesting a narrowed street space, this measure would not only induce drivers to slow down at intersections, but would deemphasize the traffic-oriented function of the street as a long channel of movement.

STREETCAR SUBURB

Streets like those illustrated in figure 27-2 were laid out at a time when the automobile was still a novelty. Nevertheless, neighborhoods in this category were designed to accommodate the car; many homes have driveways, with separate garage structures frequently in the rear of the property.

On streets with light traffic (fig. 27-2a), the introduction of speed bumps would impel the occasional car to slow down to a pace suitable for the welfare of playing children. The speed bumps could be designed as protected crossings and sitting areas—thereby making them more apparent to the driver—and constructed of brick and concrete, with short ramps striped for even better visibility. An inexpensive street bump could be made from a roll of asphalt up to 12 feet long and no more than 4 inches at its highest point. These dimensions would ensure, ideally, that the bump would not span the street, thus leaving enough room for bicycles to pass between it and the curb. They would also allow for water runoff without changing the curb drains.

Because many residents of such neighborhoods can rely on public transit to commute to nearby inner cities, public transportation should be a primary focus of new design on streets with high traffic flows (fig. 27-2b). Bus stops need to be sheltered and should have convenient and safe crossing in their vicinity. If blocks are long, additional crossings that are clearly marked through striping or pavement changes might be required at midblock locations. Clusters of tall trees would signal from a distance the narrowing of the street at the crosswalk. On intersections without traffic signals, bus stops should be located *across* the intersection so that pedestrians who are crossing the street will be visible to oncoming traffic.

If space permits, cycle trails should be provided at the sidewalk level. However, space must be sufficient to ensure, on the one hand, that trails are located well apart from pedestrian walkways, and, on the other, that cyclists avoid colliding with opening car doors. Cross traffic at intersections should be slowed to allow cyclists better continuity and speed. This could be achieved by "necking down" intersections: not only would the distance for pedestrian and bicycle crossings be minimized, but an area could be created for bus shelters or sitting.

1950 AUTOMOBILE SUBURB

Neighborhoods that were laid out at a time when planners sought above all to accommodate the automobile are characterized by wide streets offering extensive visibility. Both features encourage fast driving.

In figure 27-3a, a street that was typically 38 feet wide, that is, equivalent to the combined widths of six average cars, has been narrowed to 16 feet at the intersections. Abrupt rather than gradually curved corners discourage fast turns, and a single large tree causes changes of direction to appear more sudden than they actually are. Trees also form a gateway that enhances the street's character and identity. Chokers formed by the trees could be designed for midblock locations, dividing long streets into indentifiable segments of 200 feet or so. They could also provide a place where children could play yet be visible to drivers entering the street.

If the automobile was a key influence in the design of suburban streets, it continues to be the essential form of transportation for current residents. Low population densities result in the absence, or, at best, infrequent service, of public transit. Yet a second generation of suburban residents is taking over the homes from the first, and as their needs change, so change the issues regarding transit and other public amenities. For instance, today's young working couples require services such as child care and markets that are

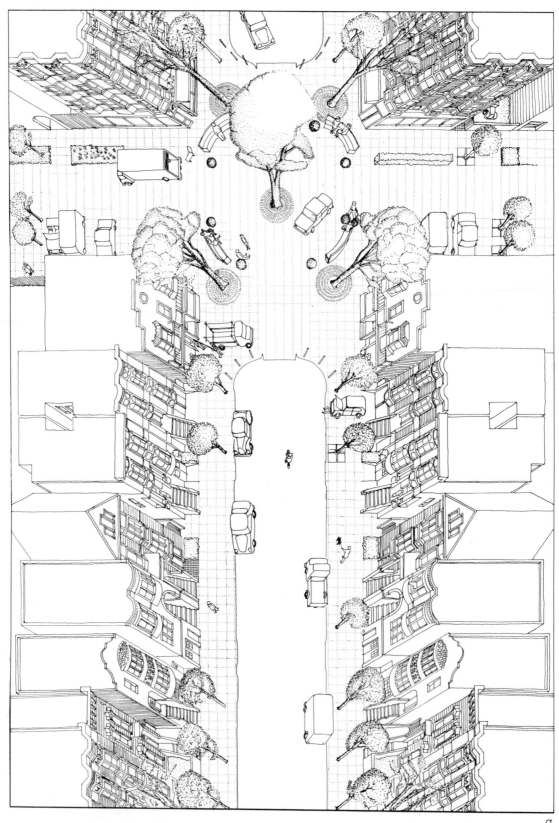

a.

27-1. Redesign of an inner-city street in a preautomobile neighborhood should <u>a.</u> effectuate cautious driving where pedestrians and automobiles share the street space—even on streets with low traffic volumes, and <u>b.</u> include measures that mitigate heavy traffic flow.

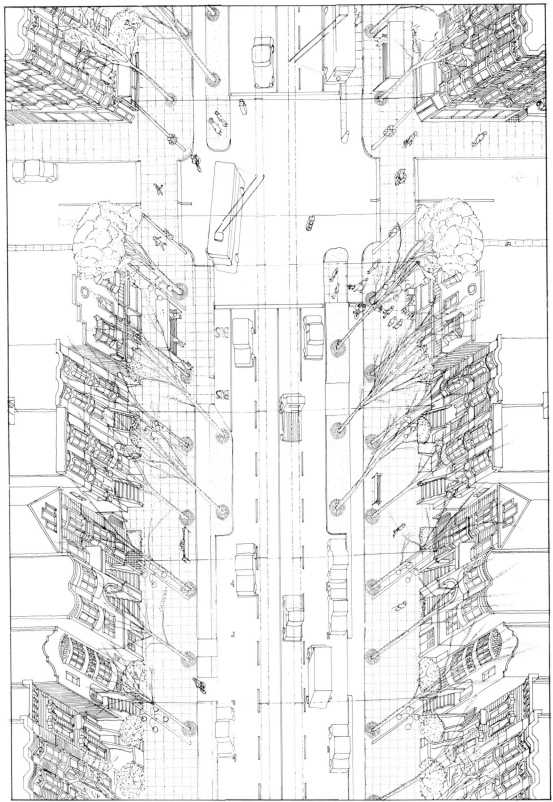

b.

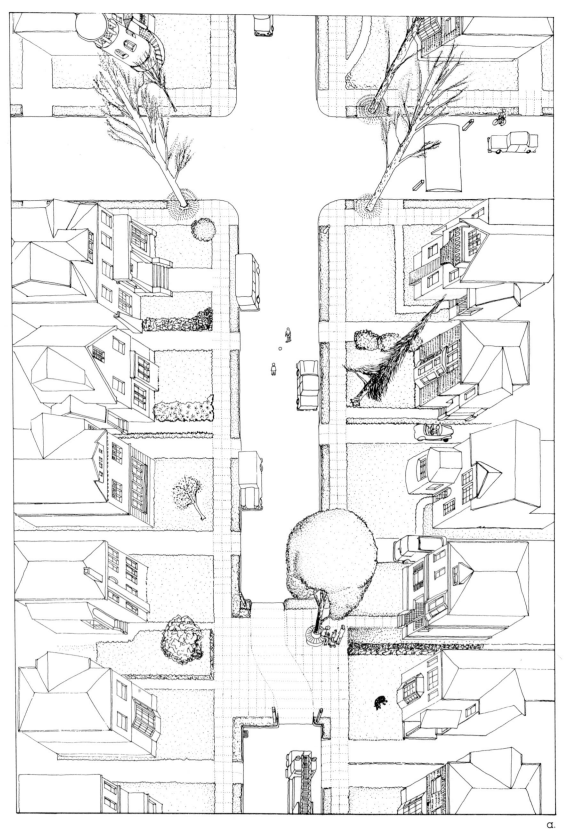

a.

27-2. Streetcar suburbs with <u>a.</u> lightly trafficked, and <u>b.</u> heavily trafficked streets would benefit from attractively designed speed bumps that could also serve as pedestrian rest areas, and from amenities, such as bus shelters, that would enhance residents' use of public transit.

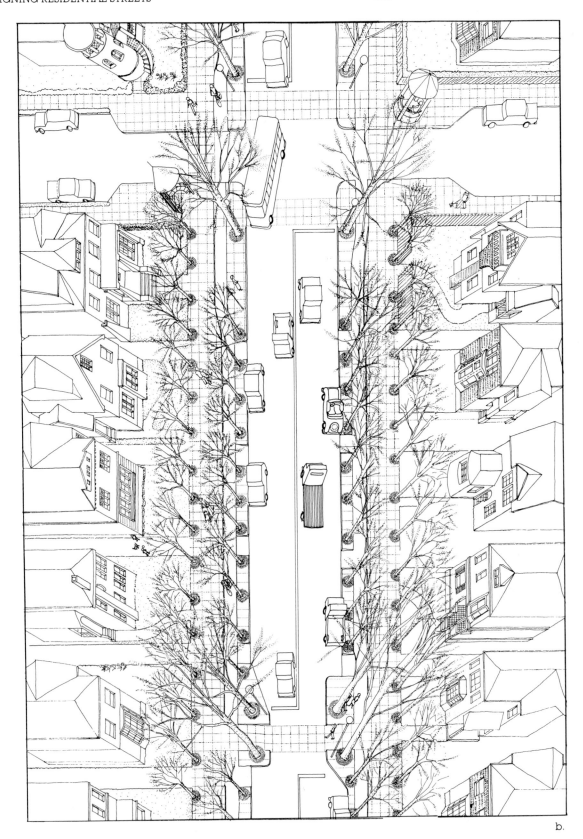

b.

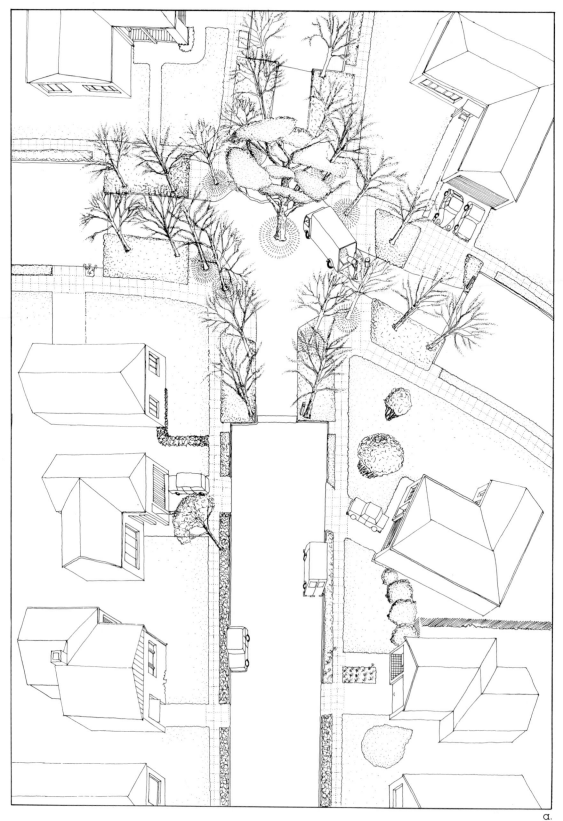

a.

27-3. Streets laid out in the 1950 automobile suburb were designed foremost as speedy and efficient channels for car traffic. The strategic placement of trees on a. a street with low traffic volumes, and b. the same street redesigned for high volumes, can enhance the aesthetic and recreational character of the street, while improving its safety.

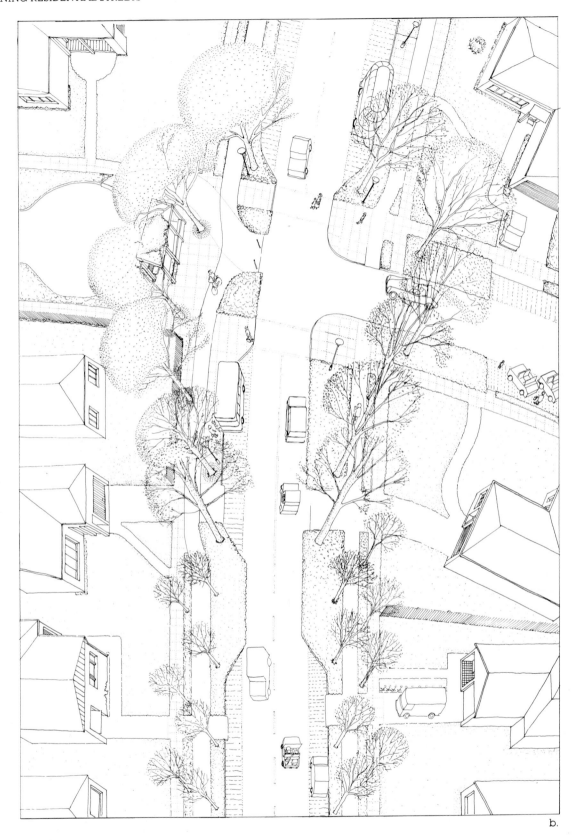

b.

close to home. Population densities continue to dwindle as families have fewer children and people marry later in life. Whereas fifteen to twenty people would have lived on an acre of land in 1960, today, the same acre would house no more than twelve people. Even so, the number of cars has increased, as more women have joined the work force and as an increasing number of unrelated adults are sharing homes. In California, ordinances that allow a second unit on single-family properties in many communities will further increase the number of car trips made in and out of these neighborhoods each day. And the trend will continue unless other means of transportation become feasible, such as neighborhood bus or van services to central transfer points located on public transit routes. Also, one can encourage bicycle travel to transit stops and markets by providing safe and interesting cycle trails and secure storage places at destinations.

In all of the changes shown in these figures, public participation is essential for a successful street improvement plan and design. Local traffic schemes arouse powerful emotions and have widespread impact. Politically, neighborhood traffic management and street improvements are controversial because some people inevitably gain while others lose. A participation process that involves the public allows for assessment and exposure of potential tradeoffs before implementation. Communication with potential opposition raises the possibility of working out compromises during the planning stage. And if adverse effects are not publicized in advance, their very existence may be used to discredit the planning process. People are also far more likely to accept a plan or take responsibility for making it successful if they have participated in its development.

REFERENCES

Appleyard, D. 1980. "Effects of Street Environment on Traffic Speed." Berkeley: Berkeley Planning Associates.

————. 1981. *Livable Streets.* Berkeley: University of California Press.

————. 1982. *Identity Power and Place.* Unfinished manuscript. Berkeley: University of California, Institute of Urban and Regional Development.

Appleyard, D., and P. Bosselmann. 1981. "Design Guidelines for Residential Streets." Working paper. Berkeley: University of California, Institute of Urban and Regional Development.

Appleyard, D., and D. T. Smith. 1981. *Improving the Residential Street Environment.* Washington, D.C.: Federal Highway Administration, May.

Bosselmann, P., and T. O'Hare. 1983. "Traffic in North American Neighborhoods." *Built Environment* 9, no. 2 (November): 127–39.

Buchanan, C. 1963. *Traffic in Towns.* London: Her Majesty's Stationery Office.

City and County of San Francisco. 1971. *Urban Design Plan.* San Francisco: City and County of San Francisco.

Giesler, H., and A. Nolle. 1984. "*Akustische Verkehrsmessungen*" (Acoustic Measurements). *Zeitschrift zur Lärmbekampfung* 31, no. 2 (March): 31–44.

Hass-Klau, C. 1986. "New Ways of Managing Traffic." *Built Environment* 12, no. 1/2 (entire issue).

Keller, H. 1985. "Report on Areawide Traffic Restraint Program." Paper presented at *Traffic Record Systems* forum. Reno, Nevada, July.

Organization of Economic Cooperation and Development, Environment Directorate. 1975. *Better Towns with Less Traffic.* Paris: Organization of Economic Cooperation and Development.

Orski, K. 1979. "Transportation Planning as if People Mattered." *Practicing Planner* 9, no. 1 (March): 22–25..

Royal Dutch Touring Club. 1980. *Woonerf.* The Hague: Royal Dutch Touring Club.

Senator für Stadtentwicklung und Umwelt. 1983. *Verkehrsberuhigung.* Berlin, FRG: Der Senator für Stadtentwicklung und Umwelt.

Urban Land Institute. 1974. *Residential Streets.* Washington, D.C.: American Society of Civil Engineers, National Association of Home Builders.

Vissers, C. J. 1982. "Evaluatie Ouderzoek in Verblijfagebieden." *Verkeerskunde* 33, no. 2: 67–81.

28.
Places versus Plazas[1]

LUCIEN KROLL

Public open spaces come in (at least) two varieties, depending on the attitudes of those who conceive them. On the one hand, some planners skillfully follow *procedures* to create a public plaza that may sometimes work—but only impersonally. On the other hand, an environment can evolve through natural *processes* that culminate in a lively, open place. Of course, the severity of this distinction does not account for spaces that become places over time by virtue of being used and becoming familiar.

Similarly, there are (at least) two geometries, mechanical and organic, that give rise, respectively, to "objects" and "subjects." Again, however, the distinction can be muddled, for use over time can eventually "fatigue" an object into a subject. This dichotomy is a modern phenomenon: herein lies the whole adventure of rational land-use planning (versus the spontaneous organization of the landscape). Herein also lies the total experience of industrialized housing (versus the use of building components by residents who aspire to build their own places, either themselves or with the help of architects).

At the scale of the neighborhood, public space is defined either mechanically or subjectively. Most designers, however, select either approach only unconsciously and with all the assurance that comes from believing that no alternative is possible. I am interested in the complementarity (and the conflicts) between these two approaches. Unfortunately, the mechanical approach is more appealing to the militaristic bureaucracies that are so prevalent nowadays. And if it often appears tamed by its aesthetics, descending from the antique genre, from the surrealism of a Chirico or a Fritz Lang or from the cinematic medievalism of a Disneyland, it always remains mercenary and imposes a rigid behavior on its residents.

HARD GEOMETRIES...

An unconscious intellectual dishonesty prompts the design professions and their clients alike to pose militaristic spaces as models and to decide tacitly that no others exist. Yet it is shocking to witness faith in an (albeit prettified) geometric order. It is worrisome to note the overriding conviction that a public space can never be conceived by the public and grow out of its own disorder. It is painful to realize that contemporary public life no longer has the right or even the opportunity to project its own organic image. Rather, it must adapt to historical travesties, private geometries, and mathematical games. By denying the apparent disorder of certain collective actions that mold the landscape and are essential to its final form, the militaristic approach rejects in a heartbreakingly obtuse way the importance of collective action and participation in the birth of urban form. It also denies centuries of slowly evolving collective forms and condemns the power that today's residents could exercise on the urban fabric and its slow colonization by familiarity. And all of this is done for the benefit of a rather exotic intellectualism and a protective artificiality, based on a game of personal power over urban space. It is absurd and nasty.

...OR SOFT

Urban edges always include pirated public spaces that manage to be vital without the assistance of urbanists.

All photos are by Atelier Lucien Kroll except where otherwise credited.

331

A superb example is developing at the Résidences du Lac in Bordeaux, whose architect had envisaged an "animated urban life" taking place on a slab that he designed to cover the parking. This space is monitored and, in fact, under the rigorous surveillance of residents from the apartments above, it is accordingly deserted and grim. But on the southern side of the project, near the exit of the parking garage, space that had not been planned to be used in any other way is being taken over little by little: people meet and chat there, children play in the sun, and merchants show their wares. Is that shameful?

Another example is the Pin de Galles, a spontaneously developed village near Toulon (fig. 28-1). One after the other, vacation cottages were built on a rugged public terrain near the sea. First, they lined the local goat path, eventually, they consolidated it, and little by little, they filled in the valley. (In fact, their development was so spontaneous that, in administrative terms, the cottages do not even exist.) People built a cable car along the ledge of the valley and a collective storage space for bicycles near the winding mountain road. Water and electricity were installed haphazardly, as needed. Just as naturally, people reserved a space large enough to accommodate a public plaza with a café, an inn, and a *pétanque* (outdoor bowling game) course. They even erected a monument to the "unknown vacationer who fell for his country." Many similar places have been created without architects, surveyors, or artificiality.

Nonetheless, I continue to maintain that an attentive architect can help such processes as long as he does not massacre natural "low-energy" interventions with hard geometries. With his help, the landscape could be woven, improved, intensified, and enriched. This is what militaristic architects cannot (perhaps, could never) believe. And I see no other means for designers to avoid creating the hard and mechanical geometries that are so likely to occur in new towns.

My position is not one of nostalgia or populism, but of developing rational, contemporary, and cordial means, first to enliven and enrich the creation of public spaces, and then to launch them into a process of continuous appropriation (the "twenty-five years later" phenomenon). These means are manifold: true participants, or those simulating the process, bring a richness of intention that is not available from designers alone or from those designated as responsible for the design process. And even if no one participates, the mere attitude of listening on the part of the de-

28-1. Le Pin de Galles, a
spontaneous contemporary village.

signer is contagious enough to help him avoid the treacheries of a militaristic route.

All of this leads to two resolutions. First, it must be known that people's creativity is not dead, that it reappears whenever need accompanied by freedom form the basis of the design process. Second, one must realize that those responsible for design are still capable of listening to people's creativity, interpreting it, and using it as a basis for their work. Because such attitudes and processes still exist, it is revolting to see the deaf and the egocentric automatically selected as the leaders of contemporary architecture, without consideration for including those who are attentive and responsive.

PLACE MARTIN V, LA MÉMÉ

Without repeating the story of Quartier des Facultés Médicales (Medical Faculty District) of Woluwé-St-Lambert in Brussels (Kroll 1975), I can summarize the origins of the project. When Catholic University, upon leaving the old Flemish town of Leuven, built its hospital in a suburb of Brussels, it invited the students to critique the facilities. Future medical doctors, more than most architects and urbanists, have

enlightened the cause-and-effect relationship that links urban design to the behavior of its residents. They refused, for instance, to apply the specialized zoning that technicians proposed, insisting, "We don't want to be a cog in this machine."

While the university still imposed most of its own conceptual framework on the project, it allowed the students to select the architect in order to mix, soften, ingrain and, together, relate the project to the neighboring residences. The students chose my team, and we experienced years of extraordinary cooperation with the university administration, the students, and the technical personnel, all of whom assisted us in interpreting, proposing, amplifying, and so on.

We had, of course, a program of user needs as well as our own convictions. The latter, however, were changed after we became acquainted with the intentions of the future residents. Particularly with regard to the conception of public places, we were able to determine their location at nodes where people met, strolled, and stopped and we surrounded them with the buildings that were needed (fig. 28-2). This procedure did not demand that we inherit a residual space (public places are no longer mere leftovers from built space), or harshly carve artificial geometries out of a landscape that did not deserve such treatment.

28-2. Quartier des Facultés Médicales, Woluwé-St-Lambert.

We have recounted elsewhere how, over the course of a few weeks' work, a group of participants used a large model to outline their instinctive and reasonable intentions (Kroll 1975) (fig. 28-3). We have also told how, by approval and refusal, the diverse functions were woven around the public places, either creating their form or taking form from them. Significantly, the focus of these crystallizations was subsequently named Place Martin V after the pope who signed the university's charter in 1425. This plaza is the site of varied activities: dwellings of different categories, administration buildings, primary school, restaurant, student union, retail shops, day-care facilities, pedestrian paths at several levels, gardens, a vegetable market, and a metro station. In short, it has everything normally possessed by a mature urban center.

In designing this plaza, we took bets on which paths would be used and which locations would become meeting places, because we were anxious to verify the validity of our scheme. Happily, our intentions often worked as planned.

OTHER PLAZAS AS PLACES

For the Vignes Blanches (White Vines) project in the new town of Cergy-Pontoise near Paris, we decided to design nothing beyond what was suggested by the future inhabitants (fig. 28-4). After some fifty participatory evening sessions, the future residents of the Vignes Blanches neighborhood proposed to reserve room for a public plaza with a bakery, a few trees, and a place to sit on Sunday mornings. People often retain memories of public (and private) spaces that may depart substantially from actual physical realities. Under exceptional circumstances, these intentions are expressed in the form of projects, which sometimes become realized when those responsible are not deaf to the suggestions. In this case, the plaza was built, but administrative bureaucracy was responsible for the failure to install the bakery. The process had therefore failed: the minimum impetus necessary to guide it to completion had not been reached, and now it will be years before the urbanization process of this particular space can actually occur (fig. 28-5).

But we also proposed a network of streets whose characteristics were defined by the series of discussions: nothing was to be rectilinear; there was to be no ribbon with rims, no sign reminiscent of the mechanical world of cars; only pedestrians and a few vehicles would be tolerated. The result has been a complete success: the street is stretched like a cloth from one building facade to the other, without curb or gutter, with small spaces reserved for planting, and with

28-3. Quartier des Facultes Médicales, model used by the participants

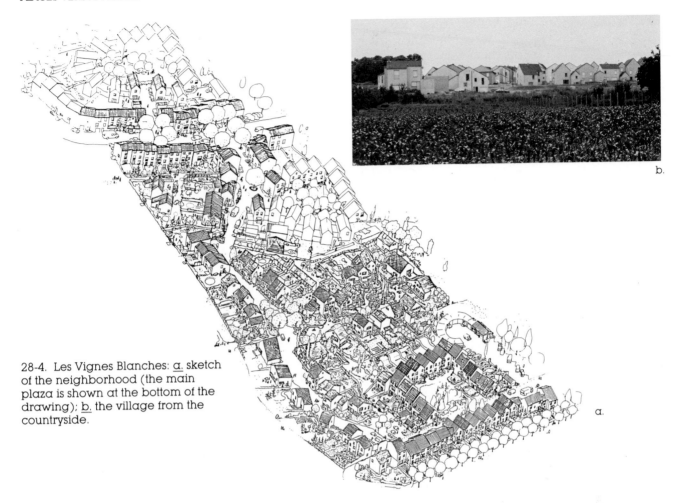

28-4. Les Vignes Blanches: <u>a.</u> sketch of the neighborhood (the main plaza is shown at the bottom of the drawing); <u>b.</u> the village from the countryside.

28-5. The main plaza of Les Vignes Blanches: <u>a.</u> arcades, parking, mailboxes, and green spaces; <u>b.</u> houses lining the plaza and green spaces with trees and benches.

street and sidewalk overlapping like village paths (fig. 28-6). Sometimes a path crosses planting areas, making it hard to know whether they are public or private: the neighboring residents voluntarily maintain these areas and sometimes enclose them with fences (fig. 28-7).

We also avoided "modern" street lighting, which the residents negatively associated with high social status. At the entry of cul-de-sacs, recycled telephone posts support strings of festive lightbulbs (fig. 28-8). A bit farther, a light switch gives the home-bound resident an opportunity to turn on the neighborhood lights at night. Sometimes one sees a neighbor leave his house grumbling, to switch the lights off and save energy.

Little by little, residents inhabited the public spaces: they planted them, arranged them, decorated them. The boundaries became fuzzy. The town bylaws require that residents maintain public areas, and everyone spontaneously took care of what was in front of his property.

Regulations obliged us to provide two parking spaces per unit, but that represented an insupportably large number of stalls to appear in parking lots. Drawing from the experience of an old, small town that had been designed instinctively, I thought of making streets that were too narrow to allow parking. Yet, in the old town, cars were all parked at a short distance from residences, because every one of the street's nooks and crannies served as parking spots and were tacitly reserved for certain persons. It was rude to park in someone else's place, yet there were no signs explaining the town's parking agreements—everything had been organized naturally over time. There were no conflicts; residents feared only the arrival of tourists, who regularly violated the system. We were con-

28-7. The "sidewalk" of Les Vignes Blanches hugs the facades with an undefined shape. Two residents spontaneously condemned it with a fence that they built themselves. They took over public space and no one complained.

28-8. Festive street lighting of Les Vignes Blanches. An opening in the shapeless street becomes a public plaza.

28-6. Streets in Les Vignes Blanches stretched like a cloth between buildings (*in black*, hard surfaces; *dotted*, soft surfaces; also shown are the individual lot lines). (Source: Anne Vernez Moudon and Anne Heasly)

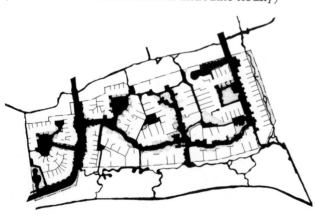

fident that this kind of self-discipline could be reproduced in the Vignes Blanches, and, indeed, only a few pockets are reserved for parking; all others park at random, as opportunity and ingenuity permit (fig. 28-9).

Over the course of rehabilitating the ZUP de Perseigne (Priority Urbanization Zone) in Alençon, we followed the diagonal paths as well as the stopping points that pedestrians spontaneously traced between the prefabricated building slabs (fig. 28-10). We then simply surrounded them with the requisite schools and the public buildings. These buildings merely gave further definition to the street and plaza whose shape already existed, if only potentially (fig. 28-11). In other words, we slowly let this urban form materialize in the way a photographic image slowly appears in a chemical bath or a Roman mosaic reveals its design bit by bit while being unearthed. Only later did we learn that this path existed in the distant past, long before surveyors erased everything to build the housing project.

Happily, we have been able to rely on instinct to design public spaces—we did not need to reinvent

28-9. Negotiating parking in a randomly formed public space in Les Vignes Blanches: a. a just-built street; b. plan at intersection.

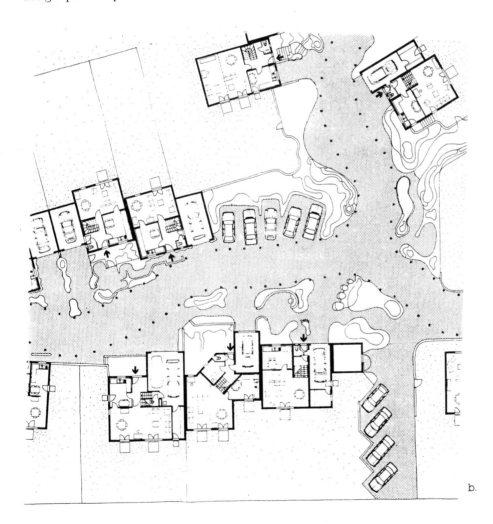

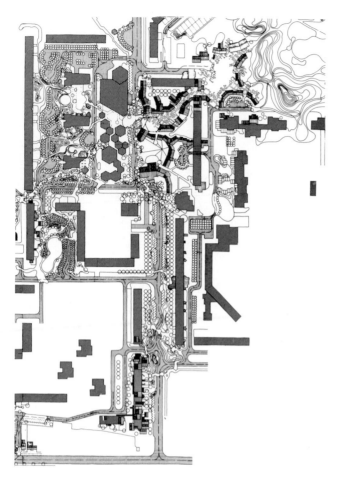

28-10. Site plan showing the existing prefabricated building slabs and the new "soft" infill contructions of ZUP Perseigne.

28-11. Urban form materializes in ZUP Perseigne along an old path.

them. We have thereby escaped being guilty of the syndrome of the colonial urbanist, who ostensibly knows and does what is good for people.

Of the old buildings of the Froidmont farm in Brussels, with its square courtyard long transversed by a service path, we created a Dominican center. Instead of emphasizing the homogeneity of a single institution, we juxtaposed more autonomous elements: church, meeting halls, public library, different types of independent dwellings where each resident could live his life (figs. 28-12, 28-13). Over the next twenty-five years this courtyard will become a truly public place surrounded by compatible neighbors. This is heterogeneity; it calls for a diversity in the building exteriors, which would otherwise (and even if nicely decorated) make the courtyard look like a cantonment.

In Gihindamuyaga (Rwanda), our design of a Benedictine monastery was based on a public plaza,

which, again, existed only virtually. After church service, Rwandans lag behind to chat, perhaps buy a few things, and then slowly return home. Such are the embryonic elements that are necessary for the birth of a public urban space. These little activities will eventually lead to buildings that slowly will be welded together and, in fifty years, will form an official plaza (fig. 28-14). In fact, this is the way that Benedictine settlements in Europe crystallized into urban textures during the Middle Ages.

Our proposal for the 100,000 square meters (39.4 square miles) of the Kronenbourg brewery in Sélestat, Alsace, broke up the homogeneity of the industrial plant into districts and blocks with real streets and plazas—not with truck routes, loading docks, or left-over spaces. We also rejected the idea of a fence around the complex: it would have stopped only honest people. The internal streets were knitted into the landscape as in any free territory.

The main street and main plaza included all the elements necessary for the first phase of the brewery's development (fig. 28-15). Other architects would oversee the second phase, or design of the street and plaza's enclosure. These architects would preferably be "enemies" with conflicting values so that a "stratified historical formation" could take place (fig. 28-16). Also, spaces were kept for unforeseen activities that enterprising people could organize, thus generating a

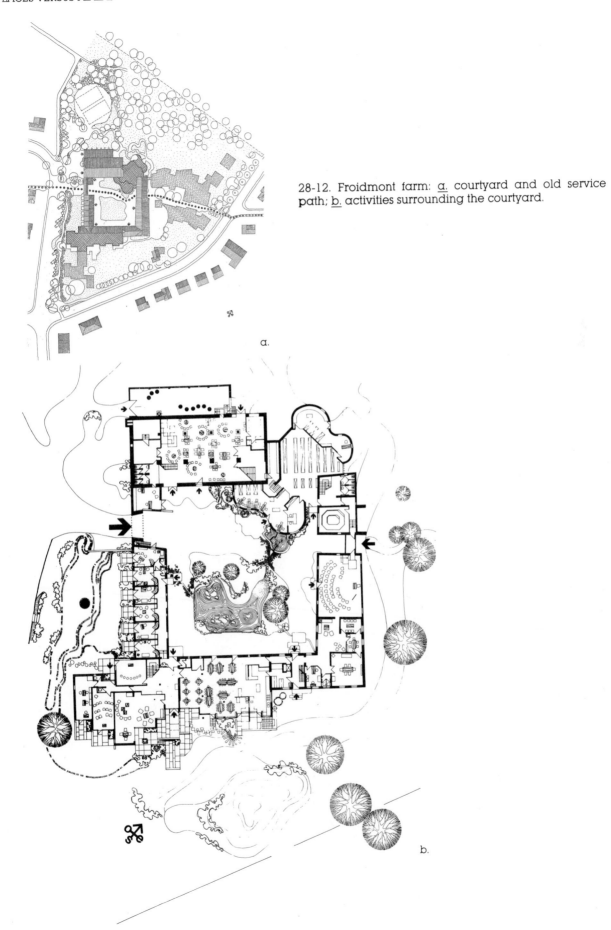

28-12. Froidmont farm: <u>a.</u> courtyard and old service path; <u>b.</u> activities surrounding the courtyard.

a.

b.

28-13. Froidmont farm path.

28-14. Monastery in
Gihindamuyaga.

28-15. Kronenbourg brewery: stratified historical formation of an industrial plant; model of first phase.

28-16. Plan of Kronenbourg brewery plant.

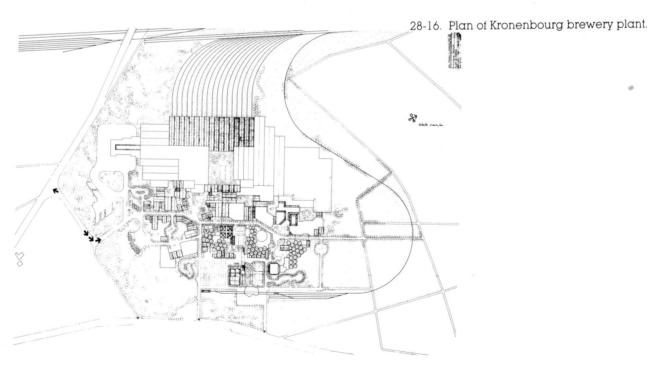

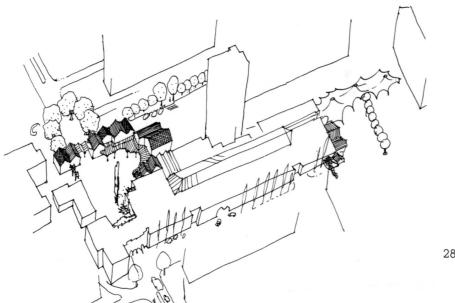

28-17. Clichy-sous-Bois.

new heterogeneity. In doing so, we hoped to avoid the oppression of rigidly uniform environments.

Today, at Clichy-sous-Bois near Paris, we are organizing a plaza that combines a large number of contradictory and perhaps explosive urban activities (fig. 28-17). Yet this is far preferable to the boredom of abstractions disguised behind technical or historical forms. A living plaza, a place, not only surrounds urban life, but sometimes creates it.

pending on the nature and location of the space. In English, however, *place* connotes both a social and a physical space, which, in French, translates to *"lieu."* In design circles, *place* has recently evolved to mean a "good" place. Lucien Kroll argues that while many places are plazas, too many plazas lack important characteristics of place—ED.

NOTE

1. The word *"place"* in French describes a strictly physical urban form, translated to *plaza* or *square* in English, de-

REFERENCE

Kroll, L. 1975 "The Soft Zone." *Architectural Association Quarterly* 4, no. 7 (December): 48–59.

Contributors

DONALD APPLEYARD was professor of urban design and planning at the University of California, Berkeley. His award-winning research focused on issues of livability and identity and of people's perception of the urban environment. Among the books he wrote are *The View from the Road* (with Kevin Lynch and John Myer, MIT Press, 1964), *Planning a Pluralist City: Conflicting Realities in Ciudad Guayana* (MIT Press, 1976), and *Livable Streets* (University of California Press, 1981).

PETER BOSSELMANN is an assistant professor of City and Regional Planning, University of California, Berkeley. He directs the Environmental Simulation Laboratory, a research facility serving the environmental design professions. His films "Livable Streets" and "Downtown San Francisco" received awards from the Environmental Design Research Association/BOSTI in New York and the International Film Festival of Films in Architecture in Lausanne, Switzerland. Professor Bosselmann is a member of the Committee on Simulation of the National Academy of Science.

MARINA BOTTA is a researcher at the Institute of Technology of Stockholm, Sweden. She recently published (with the Stockholm Town Planning Office) *God Ombyggnad* (Good Renewal) and *Vindsinredning och hiss installationer* (Design of Attic Apartments and Retrofit for Elevators). Born in Como, Italy, Ms. Botta has studied and conducted research in the United States and has been a foreign correspondent for several Italian magazines, including *Abitare* and *Arredo Urbano*. Her book *Progetti da Stoccolma* (Designs from Stockholm, Palombi, 1980) complemented an exhibit sponsored by the Swedish Embassy in Italy, the Swedish Institute, and the City of Rome.

HARVEY BRYAN is an associate professor of architecture at Harvard University's Graduate School of Design and a practicing architect. A specialist in natural lighting, he was a consultant in the New York City and Boston zoning studies. Professor Bryan has authored or coauthored over forty technical papers on natural lighting and was cochairman of the 1986 International Daylighting Conference.

LORNE CAPPE is an urban designer for the Neighborhood Division of the City of Toronto's Department of Planning and Development. Born and raised in Toronto, Mr. Cappe earned degrees in urban studies and political science as well as in architecture and urban design.

GRADY CLAY was editor for twenty-three years of *Landscape Architecture* magazine and was the first urban affairs editor of *The Courier-Journal*. He also edited several contributed volumes and is author of *Close Up: How to Read the American City* (University of Chicago Press, 1980), *Alleys: A Hidden Resource* (Grady Clay & Co., 1978), and a recently completed essay collection, *Right Before Your Eyes*. In 1981, he originated and narrated the public television documentary "Unknown Places: Exploring the Obvious." A recipient of many awards and of the Nieman and Guggenheim Fellowships, Mr. Clay has lectured and taught at several universities. He lives in Louisville, Kentucky, where he is writing an interpretive guidebook to generic North American places.

STEVE DOTTERRER is the chief transportation planner for the City of Portland, Oregon, where he has worked for the past ten years. His writings include contributions in urban development and planning in *Space Style and Structure: Building in Northwest America* (Oregon Historical Society, 1974).

RONALD B. EICHNER is an architect, planner, and a principal of a firm developing mixed-use projects in Washington, D.C. For ten years he was in charge of urban design for the public improvement program of the Pennsylvania Avenue Development Corporation. In 1980, he received a Loeb Fellowship in Advanced Environmental Affairs at Harvard's Graduate School of Design. Mr. Eichner is coauthor (with Henry Tobey) of *Urban Streetscape Analysis* (Federal Highway Administration, 1982).

BRENDA EUBANK-AHRENS is an assistant professor of visual communication in landscape planning at the Technical University of Berlin, West Germany. Her research on neighborhood traffic management and street redesign extends from her doctoral work in behavior and open space at the Technical University of Braunschweig, West Germany and from her private practice in neighborhood participatory planning as a member of the Braunschweiger Forum.

MARK FRANCIS is associate professor of landscape architecture and director of the Center for Design Research at the University of California, Davis. His work on community control of open space received an award for "exemplary design research" from the National Endowment for the Arts in 1983 and a merit award from the American Society of Landscape Architects in 1986. Professor Francis is coauthor of *Community Open Space* (Island Press, 1984) and is a member of the editorial boards of the *Journal of Architectural and Planning Research, Environment and Behavior,* and *Children's Environments Quarterly.*

KENNETH GREENBERG has directed the Urban Design Group of the City of Toronto's Planning and Development Department since 1978. The Group focused on the design of a variety of public spaces in downtown Toronto and the historic St. Lawrence area and is now involved in the preparation of a plan for the redevelopment of the Railway Lands. Mr. Greenberg has lectured widely in North America and Europe and is currently teaching at York University, Toronto. He has also contributed to several professional magazines, including *TRACE, Section A,* and *Urban Design International.*

MICHAEL S. HARRISON is head of the Long Range Planning Division of the City of Portland, Oregon. Since 1973, his work at the Portland Planning Bureau covered the development of design review guidelines, comprehensive planning, zoning code rewrite, and neighborhood and economic development planning. Mr. Harrison is a charter member of the American Institute of Certified Planners, the American Planning Association, and Urban Design International. He also teaches in the Urban Studies Department at Portland State University.

MARK L. HINSHAW is principal urban designer in the Planning Department of the City of Bellevue, Washington, where he has overseen the development of the *Bellevue Pedestrian Corridor and Major Open Space Design Guidelines* and the design review of adjacent development. Prior to joining the City of Bellevue, Mr. Hinshaw was a project planner at TRA, architects and planners in Seattle, Washington, which was involved in the initial formulation of the *Pedestrian Corridor Guidelines.* He is an officer of the Urban Design Division of the American Planning Association and the author of a number of articles on urban planning and design.

NEIL KLOPFENSTEIN was a land-use planner for the State of Alaska Department of Community and Regional Affairs in Juneau, where he provided direct planning assistance to several communities in southeast Alaska. He was a Fulbright Fellow in Norway and is currently employed as a policy planner for the State of Iowa.

LUCIEN KROLL practices architecture and urban design in Brussels, Belgium and has lectured on those subjects throughout the world. His projects in Belgium, France, the Netherlands, and Rwanda have been featured internationally in many magazines and exhibitions, and a forthcoming book on his work will be published by Hatje in Stuttgart, Germany. One of Mr. Kroll's current interests is the development of computer software that permits designers to respond to a wide variety of clients' and users' needs. His book on the topic, *Composants,* will be published in England by Batsford this year (under the title *Complexity in Architecture*) and distributed by The MIT Press.

DOUGLASS B. LEE is a principal investigator at the Transportation Systems Center, a contract research arm of the U.S. Department of Transportation. Dr. Lee has taught at the University of California at Berkeley, the University of Iowa, the Massachusetts Institute of Technology, and Boston University. He is a member of several committees of the Transportation Research Board, a full member of the American Planning Association, and Chairman of its Transportation Planning Division. He serves on the editorial board of the *Journal of the American Planning Association.* Dr. Lee lives in a historic landmark in Cambridge, an autonomous suburb of Boston, Massachusetts.

DON C. MILES is president of Don Miles Associates in Seattle and vice president of Project for Public Spaces in New York and Seattle. Both firms served as planning and design consultants for the *Bellevue Pedestrian Corridor and Major Open Space Design Guidelines.* Mr. Miles was director of urban design at the Office of Midtown Planning and Development in New York City and has been involved in numerous award-winning urban design projects nationwide. His publications include *Plazas for People* (Project for Public Spaces, 1978). Mr. Miles has taught architecture and urban design at Harvard University and the University of Washington, Seattle.

ROBIN C. MOORE teaches in the Department of Landscape Architecture at North Carolina State Univeristy, Raleigh, and is a partner in the firm of Moore Iacofano Goltsman. Educated in England and the United States, Professor Moore is past chair of the Environmental Design Research Association and vice president of the International Association for the Child's Right to Play. He is an associate editor of *Children's Environments Quarterly* and the author of *Childhood's Domain: Play and Place in Child Development* (Croom Helm, 1986).

ANNE VERNEZ MOUDON is associate professor in the College of Architecture and Urban Planning and director of the Urban Design Program at the University of Washington. She edited *Streets as Public Property: Opportunities for Interaction in Planning and Design* (with Pierre Laconte, University of Washington, College of Architecture and Urban Planning, 1983) and is the author of *Built for Change: Neighborhood Architecture in San Francisco* (MIT Press, 1986). Professor Moudon's work has earned her several honors, including a *Progressive Architecture* Research Award in 1983.

JOHN H. OWEN, JR. is a partner of MAKERS in Seattle, a firm involved in urban design, historic conservation, and neighborhood planning. Mr. Owen has led design teams for several neighborhood and downtown public improvement and redevelopment projects in the states of Washington and Hawaii. He managed the production and publication of Historic Seattle Authority's *Urban Resource Inventory*, which catalogued the historic buildings and urban design features of Seattle's older communities. Mr. Owen has taught at the University of Washington and has written on the evolution of popular styles and urban design qualities of neighborhoods.

NORMAN E. P. PRESSMAN is an associate professor of urban and regional planning in the Faculty of Environmental Studies at the University of Waterloo, Canada. He is the editor of "International Experiences in Creating Livable Cities" (*Contact* 13, nos. 2–3 [University of Waterloo, 1981]), and of *Reshaping Winter Cities* (Livable Winter City Association, University of Waterloo Press, 1985). Professor Pressman has lectured extensively throughout the world, recently in Iceland, Norway, Sweden, Switzerland, Finland, Canada, and the United States, where he is conducting research on livable urban designs and policies in cold climates.

AMOS RAPOPORT is distinguished professor in the School of Architecture and Urban Planning at the University of Wisconsin, Milwaukee. One of the founders of the field of environment-behavior studies, he is the author or editor of many books, among the most widely circulated of which are *House, Form, and Culture* (Prentice-Hall, 1969), *Human Aspects of Urban Form* (Pergamon Press, 1977), and *The Meaning of the Built Environment: A Nonverbal Communication Approach* (Sage Publications, 1982). Professor Rapoport has written more than one hundred other publications, including "Complexity and Ambiguity in Environmental Design" (1967), "The Study of Spatial Quality" (1970), "On the Perceptual Separation of Pedestrians and Motorists" (1981), "Urban Design and Human Systems: On Ways of Relating Buildings to Urban Fabric" (1982), and "The Use of Open Space in Urban Neighborhoods" (1986). Professor Rapoport serves as an editor of and editorial advisor to many professional and scholarly journals.

ELIZABETH RIVERS, a graduate of the University of Washington in fine arts and landscape architecture, is a site planner with Richard Carothers Associates in Seattle.

BEATRICE FARRAR RYAN consults in land-use planning and development. She directed the preparation of a land-use policy plan and a new zoning code for the City of Seattle's downtown and residential areas. Ms. Ryan later focused on improving the permit process and the links between land-use policy and code administration while directing Seattle's Department of Construction and Land Use. Ms. Ryan was a Loeb Fellow at Harvard's Graduate School of Design.

MANIA SEFERI was a special assistant to the Ministry of Planning in Athens, Greece. Dr. Seferi spent many years in Boston, Massachusetts, where she directed her own consulting firm and taught participatory planning at the University of Massachusetts and at Harvard University.

LINDA SNYDER is a capital projects manager for the Office of Programming in the State of Massachusetts' Division of Capital Planning and Operations. She was formerly a capital projects manager for the Municipality of Anchorage, where she oversaw urban design and zoning reviews and managed public open space and right-of-way construction projects.

ANNE WHISTON SPIRN is professor and chair of the Department of Landscape Architecture at the University of Pennsylvania. She is the author of *The Granite Garden: Urban Nature and Human Design* (Basic Books, 1984), which received the President's Award of Excellence from the American Society of Landscape Architects.

DAVID STREATFIELD is associate professor of landscape architecture and urban design and planning at the University of Washington. He was trained as an architect in Great Britain and worked in the Architect's Department of the London County Council from 1956 to 1962. The recipient of design awards from the Civic Trust and the Ministry of Housing and Local Government, Professor Streatfield is the coauthor of two pioneering works on regional landscape planning in California: *Sea Nicasio: Hidden Valley in Transition* (Marin County Planning Department, 1968) and *Early Warning System: The Santa Cruz Mountains Regional Pilot Study* (Department of Landscape Architecture, University of California, Berkeley, 1970). He is currently working on a history of garden design in California.

SUSAN STUEBING is a recent graduate in architecture from the Massachusetts Institute of Technology and was a research assistant to Professor Bryan on the project that developed the natural lighting criteria for Boston.

HENRY TOBEY is a research psychologist whose work has focused on environmental design and human factors, including analyses of transportation and pedestrian safety for the Federal Highway Administration, as well as studies of museums, naval ships, theaters, housing, laboratories, and professional offices. Currently a senior scientist with General Physics Corporation of Columbia, Maryland, Dr. Tobey is investigating control-room design of nuclear power plants.

RICHARD K. UNTERMANN is professor of landscape architecture and urban design and planning at the University of Washington. His books include *Site Planning for Cluster Housing* (with Robert Small, Van Nostrand Reinhold, 1977), and *Accommodating the Pedestrian: Adapting Towns and Neighborhoods for Walking and Bicycling* (Van Nostrand Reinhold, 1984).

CHARLES R. WOLFE is an attorney with Robinson & Cole in Hartford, Connecticut, where his practice emphasizes land-use, environmental, and local government law. Mr. Wolfe, who formerly practiced law in Seattle, served on the managing board of the University of Oregon's *Law Review* and has guest-lectured on land-use law at the University of Washington.

Index